THE
Penguin History
of
AMERICAN LIFE

FOUNDING
EDITOR

Arthur M. Schlesinger, Jr.

Praise for G. Calvin Mackenzie and Robert Weisbrot's
The Liberal Hour

"[S]hould be required reading for Democrats." —*The New York Observer*

"This is a terrific and timely book—a riveting narrative of one of the most fascinating decades in American history, as well as a brilliantly insightful account of the forces that came together to produce enduring change."
—Doris Kearns Goodwin, author of *Team of Rivals*

"Mackenzie and Weisbrot ... provide insightful and well-argued analysis of the 1960s' social, economic, and political dynamics that opened both the public and the government to great and necessary social legislation."
—*Publishers Weekly*

"*The Liberal Hour* is the most important contribution to our understanding of ourselves and our country in many years because Calvin Mackenzie and Robert Weisbrot allow us to view the 1960s whole and in all of its complexity. This gracefully written and wisely argued account focuses not simply on what we have come to see as 'The Sixties'—the counterculture, the protest movements, the music, and the anger—but also and primarily on the creative work by politicians in Washington who put into law a remarkable array of social, economic, and environmental reforms that are still with us. This is a book about our past that should affect our future."
—E. J. Dionne Jr., author of *Souled Out* and *Why Americans Hate Politics*

"Apart from a good, sturdy narrative history, there are useful lessons here for political activists and progressives."   —*Kirkus Reviews*

"Informed political history ... Strongly recommended."
—*Library Journal*

"Americans have been trying to understand the 1960s ever since they happened—possibly even earlier. To this day, the decade serves as a rallying cry to those who blindly suppress its memory, or nearly as blindly, idealize it beyond recognition. With command and eloquence, *The Liberal Hour* explains what really happened, probing the inner dynamics of the immense changes wrought by the Kennedy and Johnson presidencies, and the aftershocks we live with to this day."

—Ted Widmer, author of *Ark of the Liberties: America and the World*

"*The Liberal Hour* is a potent and insightful explanation of one of the most creative periods in the history of American public policy. The contours of the era and all of its main players emerge here in vivid detail. Anyone who wants to know how this period of great change emerged—and how it came to such an abrupt end—will find fresh and compelling answers in this highly readable account."

—Paul Light, Paulette Goddard Professor of Public Service, New York University

PENGUIN BOOKS

THE LIBERAL HOUR

G. Calvin Mackenzie is the Goldfarb Family Professor of Government at Colby College and has written or edited more than a dozen books on American government and public policy. A Fellow of the National Academy of Public Administration, he holds a Ph.D. from Harvard and was the John Adams Fellow at the Institute for United States Studies in London.

Robert Weisbrot is the Christian A. Johnson Endeavor Foundation Distinguished Teaching Professor of History at Colby College and the author of numerous books, including *Freedom Bound*, which received the Gustavus Myers Center Award for the Outstanding Book on Human Rights, and *Maximum Danger: Kennedy, the Missiles, and the Crisis of American Confidence.*

THE

LIBERAL

HOUR

WASHINGTON AND THE POLITICS

OF CHANGE IN THE 1960s

G. CALVIN MACKENZIE

& ROBERT WEISBROT

PENGUIN BOOKS

PENGUIN BOOKS

Published by the Penguin Group

Penguin Group (USA) Inc., 375 Hudson Street, New York, New York 10014, U.S.A.

Penguin Group (Canada), 90 Eglinton Avenue East, Suite 700, Toronto,
Ontario, Canada M4P 2Y3 (a division of Pearson Penguin Canada Inc.)

Penguin Books Ltd, 80 Strand, London WC2R 0RL, England

Penguin Ireland, 25 St Stephen's Green, Dublin 2, Ireland (a division of Penguin Books Ltd)

Penguin Group (Australia), 250 Camberwell Road, Camberwell,
Victoria 3124, Australia (a division of Pearson Australia Group Pty Ltd)

Penguin Books India Pvt Ltd, 11 Community Centre, Panchsheel Park, New Delhi – 110 017, India

Penguin Group (NZ), 67 Apollo Drive, Rosedale, North Shore 0632,
New Zealand (a division of Pearson New Zealand Ltd)

Penguin Books (South Africa) (Pty) Ltd, 24 Sturdee Avenue,
Rosebank, Johannesburg 2196, South Africa

Penguin Books Ltd, Registered Offices:
80 Strand, London WC2R 0RL, England

First published in the United States of America by The Penguin Press,
a member of Penguin Group (USA) Inc. 2008
Published in Penguin Books 2009

1 3 5 7 9 10 8 6 4 2

Portions of Chapter Six originally appeared in *Maximum Danger: Kennedy, the Missiles,
and the Crisis of American Confidence* by Robert Weisbrot. Copyright © 2001 by Robert Weisbrot.
Reprinted by permision of Ivan R. Dee, Publisher.

Excerpt from "The Times They Are A-Changin'" by Bob Dylan. Copyright © 1963; renewed 1991
Special Rider Music. All rights reserved. International copyright secured. Reprinted by permission.

THE LIBRARY OF CONGRESS HAS CATALOGED THE HARDCOVER EDITION AS FOLLOWS:
Mackenzie, G. Calvin.
The liberal hour : Washington and the politics of change
in the 1960s / G. Calvin Mackenzie and Robert S. Weisbrot.
p.   cm.
Includes bibliographical references and index.
ISBN 978-1-59420-170-7 (hc.)
ISBN 978-0-14-311546-5 (pbk.)
1. United States—Politics and government—1961–1963.   2. United States—Politics and
government—1963–1969.   3. Liberalism—United States—History—20th cenury.   4. Political
culture—United States—History—20th century.   5. Social change—United States—History—
20th century.   6. United States—Social conditions—1960–1980.   7. United States—
Economic conditions—1961–1971.   I. Weisbrot, Robert.   II. Title.
E841.M223   2008
973923—dc22   2008002917

Printed in the United States of America
DESIGNED BY NICOLE LAROCHE

To

LOUIS AND DORA WEISBROT
GEORGE AND MARY MACKENZIE

*Whose wisdom and love guided us through the 1960s
and all the years that have followed*

CONTENTS

"Ask not what your country can do for you" ... *"Until hell freezes over"* ... *"Segregation now, segregation tomorrow, segregation forever"* ... *Silent Spring* ... *"I have a dream"* ... *"Extremism in defense of liberty is no vice"* ... *Black Power* ... *Unsafe at Any Speed* ... *Guns and butter* ... *Give Peace a Chance* ... *Credibility gap* ... *"I shall not seek nor will I accept the nomination of my party"* ... *The new Nixon* ... *"One giant step for mankind"* ... *"The Times They Are A-Changin'."*

So vivid and affecting were the images they yielded that the 1960s survive in our national memory as a pillar of hope, a promise unkept, a continuing source of bewilderment, a scar. The passions they stirred still roil. The questions they raised still linger. Their full meaning remains unsettled.

Powerful historical forces caught up with America in the 1960s and swept through every corner of national life. It was a decade crowded with conflict; with movements for justice and against war; and with change, some superficial, some deep and lasting. Traditional notions of race relations, the role of women, the purpose of education, the responsibilities of the federal government, and America's place in the community of nations were all challenged in the 1960s as they had rarely been before. Old verities were questioned; new possibilities proliferated.

Most studies of the 1960s treat the decade as a museum of spectacles. Watts! Dallas! Woodstock! Chicago! Selma! Tet! One could hardly turn around, the histories so often suggest, without encountering some new surprise or outrage. Disbelief became the commonest of emotions.

It is not surprising that so much of the coverage of the 1960s has focused on the most dramatic moments. The brightest flame always draws the moths. But the durable legacy of that decade is more than the heat and the light, more than the sheer sense of liberation and experimentation, more than pungent images. To focus only on those is misleading.

It was an unruly decade, but one that changed the United States in profound ways. In few periods in our history has reform been so concentrated and far-reaching. A new demography, unprecedented national wealth, a relentless Cold War, and an accumulation of social and political pressures in the postwar years pushed reform onto the political agenda. The magnitude, timing, and direction of that reform were affected, sometimes deeply, by an expanding and highly visible throng of activists and critics. They took their country to task. Change could not have occurred as it did without them. But they are only one part of the story, and often not the main theme. The 1960s were also years in which the processes of democratic politics were better managed, more creative, bolder, and more responsive than they have been at any time since and rarely were before.

Government transformed American life in the 1960s, and politicians led the change. Great struggles occurred between those agents of change and the forces of resistance, but the struggles that mattered most took place within the halls of the very institutions and under the skillful direction of the very people against whom the loud voices in the street railed so often.

The story of the protest movements and the counterculture of the 1960s has been richly drawn in a vast outpouring of history, fiction, and film. But much of that story suggests that the young people of America were at war with the old; that change was a bottom-up enterprise, pushed by the powerless, resisted by the powerful.

We disagree.

The dissidents and the politicians were in this together, though few in either group recognized or admitted as much at the time. The enduring impacts on American life came from acts of Congress, from presidential leadership, and from the opinions of the Supreme Court. Yet few in government would have pushed so boldly for reform without the insistent prodding by dissidents outside the normal political channels. That the authors of the Port Huron Statement and those who marched in the streets had their say is not so much a separate truth as it is a separate part of a broader truth. The old men of Washington and the buoyant insurgents at Port Huron and Selma were not as dissimilar, let alone oppositional, as they and later writers have suggested. Both contributed in important ways to the lasting influence of the decade they shared.

The New Left, the counterculture, the intellectual dissidents, even the hippies played an important role in the 1960s, but their story is well known. They appear in this book from time to time as forces for change, but not as agents of reform. The argument here is that it was often the very targets of their wrath—the institutions of national politics and the politicians and bureaucrats who inhabited them—that produced the social and economic changes that have become the deep and enduring legacy of the 1960s.

Their story is not so well known. There are scores of books about Martin Luther King but most Americans today have little recollection of Emanuel Celler or Everett Dirksen, central players in the legal fortification of black civil rights. The legacy of Woodstock survives and its music and message are still celebrated, but Gaylord Nelson, Edmund Muskie, and Wilbur Cohen, crucial advocates for the very changes the music demanded, have little such visibility.

This was an era when demands that had lingered on the political agenda for years finally entered the realm of possibility. At long last the federal government shattered walls of privilege that white males had long regarded as natural and inevitable. It assumed new responsibilities for the poor, the elderly, the environment, the economy, even the arts and media. It enlarged rights to individual expression and political participation on a scale that had seemed improbable just a few years earlier. It subsidized health care, funded improvements in education from kindergarten through college, and strove to revive and reshape the cities. These diverse actions sprang as much from initiatives within the government as from protests and popular demands outside it.

What distinguishes the 1960s is the mysterious and momentous convergence of a public ready for change and a government poised to act. In *The Liberal Hour*, we seek to explain that convergence. This is not a comprehensive history of the 1960s. That is far too broad a topic for any single volume, and some of the wonders and curiosities of this remarkable and vexing decade are beyond our focus. We say little here about trends in fashion and popular culture, the successful effort to land a man on the moon, the seeds of movements for women's liberation and gay rights that would later bear rich fruit, and the deep impact of the decade's scientific marvels.

We focus instead on the role of government and politics in reshaping American life because we believe it is a subject of great importance that has received too little attention. We argue that the 1960s did yield uncommonly profound and lasting changes, and we will trace the roots of those changes to the hard work of practical politics. We will place the politics of that period in the context of the longer history of liberal reform in the twentieth century. And we will probe the liberalism of the 1960s to explain the paradoxes and excesses that led to its implosion by decade's end.

CONSIDER THE AMERICA that elected John F. Kennedy president in 1960. That America practiced racial apartheid in many states. Black citizens in those states could not vote or hold office; they could not serve on juries or expect even the rudiments of justice when charged with crimes. Though the Supreme Court had declared segregated education unconstitutional in 1954, nearly all schools in the South remained segregated. Even in the nation's capital, dining rooms turned black citizens away. No African Americans served in the Senate and they comprised only 4 of 435 members in the House. None had ever been a cabinet member or Supreme Court justice. To be born black almost anywhere in America was to miss the main chance at birth.

Nor were things much different for American women. Only a few served in Congress, only two had ever been members of a president's cabinet, and only two had ever served on any of the federal courts. Women were denied membership in most of the country's prestigious clubs and professional organizations. At the Cosmos Club in Washington, where the elite of the nation's press and politics gathered, women were admitted as guests only on rare occasions and only by the side door. No woman headed a major corporation. Women were not accepted as students and rarely as faculty at most of the nation's great universities and composed only tiny minorities at the best professional schools. Jury service was routinely denied to women in many jurisdictions. And the minority of adult women who worked outside their homes were often herded into jobs that were deemed, pejoratively, "women's work": nurses, teachers, secretaries, telephone operators, and the like.

In that America the highways were lined with garish billboards, stores sold products that hadn't been tested and promised much more than they could deliver, smog enveloped large cities, companies dumped hazardous waste into streams, automobiles grew larger and larger, books were removed from stores and libraries and movies banned at the whim of local censors. Cities in that America were in steep decline. Their mass transit systems were broken, their infrastructures aging rapidly, their middle-class citizens fleeing to the suburbs, their housing stocks in decline, and their schools deteriorating. Poverty, unemployment, crime: Those were the primary concomitants of urban life, and the possibilities of urban revitalization seemed increasingly remote.

The 1960s would change all of that. The transforming winds of that decade blew from all quarters, but those that prevailed blew predominantly from Washington. There, for a short time, political forces gathered and melded into a ferocious gust of reform that swept across a broad plain of issues, some old and some new. Agents of change were everywhere—in the Congress, in the courts, and especially in the White House.

How do we explain this liberal hour? Why did it happen at all? Why in the 1960s? Why so quickly? And why so briefly?

These are the questions this book seeks to answer.

This was a *liberal* hour—a time in which government was in good favor with the American people, when Americans in unusually large numbers trusted the government in Washington to act responsibly on their behalf, when government seemed the proper repository for the nation's hopes, even its dreams.

And in Washington there was a generation of proudly liberal leaders who were eager to take the federal government to places it had never been. Like earlier generations of reformers intent on enlarging federal social and economic responsibilities, liberals in the 1960s sought to expand the welfare state, extend civil rights and opportunity to vulnerable groups, protect the environment (including both the natural and the urban wilderness), and regulate the economy to ensure productivity, prosperity, and national power.

Yet for all the connections with past reform crusades, liberals in the 1960s stood apart, not simply in specific legislative priorities but in basic perceptions of the society and their own reform mission. These perceptions drew on a host of reform precedents, but they drew at least as much on distinct postwar experiences and attitudes that liberals shared with Americans of varied political hues.

Above all, liberals in the postwar era tapped a pervasive sense that Americans were living in a time of unique national possibility, marked by U.S. military and economic hegemony, burgeoning consumer abundance, and advancing technological wonders. Recent history seemed to confirm the vast and benevolent reach of American power in defeating and then demilitarizing and democratizing Nazi Germany and Imperial Japan; helping to revive war-torn European economies through Marshall Plan grants and loans; and creating the World Bank and the International Monetary Fund to promote global stability, investment, and trade. For Americans surveying a world transformed by national force, fiat, and funds, it was a short step to embracing the aspirations of liberals in the 1960s to forge an unparalleled "Great Society" in their own land.

America's unprecedented affluence in the postwar years, keyed to an industrial engine that nearly doubled its output during the 1950s and again in the 1960s, anchored the country's vast optimism and amplified the emerging liberal tide. That so many groups were enjoying higher living standards—whites and blacks; WASPs, Catholics, and Jews; men and women; entrepreneurs; professionals; blue- and white-collar workers; and farmers—defused anxieties, so acute in other eras of American history, that material gains for some must come at the expense of others. Americans could more readily embrace measures to lift those at the margins of society when the good life seemed within reach of all.

The long postwar boom further stoked the reform impulse by seeming to support liberal economic theories that expanded social programs need not drive up taxes. Throughout the early postwar years, liberal economists forecast burgeoning federal revenues with constant or reduced tax rates, thanks to gains in productivity and spiraling national wealth. The challenge to the White House and the Congress, according to these economists, was to devise constructive ways to spend these anticipated surpluses in order to avoid "fiscal drag" that could depress demand and trigger a recession.

No politician could ask for a more inviting, painless mandate—greater spending without higher taxes—and no liberal could fail to see the opening this provided to launch ambitious government projects. Americans of all backgrounds would more readily invest in the poor, in schools, in health care, in area redevelopment, and in myriad other reforms once convinced that such federal largesse would not raise their tax burden nor slow their own march toward material comfort.

Liberals also tapped a wellspring of popular faith in government that flowed from Americans' personal experience of federal relief during the Depression and federal leadership in guiding the nation to victory in two world wars. The government had achieved goals previously unimagined, exemplified by the coordination of industry, science, and the military to design and build atomic weapons with extraordinary speed during a national emergency and global cataclysm. As liberals in Congress and the White House pressed their reform agenda in the 1960s, they brandished widespread public confidence that the federal government had the resources and the expertise to implement virtually any national mandate.

When liberals enacted a dizzying succession of civil rights laws, antipoverty programs, Medicare and Medicaid, federal aid to education, and other landmark reforms, James Reston of the *New York Times* marveled in 1965, "Lyndon Johnson is getting everything through Congress except the abolition of the Republican Party—and he hasn't tried that yet." Yet even at their height in the mid-1960s, liberals were never so ascendant, let alone unbounded, as contemporaries and many later critics have claimed. Constraints of domestic politics and foreign policy wound tightly around their agendas and achievements, reflecting that the liberal experiment of the 1960s was a study less in political philosophy than in the myriad ways reform impulses are filtered by partisan pressure and historical circumstance.

While recovery from depression and the ensuing postwar boom encouraged liberals to imagine grand new government ventures, it tended to limit their vision to paths that accommodated corporate interests more fully than reform movements in the late nineteenth and early twentieth centuries. Growth, full employment, and a compensatory government "safety net," rather than government management of business, became the watchwords of reform. Liberals of the postwar era had become more "reconciled to the existing structure of the economy," wrote historian Alan Brinkley, and confident "in the capacity of American abundance to smooth over questions of class and power."[1]

The main nemesis of reform ambitions in the 1960s was neither a political party nor an ideological bloc but involvement in a distant war that two liberal presidents escalated until it discredited the White House and polarized the country more than all the decade's earlier insurgencies. The uncertain rationale for fighting in Vietnam; the heavy civilian toll from bombing, artillery fire, napalm, and "search-and-destroy" missions; the mounting costs in American lives and resources; and the receding prospects of victory all generated growing protests that shattered the liberal coalition.

The liberal hour was limited, finally, by the fragility of the consensus for reform. "It is only once in a generation that a people can be lifted above material things," Woodrow Wilson said. "That is why conservative government is in the saddle two-thirds of the time." Liberals found the political center quickly shrinking as black, feminist, antiwar, youth, and other protest movements became more radical and as Americans recoiled from street demonstrations, ghetto riots, poverty programs that fell short of expectations, and a costly, protracted war.

The reform pressures were so intense, the response so sweeping that fatigue and reaction were inevitable. By the end of 1966, a new mood was taking hold, a new era taking root. The liberal agenda of domestic re-forms had been wiped clean; little was left to enact. The financial pres-sures of all the new programs were beginning to swell. Patience with the war in Vietnam was evaporating. And a potent conservative challenge to the ideology and policies that dominated the first half of the decade was rising dramatically from the ashes of the Goldwater debacle in 1964.

As with earlier bursts of reform during the Progressive era and the New Deal, the tumult of the 1960s was at first exhilarating but in the end exhausting and alienating. The decade that once resounded with calls for a "New Frontier" and a summons to "ask what you can do for your country" faded into presidential paeans to "law and order" and "the silent majority," and warnings to "nattering nabobs of negativism" and protesting "bums."

But for a brief period of high energy and broad accomplishment in the early years of that decade, the federal government worked much as it was intended. Elections yielded governing coalitions. Leaders led. Representative institutions sensed the mood and desires of the people and responded. Americans in unusually large numbers trusted the government in Washington to act responsibly on their behalf. The goals were heady, but they were in tune with the mission of the national government framed in the preamble to the Constitution: "to form a more perfect union, establish justice, insure domestic tranquility, provide for the common defense, secure the blessings of liberty." In few periods of American history has change come with such speed, with such sweep, and with such consequence.

That was the liberal hour, and this is its story.

CHAPTER I

AMERICA IN THE POSTWAR YEARS

The photograph that seems so haunting now was taken on November 6, 1944, the last weekend of the 1944 presidential campaign. Franklin Roosevelt, looking small and gaunt, huddles in the back-seat of an open Packard, riding through the boroughs of New York City, a weak smile forcing its way onto his face, his thin hand offering an occasional ritual wave. It's cold and it's raining steadily, but Roosevelt is there campaigning for a fourth term in office. He's dying and he looks it—he would be dead a few months later.

He's there campaigning because in the 1944 presidential election, 7 percent of all of the popular votes in the country would be cast in the five boroughs of New York City, a percentage that would never be so high again. That last, exhausted ride through the streets of New York plays out like the final act in a long-running drama. It marks the end of one kind of politics in America and the beginning of another.

The war would end in a few months and the soldiers would come home. They'd start having the families they'd postponed for so long—more children in less time than ever before. With the help of the GI Bill of Rights passed a few months earlier, unprecedented numbers of Americans would get college educations and own their own homes. A million of those mustering-out soldiers would be African Americans, and their return would accelerate the great midcentury migration of their race from the South to the North. Rosie the riveter would leave the factory, turning her job back to a man who'd been in the service, but few would forget what Rosie had learned: that women could do the job as well as men. Television, invented just before the war, would become a popular consumer commodity right after it.

The country would change in profound ways, and its politics and its policies would change as well. Never again would candidates rely so heavily on personal campaigning. Soon radio and television and jet travel would become the dominant election technologies. Never again would political parties ride so high in American politics. In 1948, the Democratic Party would blow apart over the civil rights issue, and parties would never be the same thereafter. And never again would America be the urban nation that it was in 1944. No city would ever loom so large in the electoral calculus as New York did that year. The people had begun draining out of the cities and moving off the farms to fill up a whole new American frontier: the suburbs.

Franklin Roosevelt's final campaign trip to New York had not been planned as a farewell tour. But it was for him, and it was for the country in which he had come of age and which he had led through some of its darkest days.

AMERICA WAS NO STRANGER TO CHANGE. Revolution, depression, and war had all brought powerful changes over the years, upsetting traditional life patterns and challenging ancient values. But the past evolves into the present in many ways and in the postwar years the force of change was swelled not by cataclysm but by coincidence. Demographics and technology erupted and combined in ways both unsettling and enduring. By the beginning of the 1960s, there were few individuals or communities that were not feeling their effects; by the end of the decade there were none.

America spent the first century of its independence as an agrarian nation. In the first half of the twentieth century it had evolved into an urban nation. By the end of the 1960s it was neither. The older America was a land of communities: rural towns and big-city neighborhoods. Those communities were held together by deep bonds of ethnicity, religion, and tradition. But all of that was changing as the 1960s arrived. A country that had once been largely the province of local values, local industries, and local elites increasingly came under the sway of national forces it could no longer hold at bay. Much of what was happening to America in the 1960s was not unique to that decade, not something that simply materialized overnight. But many of the long-term trends of the twentieth century accelerated or peaked in the 1960s and bore fruit—bitter and sweet—that had long been ripening.

The new demographics and the new technologies of the 1960s deeply altered the political landscape, inevitably affecting American public policies as well. America in the 1960s was redefined by a population with more old people and more young people than ever before, by mobility and suburbanization, by changes in the character of the workplace, the university, and the family. And that redefinition crafted a new context for national politics, creating unique demands and constraints and opening the way for bold, substantive initiatives.

The old political order could not survive the changes that accumulated into the 1960s. The political agenda quickly filled with vexing issues—some long-postponed, others immediate products of a tempestuous time. The potent combination of so many intersecting forces gave rise to a political moment when the American people placed faith in their government and made demands upon it that had few precedents and few limits.

FRUITS OF ABUNDANCE

For centuries, beginning with the earliest explorers, visitors to America found it a land of rich and plentiful resources. J. Hector St. John de Crèvecoeur, reporting on a trip to America shortly after independence, wrote in 1782 that "there is room for everybody in America. . . . I do not mean that everyone who comes will grow rich in a little time; no, but he may procure an easy, decent maintenance, by his industry."[1] The Mississippi valley, wrote de Tocqueville in the 1830s, was "the most magnificent dwelling place prepared by God for man's abode."[2] A century later, when asked what single book he'd like to put in the hands of all Russian communists, Franklin Roosevelt replied simply, "The Sears, Roebuck catalogue."[3]

The abundance of resources and the twin forces of inventive ingenuity and productive capacity have long been themes of American development. The confidence and optimism that are common personality traits of wealthy people are characteristic as well of wealthy nations. And few nations in history have been able to match, decade after decade, the national wealth of the United States.

America entered the 1960s in a flight of optimism. The biggest economic gains lay ahead, but by 1960 the Depression was a fading memory and American families were beginning to enjoy unprecedented wealth. Personal incomes had grown by more than 80 percent between 1945 and 1960, and consumption expenditures more than doubled.[4] In 1947, fewer than 10 percent of families and single individuals had an income greater than ten thousand dollars; by 1968 the portion had grown to 33 percent.[5] This wasn't just the rich getting richer. The new wealth was widespread, across social classes and communities, regions and ages. Workers in manufacturing in 1960 were enjoying hourly wages more than three times as high as at the beginning of World War II.[6] Executive salaries spiraled upward. The middle class exploded.

Americans had never had it so good. It was a time, the economist John Kenneth Galbraith noted, "where the ordinary individual has access to amenities—foods, entertainment, personal transportation, and plumbing—in which not even the rich rejoiced a century ago."[7] And as the decade unfolded, the pace of economic growth and personal wealth expansion only accelerated. Disposable personal income, in constant dollars, grew by 33 percent in the 1950s. In the 1960s it grew by more than 50 percent.[8]

By 1960 the national economy was evolving rapidly. Physical capabilities were important criteria for fewer and fewer jobs. Blue collars were fading as white and pink collars multiplied. Education and training were more and more essential. Manufacturing was stagnant but service jobs, now often called information jobs, were growing. As a percentage of the nonagricultural workforce, labor union members reached their apogee in 1953 at 34.7 percent. By 1970 that figure would drop to 27.4 percent.[9]

But in the 1960s unions still mattered, economically and politically. And the mature labor unions of that decade, having accomplished many of their principal economic goals earlier, had turned their focus to quality-of-life issues like health care, urban revitalization, retirement, housing, and social justice. They would play a crucial role in the electoral and legislative coalitions that spawned the liberal gains of the 1960s.

In the middle decades of the twentieth century the American economy experienced a leap in productivity that produced great gains in wealth. Corporate profits soared after World War II, from $18.4 billion in 1945 to $45 billion in 1960.[10] With more money in the till, companies conducted more research and development, created more products, and built more factories. All of this added more jobs, many of them demanding higher skill levels and paying higher wages. More productive workers could earn more and work less.

When work in and out of the home required less time to produce satisfactory incomes, adults found themselves with more leisure and more money to enjoy that leisure than any previous generation. By 1960 the average American was working 1,795 hours a year, down from 1,867 in 1950 and 2,062 in 1938.[11] Americans of the 1960s tuned in for more hours of television and radio, made more visits to national parks, played and watched more sports, and took more frequent and longer vacations than any previous generation of Americans. They saw more of their own country than ever before.

As their waking hours were filled with more leisure, Americans became more concerned about the quality of their lives, not just the quantity of their incomes. Now that they could afford new consumer products, they wanted them to be safe. They wanted clean air to breathe and clean water to swim in and drink. They owned cars and drove them more and wanted better roads and safer vehicles. Only government, they soon learned, could be counted on to meet these new needs.

Nowhere were the ripple effects of this evolving economy more evident than in their impacts on the lives of American women. For all time before the middle of the twentieth century, the workplace had been a male bastion. Muscle, sweat, danger, dirty talk—all of the images and artifacts of the workplace made it, in both male and female eyes, unfit for women. Women belonged at home, or maybe, if they had no family to tend, in the office or the front of a classroom. In 1940 only 26 percent of adult women were in the paid labor force. But then there began a slow, steady climb that would take the percentage of women working for pay to more than 41 percent by 1970. And among women between twenty and sixty-four years of age, nearly half were in the paid workforce by the end of the 1960s.[12]

The long struggle to get women the right to vote had had little real immediate spillover effect in the workplace or the power centers of American life. Women could vote after 1920, but in that decade few women held paid jobs outside their homes or played visible roles in public affairs. On the eve of World War II, there were nine women in Congress, only one on the federal bench, none at the head of large corporations, and few on factory floors anywhere. Modern conveniences had eased the task of managing the home, but they provided no real escape route for women who wished to work outside the home.

But an economy that relied less on muscle and more on brains was also full of promise for American women. Employers needed a steady stream of new workers and they needed workers who had intelligence and skill. Old stereotypes died hard, but new economic realities helped to kill them. By 1960 women were beginning to emerge as a significant force in the American economy.

This was only the beginning, of course. The movement of American women into the paid workforce was one of the great social and economic revolutions of the second half of the twentieth century. It was under way when the 1960s began; it was jet propelled in that decade by economic demands, intellectual arguments, a powerful social movement, political forces, and—most significantly—changes in public law. But the backdrop and the root cause was an American economy transformed through the middle decades of the twentieth century into one much more hospitable to and needful of the labor and talents of women.

WITH WEALTH NEVER BEFORE IMAGINED, America could dream dreams never before possible. In the early years of the 1960s, national optimism reached epidemic levels. The unusual economic conditions of the postwar period began to erode American fears about scarcity and adherence to norms of frugality. As Americans individually were growing rich, America collectively began to think rich. Citizens and the groups they formed to advocate their interests came to expect that national wealth could provide a cure for many of society's ancient ills. They began to demand that government channel its share of this new wealth into radical assaults on illness, poverty, ignorance, and prejudice.[13]

And around the country and in Washington especially, they found a responsive audience. Often those in Washington made the demands and the plans without waiting for pressure from the people. "Increasingly," Daniel Patrick Moynihan wrote, "efforts to change the American social system for the better arose from initiatives undertaken by persons whose profession was to do just that. Whereas previously the role of organized society had been largely passive—the machinery would work if someone made it work—now the process began to acquire a self-starting capacity of its own . . . the machinery began to think for itself."[14]

Soaring revenues convinced many in Washington that "the wealthiest country in the history of the world," "the wealthiest country on the face of the earth"—boilerplate from the standard political speech of the decade—could accomplish whatever it set its mind to. The 1960s were presumed to be an age of unique possibilities. The wealth produced by the powerful engine of the American economy, channeled through the political dreams of Washington, made anything—and everything—seem possible.

THE OLD AND THE YOUNG

An American born in 1900 had an average life expectancy of 47.3 years.[15] Families then were work units. Those who could work, no matter how young, usually did—to support themselves and the very young and the very old. The relatively small percentage of the population that outlived their ability to work were usually cared for by their children and grand-children. There were few alternatives.

Not many Americans lived long enough to become burdens on their progeny. In 1900 only 4 percent of the population was older than sixty-five and only 0.2 percent had made it to eighty-five.[16] These figures reflect a pattern that had been typical for centuries. Many children died young. Lives were short and hard. Few people made it into old age.

All of that changed in the twentieth century. Improved water supply and sanitation and the development of modern medicines and public health practices eliminated many of the killer diseases of the past or made them survivable. Workplace safety and the replacement of manpower with machines in dangerous jobs reduced accidental fatalities. More mothers survived childbirth, more babies survived infancy, more children avoided smallpox and polio, more adults stayed out of harm's way.

The country's vital statistics reflected all these changes. By 1960 life expectancy had extended to 69.7 years. The 47 percent improvement since 1900 was the greatest change in history. More Americans were living longer lives than ever before. New language came to reflect this: "senior citizens," the "golden years," and even "retirement." The creation of a Social Security system in 1935 helped Americans contemplate a life that extended after their ability or desire to work had ended. In 1930, 54 percent of the population over sixty-five continued to work. By 1960 that percentage had dropped to 33 percent. In 1960, 8 million retired Americans were receiving pension benefits from Social Security; the number would grow to 13.4 million ten years later.[17]

The emergence and expansion of an elderly population was one of the dominant social trends of the first half of the twentieth century. It was also one of the most potent political trends. As the elderly portion of the population grew, it began to organize and to flex political muscle, seeking larger government pensions, increased access to medical care, and other federal guarantees of dignity and security.

In 1947 a retired high-school principal from Illinois, Ethel Percy Andrus, founded the National Retired Teachers Association. On the eve of the 1960s, that organization evolved into a broader American Association of Retired Persons. The mission of the AARP was to enhance the "quality of life for all as we age. We lead positive social change and deliver value to members through information, advocacy and service."[18] Aggressive recruitment added millions of members in the 1960s,[19] and AARP quickly became a visible and powerful voice for the interests of the elderly.

Responding to this expanding and increasingly demanding body of elderly constituents, politicians voted regular enlargements of the Social

Security program and expansions of its benefits. In the mid-1960s they appended extensive medical benefits to that program. By the end of the decade, the elderly were firmly established as a well-defined and some-times frightening political force. Their pet program, Social Security, had come to be called the "third rail" of American politics. "Touch it," politicians were told, "and you die."

AT THE OTHER END of the age spectrum was a rapidly unfolding development that would yield the greatest demographic anomaly in American history. For more than two decades, through depression and war, the American birthrate had shrunk. Families with desperately tight budgets during the Depression forced themselves to have fewer children. When the war came, more than 10 million American men left their homes for years on end.

In 1920 the birthrate was 27.7 live births per 1,000 population. That dropped to 21.3 in 1930 and to 19.4 in 1940. But then the economy came to life. The men came home. And Americans began having babies again. Millions of them. Live births jumped from 2.6 million in 1940 to 3.4 million in 1946. Births per year averaged 3.7 million for the remainder of the 1940s, 4.1 million through the 1950s, and 3.9 million in the 1960s.[20]

The consequence was a relentless parade of babies, then children, then teenagers, then college students and new workers that had no precedent and that reshaped every aspect of American life through the 1950s and 1960s. All across the country, new schools were built, then expanded. Schools became not just places of instruction, but social service distribution units, athletic and entertainment centers, and food service emporia. The number of K–12 students grew from 26.1 million in 1946 to 35.9 million in 1956 to 48.5 million in 1966.[21]

As the number of students grew, so, too, did the number of teachers. Between 1955 and 1970, the number of elementary- and secondary-school teachers in the United States nearly doubled.[22] Teachers organized in two large labor unions: the American Federation of Teachers and the National Education Association. By the end of the 1960s, riding the crest of the Baby Boom, they had become two of the most powerful political forces in the country. In 1965, with heavy lobbying by the teachers' unions, the Congress, for the first time, provided federal aid for local education. By 1972, 22 percent of the delegates to the Democratic National Convention were teachers, a greater percentage even than lawyers, traditionally the dominant professional group in politics.[23] A few years later, their influence gained official recognition with the creation of a Department of Education in the president's cabinet.

The front edge of the Baby Boom didn't reach the age of majority until the end of the 1960s. And the members of that generation never became an ideological or political monolith. But their political influence was a powerful, though often indirect, political element in the 1960s. Its impact was especially potent in the universities, which grew to be the nation's primary sources of social criticism and reform ideas. By decade's end, with the number of students and faculty swelling precipitously, universities would also become havens of political activism.

The Baby Boomers were the primary audience for the music and films and literature and attitudes that challenged conventional authority in that decade. Mario Savio, who led the Free Speech Movement at the University of California at Berkeley in 1964, was not a Baby Boomer, but many of those in his movement were, and the litany of protests that followed was largely sustained by other Baby Boomers on other campuses across the country.

Bob Dylan was not a Baby Boomer either, nor were the provocative folk singers Joan Baez, Phil Ochs, and Pete Seeger. But Baby Boomers were their primary audience. As cultures of doubt and dissent came to infect American politics in the 1960s, Baby Boomers were at their source. Few could vote in that decade, but they could be seen and they could be heard.

When the Baby Boom generation reached college age, American higher education changed as never before. The number of college students more than doubled in a decade, from 3.2 million in 1960 to 7.1 million in 1970.[24] New institutions were opening constantly, more than five hundred in the 1960s alone.[25] And college faculties expanded in size, character, and range of subjects. New fields and departments bloomed overnight: Black Studies, Women's Studies, Peace Studies, and so on. Students began to demand "relevance" in their courses of study, and professors scrambled to provide it.

For most of American history, universities had been places where the children of the wealthy prepared for their own lives of privileged elitehood. As gateways to opportunity, the admissions and instruction policies of American universities directly affected who would become the country's lawyers, doctors, and business leaders. Few of the best universities educated many black or Jewish students before 1960. Many, in fact, had unpublished policies limiting or preventing the enrollment of such students.

The GI Bill had begun to change the character of higher education in the decades that followed World War II. Young people who could never have dreamed of attending college were provided the means and the opportunity to do so. And they did. In the years from 1946 through the early 1950s, student populations swelled as young veterans capitalized on these opportunities. Some of the effects of this influx outlasted it. College entrance became less dependent on social and economic background. A college education came to be a requirement for more and more jobs in an expanding service- and information-dominated economy. More American families aspired to send their children to college, and more colleges welcomed them than ever before.

For young women, however, few of whom had served in World War II, change came more slowly. Until the 1960s, higher-education practices confined most female students to velvet ghettos dispersed across the educational landscape. For daughters of the very wealthy, there were the Seven Sisters and a few other elite, all-female colleges. But few of their smart, well-trained women graduates chose career paths resembling those of their male counterparts. Barbara Pierce attended Smith, the elite women's college, in the 1940s. But when she married a young Navy pilot named George Herbert Walker Bush, she dropped out to be his wife. That was characteristic behavior for the women of her time. A generation later, in the 1960s, Hillary Rodham graduated from Wellesley College and immediately set off for Yale Law School, where she met her husband, another future president. She did not drop out, nor did she shy away from the career in the law for which she had prepared. Times had changed.

Women in the immediate postwar years could also attend most of the state universities and a few coed liberal arts colleges, but most of those who did were confined by practice or policy to separate facilities and classes or to "women's fields" like education, nursing, or the humanities. In graduate and professional schools, women were rarely welcomed and constituted barely visible minorities. In 1960, only 34 percent of American college students were women. Of the master's and doctoral degrees granted that year in American institutions, only 30 percent went to women.[26]

These patterns came to an abrupt end in the 1960s. Waves of Baby Boom students and challenges to traditional practices swept across college campuses simultaneously, feeding and inspiring each other. The outside world impinged on college campuses in the 1960s as never before. Once isolated bastions of fraternities and sports and white male elitism, universities increasingly came to reflect the diverse face and compelling interests of contemporary American society. Some dropped all entrance standards, opting instead for open admissions. Recruiters began to seek out African American and other minority students. Single-sex institutions disappeared almost entirely. Men and women attended the same classes, enrolled in more of the same majors, and by the end of the decade came increasingly to live in the same dormitories. Graduate schools followed suit, and by 1970 women graduates were flowing into postgraduate education as never before.[27]

In no decade in American history did higher education change as dramatically as it did in the 1960s. The changes took root and endured. A university education has become a vital ticket not merely to the upper levels of American society but to the midlevels as well.

The changing attitudes of universities were also evident in the evolving role of faculties. The diminishing isolation of higher education from the rest of American life cleared the way for college professors to play roles beyond the traditional one of classroom instructor. Opportunities grew rapidly in the 1960s for professors to become participants in private- and public-sector decision making, employing their knowledge and analytical skills in ways that trespassed well beyond the traditional boundaries of classroom instruction and scholarly publication.

By the dozen the professors came to Washington to put their knowledge to work: Arthur Schlesinger, Jr., John Kenneth Galbraith, Walter Heller, W. W. Rostow, Daniel Patrick Moynihan, James Tobin, McGeorge Bundy. President Kennedy recruited eagerly from university faculties:

secretary of state, national security advisor, chairman of the Atomic Energy Commission, director of the Budget Bureau, ambassadors, White House aides. Presidents Johnson and Nixon followed suit. "President Kennedy has heavily raided university faculties to secure officers and administrators for his new administration," wrote A. A. Berle, Jr. "More than one college president has torn out fistfuls of hair as professorial acceptance of these appointments tore whole pages out of his catalogue of courses."[28]

College faculties were becoming an important societal resource. Corporations relied on them to hone the cutting edge of scientific research and corporate grants funneled steadily into university laboratories. Private foundations and government agencies encouraged social science research that came to play a major role in guiding social policy. And professors themselves parlayed their knowledge and analytical skills into direct roles in politics and policy making. Some of this had happened before in America, in the occasional counsel provided by a Felix Frankfurter to Woodrow Wilson or the "brains trust" to Franklin Roosevelt. But the flow of personnel between government and the universities grew to a small flood in the 1960s and a larger one in the years that followed. By the mid-1970s, President Ford's cabinet had college professors as the heads of the departments of State, Defense, Justice, Agriculture, Labor, and Health, Education, and Welfare.

This was a two-way flow. New national administrations recruited from university faculties to staff important posts in government, and former government officials often took positions on university faculties to pass on to students the lessons they'd learned in the real world. Fueled by this symbiosis, universities became not merely places to train young people for entry-level positions in the private sector, but major sources of ideas and creative analysis for a society that was pressing for social and economic changes. University of California president Clark Kerr noted in a contemporary address, "Universities have changed . . . to become the architects of progress instead of the protectors of tradition. In so changing, their role in society has become ever more important. Increasingly, the leading universities of the world have absorbed functions of intellectual leadership, and today we are all intensely aware of the link between intellect and power."[29]

PLACE

As Allied forces entered Germany to subdue the remnants of Nazi resistance in 1945, they found they could move with unprecedented speed across that country's highways, especially the autobahn, the network of high-quality, high-speed roads that connected German cities. Dwight D. Eisenhower had earlier noted the benefits these roads provided to the mobility of the German armies.[30] A gem of engineering and construction, the autobahn offered Eisenhower a vision of the role that roads could play in a modern transportation system.

That vision never left him, and when he found himself in the White House a decade later, he pushed Congress to begin a major effort in America to construct roads of similar quality. Congress responded with the passage of the National Interstate and Defense Highways Act of 1956, which created the interstate highway system. Few legislative actions in American history have had so deep and lasting an effect on the economy and sociology of the country.

While Congress had first authorized some interstate highway construction in 1938, fewer than 10,000 miles had been built. The 1956 act authorized 41,000 miles of construction, and by 1970, 32,000 miles of interstate highway were in operation. The states were inspired to improve many of their own roads and to build new ones. These were linked to the major arteries funded largely by the federal government. Road-building became a major national industry in the 1950s and 1960s. In the 1950s alone, 233,000 miles of new roads of all kinds were built in America.[31] With so many new open roads, many of the regional differences that had so long defined American society and politics would begin to diminish.

Similar development occurred in the air travel industry. Commercial air travel had begun to come into its own in the late 1930s. In 1938, Congress created a Civil Aeronautics Authority (later the Civil Aeronautics Board) to regulate the new industry. The agency immediately limited the number of certified airlines to an established few. This "competitive monopoly" served the interests of the fledgling airline industry by protecting its original companies from much direct competition. But it also served a significant national purpose by imposing a quid pro quo on the airlines. In exchange for the limits placed on competition, the airlines would have to provide regular service to smaller cities where such service promised little profit. One of the airlines would have to schedule trips to and from Burlington, Vermont; Bakersfield, California; and dozens of other such communities. But the agency would protect them from competition on those routes and guarantee them enough unfettered access to more profitable routes so that they could prosper.

Rail and mass transit, the third and fourth pieces of the national domestic travel system, were treated quite differently, however. In the nineteenth century, the federal government had played a central role in encouraging the expansion of the national rail system. But in the years that followed World War II, the Interstate Commerce Commission focused most of its attention on trucks, not trains. Many railroad companies went into economic decline as shippers and passengers found more economical and convenient ways to move their goods and their persons. In communities all across America, the trains stopped coming, weeds overgrew the track beds, and once-bustling stations closed, fell into disrepair, and were torn down. America was car country by the 1960s, and to most Americans trains had become an irrelevance.

The fourth element of the national transportation system was urban mass transit: the subways, streetcars, and buses that move people into and around cities. Mass transit had never been much of a federal priority and did not become one until the mid-1960s when many large cities were in crisis and Washington got involved in rebuilding their infrastructures. In the early years of the postwar period, however, the transportation funds coming from Washington were aimed primarily at linking the major cities with highways and airplane routes. Those funds tilted the national transportation system away from railroads and—in powerful ways—they tilted the population away from the cities.

At no time before or after World War II did any group of national planners decide that it would be wise public policy to subsidize the development of the country's suburbs. One searches in vain through party platforms, presidential inaugural speeches, and State of the Union Addresses of the postwar period for mention of the word "suburb." Yet in the years from 1940 to 1960, the federal government provided broad encouragement and enormous subsidy to the development of American suburbs. Evidence of direct intention may be absent, but evidence of profound effect is everywhere.

Although suburbanization had begun much earlier, the suburbs grew at an accelerated pace after World War II. They grew for many reasons: Returning veterans of the war needed housing as never before; the GI Bill and the Federal Housing Administration subsidized home mortgages for millions of Americans who could never have otherwise dreamed of owning their own homes; federal funds subsidized the construction of high-speed roads that linked suburban communities to central cities and suburban workers to urban jobs; mechanization was displacing the farm population at very rapid rates;[32] and Washington neglected the cities, the railroads, and urban mass transit, encouraging the use and ownership of automobiles, the sine qua non of suburban life.

There were indeed "ribbons of highways"—that splendid American image—and they all led to the suburbs. Americans happily followed. The 1920 census did not even categorize suburban residence. The people who lived outside the central cities were mostly farmers, and they constituted 49 percent of the population. If you lived in Washington, D.C., in 1920, a drive through the countryside meant a trip through the farms of Falls Church, Virginia. If you lived in Boston, you could make a similar trip through the cornfields of Concord or the dairy pastures of Beverly. So it was everywhere, with cities looming like giant towers over largely agricultural landscapes. There was little in between.

By 1940, however, the precursors of a new pattern had begun to emerge. The census that year found that 15.3 percent of the American people inhabited areas between the farm and the city, areas called the urban fringe by the census, the suburbs by sociologists.[33] Spreading automobile ownership, the declining health of the rail lines that ran into cities, and the construction by state governments of local parkways and turnpikes had made it possible for some citizens to move over the city line into the communities on the immediate periphery. In New York the initiatives of the master planner Robert Moses had produced the Throgs Neck, Bronx-Whitestone, Henry Hudson, Verrazano-Narrows, and Triborough bridges, and the Brooklyn-Queens, Staten Island, and Cross-Bronx expressways, and the Laurelton Parkway. One could work in Midtown Manhattan and live in Bronxville, Massapequa, Greenwich, or East Orange.

People of means were leaving for the suburbs in the 1920s and 1930s. But the working class was still confined to the cities, to apartments, and to public transportation—until after the war. Then came the GI Bill, more affordable automobiles, more and better roads, the onslaught of the Baby Boom, the promise of better jobs and better lives in the suburbs, and beginnings of mass suburban construction in Levittown, Long Island, and in other new tract-housing suburbs all across America. In the late 1940s, a three-bedroom house could be bought in the first Levittown for seven thousand dollars.[34] With a GI mortgage, the monthly cost could be less than forty dollars. For many Americans this was cheaper—and better— than renting in the city. So they left the cities behind.

AT THE SAME TIME, the farm economy was steadily shrinking. By the early 1960s, this movement from the cities and farms to the suburbs had passed flood stage. Between 1940 and 1959, the farm population decreased by nearly 10 million people. The farm population had composed 23.2 percent of the country's population in 1940; by 1960, the farm portion of the total was barely half that.[35] The rural-urban nation of the 1930s and 1940s was becoming a suburban nation. In the 1970 census, 75 million Americans—37.6 percent of the population—lived in the suburbs.[36] This was a larger portion, finally, than lived in urban or rural areas.

Mass advertising reflected this change. So, too, did television sitcoms and films. In *The Dick Van Dyke Show*, a leading television series of the 1960s, Rob Petrie commuted into Manhattan every morning to his job as a writer for a television show. But he commuted home every night to his home in New Rochelle and life in the suburbs where his wife and son and neighbors spent their days. It was popular, but it was also emblematic. The typical American life now resembled the image. The suburbs were ascendant.

The rapid suburbanization that occurred in midcentury affected American life in many ways. In the cities, most people had rented the residences in which they lived. In the suburbs most people owned their homes. Between 1940 and 1970 America was transformed from a nation of renters to a nation of home owners. Forty-four percent of the population owned their residences in 1930; by 1970 it was 58 percent.[37]

Home owners are stakeholders in a way that renters rarely can be. Suburban home owners wanted better roads, better schools for their children, better playgrounds and parks, and more security. In short, they wanted more government and more programs. And they got them.

With the suburbs, too, came new patterns of nationalization of the economy. Growth in the suburbs and along the interstate highways sparked the rise of shopping malls and of franchised restaurants, stores, and hotels. McDonald's, Kentucky Fried Chicken, and Holiday Inn all went into business in the 1950s. By the end of the 1960s, they were common sights in thousands of communities all across the country. A family driving from New England to Florida for a vacation in the 1940s could enjoy the wide variety of local cuisines and hospitality along the way. A similar journey at the end of 1960s wound through an endless landscape of unvarying strip malls, fast-food joints, and cookie-cutter motels. Suburbanization, ever so quickly, had nationalized and homogenized the economic and the visual landscape.

This population movement made the suburbs the new American power center. The cities were hollowed out, as the white middle class moved out and the central cities were left increasingly to the poor and to members of minority groups. Later the cities would demand federal help to revive, and they would get it. But as the suburbs gave rise to a new sense of prosperity and opportunity in the immediate postwar years, the cities sloughed into despond.

The agrarian political base dissolved almost completely. And as population shifted south and west, so too did political muscle. Between 1940 and 1970, the states of New York, Pennsylvania, and Illinois went from 104 seats in the House of Representatives to 88. In the same period, California, Florida, and Texas went from 50 to 82 seats. That transition would continue through the rest of the twentieth century. But even at the beginning of the 1960s, the rise of the South and West and the decline of the North were already significant factors in the politics of that decade.

These twin movements affected not only the distribution of citizens and voters, but also the organization of politics. The northern cities and the farm states that dominated politics for most of the century that followed the Civil War were a political organizer's dream. Farmers were always focused on a small collection of related issues: the availability of credit, transportation to market, and prices for their crops. Local and state party leaders could command their support and loyalty for generations by acting as their advocates on those issues.

In the cities the party leaders developed highly refined organizations. The leaders were often called "bosses," and the organizations became "machines." Their hierarchy extended from local neighborhoods through districts and wards to city hall and state capital. The machines were fueled by public jobs for the workers, goods and services for loyal voters, and no small amount of corruption. When new immigrants poured into the cities, the machines worked diligently and quickly to obtain citizenship for them and to turn them into grateful and reliable supporters.

The key to all of this was the ease in organizing tightly packed cities, where neighborhoods were small communities with ethnic and religious similarities. Ward leaders could organize and "deliver" their wards. Communication was efficient and effective. Before there was an Internet or even telephones, party leaders could readily know the sentiments of their constituents and respond to them.

In the South, of course, it was often simpler than that. There was only one political party of consequence in the South in the century after the Civil War, the Democratic Party. Its leaders rarely needed to pay much attention to organizing or building a party infrastructure because voters had nowhere else to go. By keeping the interests of farmers paramount and by not wavering on the overarching issue of white supremacy, southern Democrats could win election after election without worrying about partisan opposition. There was none.

These traditional patterns of political organization were all challenged and eventually undermined in midcentury. Much of that change stemmed from population movement. The dominant political party structures of the first half of the century had the rug pulled out from under them. In some places, leaders no longer had the same kind or number of followers. In others, new immigrants lacked the characteristics

or the loyalties of the citizens to whom they were becoming new neighbors. And in suburbs all across America, where political traditions were
largely nonexistent, politics lacked any clear sense of direction.

The suburbs had supported Eisenhower for president overwhelmingly in the 1950s. But so had the rest of the country, and Eisenhower's
support led to premature conclusions that the suburbs were Republican
country.[38] In 1960, John F. Kennedy drew 49 percent of the suburban vote,
closely matching his national portion.[39] In 1964, the median vote for the
Republican presidential candidate, Barry Goldwater, in a national sample
of suburbs was 33.8 percent; the Republican portion of the congressional
vote in those same suburbs was 47 percent.[40]

A large portion of the residents of the suburbs in the 1960s were still
urban refugees, still holding on to the Democratic politics they brought
with them from the cities. A generation later, the suburbs would be dominated by people born and raised there, people who had never lived in
cities or on farms. They would bear cleaner political slates. But not yet.

The suburbs established in the earlier decades of the century, a short
train ride from "downtown," were havens of the wealthy. But the suburbs
built in the 1950s, the large, carefully plotted developments where housing was much cheaper, attracted middle- and working-class folks. As political scientist Charles G. Bell notes, these newer suburbs were "populated
with Democrats who continued to vote Democratic.[41]

This was an important part of the political context for the 1960s, especially the first half of that decade when the Congress was driving full-
bore through a vast agenda of new government initiatives. There would
be a potent suburban reaction to that agenda later, but in the early 1960s,
a growing cadre of suburban representatives, both Democratic and Republican, played a major role in facilitating the policy changes taking
place in Washington. As political scientist Richard Lehne noted from his
study of congressional voting records, "The growth of American suburbs
has had unmistakable implications for congressional policy making. Increased suburban representation and the decline in the number of legislators from rural districts has enhanced support for typically liberal social
service measures. . . ."[42] "The size of the suburban delegation in Congress
has increased profoundly in the last decade," he wrote in 1975, "and these

suburbanites have been pivotal supporters of the expansive program initiatives emanating from the new Congress."[43]

The emergence of the suburbs would change American politics deeply in the last third of the twentieth century, but on the precipice of that transition, conditions were still ripe for the Democrats, for the liberal agenda, for one last great gasp of the New Deal coalition.

AMERICAN DIASPORA

The small town of Cairo sits in the center of Grady County on the southern border of Georgia. Like many small Georgia towns in the early part of the twentieth century, it had two defining characteristics: agriculture and racial segregation. Black farm laborers in that part of the South often made up a significant portion of the population. But they were economically and politically powerless.

The lives of black people in the rural South were predetermined by their race. The only way to change one's fate was to leave. And that's what Mallie Robinson did in 1920 when her husband, a plantation worker in Cairo, disappeared. She took her five young children and headed to Pasadena, California, beyond the reach of the heavy hand of Jim Crow.

Racism wasn't confined to the South in the America of the first half of the twentieth century, but outside the South, African Americans could vote, they could go to integrated schools, they had economic opportunities. Though far from perfect, the cities beyond the Mason-Dixon Line looked like the promised land to black people born in the South.

So it was for Mallie Robinson and her children. They encountered discrimination, but they confronted it with education and hard work and courage. Her youngest son attended UCLA, leaving during his senior year to enter World War II. He was confined, as all people of his race were, to an all-black unit in the segregated army of the time. Initially denied admission to Officer Candidate School, he came back again and again until he was admitted and commissioned a second lieutenant. At Fort Hood, Texas—back in the South—the new lieutenant refused to sit in the back of a local bus and was court-martialed and prevented from going to Europe with his battalion. He was eventually acquitted and honorably discharged, but with a "war record" stained by the color of his skin.

Mallie's son was a good athlete, and after leaving the Army he began to play baseball with the Kansas City Monarchs in the Negro American League. As with nearly everything in America in the 1940s, there were separate baseball leagues for blacks and whites. He played well—well enough to be discovered by Clyde Sukeforth, a scout for Branch Rickey, the general manager of the Brooklyn Dodgers.

Little more than a year later, on April 5, 1947, Jackie Robinson became the first person of his race to play major league baseball. Baseball had integrated—first a token, then a trickle, then a torrent—before the American armed forces, before the American South, before the statutes of American law. But all would follow, and soon. Jackie Robinson's appearance in a major league uniform was a moment of stunning significance in American life, widely noted at the time, deeply honored since. And it was an emblem of the challenge to racial stereotypes and racial discrimination that would flow across the following decades. But it was also an indication of the swelling consequences of one of the great population movements in human history.

Like Mallie Robinson, many southern blacks came to believe that the only way to avoid the worst dangers of racism was to escape the South. World War I provided an incentive to many. Some 360,000 African Americans served in uniform during World War I. Most came from the South, but many did not return when the war was over. They settled instead in the growing cities of the North where racism had fewer legal supports and economic opportunity was greater and more varied.

As the character of southern agriculture was transformed by the introduction of farm machinery, there was less need for the children and grandchildren of slaves who had been the primary labor for what had been a very labor-intensive economy. The disappearance of farm jobs contributed to the northward flow. By 1940, nearly a quarter of the country's 13 million African Americans lived outside the South. Most had congregated in the largest northern cities—New York, Philadelphia, Detroit, Chicago—with enough critical mass in those places to begin to establish communities and cultures of their own. Chicago became a jazz hotbed;

Harlem in New York a vibrant center of emergent black artistry. These northern black communities became magnets to those African Americans who remained in the South.

The Depression of the 1930s hit southern blacks especially hard. Desperation drove them north. When World War II grew closer and America began to arm itself and its allies, the suddenly booming northern economy sucked in workers of all colors and both sexes. Nearly a million African Americans, like Jackie Robinson, served in World War II. Hundreds of thousands more found the best jobs of their lives in the war industries in the North.

This combination of economic opportunity, political freedom, and safety from Jim Crow inspired nearly 3 million African Americans to leave the South and move north and west between 1920 and 1950.[44] Another 1.5 million followed in the decade between 1950 and 1960.[45] By the 1960s, half of the American black population lived outside the South, most of them in poor urban neighborhoods that some called "ghettos."

The relocation of the black population transfigured the North, especially its cities, and eventually it would transfigure the South as well. The economic historian William J. Collins notes that "the Great Migration literally changed the complexion of the urban North and in so doing transformed the 'Negro problem' from a rural southern peculiarity into a phenomenon of nationwide scope. Therefore, it stands as a watershed in the history of African Americans, the history of American cities, and the history of the South."[46]

Twenty percent of the citizens of the fifty largest American cities were African American by 1960. In the very largest cities, the percentage was even greater. Of those African Americans who had moved north, more than 90 percent were concentrated in the ten largest states—states whose electoral votes determined who would be president of the United States.[47]

The "black vote" began to grow in significance as politicians—white and black—realized that a motivated and unified community of black voters could tip the outcome in states that mattered in presidential politics. Some black politicians, like Adam Clayton Powell of New York and Robert N. C. Nix of Philadelphia, were elected to Congress and accumulated the seniority that was essential to power there. White politicians also began to heed their black constituents and to support causes that mattered most to African Americans: voting rights, school desegregation, open housing, and the end of discrimination in hotels and restaurants and other public accommodations.

Politicians had black constituents. Newspapers had black readers. Merchants had black customers. Blacks had begun to matter in the North. They had a voice, and it echoed in city halls and in Washington. The great American diaspora was critical to the civil rights movement of the 1950s and 1960s. That movement unfolded in the South, but its support in Washington had deepening political roots in the black communities of the North. The growth of these black communities was critical, as well, to both the substance and success of the liberal policy agenda of the 1960s.

To many African Americans, there were two great policy challenges in the 1960s. One was the old need to destroy the legal foundations of racial discrimination. The other was the newer need to rebuild American cities, where so many black Americans now resided, and to attack the poverty, poor schools, broken-down infrastructures, and crime that were becoming the common afflictions of urban life. Life in the North may have been better than life under Jim Crow in the South, but for many it was far from the good life. And it seemed natural, even essential, to turn to Washington for relief.

TELEVISION

Bill Clinton wrote in his 2004 memoir, *My Life*: "In 1956, I finally got a brother, and our family finally got a television set." He then describes how television connected him to the political world beyond his hometown and state. That first summer, he wrote, "what really dominated my TV viewing . . . were the Republican and Democratic conventions. I sat on the floor right in front of the TV and watched them both, transfixed." Later, as a teenager, "I followed the civil rights movement on the evening news . . . and Cold War events like the Bay of Pigs and the U-2 incident. . . ." Then, he writes, "one other memorable event happened to me in the summer of 1963. On August 28, nine days after I turned seventeen, I sat alone in a big white reclining chair in our den and watched the greatest speech of my lifetime, as Martin Luther King, Jr., stood in front of the Lincoln Memorial and spoke of his dream for America. . . . I started crying during the speech and wept for a good while after Dr. King finished."[48]

Like so many Americans in the 1950s and 1960s, Bill Clinton was able to experience events with more emotional intensity than had ever been possible before the advent of television as the universal national connector. Note that his recollection of seeing King's speech describes an event that "happened to me." But he was more than a thousand miles away—not reading a summary of it, or even the text; not hearing an eyewitness account, but participating as a viewer, as an audience, as part of the event. Television changed forever the concept of citizenship in the national political scheme. No event or practice—not racism, not consumer fraud, not environmental threats—would ever again be merely local.

Few inventions in its history had ever gripped America the way television did in the 1950s. Rooftops from Maine to California sprouted aluminum antennae. In 1950, 7 percent of American homes owned at least one television set; in 1960 the number had grown to 87.3 percent.[49] By 1960 the average American adult watched television about thirty-five hours per week, a total of more than eighteen hundred hours per person per year.[50] And television stations proliferated across the country, to 530 in 1960 and 673 in 1969.[51]

As the 1960s began, television had become a staple of American life, a constant presence. But television was different, in degree and kind, from any other medium of news or entertainment. The moving images gave immediacy and presence to news reports, drew in and touched the audience in ways that printed words or mere sound never had. The television image, the theorist Marshall McLuhan noted, "involves the viewer in a perpetual act of participation and completion. . . . The TV image is not a shot, nor a view of anything, so much as an experience."[52]

In the decades that followed World War II, American society underwent a process of nationalization unlike anything it had previously experienced. Local and regional differences began to melt away; a national identity took their place. Television played a major role in all this, perhaps the central role. It became a stage in every home on which each night were played out the major events of the day, a stage on which public figures loomed larger than ever before in the public consciousness.

Television quickly acquired a remarkable capacity for creating and changing the national mood, for making heroes and for destroying them, for showing humanity's deepest compassion and its darkest evil. The television networks were just that: networks. They linked American citizens. Everyone tuned in at the same time for *I Love Lucy* and *Gunsmoke* and *Ed Sullivan*.

Ed Sullivan's Sunday night program began in 1948 as *The Toast of the Town*, a New York show with a distinctively local flavor, even as its audience spread across the country. By the 1960s it was *The Ed Sullivan Show* and it reached an audience so vast that a single guest appearance could turn a comedian or a singer into a star for decades. In fact, appearing on the Sullivan show was all the evidence necessary of incipient stardom. When Elvis Presley first appeared in 1956 and the Beatles in 1964, these were transfixing national events, ensconced in reams of publicity in their own time, wrapped even now in shrouds of legend. It didn't matter whether you lived in Alabama or Michigan or Oregon; watching the Beatles on *Ed Sullivan* was a shared experience.

THE POSTWAR YEARS BONDED Americans in new networks. Interstate highways and the national air transport system tied their cities and regions closely together. National branding and marketing pulled them into similar habits in where they shopped, what they bought, and how they ate. And the narrow control exercised over the still-new medium of television by a handful of corporations and the usually friendly regulators of the Federal Communications Commission gave unprecedented power to a few broadcasters to shape fashion and taste, to manufacture celebrity, and to define the public agenda of the nation's political institutions.

It is not surprising that when national identity began to supersede local and regional identities Americans grew less willing to compartmentalize public issues. Race ceased to be just a "southern problem." The shame of the cities could no longer be left only to the urban states to address. The mistreatment of migrant workers was no longer merely a farm state concern. The ravages of hunger and poverty became topics of conversation in Greenwich and Grosse Pointe, not just Appalachia.

In a letter from his jail cell in Birmingham, Alabama, in 1963, Martin Luther King, Jr., wrote: "Injustice anywhere is a threat to justice everywhere. We are caught in an inescapable network of mutuality, tied in a single garment of destiny. Whatever affects one directly, affects all indirectly."[53]

He was not simply waxing poetic or prophetic. He was speaking a new truth of a new age. Anywhere and everywhere had come together in the 1960s. Problems that had once been "their" problems were now "our" problems. When the country came to share a growing sense of national identity, it assumed as well a new sense of responsibility. What some suffer, all must seek to cure.

Nor is it surprising that when this growing sense of national identity emerged in the 1960s Americans would logically begin to look to their national government to address issues that had long been regarded as state or local matters. Race, the care of the poor and elderly, poverty, pollution, the costs of education: All of these became national concerns in the 1960s, important to national politicians even when they had little direct impact on their own constituents.

The national agenda was growing and Washington, increasingly free from local bonds and constraints, was getting ready to respond.

CHAPTER 2

POLITICS AND THE LIBERAL ARC

When President Dwight D. Eisenhower appeared before a joint session of Congress in January 1961 to make his last State of the Union Address, he looked out on a body not much different in character from most of the earlier Congresses of the twentieth century. Most members of the Eighty-seventh Congress arrived there after years of tedious labor in the political trenches. They were products of the political parties that still dominated most American cities and much of the heartland.

Sam Rayburn, the Democratic Speaker of the House, came from Bonham, Texas. In 1960, 23 of the 24 members of the Texas delegation were Democrats. Indeed, among the 138 people representing the states of the old Confederacy in the House and Senate, 128 were Democrats. So it had been for nearly a hundred years: the solid Democratic South.

Across the benches were scores of other representatives who owed their seats in Congress to political bosses. The seat was their reward for loyalty. Make no waves. Follow the leader. In Rayburn's oft-repeated advice to new members: "To get along, go along."

A handful of barons ran that Congress: the party leaders and the committee chairs. None of them was young, for the only reliable route to power in that Congress was longevity. The barons met in private to cut their deals and define their strategy. An ironclad seniority system afforded them immunity from challenge and criticism. The invisibility of most important decision making in Congress freed them from accountability. In 1960 the powerful House Ways and Means Committee held 81 percent of its meetings in closed session. Its chairman, Wilbur Mills (D-Arkansas), cemented his authority by appointing no subcommittees. When the committee sent bills to the floor, closed rules prohibited amendments. Influence over the issues in Ways and Means' jurisdiction—tax policy, health care, Social Security—resided within the committee only, and its clever chairman guarded that hegemony jealously. "Our whole system," Wilbur Mills once said, "was to settle disputes within the committees. It's a waste of time to bring out a bill if you can't pass it."[1]

But as Eisenhower peered out over the heads of the old barons to the back benches, he could spy some members who didn't fit the mold, who were new to the Congress and who hadn't always followed the traditional trail to Washington. There was William Proxmire, senator from Wisconsin, elected in 1956 and already in trouble with the leadership, whom he seemed always willing to buck. Rep. Eugene McCarthy of Minnesota, former seminarian and college professor, was barely known to the public but was nonetheless challenging the ancient culture of the House as the leader of the ambitious and frustrated group of young liberals they were calling "McCarthy's Mavericks." Rep. Richard Bolling of Missouri, protégé of Rayburn, was already building an agenda for reform of a legislature he described as "a shambles."[2]

Scattered across those back benches and in the bulging Democratic majorities swelled by huge victories in the 1958 midterm elections were political figures whose hopes would soon come to shape the agenda of the country. They hadn't come to Congress in the old-fashioned way and they were determined not to live out their public careers that way either.

Sen. Edmund Muskie of Maine had to create a political party in his state to have a public career. The son of an immigrant Polish tailor in Rumford, Maine, he grew up in a state where only Republicans ruled. Maine had voted Republican in every presidential election in the twentieth century.[3] When forty-six of the forty-eight states supported Franklin Roosevelt in 1936, only Maine and Vermont clung to their Republican loyalties. When Muskie and a few young friends tried to forge a Democratic Party and to win the governorship in 1954, they had few allies, little money, and less hope. The joke at the time was that they held their party convention in a telephone booth. But somehow Muskie won in 1954, and in 1958, its political composition in transition, Maine sent him to the U.S. Senate. Like so many of the young liberals elected that year, he did not go to Washington to be a mere cog in a machine.

To the naked eye the Congress that Eisenhower confronted at the dawn of the 1960s might have looked comfortably typical. But beneath that familiar appearance, deep currents of change were already at work. In the decade to come Congress would begin to transform in ways that would revolutionize its membership, alter its operations, and destroy the oligarchies that had dominated it for decades. Fifty-seven percent of the members listening to Eisenhower's last State of the Union Address at the beginning of the 1960s would leave Congress before Richard Nixon's first at the decade's end. And the members who came to Congress in the intervening years would be unlike their predecessors in many ways: younger, more ideological, less experienced in and committed to the traditional deferential ways of legislatures, freer from party influences back home, and more impatient for progress on a substantive agenda of change.

The shell of the old Congress was beginning to crack in 1960, and a very different successor would emerge in the decade ahead. The new politics that emerged in America after World War II made that possible. A generation of pent-up public policy demands made it necessary.

THE LIBERAL ACCORD

The public policy initiatives that now define the 1960s in the popular imagination could not have emerged directly from the politics of the 1950s. America's political folkways and institutional arrangements were full of traps and catches that snared advocates of reform. Politics and governing institutions had to change before public policy could change.

In 1960 electoral politics was still dominated by local party leaders who viewed their quadrennial engagement with national elections as a forum for pursuit of local objectives. The Republican and Democratic parties dominated, as they had for a century, but both were little more than loose confederations of local politicians, without effective national leadership or apparent cerebral cortex. Though Democrats tended left and Republicans right, politicians in both parties were scattered so broadly along the ideological spectrum that neither party could offer the American people a coherent philosophy or distinctive platform. Both parties typically sought to control the broad center of American politics, but within each party were legions of politicians who came at the center from every direction.

In Congress, the conservatives usually dominated, even though the Democrats had claimed majorities in all but two Congresses since 1930. The party of the left was controlled, in nearly every instance, by its wing of the right. That wing drew its strength from the South and its resolve from an unshakable commitment to white supremacy. Southerners could be populist and even progressive on many matters of social policy; the New Deal had drawn significant support from that region. But in the politics of race, it gave no quarter. And it resisted any effort to expand federal authority in ways that might allow the government in Washington to determine racial practices in Atlanta or Birmingham or Tuscaloosa. Southerners colonized the Congress, shaped its rules to their needs, and made it a bastion for protecting Jim Crow at home and keeping Washington at a distance.

The presidency of the time was still a fledgling institution. The formal structure of the Executive Office had been established only in 1939. The annual "program of the president" had evolved a decade later. The postwar Congress had acquired the habit, quite novel in American history, of looking to the president for legislative leadership. Presidents in the 1950s were slowly acquiring the habit of providing it. But the modern relationship between president and Congress was still taking shape as the 1950s drew to a close.

IN THIS POLITICAL AND INSTITUTIONAL setting at the dawn of the 1960s, there resided—often awkwardly—a liberal accord. The American people had confronted an economic crisis and a world war in the previous three decades. Their government had responded with unprecedented policy initiatives: the New Deal, wartime mobilization, income tax with-holding, the GI Bill, and so on. The federal government had grown in size and scope and cost. And Americans, for the most part, approved.[4]

Most Americans, in fact, seemed ready for more. The liberal agenda was incomplete. The Depression had passed, but poverty endured. The fragility of the environment was more apparent each year. The imperfections of the marketplace and the risks posed by new products and new drugs were the subjects of gushing streams of publicity. The country's expanding wealth was a growing contrast to its shortfalls in health care, education, and housing. And always there festered the wounds of racial discrimination, more prominent and painful now in the midst of the Cold War.

The New Deal had altered the landscape of American politics in ways that would last for decades. Millions of Americans had formed attachments to the Democratic Party that survived the leader who inspired them. The Democrats would hold majorities in Congress for thirty-two of the thirty-six years between 1932 and 1968. Only a wildly popular war hero would keep them from controlling the White House through all of that period. And despite the divide between North and South, on most issues the Democratic majority—in the partisan loyalties of voters and the political control of national institutions—retained the core values of New Deal liberalism. "For two decades after World War II," wrote historian Iwan Morgan, "American politics was shaped by the existence of a liberal consensus."[5]

The prevailing accord was attached to a postwar liberalism that was uniquely American. Compared to the bold initiatives of the Labour Party in Britain or its continental counterparts—with nationalized industries, universal medical care, and a full complement of other welfare state policies—the liberalism to which American affections gravitated was a minimalist policy rooted in beneficence, but more notable for good intentions than bold actions.

The midcentury liberal accord in America was comfortable with capitalism, but not its excesses. It sought to uplift the poor without unduly burdening the wealthy. It promised new rights and opportunities for workers, for women, and for minorities, but not a social revolution that would reverse the social order or truly empower the dispossessed. As the historian Alan Brinkley has noted, "Liberal discussion of the postwar world centered on a single, highly resonant phrase: 'full employment.' . . . It was a concept that provided a reasonably coherent framework for many of the discrete and halting adjustments liberals had been making in their goals for the state since at least the late 1930s. It represented an effort to define a role for government less threatening to capitalists . . . but one that nevertheless gave the state an active and powerful part in ensuring that the capitalist economy would work on behalf of all the nation's people."[6]

The burgeoning American middle class found much to like in these notions because they were full of promise for a better life: cleaner air, improved educational opportunities, national security, racial harmony, and—most important—continuing prosperity. Godfrey Hodgson properly characterized this liberal accord as "the operational creed of a great nation at the height of its confidence and power."[7]

So powerful was the popular attachment to these New Deal values that even Republicans felt compelled to accept them. Eisenhower's presidency had sought to reverse almost none of what the previous twenty years of Democratic ascendancy had established. His "moderate Republicanism" looked different only at the edges from the New Deal liberalism that had come to dominate the American political center. When Robert Taft, the Republican Senate leader and darling of conservatives, pursued his party's nomination in 1952, he could gain little traction on this liberal landscape and Eisenhower swamped him.

But while he made his peace with the liberal accord, Eisenhower pushed it forward far too slowly for most liberals and, by the end of his presidency, for most Americans. His party could hold its majorities in Congress only for his first two years in office, and by 1958 the Republican bloc in Congress had shrunk back toward its New Deal lows. The tensions in the Congress that sat before Dwight Eisenhower in January 1961, though invisible to the public, were glaring to its members. Two Democratic senators, John F. Kennedy and Lyndon B. Johnson, would successively occupy the White House. And many other members, seemingly powerless in the old order that still dominated, would soon form the cutting edge of a new liberal surge.

But first they had to overcome the power structure of the Congress that still impeded most reform activity. The possibilities for change had been building for some time. Now it would be a test of political will—and political skill—between the old order and the new. And on that January night in 1961, the outcome remained very much in doubt.

THE PARTY'S OVER

The American political system—the one that had prevailed for most of the twentieth century—was about to collapse in 1961. It was built on legal, demographic, and technological realities that were all crumbling.

The Republican Party had dominated national politics from the time of William McKinley's election in 1896 until 1930. Only the party split caused by Theodore Roosevelt's quixotic candidacy in 1912 had prevented Republicans from holding the White House through that entire period. And in Congress Republican majorities prevailed more than 80 percent of the time. The Republican regime buckled in the midterm elections of 1930, though Herbert Hoover limped on for two more years in the White House. Democrats took control of both houses of Congress after the 1930 election, and they would retain that control for all but four of the next fifty years.

When the Seventy-second Congress organized for business in 1931, it followed the tradition of appointing as chairs the members of the majority party with the longest continuous service on each committee. This was the rule of seniority and it was ironclad. The southerners were its great beneficiaries.

The South in 1930 was still a sparsely populated, largely rural region. The Democratic Party was the only party in nearly every part of the South and all of that region's representatives in Congress were Democrats. Because southern incumbents were rarely defeated in primaries, and never in the general election, they amassed seniority much more effectively than representatives from other regions. And when the Democratic Party found itself in the majority in the House after 1930, southerners in large numbers reaped the benefits of their accumulated seniority.

Franklin Roosevelt's election in 1932 cemented the passage of power from Republicans to Democrats. Though a Yankee patrician, Roosevelt worked comfortably with southern party leaders and members of Congress. The South was a key element of the New Deal coalition that elected him four times and continued to dominate national politics after his death. In four contests for the White House, Roosevelt never lost a southern electoral vote. In the 1930s, southern representatives were solidifying their control of the Congress. No president could expect much legislative accomplishment without their acquiescence.

The politics of the midcentury decades was still organized around two major political parties. Most voters attached themselves to one of those parties and their attachments were deep and durable. They rarely changed or weakened in a lifetime. In the middle of the century, more Americans identified with the Democratic Party than the Republican. So severe were the agonies of the Depression that they set many Republicans adrift from their partisan moorings; they landed—and stayed—on Democratic shores.

Dominating the Democratic Party at midcentury was a confederation of local fiefdoms, often called party machines. Richard J. Daley ran the politics of Illinois through his positions as head of the Cook County machine and mayor of Chicago. Cigar-chomping Leander Perez was the political king of Plaquemines Parish in Louisiana. John M. Bailey in Connecticut, David L. Lawrence in Pittsburgh, Carmine DeSapio in New York, and others like them were the people who mattered in Democratic politics.[8] In many places the machines were beginning to run out of gas, but politics carried on through the 1950s and into the 1960s as though little had changed. As the political scientist Joseph Cooper has written: "In the 1950s and 1960s state and local party leaders continued to be of major importance in determining the presidential nominee, and many state and local party organizations still controlled nominations for federal, state, and local offices. As for campaigns, party organizations continued to play a major role in contacting voters and bringing them to the polls, and party identification remained strong."[9]

The political parties channeled most of the influence of special interest groups through the middle decades of the century. That term, in fact, had not yet come into vogue. Instead they were called "pressure groups," and in the Democratic Party there were only a few that really mattered: the large labor unions, the NAACP on matters of race, the Americans for

Democratic Action on the ideological left. Labor was the dominant force and the Democratic Party was its political outlet. Union members were the party's foot soldiers; union leaders sat in the party's war councils. The relationship was symbiotic and mutually beneficial. Labor unions at mid-century were at their apogee, their memberships having grown from 11.6 percent of the nonagricultural civilian workforce in 1930 to 34.7 percent in 1954.[10] Their political goals and the party's political needs were a good match.

An important contributor to the Democratic ascendancy at midcentury was the identity crisis that hamstrung the Republicans. Republicans were the party of an America that seemed to be fading away. They were the party of agrarian values in a country that was industrializing. They were the party of the urban patricians in a country where control of urban politics had fallen to the sons of immigrants. They were the party of big business in the aftermath of a Depression that had undermined much of the moral authority and political power of business leaders. As the liberal accord took form and became the ideological center of politics, Republicans could find no effective response. Hooverism had no appeal; me-tooism was a hard sell. The only handle Republicans could find was at the edges and in the excesses of Democratic dominance. The Republican campaign slogan of 1952 was all negatives: "Korea, Communism, and Corruption." The party's quiver held few other arrows. By 1960, the most important leaders in the Republican Party—Nelson Rockefeller, William Scranton, Henry Cabot Lodge, even Richard Nixon—had come to sound more and more like Democrats. None intended to turn back the liberal tide.

The Pax Democratica that settled over American politics at midcentury rested on the liberal accord described earlier but also on two important demographic foundations: urban dominance of the politics of the North and rural dominance of the politics of the South. Democrats controlled most of the northern cities, and they controlled all of the rural South. The steady growth of the cities over the first half of the century had deepened the roots of Democratic strength in the North and West. The absence of significant urban growth in the South had secured the Democratic base in that region. It was an odd mix, this party of dirt farmers and immigrants, of blue collars and blue overalls, of racists and racial minorities. But the confederational nature of the politics of the time, with politics at home more important than politics in Washington, allowed these strange bedfellows to accomplish many of their collective purposes without challenging their more cherished local values or upsetting their successful local political arrangements.

BY 1960 ALL OF THESE FOUNDATIONS of midcentury politics were cracking and all would soon crumble. When so many voters moved to the suburbs, the great urban political machines started to break down. The American population was growing rapidly, but more so in the unorganized and detached hinterlands than in the cities where the party machines had reigned. The ground was falling out from under the northern foundation of the Democratic Party. John Kennedy was one of the first to recognize this altered reality. He knew he needed the support of the bosses to win the Democratic nomination in 1960, but he also recognized that he could not count on the bosses to win him the election. So he paid lip service to these dinosaurs of Democratic politics and made the requisite visits to their realms. But he built his own national political organization and staffed its local offices with amateur activists who had few connections to the formal party organizations. "It was," wrote the political journalist David Broder, "a transitional time in politics, a time in which an equivocal political leader was attempting to cope with a shifting party situation."[11]

Just as demographic change was beginning to alter political realities in the colder states of the Northeast and Midwest, a different set of demographic alterations was emerging in the warmer climes. As the 1950s unfolded, the southern population began to swell, its farm sector shrank, its industrial base expanded, and a southern retirement became viable for hundreds of thousands of aging refugees from northern winters.[12] Southern demographic shifts, though gradual, were more rapid than changes in Southern politics because the political powers of the South were often slow in recognizing their impact.

Two durable characteristics of southern politics survived well into the early stages of the in-migration and eventually conflicted with it. One was the legacy of slavery and the politics of race. Jim Crow died hard in the South. Well into the 1960s segregation remained the political as well as the social dividing line in southern society. You were for segregation or against it. Change might have been on the distant horizon in the eyes of many southern politicians, but woe be to any of them who got ahead of it. After being defeated by the racist John Patterson when he ran a moderate campaign for governor of Alabama in 1958, George Wallace told his friend Seymore Trammell, "I was out-niggered by John Patterson. And I tell you here and now, I'll never be out-niggered again."[13] Such cynical calculation was characteristic of the southern politics of the time. The South had entered a period of social upheaval and economic development for which its politics was unready.

The other characteristic of southern politics that slowed its transition was malapportionment. Southern politics—in reality as well as in popular mythology—was courthouse politics. Counties were the important political units in the South and county politics was dominated by the "courthouse gang" of party leaders, elected officials, judges, and powerful economic interests. Their influence was rooted in their dominance of state legislatures, and that dominance rested in the 1950s and early 1960s on a fundamental flaw in the democratic process: One person did not equal one vote.

While the South became less rural, its political base did not. Because states were under no constitutional or legal obligation to redefine political jurisdictions or to reassign representative seats after each census, most of the South was stuck after World War II with legislative districts that had been created much earlier. The rural areas were shrinking or growing slowly in population. Urban and suburban areas were growing faster than those rural areas, but their portion of the representatives elected to the state legislatures was not, and neither was their portion of the representatives sent to Washington. Rural dominance of southern politics outlasted the rural character of southern populations. The courthouse gangs continued to thrive even as their constituencies went into relative decline.

Nowhere was the contrast between reality and possibility more evident than in Georgia, which had long relied on a county-unit electoral system. In this model, votes were apportioned to counties, not people. The candidate who won the plurality of the popular vote in each county received all of its unit votes. Georgia's counties were classified as urban, town, or rural. In statewide primaries—the only elections that mattered in one-party Georgia—urban counties each had six unit votes, town counties had four, and rural counties had two. But because 121 of the state's 159 counties were classified as rural, their votes always constituted a majority of those cast.

The county classifications remained essentially unchanged from their creation in 1917 until the U.S. Supreme Court struck down the system in 1963. In 1960 the three smallest counties in Georgia had a combined population of 6,980 and six unit votes. The state's largest county had 556,326 people—and six unit votes.[14] Not surprisingly in Georgia, candidates with the most popular votes often lost elections. And not surprising either was the sustenance this system provided to the rural populations that most strongly opposed racial integration and other liberal programs.

Malapportionment was a national problem and it would become a national issue in the 1960s, but in the South its effects were especially critical because they helped sustain the race issue locally and slow the progress of liberal legislation nationally. In this one-party region, where legislators found it easy to accumulate seniority and thus legislative power, the modernizing impact of first urbanization and then suburbanization were retarded by the failure to shift legislative influence away from those shrinking rural districts that were a bastion of conservative ideology and racial discrimination. That change would come in the 1960s but, until it did, the old politics of the South would live on.

THE POSTWAR DECADES BROUGHT a major new factor into the American political calculus, one that would eventually change everything. That was television. Television made much of traditional American politics obsolete.

Television by the 1960s had become the nation's major source of information. Fifty-one percent of Americans said they got the majority of their news from television in 1959; in 1967, the percentage had grown to sixtyfour.[15] The radio networks were breaking up; newspaper numbers and newspaper circulation as a percent of the population were in decline.[16] Television was rapidly becoming America's eye on the world. Increasingly, the primary connection of most American citizens to their politics and their government was electronic—not through a political party or a local politician or direct participation, but through television.

Television created an entirely new political commodity that soon became as important as experience, loyalty, or good ideas: visibility. The way to have an impact on politics—as an incumbent, a candidate, or a seeker of policy change—was to attain visibility: to be seen and heard. Joseph McCarthy and Estes Kefauver catapulted to national prominence in the 1950s when they chaired televised congressional hearings—though McCarthy later learned that those who lived by this sword could die by it as well. In 1958 John Kennedy used his large and telegenic family to good effect in his Senate re-election campaign in Massachusetts.

Other political actors soon learned the value of television: the advocates of racial change in the South, the supporters of farm workers in the West, and the opponents of the war in Vietnam. Television provided a new path to power for the powerless, and in so doing, it deepened the fissure lines in the old politics.

The bosses of the Democratic Party who thought him too young, too much a dilettante, an unelectable Roman Catholic could not keep the 1960 nomination from John Kennedy, who had used television to such advantage to promote his candidacy through the few primaries of the time. Jim Crow survived for a century before television but for only a few years after television cameras seared the images of Birmingham and Selma into the national consciousness. Even the long American disposition to support presidents in wartime could not match the impact of televised images of American soldiers at Cam Ne in 1965 "burning a village to save it" and American young people filling the streets to protest.

"Polls and television have already induced massive indirect effects upon the political process in America and undoubtedly will continue to influence the political process in the future," wrote Harold Mendelsohn and Irving Crespi in 1970. "Polls and television... have modified and reshaped our expectations of political candidates.... They are making fundamental changes in the traditional national political party structures and function.... They have introduced new techniques of mass persuasion into the political process.... In short, they have been instrumental in the emergence of a new politics on the American scene."[17]

Prominence has always been a source of power in politics, but in the television age prominence could be acquired much more quickly, with far fewer hurdles and complications, and with startling effect. Politicians with little experience and a narrow political base could emerge overnight as major political figures by using television as their key to the political kingdom. Richard Nixon accomplished this with the Checkers speech in 1952; Ronald Reagan did so with a powerful defense of Barry Goldwater in 1964. Issues could explode onto the political agenda just as suddenly when the television cameras turned on them: the travails of migrant farm workers, an endangered environment, the powerful calls to justice of a black preacher.

The sudden significance of this new factor changed the political calculus profoundly and very rapidly. Kennedy's rise in 1960 and Barry Goldwater's four years later were powerful evidence of the changes that were enveloping American politics in the 1960s. Both men captured their own political parties, and both used television and public opinion polling and brazen confrontations with the old order to push their own ambitions. You didn't have to play with the bosses any more to win the game. Connections, loyalty, dues paying—those old political virtues now counted for little. Ambition and mastery of the new techniques of visibility now counted for much. By the mid-1960s the politics of the previous hundred years was on its deathbed. Television, in many ways, was its grim reaper.

NOWHERE WAS THIS MORE APPARENT than in the precipitous decline in the importance of American political parties. It is difficult for Americans who came of age after the 1950s to imagine how important political parties had been in managing electoral politics and in captivating political loyalties. Parents would more easily tolerate a child marrying outside the family religion than outside the family's partisan preference. Those loyalties passed through the generations like family jewels. They defined the political life of whole communities and whole regions. In the great age of American immigration, the political parties turned refugees into citizens and ethnic groups into hard-core, durable partisan factions.

In a landmark study published in 1960, four political scientists drawing on data from the American National Election Study described the role of political parties this way: "… Most of our citizens freely classify themselves as Republicans or Democrats and indicate that these loyalties have persisted through a number of elections. Few factors are of greater importance for our national elections than the lasting attachment of tens of millions of Americans to one of the parties."[18]

But their conclusions had only retrospective validity. They were reporting on a political system on the precipice of great change. Within a decade of the study's publication, the strength of party identification was in free fall. Many older Americans were abandoning or loosening their traditional party loyalties; many younger Americans were avoiding commitment altogether. Political scientist Martin P. Wattenberg tracked this change and reported that "between 1964 and 1972, the percentage of respondents identifying with one of the two major parties declined from 77 to 64 percent. In addition, people who continued to identify with a party after 1964 expressed a weaker sense of identification than before."[19]

And there were easy explanations for this because political parties were losing their hegemony over the electoral process and they were no longer able to be the essential wholesaler or middleman in the policymaking process. A clever, ambitious politician no longer needed party support to get elected to public office. At the gateways to politics, parties had been replaced by direct primaries. Anybody could enter a primary, and by the end of the 1960s anybody could win. The support of the local party organization was as likely to be an albatross as an asset. Parties could no longer control or determine who their nominees would be. And one could compete for office without relying or even drawing upon party resources. Candidates raised their own funds, hired their own campaign managers and expert consultants, developed and communicated their own messages. Parties, increasingly, were bystanders, hollow shells of what they once had been in American politics.

And television was central, indeed indispensable, in these changes. Television allowed politicians to circumvent political parties whenever they desired to do so. What use were parties when candidates could speak to voters directly?

Television changed the substance of American politics, not just the process of choosing leaders. By the mid-1950s, the structure of the television universe had taken shape. Three national networks had survived the early shake-out period: ABC, CBS, and NBC. All three were providing national programming for most of the day. Local television stations had sprung up in population centers all over the country; there were 522 in operation on the day of Kennedy's inauguration.[20] Most were affiliated with one of the three networks and carried the national broadcasts through most of the day and night.

News and public affairs had begun to fall into a pattern as well. Local stations carried local news and weather; the networks provided coverage of national events and national politics. Each of the networks developed an evening news broadcast; in 1963, these would all expand to thirty minutes. They were profit centers for the networks and became highly competitive. Morning programming that included significant public-affairs coverage began with the introduction of the *Today* show in 1952. Other news coverage developed with interview programs like *Meet the Press* and newsmagazine shows like *60 Minutes*. And the networks often broke into their regular programming for presidential speeches to the nation, space launches, political conventions, or other matters of national consequence. Americans quickly acquired the habit of turning on their television when they learned of some significant breaking story like the racial confrontation in Little Rock, the Cuban Missile Crisis, or the Kennedy assassination.

Without anyone planning it, a major change was occurring in the United States: Americans were becoming—in a way never before possible—a national community. Their information about public affairs was no longer filtered through regional bias or local leaders. They didn't learn about political developments in Washington from their local party leader or even their elected representative there. They learned about them through a uniquely authoritative source: television news broadcasts. And they all learned the same things at the same time. When events had a powerful emotional content—like the fear inspired by the discovery of Soviet nuclear missiles in Cuba, or the revulsion at the sight of sheriffs beating nonviolent marchers on the Edmund Pettus Bridge in Selma, or the death of a president—the emotions were shared and they were much more powerful than they would have been had their source been the dry text of newsprint rather than the vivid images on the television screen.

Even in the history of television, this was a unique era. Beginning in the 1980s, videocassette recorders, cable, satellite broadcasting, DVDs, boutique all-news channels, video on demand, and endless new technologies would diversify television content and scatter the television audience. But for the few decades that followed the birth of network television, that's all there was—three networks around which a nation gathered to collect its information and observe its politics.

The agenda of the nation in the 1960s was full of issues that often would have been local or regional in earlier times. Race had been a regional issue. The environment was barely an issue at all. Poverty was largely invisible. Consumer protection was a local concern, often left to the Better Business Bureau, not to government. Even wars took place so far away that Americans learned of them in delayed and often heavily censored news dispatches. They didn't really see them happen, not in real time, not in their living rooms.

All of that changed in the 1960s. The power of the national community was steadily replacing the draw of local communities on the emotions and loyalties of American citizens. This change was driven by many forces—suburbanization, national branding and marketing, interstate highways and air travel, and higher educational levels—but nothing exceeded the impact of television.

REVOLT OF THE MINNOWS

It is unlikely that Howard W. Smith's featureless, grandfatherly face would ignite even a spark of recognition among any Americans who lived outside Washington, D.C., or the eighth congressional district of Virginia. But at the dawn of the 1960s Howard Smith was one of the most powerful men in American public life. Beyond Washington, that power was largely unknown; in the capital, however, it often seemed insurmountable.

Smith was born in 1883 and raised on his family's farm in Fauquier County, Virginia. He was a prisoner of the place and the time forever after. After graduating from the University of Virginia Law School at age twenty, he set up a law practice in Alexandria. Entry into local politics soon followed, and in 1922 he became a judge and was ever after known as Judge Smith. He was soft-spoken and respectful, a southern gentleman, and after he won a seat in the U.S. House of Representatives in 1930, the constituents in his largely rural, northern Virginia district regularly re-elected him.[21]

The man and the district were a near perfect fit, and for Howard Smith Washington was never much more than a place to protect the interests, the lifestyle, and the political culture of his neighbors from the constant threat of intrusions by the federal government. As his congressional colleague Carl Albert once wrote, "He was brought up believing that Yankees, carpetbaggers, Republicans, and foreigners were enemies of his people and the way of life they enjoyed. He was a white supremacist who fought racial integration to the bitter end. He opposed nearly all federal social reforms, including health, education, and welfare bills. He believed in the Constitution 'as written.' He was a strict constructionist and state's righter. He was a Tenth Amendment congressman."[22]

In many of these characteristics, Smith was not much different from a lot of southern representatives. What set him apart was his position as chairman of the House Rules Committee. When the Republicans lost their short-lived majority in the House after the 1954 midterm elections, Smith was the senior Democrat on Rules and following the iron law of seniority became its chair. With the constant support of William M. Colmer of Mississippi, the ranking Democrat, and Clarence Brown of Ohio, the ranking Republican, and the half or more of committee members who were conservative on most issues, Smith turned the Rules Committee into a graveyard for liberal legislation, especially any effort to change the civil rights status quo in the South.

Howard Smith was enormously successful at this, and thus very powerful for two reasons. One was the critical role of the Rules Committee in the legislative process in the House. Because of its large membership, the House was a more structured and orderly legislative body than the Senate. Each bill that went to the House floor was accompanied by a rule that specified the amount of time allowed for debate, the way in which that time would be allocated between supporters and opponents of the bill, and the kinds and number of amendments that could be considered. The House debated the rule before it debated a bill and if the rule were defeated then the bill, in nearly all cases, could not be called up for consideration. The Rules Committee held hearings on all bills and then recommended a rule for consideration by the House.

Or didn't. And therein lay its power.

If the committee refused to grant a rule, it effectively killed a bill. The arcane procedures for bypassing the committee were so rarely employed as to render them irrelevant. So the Rules Committee sat astride the legislative process with life-or-death power over all bills. And because committee chairs in that time had nearly absolute control of their committees and could not be dislodged, the chairman of the House Rules Committee dominated all legislative calculations. And from 1955 until 1966, that was Howard Smith, a hanging judge for civil rights and other reform bills.

Smith's power to torment liberals was only partly institutional. Perhaps the best southern tactician since Jeb Stuart, he used the rules of procedure and debate to control the flow of legislation. Richard Bolling (D-Missouri), one of the House liberals most often frustrated by Howard Smith, called him the "ablest legislator in the House."[23]

Smith's bag of tricks was bottomless, but his most effective tactic required very little cleverness. When a bill that Smith disliked came to the Rules Committee, he would often simply decline to schedule a hearing on it. "Held up in Rules" became the official obituary of much liberal legislation of the time. When a civil rights bill came to the committee in 1957, Smith didn't call the committee into session to review it. He let it be known that he'd gone back to his farm in Virginia to inspect a burned barn. Hearing this, Speaker Sam Rayburn remarked, "I knew Howard Smith would do anything to block a civil rights bill, but I never suspected he'd resort to arson."[24]

The operation of the House Rules Committee under Howard Smith is but one emblem, albeit a particularly shiny one, of the character of Congress at the time. It was a legislature run like an oligarchy. The party leaders had little formal power, though a few, such as Lyndon Johnson in the Senate and Sam Rayburn in the House, could sometimes overcome the lack of formal power with brilliant displays of political skill. The real power was in the hands of the committee chairs—chosen solely by seniority, answerable to no higher authority. Junior members found the door to power bolted shut. Only after a decade or more of service could a member of the majority party hope for a subcommittee chairmanship and a few shards of influence.

In the Senate real power was even more closely held in the hands of a few senior members who chaired the most powerful committees—the "whales," Lyndon Johnson called them, and they were few; the "minnows" were many. Because they found it so much easier to accumulate seniority than their northern and western counterparts, southerners were over-represented among the powerful few in both houses. In 1960 they chaired 65 percent of the standing committees in the Senate and 67 percent in the House. When they gathered behind closed doors to make public policy, the food was Virginia ham and collard greens, the drink was bourbon and branch water, the song was "Dixie," and the politics were conservative.

Congress had looked this way for nearly three decades. As Democratic majorities ebbed and flowed—and in two brief interims vanished— control of Congress remained safely in the hands of what came to be called the "conservative coalition." This was a loose and largely unorganized confederation of southern Democrats and conservative Republicans. There were years in which the southern wing of the Democratic Party was outnumbered by its liberal faction, but the conservative coalition dominated the Congress overall, and it enlarged and extended the formal power of the southerners who controlled the key committees.

So it was when the revolution came.

The Congress of the 1960s began to take shape in the election of 1958. Few elections in the history of Congress have wrought so significant a change in the character of its membership. Eighty-two new members were elected to the House that year, and the Democratic majority grew by 48. The party divide at the opening of the Eighty-sixth Congress was 282 Democrats to 154 Republicans. In the Senate the electoral change was at least as stunning. The Democrats gained 15 seats and held an advantage of 64 to 34 over the Republicans. But this was more than a large influx of new members, for the new arrivals were a unique generation of legislators: younger, more independent of political parties, imbued with a sense of activism, not easily intimidated by tradition or institutional expectations.

And they were liberal—Philip Hart of Michigan, Edmund Muskie of Maine, Eugene McCarthy of Minnesota, and Tom Dodd of Connecticut among many in the Senate; George Miller of California, Dan Rostenkowski of Illinois, and John Brademas of Indiana, among dozens in the

House. These new arrivals would expand the number and influence of liberal legislators in the Congresses to come.

For the core of liberals already in Washington, for Hubert Humphrey and Paul Douglas, Joe Clark and Frank Church in the Senate, for Henry Reuss, Robert Nix, and Leonore Sullivan in the House, the day after the election of 1958 was a great day: The reinforcements had arrived. The *New York Times* noted the "changed political mood that distinguishes the new Congress." "In both houses," it reported, "there are upheavals against the conservative point of view by legislators who read the November election returns as evidence of voters' demands for bolder action in foreign and domestic affairs."[25]

When that Eighty-sixth Congress convened in January 1959, expectations ran especially high. The liberals were reinforced and chomping at the bit of opportunity. The pent-up agenda of civil rights, labor, environmental, and other legislation would now roll forward in what many hoped would be an unprecedented record of progressive accomplishment.

But what the Eighty-sixth Congress produced for most liberals was little more than colossal disappointment. It passed a tepid and largely toothless civil rights bill in 1960 and granted statehood for Hawaii. But many liberal goals, including an increase in the minimum wage, federal aid to education, and an enlarged housing program, were imprisoned and died in the House Rules Committee. The most notable legislative product of that Congress was the Landrum-Griffin Act, a restrictive piece of labor legislation. Liberals shook their heads in disbelief: The Congress that began so full of liberal optimism left as its primary legacy a law that most liberals despised.

Embedded in this experience were three lessons in legislative reality. If they were ever to prevail in Congress, the liberals would first have to gain a stronger foothold in the power structure, especially the committee system. Then they would have to develop more effective mechanisms for organizing liberal members into a reliable voting bloc. And then they would have to confront the conservative coalition, match the legislative acumen of its senior tacticians, and use the rules to support rather than thwart liberal efforts. And, of course, it would help to control the White House.

The hard lessons of the Eighty-sixth Congress were soon translated into practice, in ways that would eventually reshape Congress and make it possible for liberals to transform American life. Younger members, led by Eugene McCarthy (D-Minnesota) and Frank Thompson (D-New Jersey), sensed that liberals were often outgunned in legislative struggles because they were outorganized. They sought to form an association that would serve two purposes: allow liberal members of the House to develop a consensual, substantive agenda and create a disciplined organization to maximize the impact of liberal votes. They came up with an antiseptic name, the Democratic Study Group (DSG), that they thought would not appear to pose a challenge to the formal leadership structure of the Democratic Party—even though that's what many of them hoped to do. The liberals were fighting back, and the DSG would become, in the words of Brookings political scientist James Sundquist, "probably the most elaborately organized 'party within a party' in the history of the House of Representatives."[26]

By the beginning of the 1960s the DSG had developed a whip system that allowed its leaders to count votes effectively and to galvanize a liberal coalition on significant pieces of legislation. The DSG leadership worked closely with Speaker Sam Rayburn and Majority Leader John McCormack to maximize support for bills that liberals regarded highly. The organization became a useful, indeed an essential antidote to the maverick tendencies of many congressional liberals. As Richard Bolling noted, "DSG has served to pull together liberal Democrats, who incline to independence and even irascibility, into a semblance of a cooperative group that grasps the importance of legislative technique, the 'how' of legislative endeavors."[27] In the years that followed, the DSG would play a central role in shaping and guiding liberal efforts to reconstruct Congress and to advance an ambitious substantive agenda.

The first critical test in the confrontation between the liberals and the old order came soon after John Kennedy's election. Kennedy had spent fourteen years in Congress and was intimately familiar with the power, the skills, and the passionate resistance of the conservative coalition to liberal ideas. He realized that his legislative agenda was likely to go nowhere in a Congress it controlled. His own vote counting told him that the legislative losses his party suffered in the 1960 elections—when it lost twenty seats in the House and one in the Senate from the 1958 election high-water mark—would make the liberal-conservative split in Congress, especially in the House, very, very close. But he also recognized that his legislative opportunities would quickly shrink to the vanishing point if he did not encourage an effort to break down the institutional underpinnings of conservative power. And the focal point of that challenge had to be the Rules Committee. If Howard Smith were to remain a Colossus astride the legislative process, few of Kennedy's legislative proposals would make it to Rhodes.

So discussions among the president, Vice President Johnson, Speaker Rayburn, and other congressional leaders yielded what seemed a simple strategy: The House would vote to add three members to the Rules Committee, Rayburn would appoint two sympathetic liberals, and this would tip the balance away from the conservatives in Smith's committee. At the end of the previous Congress, Rules had twelve members, evenly split between liberals and conservatives. Smith could control that committee and turn it to his own purposes. If the enlargement were approved and the expected appointments made, Smith stood to be outvoted in his own committee on divisive legislation.

What seemed so small a change would, however, become a large pivot point in the emergence of liberal opportunities in Congress. No one in Congress—not liberals, not conservatives—failed to recognize the significance of this effort to expand the Rules Committee. If it succeeded, Smith would lose; if it failed, Kennedy would lose.

Kennedy called Sam Rayburn to Florida after the election to discuss the change in Rules and there began more than two months of the most delicate politicking in the modern history of Congress. This would be a fateful event, but to most Americans it was invisible: the kind of insider conflict whose immense significance is understood only among the powerful. The great special interests began to take sides: the National Association of Manufacturers, the Chamber of Commerce, and the Farm Bureau Federation against the enlargement, the major labor unions and civil rights groups supporting it.

But, as often occurs in legislative struggles, the outcome was determined by the interplay of personalities. Howard Smith was seventy-eight years old; Sam Rayburn was seventy-nine and infected with cancer. Some journalists likened them to ancient gladiators fighting one last titanic battle. In reality they were two country boys—the chairman from Broad Run, Virginia, the Speaker from Bonham, Texas—who'd risen to national power and did not want defeat as their legacy. Smith told colleagues he was "ready for a fight." Rayburn was gearing up for what he later called "the worst fight of my life."[28]

So Rayburn, the old poker player, threw in his whole stack. Lyndon Johnson roamed congressional corridors, still in his element but now the enforcer for the new administration to which he'd hitched his star. Kennedy tried to show appropriate deference to what he publicly called a "House matter." In reality, however, every resource of patronage, campaign commitments, and federal action was injected into the fight on Capitol Hill.[29]

With much effort Kennedy and Rayburn succeeded in securing the key support of Carl Vinson of Georgia. Vinson, born in 1883 and then serving his forty-seventh year in the House, commanded wide respect in Washington, especially among southerners. His detachment from the conservative coalition—rumored to be in exchange for a quid pro quo that was never revealed—would turn out to be the turning point in this confrontation.

On January 31, 1961, the day of the House vote, Rayburn left the rostrum to make his final plea. Vote switching occurred even as the roll was being called. The final tally—217 votes to enlarge the Rules Committee, 212 to prevent it—was both an indication of how evenly divided the two sides were and how critical this institutional change would be in allowing Kennedy and the liberals in Congress to advance their agenda. Rayburn had won his last great fight. He succumbed to cancer ten months later.

The 1961 vote to enlarge the Rules Committee was applicable to that Congress only. This was sold to the members as a temporary enlargement. But two years later when the new Speaker, John McCormack, proposed a continuation of the enlargement, it passed the House by thirty-nine votes. Opportunities for significant change in the operations of Congress had been barely in evidence in 1961. By 1963, they looked much more promising, and in the years that followed they would materialize in ways that permitted a far-reaching restructuring of power in both houses of Congress.

The conservative coalition would remain a potent element in the public policy struggles of the 1960s, but its high-water mark had passed. Rules changes in Congress would continue to unfold, and their primary effect would be to weaken the committee chairs and strengthen the capacity of junior members to participate in the legislative process. The rigid seniority rule would eventually fall by the wayside. The number of subcommittees would rapidly expand. Committee and personal staff would explode in size. This would not happen overnight, but the door that opened in 1961 to a new kind of legislature would open wider in each succeeding Congress.[30]

Other changes were about to occur as well. The declining strength of the political parties, especially in the urban areas where they had been strongest, would lead to the disappearance of a once-flourishing breed of member: the political hacks enjoying a sinecure as their reward for loyal service to the party boss. They would be replaced by younger members, not beholden to any boss and eager for an active role in policy making.

The dominance of southerners would begin to fade as well, at least in the way it had prevailed for the middle decades of the twentieth century. The 1960s would see a vast expansion in the number of black voters in the South. Reapportionment imposed by the Supreme Court in its "one person, one vote" decisions in the first half of the decade would weaken the rural, and mostly conservative, faction in southern politics.[31] Howard Smith himself would fall victim to reapportionment and lose in the Democratic primary in his newly refashioned district in Virginia in 1966. Population in-migration, industrialization, suburbanization, cultural homogenization, the Goldwater candidacy in 1964, and the presidential pursuits of George Wallace would all combine to remake the landscape of southern politics. The long tradition of the "solid Democratic South" evaporated rapidly in the 1960s; the South would not soon again be either very solid or very Democratic.

The party leadership of Congress was changing as well. In the 1950s two Texans, Lyndon Johnson and Sam Rayburn, had provided Congress with some of the most effective leadership it had ever had. Neither had expansive formal powers, but both were masters of the legislative process and brilliant practitioners of the arts of personal persuasion. Johnson was the more overt, Rayburn the more subtle, but each had a genius for counting votes, for devising successful strategies of coalition building, for working with counterparts across the aisle, and—in the Texas tradition—for rounding up strays.

But they were both gone from the Congress by the end of 1961 and their replacements, the limited John McCormack of Massachusetts in the House and the taciturn, easygoing Mike Mansfield of Montana in the Senate, were not the equals of their predecessors. In fact, no leaders of similar capacity have since ascended the congressional party hierarchy.

So the Congress that John Kennedy confronted at the other end of Pennsylvania Avenue was an institution in the early stages of what would become a major reformation. It was a time of transition. The Democrats remained in control, as they would throughout the decade. But the southern base of the party was starting to show signs of decay. The stranglehold that committee chairs and the Rules Committee had long exercised on the legislative process was beginning to weaken. Membership was changing as older members representing malapportioned rural districts and boss-dominated urban districts were leaving, and younger members with heterogeneous metropolitan constituencies and significant political independence were arriving.[32] The leadership capacity of the legislature, from its committee chairs and its party leaders, was deteriorating.

None of these changes was sudden; all would unfold in stages over the decade that lay ahead. The forces of resistance to liberal policies would not quickly disappear. But the dawn of the 1960s, to those clear-eyed enough to recognize it, was an instant of opportunity. Especially significant to the opportunists was the growing leadership void in Congress and the prospect it posed for presidents to expand their own leadership role in the policy-making process. The question, of course, was whether presidents would be up to the task.

THE VITAL CENTER

In the weeks that followed his election John Kennedy retreated to his home in Georgetown and later to the family home in Palm Beach, Florida. There he entertained a steady stream of invited guests. Some came to audition for appointments in his administration. Others came to discuss specific matters of public policy: the budget, international relations, civil rights. And some came to help Kennedy figure out how to be president.

One of those was Richard Neustadt. Neustadt had served as a staff member in the Truman administration before resuming his academic career, first at Columbia, then at Harvard. He was a scholar of the presidency, and the book on which he had been working for some time was published in April 1960. That book, *Presidential Power*, would go through many editions over the next thirty years and would be read by tens of thousands of college students, journalists, and future presidents. Neustadt's reputation as a sensible, insightful, practical scholar was known to Kennedy, who had read and admired *Presidential Power*. The president-elect asked the scholar to prepare a memo on how to be president. Neustadt did so, and on September 18, 1960, he met with Kennedy in Georgetown to discuss the memo.

Neustadt was one of the leaders of an emergent stream of presidential scholarship that depicted the startling growth of the presidency in the twentieth century as logical, inevitable, and beneficial. Neustadt observed that the expansion of presidential power during the Depression and World War II no longer appeared to be emergency deviations from the norm. It had become the norm. To function effectively, the American political system in the postwar world needed an active, vigorous executive as the "vital center," the guiding and driving force of American politics.

Neustadt urged Kennedy to avoid comparisons with Franklin Roosevelt's first hundred days, when the conditions for action were very different. But he did lay out a number of practical steps for devising a presidential program, communicating it rapidly and effectively to the Congress, and putting into place a team of aides and appointees who could give his administration the kind of brain power and muscle power that modern presidential leadership required. The first priority, Neustadt argued, was to make critical decisions on the "substance, timing, publicity, and priority of legislative proposals to Congress."[33]

In *Presidential Power*, Neustadt had suggested that presidents needed to build and carefully tend their influence in order to make their public policy objectives viable. By seeking power, he argued, a president "contributes to the energy of government." And, in a prescient comment about the roles played by John Kennedy and Lyndon Johnson in the legislative record of the 1960s, Neustadt wrote: "Viability in policy has three ingredients. First is a purpose that moves with the grain of history, a direction consonant with coming needs. Second is an operation that proves manageable to the men who must administer it, acceptable to those who must support it, tolerable to those who must put up with it, in Washington and out. Timing can be crucial for support and acquiescence; proper timing is the third ingredient. The President who sees his power stakes sees something very much like the ingredients that make for viability in policy."[34]

This was not a concept of the chief executive envisioned by the framers of the Constitution, most of whom were worried even about the limited grant of executive authority their document provided. The first century of political experience had demonstrated occasional flashes of presidential potency, but for the most part Congress ran the country. As the astute British scholar James Bryce noted in 1889 in his landmark study of American political folkways, "The expression of [the president's] wishes conveyed in a message has not necessarily any more effect on Congress than an article in a prominent party newspaper. . . . In fact, the suggestions which he makes, year after year, are usually neglected."[35] A prominent senator of the late nineteenth century, George F. Hoar, wrote, "The most eminent senators would have received as a personal affront a private message from the White House expressing a desire that they should adopt any course in the discharge of their legislative duties that they did not approve. If they visited the White House, it was to give, not to receive, advice."[36]

Even the young political scientist Woodrow Wilson wrote in 1885 in the first genuine classic of that discipline that Congress was "unquestionably, the predominant and controlling force, the centre and source of all motive and all regulative power." "I know not how better to describe our form of government in a single phrase," he wrote, "than by calling it a government by the chairmen of the Standing Committees of Congress."[37]

A revolt against the Speaker of the House on the eve of Wilson's presidency provided him with an opportunity that few of his predecessors had possessed: leadership of the legislative process. Wilson grabbed at it eagerly, having spent decades as a scholar arguing that presidents ought to fill just such a role. During World War I, the government in Washington expanded to an unprecedented degree and new agencies popped up like spring crocuses. Wilson did his best to manage this spreading enterprise, mostly with ad hoc inventions: borrowed staff, temporary commissions, and diligent personal efforts. But few of his attempts to centralize executive authority to manage the war effort in Europe survived the armistice. The presidency he abandoned in 1921 was a formal institution little changed from the one he had inherited eight years earlier. And the three Republicans who succeeded Wilson found little reason to expand presidential authority or resources, even after the stock market crashed in 1929.

The presidency that fell to Franklin Roosevelt in 1933 was barely an institution at all. A national budget, and a Bureau of the Budget to construct and implement it, had existed for barely a decade. The White House provided some household help and a clever president could find money in the budgets of some of the departments to bring in a few secretaries and assistants, but there was no formal authorization for a White House staff. The rococo Executive Office Building that had sat grandly to the west of the White House since 1871 housed the departments of State, War, and the Navy during most of Franklin Roosevelt's tenure. The small office quarters in the west wing of the White House were adequate for the handful of people who worked directly for the president.

But a new concept of the American presidency began to emerge in the 1930s and it would expand and deepen in the decades that followed. In 1937 Roosevelt appointed a small committee of public administration specialists to examine executive branch operations. The Brownlow Committee, as it was called after its chairman, Louis Brownlow, issued a report that began: "The president needs help." It went on to detail the growing burdens on the president and the dearth of management resources at his disposal. Some of the report's recommendations found their way into law when the Congress passed the Administrative Reorganization Act of 1939.

That act established the Executive Office of the President, moved the Bureau of the Budget there from its location in the Treasury Department, and authorized the president to employ six staff aides. For the first time, in a formal sense there was a presidency as well as a president. The chief executive was becoming an institution.

In the years that followed there were further expansions of the Executive Office. The Employment Act of 1946 authorized a Council of Economic Advisors. The National Security Act of 1947 created the National Security Council, the Joint Chiefs of Staff, and the Central Intelligence Agency, all reporting directly to the president. Further elaborations of the institutional presidency would continue to occur in the decades ahead as new needs were identified and new staff resources created to meet them.

As the size and scope of the institutional presidency grew, so did the role of the president in the American political system. Presidential leadership of the policy-making process became habit-forming. Congress retained formidable powers of resistance and frustration, but it began to cede the legislative initiative to the president. By the early 1950s a routine had emerged in the Executive Office around the creation of an annual "program of the president." Coordinated in the Bureau of the Budget and revealed in the first two months of the year in the State of the Union Address, the Economic Report of the President, and the president's budget recommendations, the "program of the president" identified the chief executive's policy priorities—and much of the congressional agenda. In the policy-making process, the presidency was developing focus, discipline, and a single—often very loud—voice.

As the president was learning to lead, so was Congress learning to follow. By the late 1940s, a new practice had begun to take hold in Congress. Party leaders would not move forward on legislative proposals until they had been referred to the White House. Presidents often treated this as an invitation to submit a bill, which then became the focal point of legislative discussion.

By the end of the Truman administration these new routines had become part of the daily life in the White House and on Capitol Hill. Presidential leadership of the legislative process was beginning to look like the new norm of Washington policy making. But scholars and journalists wondered whether these approaches would survive an Eisenhower presidency. Would a Republican be as active a chief executive, as aggressive in exercising the new leadership capacities and prerogatives of the White House as the Democrats had been? Or would he revert to the much more passive leadership style of the Republican presidents who preceded Franklin Roosevelt?

The answer was not long in coming. While Eisenhower had a more limited policy agenda than his Democratic predecessors, he was not reluctant to use the executive resources he inherited from them. He, too, turned out an annual program, pushed hard for his budget priorities, and used his staff to extend his reach into the executive agencies and the legislative process. And though he was not a naturally gifted communicator, Eisenhower recognized the recently expanded public dimension of the presidency. He was the first president to allow his news conferences to be filmed and to provide the film to the television networks and movie newsreels. He made regular televised addresses to the nation on key policy matters. And he kept a speechwriting staff busy with addresses to special-interest groups, college commencements, and other audiences around the country.[38]

One area in which these efforts unfolded was in the management of presidential relations with Congress. In previous administrations, these relations had tended to follow party channels. Party leaders, in and out of government, were often the primary conduit for political communications on legislative matters. If the president needed the votes of Illinois Democrats, he might contact the leader of the Cook County Democratic organization. When he was a senator, Harry Truman once complained to President Roosevelt that the latter should ask him directly when he wanted Truman's vote and not go through the Pendergast machine in Missouri.[39] Roosevelt and Truman both had people on their staffs or in their cabinets whose close connections to party leaders made them de facto legislative liaisons, but their functions were informal and incomplete.

Eisenhower sought a different approach, establishing an expanded legislative liaison operation within the White House. He wanted to keep his distance from the Republican Party organization that too often regarded him as an outsider. For all but his first two years in office, Congress was dominated by the opposition party, so his own party organization was of limited value in forging legislative coalitions. And he had a natural predisposition for structure and organization that inclined him to see every task, even the overtly political, as a management challenge.

In the interim between the New Deal and the Fair Deal on one end and the New Frontier and the Great Society on the other, the Eisenhower presidency left a relatively slender legacy of presidential policy initiatives. But it left a significant legacy of presidential institutionaliza-tion. Eisenhower enlarged the White House staff, expanded his capacity to present his objectives to the public, and built a broader foundation for the president's new role as chief initiator in the legislative process. By not turning back the clock to the 1920s, or even contemplating this, Eisen-hower made it clear that the evolving modern presidency was not simply the Democratic approach to executive leadership. It was the new norm for both parties. Debates of old about whether the president should be an active promoter of public policy or merely the chief clerk of the na-tion were over. That question would never be debated again.

KENNEDY AND JOHNSON WERE rarities among presidents in that both had lengthy service in Congress before coming to the White House. Ken-nedy had served for fourteen years, six in the house, eight in the Senate. He had seen congressional life from both the majority and minority sides of the aisle. But even more than Kennedy, Johnson had the soul of a legislator. As a boy he had accompanied his father on the rounds of his Texas state legislative district, meeting constituents and hearing their problems. He'd gone to Austin as well and sat in the galleries of the state-house, watching the legislature at work. "I loved going with my father to the legislature," he told Doris Kearns. "I would sit in the gallery for hours watching all the activity on the floor and then would wander around the halls trying to figure out what was going on."[40] At twenty-three, Johnson took a job as legislative secretary to Representative Richard Kleberg of Texas's fourteenth congressional district and grabbed a train to Wash-ington where he began a long career that would take him through six years as a congressional staff member, eleven years in the House, twelve years as a senator, and three more during his vice presidency as president of the Senate. Only three earlier American presidents had more congres-sional service before coming to the White House than John Kennedy. None had more than Lyndon Johnson.

But Kennedy and Johnson had had very different legislative experi-ences. Kennedy had never acquired much seniority, nor had he been especially skilled at the inside game of legislative coalition building. If members of Congress were split between "show horses" and "work horses," in Sam Rayburn's famous taxonomy, Kennedy would have likely been categorized as the former. And in a body dominated by men who were elderly and southern, Kennedy was neither. As president it took him a while to adjust to dealing on a level plane with the legislative leaders who had often loomed over him during his years on Capitol Hill.

The promising beginnings of his first year in office had failed to yield a very large legislative product, and Kennedy was sometimes criticized for his failures of leadership, especially in dealing with Congress. It was a charge that even his friendliest biographers could not dismiss. "Kennedy, particularly in his first year ... felt somewhat uncomfortable and perhaps too deferential with these men who the previous year outranked him," wrote Theodore Sorenson. "He knew he had always been too junior, too liberal, too outspoken, and too much in a hurry to be accepted in their inner ruling circles."[41] Kennedy reflected on his first year in office: "There is no sense in raising hell, and then not being successful. There is no sense in putting the office of the Presidency on the line on an issue, and then being defeated." Mindful of his narrow victory in 1960, Kennedy would often quote Thomas Jefferson: "Great innovations should not be forced on slender majorities."[42]

But these initial trials were a learning experience and the president himself and the team he built in the White House soon became much more proficient at developing legislative initiatives, presenting them in compelling fashion to the press and the public, and building support in Congress. The congressional liaison operation that Eisenhower had established became under Kennedy and Johnson a "well-oiled machine."[43] Larry O'Brien, whom Kennedy had plucked from the rough-and-ready school of Massachusetts politics, took over as the chief legislative liaison for both presidents and quickly became as good as anyone who ever held that job. On September 1, 1961, O'Brien, with a backdrop composed of a carrot and stick, became the first and only presidential assistant for congressional liaison to be pictured on the cover of *Time* magazine.

O'Brien enlarged the staff and honed its routines. He devoted enormous attention to detail. Members of Congress now had a place to go when they needed something, information or a favor, from the White House. Kennedy and Johnson now had reliable head counts and insightful analysis as they sought to build legislative coalitions. In an age when political parties were in steep decline, when presidents could no longer count on party loyalty to generate broad support for their programs, it became essential to build new bridges between the White House and the Capitol. That work was well under way in the first year of Kennedy's presidency, and it would become an important element in the legislative battles that lay ahead.[44]

The groundwork that Kennedy laid in expanding ties with Congress and building public support for a legislative program would ably serve his successor, Lyndon Johnson. Johnson had never been a Kennedy intimate and he was largely invisible during much of Kennedy's presidency, but when tragedy called him to power, he was unusually well prepared to exercise it. If Kennedy had been slow to acquire the knack for legislative leadership, Johnson seemed born with it. If Kennedy had been reluctant to confront the elderly southerners who occupied the primary positions of power in Congress, Johnson was eager to do so. These were his old friends.

Richard Russell (D-Georgia), perhaps the most respected of all senators, had been Johnson's guiding star during his years as Senate majority leader. Senators Russell Long (D-Louisiana), who chaired the Finance Committee, and Carl Hayden (D-Arizona), who chaired Appropriations, had been Johnson's allies in scores of legislative battles. He had crossed swords and cocktail glasses on many occasions with Rep. Clarence Cannon (D-Missouri), who chaired House Appropriations, and Rep. Wilbur Mills (D-Arkansas), who headed Ways and Means. These were Johnson's people. He knew their families and their constituencies, he knew what cigars they smoked and what they drank with their bourbon, he knew whether they could be bluffed by drawing to an inside straight. And he knew what it took to get their votes.

Johnson also knew intimately a man who was not a southerner, not a committee chairman, not even a member of the majority party, but who would become the pivot point in many of the key legislative debates of the 1960s. That was Senator Everett McKinley Dirksen of Illinois.

Dirksen was born to a family of small farmers in Pekin, Illinois, a suburb of Peoria, in 1896. He served in the Army during World War I and began a political career as a Republican in the 1920s. Elected to the U. S. House of Representatives in 1932, he served there until an illness that severely affected his eyesight forced his retirement in 1946. But he recovered and was elected to the Senate in 1950, defeating Scott Lucas—then the majority leader of the Senate—in a contest in which Dirksen employed tactics not unlike those used by Joseph McCarthy.

Dirksen soon emerged as a leader among Republicans, known for his practical approach to legislation and his ability to work with members of both parties. Long before Senate Republicans chose him as their party leader in 1959, Dirksen had developed a solid working relationship and a growing personal bond with his Democratic counterpart, Lyndon Johnson. Dirksen had also become something of a national figure. His wavy white hair, rumpled appearance, mellifluous voice, and old-fashioned, ornate oratory made him unusually recognizable. Some called him the "wizard of ooze."[45] Dirksen was easy to caricature, but he was a ferocious legislative craftsman and tactician, one worthy even of Lyndon Johnson's steel.

Dirksen believed in negotiation and compromise. "The Senate is a public institution," he would say; "it must work; it's a two-way street; and that requires the efforts of both parties."[46] Dirksen never feared criticizing Johnson, and he did it regularly when the latter was in the Senate and when he was in the White House. But he believed that "the oil can is mightier than the sword."[47] And when a deal needed to be made . . . well, these were deal-making men. Johnson's long and intimate acquaintance with Everett Dirksen would be a sturdy and constant thread in the fabric of his legislative accomplishments.

THERE IS NO SINGLE EXPLANATION for the remarkable legislative explosion that occurred in Washington in the 1960s, but one cannot underestimate the significance of the personal relationships that existed among the most powerful players. Nor should one underestimate the significance of the most skilled and ingenious legislative leader of that generation, perhaps of all time: Lyndon Baines Johnson. Skills and experience of the sort he possessed are rare in any setting. Among presidents of the United States, they were unique.

Their legislative experience and their political sensitivities imposed a powerful understanding on both Kennedy and Johnson. Little that they hoped to accomplish legislatively could get done without Republican help. The southern dominance of Congress and the southern strangle-hold on the Democratic Party might have passed its high-water mark, but it would recede slowly. Unable to count on many southern votes for social welfare legislation and virtually none for civil rights, both presidents knew they had to find and nurture Republican support.

Kennedy came from a state where Democrats dominated in the legislature and among voters, but Republicans often held the top offices. He was the grandson of John "Honey Fitz" Fitzgerald, a classic Irish pol of the early twentieth century. His own entry into politics came at a time when James Michael Curley, another of that ilk, was the dominant figure in his state. Kennedy, in fact, succeeded Curley as the representative in Washington of the eleventh district. But Massachusetts was also the state of Oliver Wendell Holmes, the great Republican jurist; the Republican senator Henry Cabot Lodge, who had led the effort to scuttle Woodrow Wilson's League of Nations; his son, Senator Henry Cabot Lodge, Jr., who had played a critical role in launching Eisenhower's candidacy in 1952—an effort that distracted him from his own, ultimately unsuccessful defense of his Senate seat against a young congressman named John F. Kennedy. Massachusetts was a complex polity in Kennedy's time, and Yankee Republicans were a prominent part of the landscape. Kennedy had learned to work with them.

During his eight years in the Senate, John Kennedy was the junior senator from Massachusetts. The senior senator was Leverett A. Saltonstall, an exemplar of the Yankee Republican breed. Saltonstall's ancestors had come to Massachusetts on the *Mayflower*. Like ten generations in his family before him, he had gone to Harvard College, and he followed many of his relatives into politics. Saltonstall was a graceful politician whose Brahmin roots never prevented him from connecting with the working-class citizens who helped elect him governor three times and senator four. Curley said of Saltonstall that he had a "Harvard accent with a South Boston face,"[48] and at the annual St. Patrick's Day breakfast at Dorgan's in South Boston, the local wit, Billy Bulger, introduced him as a man who was "Irish on his chauffeur's side."[49]

People like Leverett Saltonstall were a familiar species in Congress in Kennedy's time. Born to wealth, tolerant, internationalist, progressive, and committed to public service, they were often called "moderate"

Republicans. Members like Clifford Case (R-New Jersey), Kenneth Keating (R-New York), and John Sherman Cooper (R-Kentucky) in the Senate and Ogden Reid (R-New York), Rogers Morton (R-Maryland), and Peter Frelinghuysen (R-New Jersey) carried social pedigrees and political preferences not unlike Leverett Saltonstall's. On many issues they found themselves on the same side as liberal Democrats. In fact, the conservative coalition of right-wing Republicans and southern Democrats often confronted a similar coalition of moderate Republicans and liberal Democrats. Kennedy and Johnson had often joined those progressive coalitions in Congress and were comfortable working with congressional Republicans when they sought to build such coalitions from the White House.

Neither Kennedy nor Johnson had begun their congressional careers with notable reputations as liberals. Kennedy had been a reliable supporter of President Truman while in the House, but in the Senate he had been one of the last Democrats to condemn Joseph McCarthy. In 1957, he voted for the civil rights bill of that year on final passage, but had earlier supported the "jury trial amendment," which many liberals thought removed the real teeth from the bill. When Kennedy's name was placed in nomination for vice president at the 1956 Democratic convention, he drew significant support from the South (and vociferous opposition from Eleanor Roosevelt) against the more liberal Estes Kefauver and Hubert Humphrey. Kennedy was no darling of the liberals in the 1950s.

But as he formulated plans to run for president in 1960, Kennedy began to reposition himself ideologically. This was less a change of heart than it was a change of emphasis, superimposing some of his instincts over others. He was not by nature confrontational, and he'd had little experience leading progressive efforts. But to win the presidency he would have to convince Democratic leaders and Democratic voters that he shared their dreams and that he possessed the skills and commitment to help realize them.

The liberal Democratic resurgence in the 1958 midterm election was a potent demonstration to Kennedy of the direction in which his party and the country were going, and he quickly made visible efforts to join the liberal bloc on welfare, civil rights, and other issues. This was a carefully considered ideological positioning, for Kennedy wanted to win liberal hearts without trespassing beyond the comfort zone of the southern voters whose support he would desperately need in 1960 and the southern legislators with whom he anticipated a fragile relationship after the election.

But ultimately Kennedy experienced a conversion that is not uncommon in presidential politics. In the glare of a national campaign and the constant scrutiny of the White House, presidents come to believe what they say. The uncertainties, the waverings, the inconsistencies, the changes in course that are permitted to a legislator or even a governor are fodder for intensive criticism in a presidential candidate and a president. Because every position a candidate or a president takes is so much more visible and much more open to attack, clarity, resolve, and commitment become paramount. Uncertainties that may occur in deciding on a policy position are suppressed in the articulation and defense of it.

So the tentative ideological tendencies often observed early in a president's political career—the caution in taking clear positions on issues—become much less subtle, much more unshakable in the White House. No president wants to admit doubts or errors. And they rarely do. This can be a path to pathology, as it later became for Lyndon Johnson; but it also ensures that the highly visible modern presidency will force its incumbents to come out from behind their doubts, to stand for something, and to stand for it without cavil or concession.

And so it was for John Kennedy. There was no hiding from confrontation on the campaign trail or in the White House. He had to respond to Hubert Humphrey's questions about his liberalism during the presidential primaries, and he defended his religion and rebuffed Nixon's attacks on his inexperience during the election campaign. The testing hardened him, as it did in the White House when Roger Blough, the president of U.S. Steel, dismissed Kennedy's demands for a price rollback, when Nikita Khrushchev placed missiles in Cuba, and when Governor Ross Barnett challenged federal authority in Mississippi. In this cauldron of politics and leadership, Kennedy became Kennedy. He may not have been much of a liberal in 1956 and only a tepid one early in 1960. But he came to believe fully the words of aspiration and hope that filled his handsome speeches, and he had come to acquire the skills and self-possession to convert them into public policies.

Lyndon Johnson required little such conversion by fire. Though few distant observers of his early political career would have noted it, Johnson was in many ways a natural liberal. James H. Rowe, Jr., a well-connected Washington lawyer who knew both men well, said of Johnson, "Instinctively, he's a helluva lot more liberal than Kennedy."[50]

Kennedy had been born to genteel wealth, Johnson to genteel poverty. Kennedy's father was a multimillionaire and a businessman. Johnson's father was a dirt farmer and cattle trader, a rider on the reckless farm-market roller coaster, and a drinker. He was also, for a time, the elected representative in the state legislature of some of the poorest folks in the country. Kennedy had gone to Harvard and toured Europe as an ambassador's son. Johnson went to a teacher's college and had to drop out for a year, earning money to continue by teaching Mexican American children in a run-down elementary school in Cotulla, Texas. With much help from his wealthy father, Kennedy turned his college honors thesis into a best-selling book, dated movie stars, and hobnobbed with an international elite. Johnson spent his postcollege years as a congressman's secretary and then as head of the New Deal's National Youth Administration in Texas. As young men, one showed little interest in politics; the other became an ardent New Dealer. Kennedy had to sharply hone his liberalism to become a successful national politician in the 1960s; Johnson had to mute his to survive the rigors of Texas and congressional politics.

Survival in Texas politics required Lyndon Johnson to keep his liberal instincts submerged during much of his congressional career. His major legislative accomplishment during eleven years in the House was securing electrification for the farm families in his rural Texas district. He assured a constituent in a letter written as his House service was ending that he had "voted against all anti–poll tax, anti-lynching, and all FEPC [Fair Employment Practices Committee] legislation since I came to Congress."[51]

In the Senate, especially after he became his party's leader in 1953, his voting record became more complex and subject to divergent interpretations. He never lost sight of the constraints on every southern member intent on a long congressional career. But, with a Republican president settling in, he was also the leader of the opposition. There would be battles to fight, and in many of them, his party stood to the left of the president. Johnson, then, would have to lead from the left, and thus balance his own electoral survival imperatives with the diverse views of the members of the party he led. He worked hard, and with widely admired political skill, to obtain enough "elbow room" from his southern colleagues that he could maintain good relations with Senate liberals and fit many of their priorities onto the Senate's agenda.[52] Richard Russell of Georgia, dean of the southern Democrats, continued his deep affection for the man he hoped would be the next southern president. But, at the same time, Hubert Humphrey and other liberals found growing reasons to trust Johnson as he placed them on significant committees and provided them a modicum of influence that had never been theirs before he became their party's Senate leader. On many days it was a balancing act worthy of a tightrope artist, but it worked.

Johnson's navigation of a civil rights bill through the Senate in 1957 was a tour de force of legislative legerdemain, and even those liberals disappointed with some of its contents had to admit that without Lyndon Johnson at the helm there would have been no bill at all. In the days following its passage, liberal publications like the *New Republic* and the *Reporter* complimented Johnson's leadership. The *Washington Post* called it Johnson's "masterpiece," and an editorial noted that Johnson had come out of the debate "a national rather than a regional figure."[53]

As a legislator, Johnson's ideology was easier to caricature than to categorize. He was a stalwart defender of his home state and of the oil and gas industry that dominated its politics. He had managed to build a personal fortune with "timely" investments, especially in local television and radio stations. He kept close company with some of Congress's most conservative members. And he came from a state where developing a reputation as a liberal was rarely a good career move. So there were many reasons for liberals to be skeptical of Lyndon Johnson and to see his flirtations with their causes as the opportunism of an ambitious politician with eyes on the presidency.

Civil rights, of course, was the key test for liberals. And for Lyndon Johnson, it was a constant but silent agony. As the civil rights movement unfolded, he walked a fine line, trying to keep sizable majorities of his colleagues to his right and his left, holding his support at home and among the southern committee barons while simultaneously protecting his national political options.

His voting record demonstrates this. To conservatives, Johnson was a "consistent liberal." The conservative interest group Americans for Constitutional Action called Johnson's Senate record during 1959–60 "one of the most liberal . . . in the Congress." On ninety key roll calls, according to ACA, Johnson took the conservative position only 10 percent of the time. The Committee on Political Education (COPE) of the AFL-CIO also rated members of Congress. A high COPE score was widely regarded as evidence of a member's liberalism. For Johnson's entire twelve years in the Senate, he earned a COPE score of 73 percent; that is to say that on key votes the country's largest labor union approved of Johnson's position nearly three-quarters of the time.[54] Perhaps a broader measure of a member's ideological position is the score reported each year by the liberal interest group Americans for Democratic Action (ADA). During his time in the Senate, Lyndon Johnson's ADA score inclined upward, averaging 58 percent overall.[55]

After the Supreme Court struck down school desegregation, outrage in the South led to the drafting in Congress of a "Southern Manifesto" that vigorously opposed racial integration. Of the twenty-two senators from states of the old Confederacy, only three declined to sign it. Lyndon Johnson was one of those.

But Johnson's heart-of-heart's ideology remained elusive even to the most diligent observers. He was capable of saying quite opposite things to different audiences. And like most politicians with extensive public records, his votes and public statements had taken him on a winding road over the ideological landscape. The year 1960 provides a good example. Johnson campaigned that fall for two offices, for vice president on the Democratic ticket and—hedging his bets—for re-election to his Senate seat from Texas. The state platform of the Democrats in Texas was in many ways the polar opposite of the Democratic national platform on issues like right-to-work laws and the oil depletion allowance. The national platform called for many expansions of federal programs and federal authority; the state platform stood firmly against "federal encroachment."[56] Yet Johnson campaigned on both, apparently unperturbed by the contradictions.

But all of this was mere prelude. Some presidents have thought of the White House, as Harry Truman did, as a prison. But for Lyndon Johnson, it was the first place in his public life that allowed him to be fully himself. And he moved quickly to quell the doubts about what he believed. On his first full night as president, he told Walter Heller, the chairman of the Council of Economic Advisors, "Now, I want to say something about all this talk that I'm a conservative who is likely to go back to the Eisenhower ways or give in to the economy bloc in Congress. It's not so, and I want you to tell your friends—Arthur Schlesinger, Galbraith and other liberals—that it is not so. . . . If you looked at my record, you would know that I am a Roosevelt New Dealer. As a matter of fact . . . John F. Kennedy was a little too conservative to suit my taste."[57]

Ideology doesn't slice well, and ideological purity is a goal that successful politicians rarely pursue. So there is little to be gained from trying to put too fine a point on the liberalism of either Kennedy or Johnson. Though they arrived by different routes, both had become as presidents deeply committed to liberal political goals. And they would have unimagined opportunities to act on those commitments.

1963–66: THE PERFECT STORM

Periods of great policy upheaval are rarities in American history. The American system of governance is by nature conservative. It is a collection of traps and catches, designed to hamper majorities, to slow the process of change, to favor the status quo. Most of the time, inertia is the most powerful force in government. Those who seek change have to succeed at dozens of potential veto points. Those who seek to prevent change usually have to succeed at only one. Reform movements, as a popular book of the time noted, often succumbed to the "deadlock of democracy."[58]

This was a lesson fully understood by the southerners in Congress. They didn't need to have majorities on their side, they didn't need to have public opinion on their side, they didn't need the president on their side. They only needed to have the rules on their side. And they did. In a Congress where committees reigned, where it was nearly impossible to get legislation to the floor without committee support, committees became the ultimate power centers. As long as the rules favored committees, as long as the rules gave chairmen nearly absolute control of their committees, and as long as seniority remained the only route to a chairmanship, the status quo would remain well fortified. It would take a rare and overwhelming combination of elements to challenge it.

But in the years that began near the midpoint of John Kennedy's presidency, those elements began to gather. They would come together with a force and a furor that no one could have predicted. They would yield a public policy accumulation that challenged all precedent. And then they would dissipate and the storm would pass. While its fury might have been brief in historical time, the effects of that liberal hour would endure for generations, remaking American life.

Even the most hopeful liberals could not have imagined this perfect storm. By late 1962, having confronted the racial violence surrounding the integration of the University of Mississippi and the dangerous nuclear threat of the Cuban Missile Crisis, Kennedy was becoming a stronger, more popular president. In a Gallup Poll in December of that year, 76 percent of the American people expressed approval of the job he was doing as president.[59] Increasingly he was emboldened to shake the constraints of his narrow victory in 1960 and to push more forcefully for the key elements of his program: federal aid to education, manpower retraining, aid to depressed areas, increases in the minimum wage, and expanded Social Security benefits, among others.

In 1963 successes began to emerge. An urgent tax cut bill was moving forward, the Senate ratified the Nuclear Test Ban Treaty, new funds were appropriated for mental illness treatment and medical school construction. Air pollution control programs were enlarged. The Kennedy agenda for the Eighty-eighth Congress was expansive, but as he told his last press conference, "I'm looking forward to the record of this Congress, but . . . this is going to be an 18-month delivery."[60]

The year 1963 was also when the civil rights movement grabbed the full attention of the American people: the televised pictures of cattle prods, fire hoses, and police dogs used against nonviolent marchers; the ghastly images of the Sunday school where four young black girls were killed by a racist's bomb; the growing stature of Martin Luther King, embellished by an unforgettable speech in front of the Lincoln Memorial in August. Civil rights was becoming a national issue at last and it was fueling a spreading clamor for social justice in many forms. Kennedy had introduced the most sweeping civil rights bill ever set before Congress by a president and, as 1963 rounded into the year ahead, signs pointed to a real opportunity for passage.

And then Kennedy was assassinated.

In their grief, liberals worried that Lyndon Johnson—their caricature of Lyndon Johnson—could not possibly carry forward the policy momentum of 1963. But Johnson surprised them. In the hours after his return from Dallas, he drew on all his years of experience and all of his formidable energies not only to continue that momentum but to accelerate it. He called on the country to honor the martyred president by continuing the legislative momentum Kennedy had initiated. "The dream of education for all of our children," he told Congress on November 27, "the dream of jobs for all who seek them and need them—the dream of care for our elderly—the dream of an all-out attack on mental illness—and above all, the dream of equal rights for all Americans, whatever their race or color—these and other American dreams have been vitalized by his drive and by his dedication. And now the ideas and the ideals which he so nobly represented must and will be translated into effective action."[61]

In private he held countless meetings and conversations with key legislators of both parties and drove his staff, both his own old hands and those he inherited from Kennedy, to turn out bold proposals for 1964. In a phone call to Senator George Smathers (D-Florida) the day after the assassination, Johnson said, "We've got to carry on. We can't abandon this fellow's program, because he is a national hero and there are going to be those people who want his program passed and we've got to keep the Kennedy aura around us through this election." To Speaker John Mc-Cormack, he said, "I can't sit still. I've got to keep the government going." With Whitney Young, executive director of the National Urban League, Johnson shared strategy for pushing the legislative program forward: "I don't know what we're going to get out of them in the way of tax and civil rights. . . . But we're just beginning to fight." Pushing for action on the tax-cut bill, he told Everett Dirksen, "We can pass the tax bill in a week. . . . We ought to show some evidence of progress. . . . You be thinking about how you can help us get that tax bill out." "What's the difference between a Texas Ranger and a Texas sheriff?" he asked in one conversation. "Well, when you hit a Ranger he just keeps coming. So that's the kind of fight we're in."[62]

The list of pent-up issues was long. He told an aide late on his first night in office, "You know, when I went into that office tonight and they came in and started briefing me on what I have to do, do you realize that every issue that is on my desk tonight was on my desk when I came to Congress in 1937?"[63] They would not stay there long.

As 1964 unfolded, Johnson's relentless energy, his skill in leading Congress, his frequent evocation of Kennedy's legacy, and the ripening liberal mood[64] paved the way for a remarkable legislative explosion: a major civil rights act, antipoverty legislation, the tax cut, food stamps, aid for urban mass transit, hospital construction, creation of the National Wilderness System, and on across the spectrum of national interests. "This has been a year without precedent," Johnson told members of Congress at a reception in their honor on August 19, 1964. "This session of Congress has passed more major legislation, met more national needs, disposed of more national issues than any other session of this century or the last."[65]

That year was also an election year. In a monument to bad timing, the Republican Party that year turned hard to the right. It nominated Barry Goldwater, a senator from Arizona who had voted against civil rights, who pledged to undo the Social Security program, and who hinted darkly at the wisdom of using nuclear weapons in Vietnam. Rarely has a major-party candidate positioned himself so far from the prevailing mood of his time, and Goldwater paid dearly. Johnson won the largest percentage of the popular vote ever recorded up to that time and carried the electoral votes of all but six states. The Republican Party paid dearly as well, losing thirty-eight seats in the House and two in the Senate. The Goldwater debacle further quickened the liberal legislative momentum as the Eighty-ninth Congress gathered in 1965.

Johnson had lived through many political cycles, and he knew the good times wouldn't last. So he pushed feverishly to get new proposals to Congress and then to bring them to law. "I have watched the Congress from either the inside or the outside, man and boy, for more than 40 years," Johnson told a group at the White House, "and I've never seen a Congress that didn't eventually take the measure of the President it was dealing with."[66]

By mid-1966 the liberal storm was passing. But while it raged, this confluence of elements—the pent-up liberal policy agenda, the burgeoning national support for black rights, the programmatic foundation that Kennedy had built, his assassination and martyrdom, the skill and bottomless drive of Lyndon Johnson, the overwhelming defeat of Republican congressmen and conservative ideas in 1964, the changes in membership and rules in Congress that weakened the forces of resistance, the unique opportunities for bipartisanship, the liberal accord that prevailed in American public opinion—produced the public policy equivalent of a perfect storm. It came suddenly and raged briefly, but it left a deeply altered landscape in its wake.

CHAPTER 3

THE FEDERAL COLOSSUS

January 20, 1961. A Friday. Across the country, the workweek was ending. The morning papers focused on Washington and the inauguration that day of John F. Kennedy. Editorials speculated on what his new administration and this unfolding decade might bring—unaware that some clues were available only a few pages away. The classified ads had categories of jobs for men and jobs for women. "Gal Friday needed" was a common lead. News stories reported on the continuing pattern of slow economic growth. Small items here and there mentioned the emerging American presence in Southeast Asia and the consequences of President Eisenhower's decision to break off diplomatic relations with an increasingly provocative new dictator in Cuba. *Time* magazine reported on the travails of Charlayne Hunter, the first black woman to enroll at the University of Georgia, who was taunted with chants of "make way for the nigger" when she walked to class.[1]

A prospector looking for a nation's agenda would find plenty of hints in the news of that week. The economy had been lagging for several years and needed a boost. Cuba was becoming an ever sharper thorn in the side of its northern neighbor. Instability was growing in a distant place that many Americans still knew as French Indo-China but that would soon become more familiar by its other name: Vietnam. The Baby Boomers were flooding the country's schools and putting enormous pressure on local education budgets. The rising tide of southern black protest was beginning to command national attention. Health costs were rising faster than the incomes of America's growing community of older people. Skies grew darker and rivers smellier as the by-products of an industrial economy filled the air and water with toxins. There was an agenda there, all right, but an attendee at John Kennedy's inauguration would have heard little about it.

THE KENNEDY PRELUDE

John Kennedy delivered a memorable inaugural address, remarkable more for its poetry than its particulars. It was a Cold War anthem, with barely a mention of domestic policy. He called on Americans to ask not what their country could do for them, but what they could do for their country. But he offered few hints about what, precisely, that might be— not about racial bigotry or the environment or education or health care or poverty.

For all the talk about torches passing and new generations taking over the leadership in the country, there was little reason for most people to see the Kennedy inauguration as a pivot point in history. The election of 1960 had been exceedingly close, the issues separating the candidates narrow. The electorate was not in revolt, the country seemed at peace with itself. The country's leading political commentator, Walter Lippmann, had written in the election year that "the public mood of the country is defensive, to hold on and to conserve, not to push forward and to create. We talk about ourselves these days as if we were a completed society, one which has achieved its purposes, and has no further great business to transact."[2]

Lippmann's lament belied the anxiety with which Americans were groping for new leadership. The publisher of *Life*, Henry R. Luce, understood the depth of this malaise. The United States was "the greatest nation in the world," Luce wrote in an anthology he commissioned in 1960 entitled *The National Purpose*. "But what shall Americans do with the greatness of their nation? And is it great enough? And is it great in the right way? From all over the land, there is evidence that this is what

Americans are worrying about. A group of citizens may begin by talking about the price of eggs or the merits of education but they end by asking each other: What are we trying to do, overall?"[3]

But while liberals might clamor for change, America in 1961 was not a country in crisis. The economy had recently suffered through several periods of recession, but it was not devastated as it had been the last time a Democrat replaced a Republican in the White House. Concerns about civil rights had been growing over the previous half-decade and serious voices had begun to call for federal action to confront racial segregation in the South. But in 1961 race remained a secondary issue to most Americans, Kennedy included. And while the new president had called during the campaign for health care for the elderly, federal aid to education, and other perennials of the liberal agenda, he seemed in no hurry to aggressively mold public opinion.

Intellectuals around the president agreed that summoning the nation to an ambitious reform agenda would require patient preparation. Richard Neustadt, the Harvard professor who counseled Kennedy during the transition, warned him against trying to compete with Franklin Roosevelt's legendary "first one hundred days" during the nadir of the Great Depression. "In terms of legislative action, the analogy to 1933 is not apt," wrote Neustadt. "Postpone whatever is postponable."[4]

Neustadt's advice seemed to mesh with Kennedy's political moderation. In his years in the House and Senate and his yearlong quest for the presidency, Kennedy had always seemed more comfortable with foreign policy than domestic. He had never been one of the people who came to mind when commentators spoke of "congressional liberals." And his record in Congress had not excited liberals in his own party when he announced his campaign for president.[5] He had never joined Americans for Democratic Action or the Democratic Advisory Council, organizations that had played important roles in formulating the liberals' agenda.[6] "Kennedy seemed too cool and ambitious, too bored by the conditioned reflexes of stereotyped liberalism, too much a young man in a hurry," wrote Arthur M. Schlesinger, Jr. "He did not respond in anticipated ways and phrases and wore no liberal heart on his sleeve."[7]

On entering office Kennedy had little faith that Congress was ready for bold action on any matter, especially for new programs that would enlarge the role of the federal government and put new pressures on the federal treasury. He took conservative opposition seriously, perhaps inflating its magnitude. Joseph Kraft, a leading Washington columnist who knew Kennedy well, wrote, "By nature, he was cautious. He made decisions at the margin, committing himself little and leaving room for escape. He had par excellence the ability to separate out things—the analytic capacity. Politically, he tended to court the opposition and ignore his friends. He gave high office to many Republicans, and always clothed soft-line sentiment in hard-line dress. His motto might have been: no enemies to the right."[8]

But Kennedy's natural caution was far from terminal. Liberals in his own party and his own administration were pushing him to initiate legislation on a number of domestic fronts. Conditions in the country, particularly the signs of weakness in the economy, demanded attention, and Kennedy's confidence seemed to grow as the months in office passed. House Speaker Sam Rayburn's success—in which the president and his staff played a key role—in altering the ideological balance of the House Rules Committee also offered greater promise for the Kennedy legislative program.

While Kennedy's credentials as a liberal were never very impressive in his prepresidential years, he was a government man—a federal government man. His grandfather had been a mayor, his father a federal regulator and an ambassador. He had come of age as a naval war hero, been elected to Congress at twenty-nine, and lived much of his adult life in Washington. He is one of only two presidents buried in Arlington National Cemetery. Though never a liberal ideologue, Kennedy's view of the political world as centered in Washington was deeply internalized, the product of a life in which the nation's capital and the nation's government had dominated his every predisposition.

One of the strategies Kennedy adopted to cope with the congressional constraints he confronted was the aggressive use of executive authority. In his first year in office he issued sixty-nine executive orders. Executive Order 10924 established the Peace Corps. To stimulate the national economy, he ordered the Veterans Administration to accelerate the payment of GI life insurance benefits. He ordered a speedup in post office construction and faster distribution of income tax refunds. Employees of the executive branch were on notice to spend faster and sooner the funds appropriated for fiscal year 1961.

Though he used executive authority more assertively than most of his predecessors, Kennedy knew well that he had to work with Congress for significant policy changes. "Kennedy and I both believed," his legislative assistant Larry O'Brien later wrote, "that he, and I also, would have to take an active, aggressive role with Congress if he was to have any chance of passing his program.... [W]e believed that Kennedy's only hope of legislative success was to establish a liaison relationship with Congress ... that was new and, in the context of Capitol Hill, revolutionary."[9]

Though he had only a five-person White House staff, O'Brien organized the legislative relations staffs of dozens of departments and agencies into a coherent unit working for the president's program. He and the president held regular breakfasts with the legislative leadership and found many other opportunities to include legislators in White House events and the president's schedule. They used patronage creatively, often shamelessly, to woo legislative support. Kennedy's narrow electoral victory—which provided no coattails for legislators in 1960—and the enduring strength of the conservative coalition in Congress made such courtship indispensable for the new administration.

Kennedy's primary domestic policy concern in that first year was the economy. A recession had been under way for most of Eisenhower's last year. Economic growth was stumbling along at less than 3 percent. Capacity utilization in manufacturing was less than 80 percent. Unemployment was above 6 percent.[10] The issue in early 1961 was not whether to act, but how.

Kennedy became president during an upheaval in the field of economics. The ideas of John Maynard Keynes—especially the notion that governments should operate countercyclical fiscal policies—had first emerged in 1936 with the publication of his *General Theory of Employment, Interest and Money*. By the early 1960s they had taken hold among many of the country's leading economists. The men whom Kennedy appointed to his Council of Economic Advisors—Walter Heller, Kermit Gordon, and James Tobin—were among those who had come to share this view of government's role.

Before this, deficit spending by the national government had typically been explained as an accident or a necessity justified by national emergency, such as war or depression. That government might spend more than it took in as a strategy for improving the national economy was the gist of the Keynesian argument and the basis of what came to be called in Kennedy's time the New Economics.

Though differing in emphasis, Kennedy's economic advisors were in broad agreement, Theodore Sorensen reports, "that unemployment was too high, that budget deficits at such times were both unavoidable and useful, and that consumer purchasing power should be more strongly supported by Federal actions than had been true under the previous administration."[11]

Kennedy came to this view reluctantly. The fiscal 1961 budget deficit of $3.3 billion was not planned and troubled him.[12] His conversion to Keynesianism would come gradually, but he accepted the analysis of his advisors that growth was the economy's primary need and that federal action to kindle economic growth should be a priority. The administration's goal was to stimulate demand, thus to enlarge use of the economy's capacity and get people back to work.

In the first two years of the Kennedy administration, this approach was implemented with quite traditional measures: investment tax credits, accelerated government transfer payments, investments in public works, more generous depreciation allowances, an extension of unemployment insurance, and increases in the minimum wage and Social Security benefits and coverage. The economy did begin to grow but not fast enough for Walter Heller, chairman of Kennedy's Council of Economic Advisors. In 1962, Heller suggested to the president the need for a tax cut to further stimulate economic demand. Kennedy hesitated. Budget deficits remained a worry to him and only a Keynesian, perhaps of the romantic variety, could see clearly how a tax cut would yield sufficient economic growth to generate new revenues that would compensate for those lost through the cut itself.

Heller argued that more growth was needed to bring the economy to its maximum potential, what came to be called the "full-employment economy." But as James Tobin, a Yale economist also serving on the Council of Economic Advisors and later a Nobel laureate in economics, recalled, "Kennedy was afraid of offending two establishments: the conservative Democrats in Congress and the wider financial establishment. He had been a junior senator, and in the minds of many of the older Democratic committee chairmen, he was an upstart. Those of us at the Council were disappointed by his caution at the beginning of the administration. We tried to persuade the president to be more audacious in economic policy."[13]

Eventually, the administration moved in the direction of its Keynesian advisors, undertaking what one critic called "one of the grandest experiments in social theory of this century."[14] The tax cut that Heller advocated became the major economic policy initiative of the Kennedy administration, though it did not come to fruition until after his death. It required action by Congress, and Congress was as reluctant to cut taxes as Kennedy himself had been initially. Pursuit of the elusive full-employment economy would become Lyndon Johnson's burden.

Among Kennedy's other legislative priorities were two holdovers from earlier Democratic administrations: federal aid for education and health insurance for the elderly. Though he proposed these in 1961, neither was enacted by Congress during his administration. The same fate awaited the civil rights legislation that Kennedy proposed in 1963 after a season of black protest across the South. Kennedy had no long history as a leader or even a prominent voice on civil rights, but no president of either party in the early 1960s could have denied the momentum for federal action on this increasingly visible issue.

While Kennedy made limited headway in the Congress, he did much to educate the public on the need for active government. In speeches, conferences, and meetings with congressmen, he identified problems such as environmental blight, economic stagnation, racism, and poverty as national in scope, and he urged greater federal as well as state and local redress. His proposals to the Congress encompassed such diverse aims as area redevelopment, extension of the minimum wage, aid to education, regulation of air quality, construction of mental health facilities, and a new program of manpower development and training.

After the midterm election in 1962, Kennedy also began to explore possibilities for federal intervention to reduce poverty. Kennedy, of course, was the son of one of the wealthiest men in the country. What he knew about poverty he learned from his constituents in Massachusetts, from people he had met on the campaign trail in West Virginia and other places in 1960, and from his reading. And like many Americans, he was reading Michael Harrington.[15]

Harrington wrote one of the books that helped shape the liberal agenda in the 1960s. Published in 1962 to exhilarating reviews and wide comment, Harrington's *The Other America* told of the magnitude and the pain of poverty—a national embarrassment in an age of affluence.

Born in St. Louis, Missouri, Harrington was a graduate of Holy Cross College and had been an editor of the *Catholic Worker* in the 1950s. But he gradually lost confidence in his church and became more involved in leftist politics, eventually becoming a socialist and prominent social critic. His contribution was not simply in noting the extent of poverty in America—he estimated that there were 40 to 50 million poor people—but in suggesting the shame this ought to produce among political and economic leaders whom Harrington believed had been derelict in not recognizing the problem. "That the poor are invisible is one of the most important things about them," he wrote. "They are not simply neglected and forgotten as in the old rhetoric of reform; what is much worse, they are not seen."[16]

The Other America brought them into view. And among those who noticed was Walter Heller. Not surprisingly, Heller regarded poverty as an economic problem, the mitigation of which would come through improved economic conditions. In a year-end discussion of economic issues in 1962, Kennedy urged Heller to proceed with an analysis of poverty and to develop a policy response. Heller recruited Robert Lampman, an economist from the University of Wisconsin and himself the author of a respected study of poverty, to guide the council in its antipoverty explorations. Lampman worked with federal employees in the Social Security Administration, the Bureau of the Budget, and the Department of Health, Education, and Welfare. They struggled to come up with a consensual definition of poverty and to develop program initiatives. Kennedy encouraged their efforts, asking Heller to pull together a set of antipoverty proposals for 1964. On November 19, 1963, he again spurred Heller to move forward on the antipoverty initiative.[17]

Kennedy's death later that week did not slow the momentum for an antipoverty program. Lampman's work yielded a significant chapter on poverty in the Economic Report of the President that was submitted to Congress in early 1964. This became the basis for the Economic Opportunity Act and other elements of the war on poverty that Lyndon Johnson would launch in his first State of the Union Address in January

Measured in legislative accomplishments at the time of his death, the Kennedy record is hardly exceptional.[18] The constitutional separation of powers, the traditional weakness of political parties, and the separate election cycles of presidents and legislators always make it hard for American chief executives to dominate the policy-making process. But Kennedy and his team were moving forward in 1963. His civil rights bill had been reported by the House Judiciary Committee and appeared ready to survive the rest of the legislative gauntlet it faced. The House had passed the president's tax-cut proposal and the Senate seemed likely to follow suit. Other elements of his program were advancing as public support began to crystallize, legislative opposition wore down, and John Kennedy grew steadily better at being President Kennedy.

The thirty-four months of Kennedy's presidency were a bridge between an era of national politics dominated by congressional conservatives and a liberal hour that was just beginning. The Kennedy program had provided much of the agenda. His death and martyrdom gave it potent emotional validation. It wanted now only a guiding force.

MAKING NEVER NOW

After flying back to Washington from Dallas and making a brief and graceful statement to the nation from the tarmac at Andrews Air Force Base, Johnson stayed up late into the night of November 22, 1963, conducting phone calls with one ear and personal conversations with a stream of aides and administration officials with the other. The relentless energy that had been so apparent through his congressional career and so stifled during his years as vice president revived immediately on that day and quickly became the dominant power source in Washington. The jolt he provided would supercharge national politics for the next three years and leave its mark on the nation for generations.

The hallmark of the president's style, wrote the columnist Joseph

Kraft after years of close observation, was "cyclonic activity." "He is not only big physically. He hates more, loves more, worries more, boasts more, talks more, cries more, laughs more, eats more, conceals more, exposes more, works more, plays more than normal men. He is a giant in all things, something larger than life and out of size. . . . His genius is to be the average writ large."[19]

This was the common view of Lyndon Johnson. "He was an awesome engine of a man," wrote his long-serving aide Jack Valenti, "terrorizing, tender, inexhaustibly energetic, and ruthless; loving of land, grass, and water; engulfing, patient, impatient, caring, and insightful; devoted to wife, family, and friends; petty, clairvoyant, and compassionate; bullying, sensitive, tough, and resolute; charming, earthy, courageous, and devious; full of humor, brilliantly intelligent; brutal, wise, suspicious, disciplined, crafty, and generous."[20]

Lyndon Johnson had always been a man in a hurry. "When you have something to do," he told his aide Eric Goldman, "don't sit there. Do it, and do it fast." Lady Bird Johnson, the new president's wife, said simply, "Lyndon acts as if there is never going to be a tomorrow."[21]

And he was ambitious. He won a special election for a seat in Congress in 1937 when he was twenty-eight. Little more than a decade later he won, by the narrowest of margins, a long-shot race for the Senate against a popular governor. He was elected leader of his party in the Senate while still in his first term and majority leader at the beginning of his second.

But his eyes were always on the prize, the presidency. He ran for it as soon as Eisenhower's time was up and when he lost the nomination, he shocked everyone—including the man who offered it—when he accepted the vice presidential nomination. Kennedy's death brought him to the White House at last, but this hardly sated his ambition. He didn't want simply to be president, he wanted to be a great president, "the greatest of them all."[22] "He had one goal," Valenti wrote, "to be the greatest president doing the greatest good in the history of the nation."[23]

Johnson was an optimist, and his optimism infused the nation's politics in the early years of his presidency. He'd spent the bulk of his adult life as a political infighter. He knew that there were windows of opportunity in politics, and he knew that they shut quickly. His eagerness to move forward was not mere impatience. He sensed the opportunities of the moment—a booming economy, a high level of citizen trust in government, a lull in the Cold War, the Kennedy martyrdom. But he also sensed that none of that would last long, that if his administration did not strike quickly, it could not strike with the reach and success that he so desperately sought. All his life, Johnson later said, he had heard cries of "Never." He wanted, in his presidency, to "make never now."[24]

THE GREAT SOCIETY

Wilbur J. Cohen and Lyndon Johnson would seem at first blush to have had little in common. Cohen's grandparents had escaped the pogroms of Eastern Europe by emigrating to America in the nineteenth century, one family from Russia, the other from Poland. Raised in Milwaukee where his parents ran a succession of small stores in ethnic neighborhoods, he came early to know the sting of anti-Semitism and the reality of life on a financial knife-edge.

Hard work in school opened the door to higher education for Wilbur Cohen, and he graduated from the University of Wisconsin in 1934. Like many bright young men of the time, he headed immediately to Washington to save the country. He found a job as a research assistant with the congressional committee that wrote the Social Security Act. He studied the issues relentlessly, and for most of the years that followed he worked in or around the federal government as one of the modern American welfare state's great technicians. Joseph Califano summarized the common perception when he called Wilbur Cohen "one of the most effective public servants of the twentieth century."[25] He became invaluable to the liberal leadership of his era, almost indispensable.

Cohen was for most of his life one of those invisible public figures whose intelligence, knowledge, and creativity are the foundation upon which politicians build public policies. Cohen's anonymity evaporated during the 1960s as he played a major role in the expansion of Social Security to include Medicare and Medicaid. Kennedy and Johnson relied on him heavily and constantly. When Johnson chose him to be secretary of health, education, and welfare in 1968, the appointment merely certified what most people in Washington already knew: that Wilbur Cohen was the brains of the outfit.

The policy inventions of the 1960s were the work of politics, and politicians get most of the credit. Their names fill the history books and adorn the monuments. But policies are born from ideas and analysis. Politicians may give new policies life, but experts give them shape and content. And in the 1960s experts came to play a role in policy development that was far broader and of much deeper impact than ever before.

Neither Kennedy nor Johnson were idea men. Neither had any significant professional training in economics or social science, nor were moments of creativity or great substantive insight notable in their lives. But both understood the need for ideas as the fodder of policy making. The task forces that proliferated under Sargent Shriver's leadership during the months after Kennedy's election yielded some of those ideas, and no small number of the people who shone in that work were appointed to positions in the Kennedy administration.

Johnson was as aggressive as Kennedy, perhaps even more so, in his pursuit of new ideas for policy initiatives. No intellectual himself, Johnson came to feast on the products of those who were. In a speech at the fiftieth anniversary of the Brookings Institution in 1966, Johnson said:

> There is hardly an aspect of the Great Society's program that has not been molded, or remolded, or in some way influenced by the community of scholars and thinkers. The flow of ideas continues—because the problems continue. Some ideas are good enough to stimulate whole departments of Government into fresh appraisals of their programs. Some are ingenious; some are impractical; some are both. But without the tide of new proposals that periodically sweeps into this city, the climate of our Government would be very arid indeed.[26]

"I am determined to do things that will make opportunities better for ordinary Americans. . . ." Johnson told Eric Goldman. "But I badly need help—I badly need it. And I especially need the help of the best minds in the country."[27]

Getting the "best minds" and putting them to work became a preoccupation of the president and the White House. From universities and think tanks, policy specialists came to work on the White House staff and at key positions in the departments and agencies. Some were recruited for short-term assignments in their areas of expertise; others took regular appointments in the government. Johnson also developed his own network of task forces and study groups to translate ideas into specific policy proposals.

Richard Goodwin had come to work for Senator John Kennedy in 1959 when he was twenty-seven, later following him to the White House. From Massachusetts, first in his class at Harvard Law School, law clerk to Felix Frankfurter, he was not like Jack Valenti, Walter Jenkins, Harry McPherson, and other typical Johnson staff aides over the years. But Johnson kept him on because Goodwin could help him bring the "best minds in the country" into the president's increasingly insatiable idea factories.

"Designing the Great Society was a multilayered process," Goodwin later wrote. "The task forces that Johnson promised were assembled, bringing together not merely experts and specialists, but the philosophical explorers of American public life. . . . From their discussions (attended by members of the White House staff) we attempted to extract a coherent program of public policy, then to make necessary compromises to accommodate the demands of 'interest' groups that had the power to obstruct, perhaps defeat, our proposals."[28]

Much of the intellectual energy that fueled the Johnson policy machinery came not from outside experts or professors on leave from their universities but from the permanent employees of the national government. By the 1960s the federal bureaucracy had become a thriving center of knowledge and expertise. It employed thousands of Ph.D.'s, M.D.'s, and J.D.'s. These scholars and doctors and lawyers and many others from the professions were not mere implementers of public policy, nor were they ideological or political neuters. They were people with ideas and with sharp opinions on what the government could do—and should do—for American citizens. And they played a large role in identifying problems and proposing and formulating the policy solutions that would come to mark this era.

Washington in the 1960s was bursting with people whose career paths resembled Wilbur Cohen's. They were liberals, believers in the capacity of government to be a positive force in American lives, and eager to make it so. For them, the bureaucracies of Washington were not merely places to earn a living and accumulate a pension, but places to exercise their knowledge, their skills of analysis, and their imaginations in pursuit of social justice.

In every area of public engagement, bureaucratic experts formed the core of government knowledge and understanding. But they were not simply resources waiting to be called upon. In many cases, they were pushing aggressively for government action to address the problems that absorbed their daily attention. "The main pressure for a massive government assault on poverty," wrote Daniel Patrick Moynihan, a firsthand observer, "developed within the Kennedy-Johnson Administration, among officials whose responsibilities were to think about just such matters. These men now exist, they are well paid, have competent staffs, and have access to the President. . . . Most importantly, they have at their command an increasing fund of information about social conditions in the United States."[29]

This approach to policy making, which some have labeled "top-down," bore echoes of the Progressive reform initiatives of the early decades of the twentieth century. Progressives combined an interest in popular rule with calls for efficiency, scientific planning, and expertise. Similar approaches prevailed in the 1960s. The domestic problems identified by Washington experts in the latter period were not matters of significant concern to most Americans. With the exception of race, most of these issues had not inspired or energized heavy citizen pressure on government. Robert Lampman, one of the creators of the federal anti-poverty proposals, noted, "The initiatives for a poverty program came from inside government. . . . They certainly did not come from well-organized pressure groups. . . . It was an elite group inside the Kennedy administration that started talking about this."[30] And so it was with most of the issues that came to define the policy corpus of the 1960s: The federal government was acting not as the agent of the American people responding to their demands, but as an independent force seeking to solve problems that its experts had identified and to which they had applied the tools of modern analysis.

FROM THAT FIRST long day in office, November 22, 1963, Lyndon Johnson prodded and pushed his government to action. His schedule overflowed with meetings. The telephone was so often at his ear that it could easily be mistaken for an appendage. The phone, said Valenti, was Johnson's "Excalibur."[31] Johnson observed no proprieties of the clock, calling aides and members of Congress and others at all hours of the night and day. Douglass Cater, a Johnson aide, tells the story of one senator who was awakened at 5:00 A.M. by a phone call from the president. Johnson began the conversation by asking, "Hi. What are you doing?"

"Oh nothing, Mr. President," came the reply. "Just lying here hoping you'd call."[32]

By 1964 the legislative ground had been well prepared for Johnson's style of leadership. The Kennedy program had been moving forward before his assassination and Johnson was able to build upon and in some cases to accelerate its momentum.

Johnson's first priority was legislative approval of President Kennedy's tax-cut proposal. This occurred on February 26. The civil rights bill, too, was slowly navigating through and around the rear-guard assaults of the southern conservatives. Johnson was not shy about calling on his old Senate friends, like Richard Russell of Georgia, to indicate his powerful desire to see this bill passed. He switched no southern votes for civil rights, but he made it clear that he would not lie down for any dilatory tactics. This emboldened the bill's supporters and sharpened the handwriting on the wall for its opponents.

The House had passed the bill by a vote of 290–130 on February 10. But the real roadblock was in the Senate, where an unfriendly Judiciary Committee and the likelihood of a filibuster stood in its way. Neither was fatal, however. On June 10 the Senate voted for the first time to end a filibuster on a civil rights bill, and on June 19 it passed the bill by a vote of 73–27. One of those who voted against the bill was Senator Barry Goldwater of Arizona, who a few days earlier had upset New York governor Nelson Rockefeller in the California Republican primary, thus moving him closer to his party's presidential nomination.

The legislative successes began to accumulate in 1964, and the press and the public took notice. Johnson's job approval ratings in the Gallup Polls during the first half of 1964 never fell below 74 percent.[33] But Johnson wanted more, much more. It was not enough to be the executor of the Kennedy legacy, although he was happy to play that role when it served his purposes. He wanted election to his own term as president, and he wanted public policy initiatives that would reshape the country and awe posterity. And in those bold pursuits, not a day of 1964 could be wasted.

In the spring of that year Johnson accepted an invitation to give the commencement address at the University of Michigan. He used that occasion to lay out a vision of America that would drive his legislative program and give the era its name. The speech had been written largely by Richard Goodwin, but its tone and tenor grew out of White House staff discussions that sought to crystallize a sense of direction for the Johnson legislative program.

On that May afternoon in 1964 Johnson told the ninety thousand people in the commencement audience at Ann Arbor about his vision for a "Great Society." The phrase had been used before in Johnson speeches, but never had he sought to color in the vision as he did that day. What he wanted especially was to go beyond the traditions of Populism and Progressivism, beyond the New Deal and the Fair Deal, beyond even the specific programs like aid to education and health insurance for the elderly that were then in the legislative mill. "My mandate as I understood it," Goodwin later wrote, "was not to produce a catalogue of specific projects, but a concept, an assertion of purpose, a vision, if you will, that went beyond the liberal tradition of the New Deal."[34]

Johnson began by noting the accomplishments of his predecessors. "For a century we labored to settle and to subdue a continent," he said. "For half a century we called upon unbounded invention and untiring industry to create an order of plenty for all of our people."[35] But wealth and comfort would not be adequate measures of success in the decades that followed: "The challenge of the next half century is whether we have the wisdom to use that wealth to enrich and elevate our national life, and to advance the quality of our American civilization."

Johnson proposed taking that next step, "to move not only toward the rich society and the powerful society, but upward to the Great Society," which he described in this way:

> The Great Society rests on abundance and liberty for all. It demands an end to poverty and racial injustice, to which we are totally committed in our time. But that is just the beginning.
>
> The Great Society is a place where every child can find knowledge to enrich his mind and to enlarge his talents.... It is a place where the city of man serves not only the needs of the body and the demands of commerce but the desire for beauty and the hunger for community....
>
> It is a place where men are more concerned with the quality of their goals than the quantity of their goods.
>
> But most of all, the Great Society is not a safe harbor, a resting place, a final objective, a finished work. It is a challenge constantly renewed, beckoning us toward a destiny where the meaning of our lives matches the marvelous products of our labor.

The Great Society would come to be attached to Lyndon Johnson's presidency as a description of its goals and later as an emblem of its over-reaching. What Johnson sought was not merely a continuation of the liberal tradition of the twentieth century that attempted to provide legal protections and a social safety net for the poor and dispossessed. He wanted that, of course: more protections and a stronger safety net than ever before. But he also wanted to clean up the air and water, to beautify the countryside, to make the cities livable and manageable, to protect consumers, to fund the arts and culture—to make government the engine of a new kind of progress, far broader in focus than the liberal programs of the past.

Johnson did not invent these notions; some liberals had been suggesting for years that the country's resources were substantial enough to permit government to lead society to a higher state.[36] But Johnson was the first to propose making this a driving vision of the country's capabilities and its goals.

In his first State of the Union Address, in January 1964, Johnson had called for an "unconditional war on poverty." That call was followed on

March 16 by the president's poverty message to Congress explaining the need for and laying out the details of Johnson's antipoverty program. Eliminating poverty, Johnson said, was "the great unfinished work of our society."[37]

Johnson's goal was not simply to give more financial aid to the poor, but to cure poverty by attacking and eliminating its causes. When Walter Heller had first interested Kennedy in an antipoverty program, poverty was conceived largely as an economic problem that could best be addressed by adjustments in the national economy, especially incentives to economic growth that would produce new jobs. But the prevailing view among Johnson's advisors, and among many in the social-science community at the time, was that poverty was the result of a set of interlinked sociological and cultural conditions that fed upon one another. There was, thought many students of the problem, a "cycle of poverty" that could only be broken by a concerted attack on each of its contributing elements.[38] The "treadmill of poverty," Johnson called this in his memoirs. "A man was poor if he did not have enough money to live on, but that was only part of it. If he was poor, the consequences were that he had little education, that he received inadequate medical care and substandard nutrition, that he lived in crowded and substandard conditions. He had no real chance to train for a decent job."[39]

This was a different view of the causes and character of poverty than had prevailed among New Deal reformers. New Dealers believed that the root problems of the poor and unemployed lay in a flawed economy. Their proposed remedies included tighter federal regulation and restructuring of business, promotion of labor unions, public works and relief programs to give cash to people in need, and national economic planning through such agencies as the Agricultural Adjustment Administration and the National Recovery Administration. Liberals in the affluent society, by contrast, focused their efforts on the limitations of poor people themselves.

An attack on all of the elements in the cycle of poverty was Johnson's goal: a "war on a domestic enemy which threatens the strength of our nation and the welfare of our people." To accomplish this, Johnson proposed legislation that would become the Economic Opportunity Act of 1964. While some of the components of the bill had been proposed before, this was the first major legislation to bear fully the stamp of Lyndon Johnson and he was relentless in his pursuit of its passage.

When the bill cleared Congress on August 11 it contained virtually everything the president had requested and authorized $947.5 million in fiscal 1965, only $15 million less than the administration proposal. Among its key provisions were the creation of a Job Corps to provide young people with two years of education, vocational training, and work experience; programs to raise the incomes and living standards of low-income rural families and migrant workers; incentives for small businesses to hire the long-term unemployed; creation of the Volunteers in Service to America (VISTA) to work with state and local agencies in efforts to combat poverty at the local level; and a federal Office of Economic Opportunity (OEO) to coordinate administration of the program.

Title II of the Economic Opportunity Act established a new approach to local efforts to eliminate poverty and ultimately became the most controversial piece of Johnson's Great Society: the "community action programs" (CAPs) that were intended to improve the conditions under which the poor lived and work. What distinguished them was their creation outside the normal administrative framework of government. They would be nonprofit organizations engaging the "maximum feasible participation" of local residents, who would design and operate antipoverty programs unique to their communities' needs. In effect, the poor would design and run programs to cure their poverty.

These community action programs were problematic from the start. For some of those who helped design this legislation, CAPs seemed an effective device for getting around the resistance of government bureaucracies at all levels. Others saw the CAPs less as administrative devices than as sources of community activism. They believed that a key to combating poverty was for the poor to take control of their own lives, to play an active rather than merely passive role in federal antipoverty efforts.[40] The CAPs, they thought, would challenge the political establishment, not be its handmaiden.

While their experiences varied widely, many of the local community action programs did become hotbeds of community activism. This was threatening to local political leaders who saw the CAPs as alternative power structures in their own communities, funded and encouraged by the federal government. Complaints to Washington were not long in coming.

Equally troubling to some antipoverty activists were the failures of many of the community action programs to demonstrate any progress in the war on poverty. It became apparent that the poor were not especially effective at designing or implementing antipoverty programs. Community action, in the words of historian Mark Gelfand, became the "loose cannon" in the War on Poverty. "What had originally been touted as an instrument for more efficient local coordination of extensive federal effort," he writes, "turned into a federally supported device for challenging the local political and welfare structure. The ruckus CAP created was blown far out of proportion to the threat it actually posed, but the bad publicity dealt the War on Poverty a blow from which it never recovered."[41]

Two other antipoverty programs, though not part of the original legislation, were created by the Office of Economic Opportunity and eventually outlived it. One of these was Head Start, a program that provided educational and social services to four- and five-year-old children to improve their ability to succeed in school and in life. The other was Legal Services, a program that provided free legal assistance to the poor in such matters as contracts, disputes with landlords, and criminal cases.

The year 1964 also saw the creation of the food stamp program. Initially conceived as a source of relief for farmers facing stockpiles of agricultural surpluses, the program allowed poor people to purchase food stamps, which they could then use as currency at the supermarket. The value of the stamps exceeded what they cost; six dollars, for example, would purchase ten dollars' worth of food stamps. President Kennedy had been a strong advocate of this program and President Johnson called for its permanent enactment in his 1964 agricultural message. In practice, food stamps became a significant component of federal antipoverty efforts, eventually providing a federal food subsidy to almost 10 percent of the American people.[42]

The accomplishments of the antipoverty effort were mixed and they remain controversial. But they bore many of the characteristics of 1960s liberalism. There was, first, an overriding optimism fueled by a burgeoning economy, and a sense of unprecedented opportunity to overcome the ancient plagues of mankind. "For the first time in our history," Lyndon Johnson noted in his antipoverty message to Congress, "it is possible to conquer poverty." Historian David Burner wrote, "Liberals were addressing the issue of poverty in the confident spirit of the Kennedy era, convinced that with enough dedication the country could reduce or eliminate want, as it could hurl a spaceship into the sky."[43]

Second, there was a prevailing faith that social science could diagnose the causes of human problems and develop sound and effective public policy cures. Social scientists colonized the Kennedy and Johnson administrations. Their studies of family breakdown, juvenile delinquency, urban blight, and many other topics were impressive and persuasive. Often they forced lawmakers into action, inspiring a suspension of disbelief—and sometimes common sense—in the face of such a wealth of statistics and data and theorizing. "The new initiatives," wrote Johnson aide Robert Wood two decades later, "derived for the most part from the capital stock of the social sciences as understood and practiced a generation ago."[44]

Lyndon Johnson bought into most of this. He was not a trained or even very interested consumer of the social science studies that guided so many administration efforts. But he was happy to employ them and the advocacy provided by the "best minds" who produced them to legitimize his own efforts to use the instruments of public policy for the substantive purposes in which he believed. Johnson turned to the experts because he wanted a "tremendous infusion of objective thinking and new and original ideas," thinking and new proposals that were "imaginative and not bound by timid, preconceived notions."[45]

The antipoverty efforts of the 1960s were characteristic of the liberal reform efforts of that period in a third way as well. They demonstrated the sheer impetus of capability, the willingness to do something merely because it could be done without regard to its likely outcome or success. Did the social value of a manned space program equal its costs? Would a land war in Asia protect the United States from the spread of communism? Could all the instruments of public policy, wound together in an "unconditional war," actually eliminate poverty? Too often those questions were set aside, overshadowed by the sheer capacity of the American system to send a man to the moon, to conduct a war in Asia, to build a vast network of antipoverty programs.

By the summer of 1964 Lyndon Johnson had become master of his universe. The policy-generating process in the executive branch was humming. Under his guidance, the legislative process in Congress was yielding to presidential leadership as it hadn't in decades. The Supreme Court rarely thwarted the president on any matter and often pushed ahead even of his own aggressive agenda of liberal reform. And then came the election of 1964 and the accelerator hit the floor.

THE GOLDWATER DEBACLE

When Michel Goldwasser emigrated to the Arizona desert in 1835 from the Jewish shtetl in Konin, Poland, he brought with him little more than a capacity for hard work. It was a habit that passed to his son, along with the string of enterprises that Goldwasser had started. The family name was changed to Goldwater in the nineteenth century, and its members became successful merchants in Phoenix. As Arizona grew in population and wealth, the Goldwater name and fortune spread.

One of Michel Goldwasser's sons, Baron Goldwater, converted to the Episcopalian church when he married Josephine Williams. Among their children was an adventurous young man named Barry Goldwater. Though raised in a privileged environment, he was an indifferent student and dropped out of college. He joined the family business but had little passion for it and spent much of his time pursuing other interests: rafting, airplanes, photography. He became a well-known lecturer in Arizona, entertaining audiences with films of his exploits. During World War II, he served as an Air Corps pilot, though not in combat. He remained in the Air Force reserves after the war, eventually rising to the rank of major general.

Goldwater ran successfully for the Phoenix City Council in 1949 as a reformer. In the Eisenhower landslide of 1952, he was able to win election to the United States Senate. There he was a backbencher in the minority party for ten of the next twelve years—years in which Democrats often had huge majorities. Finding little to absorb his attention in the Senate, he traveled widely around the country, giving speeches and becoming a prominent critic of Democrats and liberals.

Goldwater's conservatism was more practical than theoretical, drawing heavily on the successful experiences of his family in Arizona. He had no grounding nor much interest in ideology as an intellectual matter. His reading in the literature of conservatism seemed to be slender and rarely informed his thinking or his speeches. He emerged as a darling of conservatives after publication of his book *The Conscience of a Conservative* in 1960, but the book was almost entirely ghostwritten by Brent Bozell, one of his speechwriters.

Goldwater contributed little to the intellectual construction of modern conservatism. But in the midst of the liberal hour, he became its leading front man. And when he acceded to the pleas that he run for the Republican nomination for president in 1964, he electrified the right wing of his party and appalled its moderate core. Goldwater inspired strong emotions.

Had there been a coordinated effort by Republican moderates to deny Goldwater the 1964 nomination, they might well have succeeded. The bulk of his support came from outside the mainstream of the party, and most prominent Republicans were sure that with Goldwater as the nominee, he and many of the party's congressional candidates would suffer overwhelming defeat. Governor Nelson Rockefeller of New York seemed the best hope to block Goldwater, but Rockefeller was handicapped by a controversial divorce and remarriage a few years earlier. And Rockefeller would in 1964 and again in 1968 prove to be a diffident, often inept national campaigner.

When Rockefeller failed to stop the Goldwater juggernaut in the 1964 primaries, another moderate, Governor William Scranton of Pennsylvania, emerged on the eve of the convention to rally the anti-Goldwater forces. But his opposition was too little too late, and a wild celebration ensued on the floor of the Cow Palace in San Francisco when Goldwater won the nomination on the first ballot.

In his acceptance speech, Goldwater lamented the direction in which the country was moving. "The tide," he said, "has been running against freedom. Our people have followed false prophets." Without naming any names, he castigated Lyndon Johnson and the Democrats who dominated Congress as "those who seek to live your lives for you, to take your liberty in return for relieving you of yours, those who elevate the state and downgrade the citizen." Toward the end of his speech, Goldwater uttered the lines that would echo throughout—and haunt—his campaign: "I would remind you that extremism in the defense of liberty is no vice! And let me remind you also that moderation in the pursuit of justice is no virtue!"[46]

The normal approach to presidential politics is for a major-party candidate, having secured the nomination by energizing a faction of his party, to then reach out to other factions within the party and move toward the center in the general election—to pursue the support of independents and even weak supporters of the opposition party. But Goldwater was having none of that. He and his advisors were true believers. They hoped to engage the Democrats in a campaign that would serve as an ideological plebiscite, a contrast of the dominant liberalism of the time with Goldwater's conservative credo.[47] "Some Republicans," wrote the political scientist Aaron Wildavsky, "were so intensely committed to a conservative victory at the convention, and so frustrated at their previous inability to win the nomination, that they convinced themselves that a 'hidden conservative vote' would emerge to help them at the state level."[48]

But Lyndon Johnson had no interest in ideological combat. The Democrats sought instead to paint Goldwater as an extremist and Johnson as the candidate, not just of the liberals, but of all Americans. For Johnson, the 1964 campaign was not a recess from governing but an opportunity to build support and momentum for his programs. He emphasized consensus to suggest the broad appeal of what he was hoping to accomplish. Theodore H. White, the great chronicler of the presidential campaigns of the 1960s, noted, "All Lyndon Johnson's life and political art had been spent in trying to reconcile differences, to bind and hold them together and, out of them, to make law." This constant call for consensus and unity would, White pointed out, "become the campaign program, the campaign theme."[49]

Goldwater was fond of quoting Henry Clay's declaration that "I'd rather be right than president." And he campaigned in that mode: voting against the Civil Rights Act, questioning the value of Social Security, suggesting the use of nuclear weapons to defoliate the jungles of Vietnam, urging the sale of the Tennessee Valley Authority (TVA), calling for an end to farm subsidies.

There were no presidential debates in 1964 as there had been in 1960 and thus there was no opportunity for Goldwater to confront Lyndon Johnson and force him to defend the expansions of government activity that were central to the Great Society agenda. Johnson was free to move about the country, drawing huge crowds and speaking homilies about the importance of unity and the dangers of divisiveness.

Vietnam was an issue in 1964, but Goldwater was the candidate advocating more vigorous military action. Johnson said he had no intention of sending "American boys to do the job that Asian boys should be doing." Vietnam rarely consumed much space in his speeches in the autumn of 1964. His campaign aired a television commercial of a young girl picking petals off a daisy in a meadow while a countdown took place in the voiceover and a mushroom cloud emerged on the screen. "These are the stakes! To make a world in which all of God's children can live, or to go into the dark. We must either love each other, or we must die," said the tag line. And that was a consistent Johnson message: Goldwater's views were not just extreme; they were dangerous.

The voting on November 3 gave Lyndon Johnson one of the great election victories in American history. Landslides are hard to compare because of the impact of third parties, but surely Johnson's 61.1 percent of the popular vote ranks with the victories of Theodore Roosevelt in 1904, Warren G. Harding in 1920, and Franklin Roosevelt in 1936. (Richard Nixon's victory over George McGovern in 1972 would later join that group.) The president's long coattails brought a net gain of thirty-eight Democrats in the House and two in the Senate, yielding the largest Democratic majorities in Congress since 1936.

Johnson thought his mandate was clear. "The program we submitted to the voters during the 1964 campaign," he later wrote, "would commit the nation to press on with the War on Poverty, to provide greater educational opportunities for all American children, to offer medical care to the elderly, to conserve our water and air and natural resources, and to tackle the country's long-standing housing shortage. The people responded to that program with an enthusiasm that made its mark on American history."[50]

A *Washington Post* editorial noted the primary question before the American people: "Do you wish the government to continue its intervention in affairs which before 1932 were largely left to private decision?" "To that question," said the *Post*, "the voters have answered 'Yes!'"[51] Walter Lippmann concluded that "the Democratic Party has become what John F. Kennedy intended and Lyndon Johnson has achieved—a party which represents the vast center of American public life."[52] To the *New York Times* the "overwhelming vote for the Johnson-Humphrey ticket reflects the popular attachment to the policies of moderate liberalism that have prevailed through more than three decades of Democratic and Republican rule....The real obligation of the next four years will be to speed progress toward better schools, better homes, better jobs, and all the other ingredients of the 'Great Society,' whose cloudy outlines were sketched by President Johnson during the campaign."[53]

What was missing in the contemporary commentary, and would become more apparent later, was recognition of some of the countercurrents in this sweeping Democratic tide. Democrats far too facilely assumed that the election result demonstrated the overwhelming liberal disposition of American citizens and was a mandate for new liberal programs. But subsequent analysis of the vote did not, in fact, support those assessments. The country, though responding negatively to Goldwater the candidate, was offering a much less dramatic judgment on Goldwater's—or Johnson's—political ideology. Most voters could not be characterized as ideologues in their political behavior, and in 1964 only 11.5 percent of a national sample queried by the Survey Research Center at the University of Michigan characterized the reasons for their electoral choice in liberal-conservative terms.[54] America was not as liberal as the outcome of the 1964 election suggested to some contemporary commentators.

Also unnoted in most analyses at the time was the role that Goldwater's candidacy had played in energizing conservatives. The Goldwater campaign was an inspiration or training ground for many young people—some still in college—who would later play significant roles in a conservative resurgence in American politics: William Baroody, William Rusher,

George Will, L. Brent Bozell, Clifton White, and Lyn Nofziger, to name a few. In California toward the end of the 1964 campaign, an actor named Ronald Reagan, a lifelong Democrat who'd lost faith in his party, made a speech for Barry Goldwater called "A Time for Choosing." In it he articulated eloquently many of the themes that resonated so vibrantly with Goldwater's supporters. The speech was broadcast nationally on network television. It was not enough to save Goldwater, but it led some California businessmen to encourage Reagan to seek the governorship of their state and thus to launch his own political career two years later. The Goldwater campaign may have failed miserably in winning the 1964 election, but it succeeded famously in midwifing a modern conservative politics in America.

Also little noted in the popular analysis of the 1964 campaign was the shifting political seismology of the South. In the electoral vote, Goldwater had carried only his own state of Arizona and Alabama, Georgia, Louisiana, and South Carolina. Liberals dismissed this as the "bigot vote" and thus an aberration in the long and deep Democratic dominance of the South. But it was not an aberration. Lyndon Johnson had once said to an aide on the day after signing the Civil Rights Act, "I think we delivered the South to the Republican Party for your lifetime and mine."[55] The 1964 election provided the first evidence of the accuracy of that prediction. Though little noted in the heady aftermath of Johnson's great victory, the "solid Democratic South"—after a hundred years—had come to an end.

The year 1964 was, as the historian Robert Mason wrote, "a record low for Republican fortunes."[56] But the Republicans would rise from these ashes much more swiftly than anyone would have dared predict on the day after the 1964 election. New opportunities in the South, the chastening lessons of the radical Goldwater candidacy, the energy and experience of many bright young conservatives, and the certainty of Democratic over-reaching in the aftermath of an election they defined as a formidable mandate would all contribute in the years ahead to the revitalization of the Republican Party and the reconfiguration of the American political map.

THE EIGHTY-NINTH CONGRESS AND BEYOND

On January 4, 1965, at 9:04 P.M., Lyndon Johnson arrived in the House chamber to deliver his State of the Union Address. Cascades of applause greeted him and punctuated his speech. As he looked out upon the assembled members of Congress, the "aisle" separating Republicans from Democrats was as far to his left as it had been since 1936. Nearly four dozen of the Democrats had not been in the Eighty-eighth Congress, and many of them were fully cognizant of the contribution the Johnson landslide had made to their own electoral success.

"We are in the midst of the greatest upward surge of economic wellbeing in the history of any nation," Johnson told the audience in the chamber and at home. "We worked for two centuries to climb this peak of prosperity. But we are only at the beginning of the road to the Great Society. Ahead now is a summit where freedom from the wants of the body can help fulfill the needs of the spirit."[57]

And then he began to list what would become the table of contents for the astonishing work of the two years that lay ahead:

A program in education to ensure every American child the fullest development of his mind and skills.

A massive attack on crippling and killing diseases.

A national effort to make the American city a better and a more stimulating place to live.

An increase in the beauty of America and an end to the poisoning of our rivers and the air that we breathe.

A new program to develop regions of our country that are now suffering from distress and depression.

New efforts to control and prevent crime and delinquency.

Elimination of every remaining obstacle to the right and the opportunity to vote.

Support for the achievements of thought and the creations of art.

Inflated rhetoric is the currency of State of the Union Addresses. What distinguished this moment was the widely shared belief that this president and this Congress could actually enact most of the programs on Lyndon Johnson's laundry list.

And they did.

No sooner had the applause ceased to echo through the House chamber than Johnson began to send bills and messages to Congress outlining the specifics for the Great Society. And no sooner did they arrive on Capitol Hill than congressional Democrats moved them forward. In March, the Appalachian Regional Development Act, providing more than a billion dollars to that depressed area, became law. In April the president signed a law providing federal aid for elementary and secondary education, a long-standing Democratic priority and the first major involvement ever of the federal government in the funding of local schools. In June the Congress enacted a major reduction in federal excise taxes. In July it created the Medicare and Medicaid programs. These medical insurance initiatives for the elderly and indigent had been part of the liberal agenda for decades and would soon become a prominent—and expensive—component of the nation's social welfare safety net.

In August the president signed the Voting Rights Act. In September the Department of Housing and Urban Development, the first new cabinet department in thirteen years, was created. September also brought a major crime control initiative, establishment of the National Foundations for the Arts and Humanities, and a number of new national parks and recreation areas.

In October the pace quickened. The Water Pollution Control Act was signed into law on the second, the Immigration and Nationality Act on the third, an act to establish new regional research and treatment centers for several diseases on the sixth, a major expansion of the war on poverty on the ninth, a sweeping Motor Vehicle Pollution Control Act on the twentieth, and a highway beautification act on the twenty-second. And then before adjournment in November the Congress sent to the president an omnibus farm bill, significant amendments to the Vocational Rehabilitation Act, and a new Higher Education Act providing unprecedented support for students attending college.

When the Eighty-ninth Congress returned at the beginning of 1966,

Johnson congratulated the members on their accomplishments in 1965. He noted the expansion of the war in Vietnam and the concern that was causing in some quarters that the nation could not afford both the war and the Great Society. But then he disagreed firmly with that view: "I have come here to recommend that you, the representatives of the richest Nation on earth, you, the elected servants of a people who live in abundance unmatched on this globe, you bring the most urgent decencies of life to all of your fellow Americans.... Time may require further sacrifices. And if it does, then we will make them. But we will not heed those who wring it from the hopes of the unfortunate here in a land of plenty. I believe that we can continue the Great Society while we fight in Vietnam."[58]

Johnson's support in the country and in Congress began to recede by the beginning of 1966, and it would continue to fall during the year. Having averaged 75 percent job approval in his first year and 66 percent in his second, Johnson's approval would average only 50 percent in 1966.[59] But the forceful momentum of the first session of the Eighty-ninth Congress continued into the second, where hundreds of new public laws were passed, including an Urban Mass Transportation Act, Highway and Motor Vehicle Safety acts, federal minimum wage increase, creation of a Department of Transportation, Model Cities Act, Clean Water Restoration Act, and Truth-in-Packaging and Truth-in-Labeling acts.

It was a breathtaking performance by a Congress, as if a long-distance run had been completed at the pace of a sprint. A typical American Congress produces just a few pieces of significant legislation among its routines of appropriating funds for federal agencies, refining and renewing prior legislation, and naming post offices after retiring members. The Eighty-ninth Congress produced major legislation almost every month— "the way Detroit turns super-sleek, souped-up autos off the assembly line," wrote Tom Wicker in the *New York Times* in the midst of the flow.[60] Often the bills it passed were items that had been on the legislative agenda for years, sometimes for decades. When Lyndon Johnson signed the Medicare legislation into law, he traveled to Independence, Missouri, and conducted the signing ceremony in the presence of Harry Truman, who had first called on Congress to enact such legislation twenty years earlier.[61]

That same pace would not continue in the Ninetieth Congress. The

1966 elections produced a reversal of the surge the Democrats had enjoyed two years earlier. Republicans achieved a net gain of forty-seven seats in the House and three in the Senate. The irresistible Democratic majorities of the Eighty-ninth Congress were gone.

But gone, too—or at least substantially diminished—was the capacity of Lyndon Johnson to urge and prod Congress as he had in the previous two years. The war in Vietnam was steadily eroding his political capital, especially his popular support.

Johnson was the most astute barometer of political conditions and he recognized that his window of opportunity was closing rapidly. The Ninetieth Congress was far from barren, but its products paled in comparison to those of the Eighty-ninth. It passed a major tax increase, the Public Broadcasting Act, a significant air quality act, an omnibus crime-control act, the creation of the Consumer Products Safety Commission, and the era's last significant civil rights act, banning racial discrimination in the sale or rental of housing.

Taken together, these two Congresses are matched in the twentieth century only by those of the early New Deal in the sweep of their impact on national life. With Lyndon Johnson as their guide and goad, they put the full force of federal authority behind the voting rights protections of the Fifteenth Amendment and outlawed racial discrimination in the national housing market. They identified consumers as a class worthy of federal protection and passed laws that required accurate packaging and labeling, enhanced the safety of roads and automobiles, and required safety testing for consumer products. They created broad federal initiatives to protect the country's environment, especially its air and water, and they placed millions of acres of land into national parks and other forms of protected use. They recognized the glaring needs of American cities and authorized billions of dollars of federal funds to help rebuild their infrastructures, provide for safety from crime, and encourage their development in the future. They reconfigured national housing and transportation policies. And they created new programs to encourage artists and scholars, to protect national treasures, and to provide a public broadcasting system.

Only rarely in the nation's history had the flow of new public policy reached a flood stage so high. Like all floods, this one would soon recede. But the marks it left behind would linger for decades.

THE WARREN COURT

It was easy, in October 1962, to overlook the start of a revolution. Riots broke out that month in Oxford, Mississippi, when a black student sought to enroll at the university there. The construction of Soviet nuclear missile sites in Cuba had been detected by surveillance flights and led to the most threatening confrontation of the Cold War.

So it is understandable that the normal convening of the U.S. Supreme Court on the first Monday of that October would barely penetrate the public consciousness. But that Court would be a major force in the floodtide of liberal policies in the next half-decade. Long after the clash at Ole Miss and the Cuban Missile Crisis had become entries in the history books, the decisions of that Supreme Court would continue to shape American life.

What was most notable about the Supreme Court that convened on October 1 was the absence of one of the towering legal figures of the twentieth century. Felix Frankfurter had been appointed to the Supreme Court in 1939 by Franklin Roosevelt. A founder of the American Civil Liberties Union, Zionist delegate to the Paris Peace Conference, defender of the anarchists Nicola Sacco and Bartolomeo Vanzetti, Frankfurter had come to the Court with the reputation of a liberal.

But no ordinary liberal. For the twenty-five years before his appointment to the Court, Frankfurter had been a popular teacher at Harvard Law School and one of the country's most admired legal scholars. The New Deal was heavily populated with Frankfurter's students, and he was closely connected to many of its leading figures. It was widely assumed at the time of his appointment that Frankfurter would be a dominant force on the Court, a dominant force for progressive and liberal interpretations of the Constitution and laws, and a potent corrective to the rigid jurisprudence that had bedeviled Franklin Roosevelt during his first term in the White House.

Frankfurter did become a powerful force on the Court, but instead of advancing the liberal momentum of the New Deal his brilliance often thwarted it. Frankfurter had enjoyed a close friendship with Oliver Wendell Holmes, Jr., and revered his philosophy of judicial restraint. Frankfurter did not believe the courts should substitute their judgment for that of elected legislatures. True, legislatures might sometimes transgress in ways no conscientious court could permit—by imposing racial segregation, for example. But in general, he believed that courts should not interfere in policies determined by the elected branches of government. Even when state legislatures declined to address the inequities of grossly malapportioned legislative districts, Frankfurter refused to override them. That, he wrote, was a "political thicket" into which the courts should not trespass.[62]

As appointments by Roosevelt and Truman and even Eisenhower transformed the Court from the conservative bastion of the early 1930s into one with substantial liberal sympathies, Frankfurter's devotion to judicial restraint became an anchor the Court could only rarely drag to the left. Frankfurter was not just a legal impresario, he was also an inveterate proselytizer. Every new appointee to the Court became a target of Frankfurter's charm, as he sought through personal relations and legal arguments to expand his sway. Long, fawning letters to new appointees, encouraging notes passed in the weekly conference of the justices, assistance with opinion writing—Frankfurter rarely missed an opportunity to cultivate a potential ally on the Court.

Through much of the 1940s and 1950s Frankfurter was able to keep a liberal majority from ever gaining control of the Court. Even as liberals gained influence in the late 1950s, he shielded the old order with his insistence on judicial restraint. It was the law made by legislatures, in Frankfurter's view, not judicial interpretations of that law that was the "instrument and offspring of reason."[63]

By the early 1960s even so formidable a combatant as Felix Frankfurter could not stay the forces of change. In his last year on the Court, two cases revealed the diminishing appeal of judicial restraint. In *Mapp v. Ohio*, the Court voted 6–3 to void a conviction against an Ohio woman based on evidence that had been obtained illegally. The case involved the "exclusionary rule," a practice in federal courts in which judges would exclude from a case any evidence that was improperly obtained, based on the Fourth Amendment prohibition of "unreasonable searches and seizures." Until this case, the Supreme Court had never applied the exclusionary rule to cases in state courts. The Bill of Rights, Felix Frankfurter had long argued, was a constraint on the federal government, but rarely applied to the states. But in this case, it was becoming clear that Frankfurter could no longer hold off the majority's growing desire to incorporate the Bill of Rights into its review of state actions.

Later in the term, the Court decided one of the most important cases of the twentieth century, *Baker v. Carr*. This was a legislative apportionment case from Tennessee. The Court had typically followed Frankfurter's logic in apportionment cases that these were "political questions," and the Court should not seek to resolve them. As Frankfurter had written in the majority opinion in *Colegrove v. Green* in 1946, the Court must not give "what is beyond its competence to grant," but must refuse to intervene out of "due regard for the effective working of our Government."[64]

But in *Baker v. Carr* six justices set aside the political-questions doctrine and decided that legislative apportionments were proper matters for judicial review. Frankfurter deplored the majority's decision as "an odd—indeed an esoteric—conception of judicial propriety" and an assertion of "a destructively novel judicial power."[65] But only Justice John Harlan joined his dissent.

So the handwriting was beginning to appear on the wall even before Frankfurter suffered a series of strokes in the spring of 1962 and had to retire from the Court. Charles Whittaker, an Eisenhower appointee who was never a comfortable fit on the Court, departed almost simultaneously. President Kennedy now had two appointments to a Court that was already growing bolder in superimposing its views on important matters of public policy. With Frankfurter and Whittaker gone, no political thicket would be safe from what quickly became the most assertive Supreme Court in American history: the Warren Court.

THE WARREN COURT. An odd name for a Court composed of such diverse, brilliant, and fiercely individual justices. Some legal scholars argued that because of its jurisprudential leanings it should be called the

Brennan Court, others would opt for the Black Court, but neither name caught on outside the narrow confines of the law reviews. To Americans in the 1960s and ever since, it has been the Warren Court, taking the name of the man who was chief justice of the United States from 1953 until 1969, Earl Warren.

Its senior justice was Hugo L. Black of Alabama, a senator at the time that Franklin Roosevelt appointed him in 1937. The last of eight children raised in poverty in Clay County, Black graduated from the state university where he studied law. He went into solo practice as a young man and eventually became a county prosecutor. His political career blossomed and he was elected to the U. S. Senate in 1926. After Roosevelt's election, Black was a consistent New Deal supporter, even breaking with most of his congressional colleagues to support Roosevelt's court-packing plan in 1937. Some speculated at the time that Black's appointment to the Court was a reward for that support.

As a liberal bloc formed on the Court in the years that followed, Black was a consistent but peculiar member. On some legal matters, such as civil rights and freedom of expression, he helped define the liberal, and eventually dominant, position. On others, such as the right to privacy, he disagreed with his liberal colleagues. While his membership in the liberal majority became less reliable toward the end, he was a central figure in the Warren Court's assault on many of the legal doctrines the Court inherited.

Black's constant colleague, in membership on the Court and in voting on cases, was William O. Douglas. Douglas's thirty-six years on the Court remains the longest tenure of any justice, and he wrote more opinions than any other as well. Douglas was raised in Yakima, Washington. His father died when he was six, leaving the family with little money. Douglas attended a local college on scholarship and then taught school. He eventually made his way east, attending Columbia Law School, teaching law, then joining the new Securities and Exchange Commission. He was chairman of that commission when Franklin Roosevelt selected him to replace Louis D. Brandeis on the Supreme Court in 1939.

Douglas soon established himself on the Court's left pole, a vigorous and rigid defender of individual rights against the government and a literal reader of the First Amendment's dictum that "Congress shall make *no* law. . . ." Douglas could be unpredictable to the point of eccentricity and often frustrated liberals outside the Court who expected him to play a more effective role in building Court majorities for his own views. Nevertheless, he was a consistent vote with the majority of the Warren Court in the 1960s.

The other titan of the Warren Court was William J. Brennan. Brennan was appointed by Eisenhower, who developed a knack for making judicial appointments he later came to regret. Eisenhower wanted to appoint a Roman Catholic to the Court and wanted someone relatively young. Brennan, one of eight children of barely educated Irish immigrants in Newark, New Jersey, a Roman Catholic, and fifty years old, fit the profile. Eisenhower, apparently paying little attention to Brennan's opinions on the New Jersey Supreme Court, could not have envisioned that he would become, in the words of Professor Lucas A. Powe, Jr., "the most important jurist of the second half of the century and Warren's best friend and ablest lieutenant."[66]

Brennan's winning personality and his sensitivity to the whims of his colleagues made him a central figure in the development of the Warren Court's jurisprudence. Because he was a much more skillful legal gymnast than Warren himself, the Chief often assigned him the opinion-writing chores in cases that he knew would be contentious internally and controversial when made public. It was a role for which Brennan was almost perfectly fitted.

After the departures of Frankfurter and Whittaker, the Warren Court majority was solidified by four other appointments in the 1960s. Kennedy chose a senior Justice Department official, Byron (Whizzer) White, to replace Whittaker. White turned out to be a less consistently liberal vote than Kennedy may have intended, but his vote quickly became less significant when the president selected Arthur Goldberg, his secretary of labor, to replace Frankfurter. Goldberg was the eleventh child of a Russian Jewish immigrant peddler in Chicago. He excelled at Northwestern University Law School and as a labor lawyer, culminating with his work as a negotiator and chief legal counsel for the CIO in its merger with the AFL in 1955. On the Court, he became one of the most reliable liberal votes.

When Lyndon Johnson persuaded Goldberg to take the post of ambassador to the United Nations in 1965 so he could appoint his friend Abe Fortas to the Court, the liberal majority remained intact. Fortas's voting record was almost as liberal as Goldberg's had been. And when Tom Clark, a Truman appointee, stepped down in 1967 so that his son Ramsay could become attorney general, Johnson appointed Thurgood Marshall, the Court's first black justice and another reliable liberal, to replace him.

From the beginning of the 1962 term through the middle of 1969 the associate justices always included at least four and often five or six solid liberals. But it was not just ideology that made this a unique group. The members of this liberal majority were distinguished by two other traits. One was the similarities in their life stories. Born poor or close to it, often in large families, not uncommonly to immigrant parents, forced to get ahead in life by their own wits and intelligence and relentless ambition: It was almost as if this was the job description for Black, Douglas, Brennan, Goldberg, Fortas, and Marshall. Journalists love to call this the American dream: poor boy rises to great heights. But for the justices who traveled it, this hard road to success rarely seemed like much of a dream. It was, however, a source of deep lessons and profound convictions.

The other common characteristic was that these were government men, mostly federal government men: U.S. senator, regulatory commission chairman, cabinet secretary, powerful Washington attorney, solicitor general. Of the associate justices who composed the liberal majority on the Warren Court after 1962, only William Brennan had served no prior tour in Washington.

Of that group, only Brennan in New Jersey and Marshall very briefly on the Second Circuit had been judges before they became justices. The Warren Court majority was composed of individuals much more drawn to action than to constitutional theory. Brilliant though some of them were, it was their practical experience that informed their jurisprudence. The Warren Court was, in its dominant strain, a group of men seeking—and often manufacturing—judicial theories to support their remedies for practical problems.

So it is no surprise that the emerging liberal consensus of the 1960s wove its way into the decision making of the nation's highest court. Here were justices who knew poverty, who had experienced discrimination, who had been blessed by educational opportunity, and who were comfortable with the notion that government could be a positive force in citizens' lives. Their legal reasoning was guided by the lessons of the lives they had lived before they came to the Court.

AND THEN THERE was Earl Warren. The 1960s raised the curtain on many second acts. Kennedy, the diffident aristocrat, became the voice of justice at home and steadfastness abroad. Johnson, the archetypical southerner, dripping in oil and tolerant of his region's caste system, became the leading warrior against inequality. Richard Nixon, left on the ash heap of national politics at the beginning of the decade, rose from the ashes at the end. But of Earl Warren it may be said that he had the most surprising second act of all.

Like so many of his Court colleagues in the 1960s, Warren started life a long way from the limelight. Bakersfield, California, where Warren was born in 1891, was a rough-and-tumble town, dominated like much of California by the Southern Pacific Railroad. The railroad was the most powerful force in the state, a symbol to many of the weakness of individuals and government in the face of dominant corporations. Frank Norris wrote of the Southern Pacific in *The Octopus*, a novel published when Earl Warren was ten years old:

> The galloping monster, the terror of steel and steam, with its single eye, cyclopean, red, shooting from horizon to horizon ... the vast symbol of power, huge, terrible, flinging the echo of its thunder over all the reaches of the valley, leaving blood and destruction in its path; the leviathan, with tentacles of steel clutching into the soil, the soulless Force, the iron-hearted Power, the monster, the Colossus, the Octopus.[67]

Few who lived in its sway felt much different.

Warren's mother was a Swedish immigrant, his father a laborer for the railroad. The Warrens lived in a small row house; money was always scarce; and insecurity—the bane of railroad employment—was a constant in their lives. Earl Warren himself worked for the Southern Pacific before escaping to the state university at Berkeley.

A young man in turn-of-the-century Bakersfield saw many things: gambling, drunkenness, prostitution, police brutality, and government corruption. He also saw, sometimes through the eyes of his own parents, what unbridled corporate power looked like. Later in life, he would remind listeners that powerful corporations used up people, then cast them aside.[68]

I saw every man on the railroad not essential for the operation of the trains laid off without pay and without warning for weeks before the end of a fiscal year in order that the corporate stock might pay a higher dividend.... I helped carry men to the little room called the emergency hospital for amputation of an arm or a leg that had been crushed because there were no safety appliances in the shops or yards to prevent such injuries. I knew of men who were fired for even considering a suit against the railroad for the injuries they sustained. There was no compensation for them, and they went through life as cripples....

The things I learned about monopolistic power, political dominance, corruption in government, and their effect on the people of a community were valuable lessons that would tend to shape my career throughout life, although I did not then foresee any such results.[69]

Berkeley was Earl Warren's escape route from all that. He studied hard and prepared for a career in law. He also became involved in politics while a student, Progressive politics. California was a fertile breeding ground of Progressivism when that movement flowered in the first decade of the twentieth century, and Hiram Johnson was its leading light. Warren was not old enough to vote in 1910 when the Progressive League nominated Johnson as its candidate for governor. But Warren was drawn to the man and his ideas and worked on his campaign.

Hiram Johnson won that election and initiated profound changes in the way California was run. "A different set of political values were injected into public affairs," writes Warren biographer G. Edward White. "Three such values were especially prominent: the value of honesty and openness in government; the value of affirmative governmental action in the 'public interest,' as opposed to 'special' economic or class interests;

and the value of fidelity to public opinion, which was taken to be enlightened, forward-looking, and honorable."[70]

As Warren's public career unfolded from bureaucrat to county attorney to state attorney general to governor and then to the Supreme Court, he never abandoned these values. One of the legacies of Progressivism in California in the middle of the twentieth century when Earl Warren was its dominant politician was its muted partisanship. When forced to choose, Warren called himself a Republican and he took a leading role in that party's statewide activities. He was elected governor of California as a Republican in 1942. But the election laws of the state permitted cross-filing and Warren was the candidate of both the Democrats and the Republicans when he ran for re-election in 1946.

At his ideological core, however, there abided not a Republican nor a Democrat but a Progressive. His emergence to national prominence came at a time when Republicans were challenging the policy and ideology of the New Deal. The party chose him in 1948 to run for vice president on its ticket with Governor Thomas Dewey of New York. But Warren was a misfit in this role, and he found little pleasure in it. "I never felt like I was making any great contribution," he wrote in his memoirs. "I was entirely detached from the main campaign."[71]

Attacks on the New Deal were an odd role for a governor of California who had advocated programs similar to those that the New Deal had brought to Washington—a massive public works program, broad investment in schools and the state system of higher education, new housing, a major commitment to state-run economic planning, aggressive but ultimately unsuccessful efforts to establish state-provided, single-payer health insurance for California citizens. Critics sometimes said that Warren was trying to "out–New Deal the New Deal."[72] The *New York Times* claimed in 1944 that Warren was pursuing "the most farsighted, intelligent and thorough postwar planning program" in America.[73]

But little in Warren's life before 1953 identified him as a leading candidate to be chief justice of the United States. He had never been a judge, never associated himself with any sophisticated legal or constitutional theory, never served in any civilian capacity in the federal government, not even argued a case in court for more than a decade. As his third gubernatorial term neared its end in 1953, he was planning to leave government completely. But those plans were interrupted when the legacy of a vague promise made Earl Warren the leader of the nation's highest court.

Dwight D. Eisenhower was grateful to Warren for having delivered much of the California delegation to his camp at the 1952 Republican convention. But he barely knew Warren and found no place for him in his cabinet. As a consolation, he called Warren and told him that he intended to nominate him for the first vacancy that came up on the Supreme Court. Neither man could have known that the vacancy would occur when Chief Justice Fred Vinson died of a heart attack on September 8, 1953, just a few weeks before the start of the new Supreme Court term. When Eisenhower sought to suggest that he hadn't intended his pledge to include appointment as chief justice, Warren reminded him that there had been no such caveat.

So, with little enthusiasm, Eisenhower appointed Earl Warren. He presumed that Warren was like him—a middle-of-the-road Republican likely to bring moderation and common sense to his work on the Supreme Court.[74] And, in the most visible ways, Warren seemed to fit that image. A bland public speaker, competent but not charismatic, deeply devoted to his family, diligent, sincere, incorruptible, Warren bore many of the traits of the cautious moderate Eisenhower took him to be.

But less visible influences also stirred Warren, sharpening his discontent with society and his faith in government remedies. Warren was a Californian, and California was the cutting edge of a new America where technology and growth and immigration were affecting every aspect of human life. He had been a crime-busting district attorney, but he had also seen firsthand the dark side of the criminal justice system. He had had a clear preview in California of what a more diverse America would look like, and he had been seared by his regrettable participation in the uprooting and forced relocation of so many Japanese American Californians at the outbreak of World War II. He had been a public employee for most of his adult life and had ample reason to believe in government as a force for good in the lives of ordinary citizens. And his own biography was full of lessons about poverty, corporate greed, and the value of education. He was in many ways, wrote the journalist David Halberstam, "the perfect twentieth-century American liberal hybrid, in his roots, his personal experiences, and his optimism."[75]

Earl Warren's second act put him in the Chief's chair for sixteen years during which the Supreme Court of the United States was often at the center of the great issues and upheavals of a tempestuous time. During the latter years of that tenure, he presided over a Court the majority of whose justices had lived lives much like his own and who shared values and views much like those he then possessed.

Earl Warren wrote few memorable opinions. His words do not ring down through the constitutional law classes like those of Holmes or Brandeis or Cardozo. He spent no time in the vanguard of constitutional theory. But as the presiding justice of a powerful decision-making body at a turning point in American history, he brought a critical talent for molding consensus. His colleague William J. Brennan said of Warren, "His great gift was his sensitivity to the diverse and conflicting opinions held by his brethren. He had about him a grace and courtesy that we all respected deeply, and he set a tone that ensured that even the most heated discussions would be conducted with decorum and consideration. Thanks to him, our decisions always were the product of robust debate. . . . He was a man of integrity and fairness, and no one ever brought more of a sense of humanity and quiet wisdom to the Court than he did."[76]

Engraved on Earl Warren's tombstone at Arlington National Cemetery are words he spoke at the time of his retirement from the Court: "Where there is injustice, we should correct it; where there is poverty, we should eliminate it; where there is corruption, we should stamp it out; where there is violence, we should punish it; where there is neglect, we should provide care; where there is war, we should restore peace; and wherever corrections are achieved we should add them permanently to our storehouse of treasures." On the Court he led in the 1960s, those were fighting words.

THE SUPREME COURTS of American history had often served the dominant interests in American society: rich over poor, management over labor, white over black, the rights of property over the rights of individuals. In the first four decades of the twentieth century, the Court often applied the brakes to liberal reform. But in the first important case of his tenure, *Brown* v. *Board of Education*, Warren's ability to craft a unanimous decision declaring racial segregation in schools unconstitutional was a clear preview of what lay ahead. Here the Court overturned a precedent it had shied from confronting in the previous two decades: the holding in *Plessy* v. *Ferguson* (1896) that states could impose racial segregation as long as their separate facilities for each race were equal.

In the years that followed, the Warren Court overturned 133 precedents, 45 more than all the previous Supreme Courts in American history.[77] When faced with a conflict between precedent and principle, the Warren Court never hesitated. The sound of precedents falling was one of the loudest noises coming from Washington in the 1960s.

The Warren Court of the 1960s was not a gathering of legal theorists. Law reviews of the time often criticized the Warren Court, sometimes brutally, for its failures in "reasoned exposition," its too-frequent reluctance to encase its decisions in the protective covering of flawless legal justification.[78] Nevertheless, two legal theories became deeply embedded in the jurisprudence of the later Warren Court.

One was the doctrine of incorporation, the notion that the Fourteenth Amendment "incorporates" the Bill of Rights and thus imposes its restrictions on state governments as well as the federal government. Until the middle of the twentieth century, the Court had regularly held that the specific restrictions in the Bill of Rights applied only to the actions of the federal government. But the Roosevelt appointees, especially Hugo Black, began to seek expansions of the coverage of the Bill of Rights. Black believed in total incorporation—that the entire Bill of Rights applied to the states. In the 1940s and 1950s, this deeply divided the Court, with Black unable to muster a majority of justices to this view, though he did begin to win some battles on the incorporation of specific guarantees of the Bill of Rights. After Whittaker and Frankfurter retired, however, the incorporation doctrine finally had its majority, and by the end of the 1960s nearly all of the "thou shalt nots" in the Bill of Rights had been applied to the states.

Haunting the early Warren Court and inspiring the later was the famous Footnote Four, evidence of the way that wide legal turns can sometimes occur on the smallest of pivots. Footnote Four emerged from a minor Supreme Court case in 1938, *United States* v. *Carolene Products Co.*, in which the Court upheld a federal law that banned skimmed milk mixed with nonmilk fat from interstate commerce. The majority argued that the law was "presumptively constitutional" and noted that the presumption of constitutionality, i.e., that the act of a legislature deserved the benefit of the doubt, should be the normal approach of the Court. But in a footnote to the majority opinion—Footnote Four—Chief Justice Harlan Fiske Stone noted certain conditions where that presumption of constitutionality would not be valid or appropriate.[79]

Any law that seemed directly to challenge a provision of the U.S. Constitution or that attempted to undermine the ability of the political process to produce a fair or representative outcome or that affected the rights of minorities, Stone argued, did not deserve the presumption of constitutionality and should be subjected to strict scrutiny.

Footnote Four had little immediate impact on the work of the Court. But when the liberal majority of the 1960s sought to impose its own public policy views in place of those adopted by state legislatures, it confronted a significant dilemma. The Progressive roots of midcentury liberalism were also constraints on its development.[80] At the core of Progressive thought was the simple notion that majorities should rule, that government processes should be uncluttered by party bosses, smoke-filled rooms, and even judicial review. Legislatures should be representative of the people, everyone should be able to vote, and then legislatures should be trusted with the business of making public policy.

But for liberals in the 1960s, the problem was that legislatures sometimes acted in illiberal ways: They restricted free speech, they permitted state-sanctioned religious practices, they afforded too little protection to individual rights and too much protection to corporations and petty government officials. How to square the Progressive faith in legislative majorities with the growing liberal dissatisfaction with their products? Footnote Four lit the path out of this dilemma that haunted liberal reform in the middle of the twentieth century. It proposed that there were certain "preferred freedoms" and that these demanded the special attention of courts and, when necessary, action by courts in contravention of legislative majorities when these freedoms were challenged.

So armed, the Warren Court, composed as it was of practical men seeking legal solutions to societal problems, became the most assertive Supreme Court in American history. Not merely responding to policies made by other institutions, nor merely judging them, it often played the role of initiator: moving public policy in new directions that it mapped out. This was a risky role for any court, and the Warren Court provoked bitter opposition. But it also had some advantages in the politics of the 1960s. One was the steady support of Presidents Kennedy and Johnson. They agreed with most of the Court's decisions and expressed public support for even the most controversial.

Another was the repudiation in 1964 of one of the Court's harshest critics, Senator Barry Goldwater of Arizona. As the Republican presidential candidate in 1964, Goldwater frequently attacked the "liberal decisions of the Supreme Court." Goldwater's defeat sustained and encouraged the Warren Court.

Most of the Court's decisions also fit the tenor of the time. The Court could certainly anger segments of the population with its decisions. The early desegregation decisions yielded a violent reaction in the South. The Court's decisions on prayer in schools and on protections for criminals seemed to be over-reaching to many Americans. But the general flow of Court decisions—to enlarge racial equality, to ensure fair procedures in police stations and courtrooms, to broaden the scope of the First Amendment—not only followed the mainstream of liberal reform in the 1960s, but, in important ways, helped to define it.

When asked in a 1966 poll in which institutions of government they had "a great deal of confidence," half the American respondents named the Supreme Court. In the same poll, 42 percent named Congress and 41 percent named the executive branch of the federal government.[81] The Warren Court had its critics—plenty of them—but it had its supporters as well.

THE WARREN COURT confronted the ancient issue of race in a way that no other American institution ever had. The racial policies of the United States before Warren were built on permissions granted by the Supreme Court. In *Dred Scott* v. *Sandford* (1857) and *Plessy* v. *Ferguson* (1896), the Court had permitted state and local governments to establish and maintain policies of racial apartheid. But in *Brown v. Board of Education* and in many other decisions in the 1950s and 1960s, the Court sought to undo what had largely been its own doing. It developed a concept of equality as a constitutional standard, then spent much of its subsequent efforts refining that standard and overseeing its implementation. "The motif on the facade of the Supreme Court building reads: 'Equal Justice under Law,'" wrote legal scholar Philip Kurland. "If earlier Courts emphasized the words 'Law' or 'Justice,' the Warren Court has accentuated the word 'Equal.'"[82]

On matters of criminal procedure, the Court was a revolutionary force. Policing and judging would never be the same. Before the interventions of the Warren Court, police routinely searched private homes without proper warrants and judges allowed convictions on the evidence so obtained. Suspects were arrested, questioned, beaten, and coerced into confessions without ever being informed of their rights to counsel and against self-incrimination. Defendants unable to afford attorneys went without. But in cases such as *Mapp v. Ohio* (1961), *Gideon v. Wainright* (1963), *Escobedo v. Illinois* (1964), and *Miranda v. Arizona* (1966), the Warren Court ruled that it was time to hold all the police and criminal courts in America to the rule of law.

The Warren Court again made equality its preeminent goal in redefining the character of representation in American legislatures. In his memoirs, Earl Warren cited *Baker v. Carr* (1962) as the most important case decided by the Court during his tenure as chief justice.[83] *Baker v. Carr* reversed the Court's long-standing disinclination to consider legislative apportionment issues and opened the door to a series of cases that applied the "one person, one vote" standard to every legislature in America except the United States Senate. American politics and government, in both the short and the long term, were deeply altered by these decisions and the consequent shifting of political power from sparsely populated rural areas to the cities and then soon after to the burgeoning American suburbs. The Court's decisions in this matter opened up the other institutions of government to a fresh flow of new personnel and undermined the conservative forces that were the leading benefactors of malapportionment and the primary opponents of postwar liberals.

The Warren Court contributed as well to the expansions of free expression and the abandonment of obscenity proscriptions that occurred with startling rapidity in the 1960s. The Supreme Court did not liberate sexual mores in that decade, but it made no effort to impose significant legal constraints on that outburst of liberation. The last vestiges of the Victorian era reached their end point in the 1960s. A wave of sexual freedom in expression and behavior swept across the country, as it did much of the rest of the world. The capacity of censors and the power of prudes crumbled in its wake. When legislatures fought this new openness, the Court was asked to apply the First Amendment to protect artists, booksellers, pornographers, and advocates of birth control. And it did so.

In *Roth* v. *United States* (1957), the Court established a new standard for judging obscenity: "Whether to the average person applying contemporary community standards, the dominant theme of the material, taken as a whole, appeals to the prurient interest." In subsequent cases, the Court struggled to define those standards or to determine whether they were national or local. In *Jacobellis* v. *Ohio* (1964), the Court overturned an obscenity conviction against a theater owner for showing a film that local officials deemed obscene. But in that case, the justices could not agree on an applicable principle. Justice Potter Stewart reflected their frustration in trying to find legal nostrums for dirty pictures. "I shall not today attempt further to define the kinds of material I understand to be embraced within that shorthand description; and perhaps I could never succeed in intelligibly doing so," he wrote. "But I know it when I see it, and the motion picture involved in this case is not that."

It took almost a decade after *Jacobellis* for the Court to come up with a test of obscenity to which a majority of the justices could agree. In the meantime, with little constraint from the nation's highest court, "anything goes" became the dominant criterion in the marketplace of free expression.[84]

While the Court seemed to mirror popular tastes in these decisions, they inspired no shortage of criticism. When Justice Abe Fortas was nominated by Lyndon Johnson in 1968 to be chief justice, Senator Strom Thurmond of South Carolina sought to rally opposition to the nomination by using a room in the Capitol to show adult films that the Court had refused to declare obscene.[85] It was one of the more curious spectacles in the political history of the 1960s.

The First Amendment's dual commands that Congress shall neither establish a religion nor limit the free exercise thereof have long engaged the nation's courts. Most of what constitutes federal religious policy is the product of court decisions. The Warren Court was most active on the establishment clause of the First Amendment. In *Engel* v. *Vitale* (1962) and *Abington Township* v. *Schempp* (1963), the Court ruled that a nondenominational prayer written by the New York Board of Regents for use in schools and even the reading of the Lord's Prayer or the Bible by a teacher in a public school were violations of the establishment clause. In the *Abington Township* case, the Court ruled out prayers in public schools. In all of its major rulings on religious matters, the Warren Court sided with those who wanted greater distance between church and state.

THE SUPREME COURT is a constantly evolving organism. Every new appointment, as Justice Byron White was wont to say, creates an entirely new Court.[86] Even without changes in personnel, the views of individual justices change or harden over time, personal animosities or friendships among the justices can develop into voting blocs, new issues challenge old doctrines, and changes in the country's politics extend their effects into the Court's chambers.

So it was with the Warren Court. It was the product of a peculiar accumulation of presidential personnel decisions following no discernible theory of judging or constitutional interpretation. Yet the Warren Court, especially from 1962 through 1968, took on a unique and clearly defined character.

The Warren Court was not the first activist court in American history, but it was the first (and only) liberal activist court. In the past, activism had meant striking down federal and state statutes to protect narrow interpretations of the Constitution, usually in favor of the powerful. Under Warren, activism came to mean striking down federal and state statutes to expand constitutional interpretations, often in favor of the powerless and the downtrodden. "Because it was libertarian and egalitarian in its judicial activism," wrote Professor Leonard Levy, "and because it dared to lead the way, redressing injustices to which state courts, policemen, and politicians both state and national had been stone blind, neglectful, or unable to redress, the Warren Court became the conscience of the country. . . . Even within its own ranks, the Court's departure from its traditional role as a defender of the status quo and its novel assumption of the role of St. George exposed it to scathing criticisms."[87]

Courts do not always align with their times. Certainly the Supreme Court in place during FDR's first term was out of step with the forward rush of American history. But there are occasional periods of colossal coincidence when a court is poised to join, even to escalate, the movements of its era. The 1960s were one of those rare periods. "The Warren Court was a liberal Court," wrote Professor Mark Tushnet, "in that its decisions were compatible with the policy agenda of political liberals during the 1960s and 1970s. Perhaps because political liberalism in the contemporary sense had never been a dominant force in national politics before, no Supreme Court had been liberal in that sense either."[88]

For a brief span in the 1960s the Supreme Court was the hammer of liberalism, unconstrained by the need to compromise in breaking the bonds of conservatism. In its reapportionment decisions, for example, it freed the growing urban and suburban majorities to finally take control of their legislatures from the countryside courthouse gangs whose power—though very real—rested on a rapidly vanishing foundation of representation.

Warren and his majority resembled Lyndon Johnson in an important way. Neither was shy about using the power he possessed. Johnson's confidence came from the election of 1964, Warren's from the personnel changes of 1962. Both pushed the limits of the power of the institutions they headed. This permitted them to contribute to unusually broad changes in public policy.

The Warren Court caused such controversy because it was so effective at altering the balance of power in American society. It opened up opportunities, for the first time, to blacks, women, the poor, atheists, and others who had long been excluded from meaningful participation in American society by the legal rules and practices the Warren Court demolished.

The Warren Court was significant in certifying and implementing the values of the left, but so, too, was it significant in inspiring and coalescing the opposition to those values on the right. Long before the right turned against Lyndon Johnson, it demonized Earl Warren and his liberal brethren. It was Warren, not Johnson, whose impeachment was advocated by billboards that dotted the landscape for more than a decade. It was the Warren Court that became liberalism's most-targeted lightning rod, its clearest symbol of the profound changes that had come to America in the middle years of the 1960s.

CHAPTER 4

FREE AT LAST

On February 1, 1960, Franklin McCain, Joseph McNeil, Ezell Blair, Jr., and David Richmond sat down on stools at the Woolworth's lunch counter in Greensboro, North Carolina, and waited to order. But no one came to take their order, not that morning, nor all day long. They sat there peacefully until the store closed, yet no service was offered them, even as other customers ate and drank.

The next day they returned with twenty other students from nearby North Carolina Agricultural and Technical College, the all-black school at which they were freshmen. Still they were not served; still they waited in peace. Their seemingly innocent act began to attract notice and soon similar "sit-ins" were under way at segregated public facilities all over the South. Merchants who had long refused to serve African American customers now found themselves the subject of widespread publicity. Some of the sit-ins inspired violent reactions from local white citizens. The publicity spread. None of this was good for business.

The students, of course, wanted more than a bite to eat, more than just service. They wanted freedom, and the dignity and respect that came with it. The four freshmen from North Carolina A&T were not out to change the world. But their simple act of defiance soon became part of a broader effort, across the South and across the nation, to challenge the assumptions and the policies that had for so long been the foundation of racial segregation in America.

In July Woolworth's ended its discriminatory practices and integrated all of its stores and their lunch counters. One barrier had fallen. Others would soon follow in a cascade of dominoes that would lead all the way to Washington and into the darkest recesses of American public policy.

ORIGINS OF "THE NEGRO REVOLUTION"

The ninety-five years from the end of slavery to the advent in 1960 of mass protests against racism marked a twilight period in black history during which racial equality was often discussed but rarely accomplished, in which glints of possibility were always quickly overshadowed by the dark curtain of reality. In the decades following the Civil War, the heart of the old slave system in the South, black dependence on white land-owners, continued to beat vigorously. By the late nineteenth century, it was almost as if there had been no Civil War. Black Americans were free, but it was a most peculiar kind of freedom, hemmed in on every side by the racial attitudes of white citizens who monopolized political and economic power. Those attitudes often found their way into laws and customs that made submission and humiliation of blacks a central thread in the daily fabric of southern life.

In education, lodging, transportation, and other public services, separate and second-class facilities marked the lot of African Americans. Whites used rest rooms designated "Men" or "Women" while blacks followed signs for "Colored." Separate entrances to buildings were standard in southern towns, except in polling places, where there seemed to be no entrance for blacks at all. Racist registrars and administrative technicalities such as poll taxes and literacy requirements kept most black citizens at bay on election day. Those who challenged them did so at their peril, for violence and murder were ever-ready last resorts of the old South that would not let go. Even in death, where all presumably were equal, cemeteries and funeral notices in local papers were racially segregated.

The southern caste system flourished on the periphery of American attention through the 1950s. Yet its vulnerabilities were beginning to show. With the expansion of textile, oil, lumber, and chemical industries 60 percent of the region's population had come to reside in urban centers, diminishing the centuries-old grasp of the plantation culture and its strict distinctions of race and class. Such business growth required a more widely educated labor force, selected by merit rather than color, and a domestic market unhampered by racial division of consumers or disruptive social tensions. To a rising, if reticent, minority of merchants, manufacturers, and professionals, Jim Crow was becoming an embarrassing and costly anachronism.

Demographic trends further accelerated the pressure on southern traditions. Until 1910 some 90 percent of all blacks lived in the South, and for most Americans, race was a regional, not a national issue. But the massive population movement that began after World War I reduced the proportion to less than 60 percent over the next half-century. This liberated more African Americans from Jim Crow laws and disfranchisement than the Fourteenth and Fifteenth Amendments had ever done.

The New Deal and the reforms it brought added to the changing conditions for African Americans. The federal safeguards advocated and advanced by liberal reformers began to open doors for African Americans. A new welfare structure, designed in and funded from Washington, D.C., advanced the ideal of aiding "forgotten Americans." Few were more forgotten than African Americans, and—while racial equality was rarely a stated goal—the New Deal opened for them new avenues of participation in American life.

Despite the local prejudices that infected the implementation of federal assistance programs, the substantial inclusion of blacks as recipients of federal aid strengthened the ties between blacks and liberals. In 1936, blacks voted in record numbers for the Democratic president, Franklin Roosevelt, responding to his job and relief measures at a time when work even as a salesclerk could garner front-page coverage in Harlem papers. Blacks who had moved to the North found a political home in the Democratic Party and formed a growing counterweight to the party's white southern wing.

The rise of industrial unions in the mid-1930s promoted the convergence of black and white interests. Unlike the established craft unions that openly excluded blacks, industrywide unions in steel, automobile, and other mass-production fields recruited blacks rather than risk letting companies hire them cheaply as strikebreakers. Walter Reuther of the United Auto Workers and John L. Lewis of the United Mine Workers spoke out against the caste system that divided labor in the South and impeded union organizing. As black employees increasingly joined strikes and factory "sit-downs," helping to win heftier pay envelopes for all union members, white coworkers warmed to the cause of racial tolerance as sound philosophy and still better economics.

In the 1920s Republican administrations had championed corporate interests while showing little concern for either the poor or ethnic minorities. But the Depression discredited both business leadership and the idea of single-interest government and opened the door to political influence for many groups that had rarely enjoyed national influence: Catholics; Jews; Irish, Italian, and Slavic Americans; the Farm Bureau; women's organizations; social workers; and intellectuals. Though by no means the strongest of these forces, blacks, too, began to take a place in the New Deal coalition that would dominate American politics in the middle of the twentieth century. Respectful treatment of them by President Roosevelt and by northern congressmen signaled a turn from the politics of white supremacy.

What the Depression had begun in forging a change in racial attitudes, World War II accelerated. Four years of war against Hitler's Germany had alerted many Americans to the dangers of racial ideology. Although racist policies at home were less extreme than Nazi atrocities in the name of Aryan supremacy, they seemed to many Americans uncomfortably similar in spirit. Growing numbers of religious, civic, labor, and intellectual spokesmen addressed the issue of segregation, not just as a "Negro problem" or a regional one, but as a challenge to national values.

Blacks also found an ironic but potent ally in the anticommunist fervor that gripped the country after 1945. Although this mood lent itself to political conformity, the obsession with "godless communist tyranny" encouraged a celebration of American society for its guarantee of freedom for every citizen. And, as the Cold War unfolded, America found itself in fierce competition with the Soviet Union for the favor of emerging nonwhite nations in Africa and Asia. Racial segregation was a damaging embarrassment for a people claiming for themselves the virtues of a democratic society, a vast hypocrisy that Soviet leaders and Soviet propaganda rarely failed to point out. The preoccupations of the Cold War thus encouraged Americans to achieve at home the ideal of liberty on which they based their assertions of moral superiority abroad.

By the end of the 1950s, the robust postwar economy and growing influence of blacks in northern urban politics created a new context for the race issue and new opportunities for those who wished to use the federal government to attack the remaining vestiges of legal segregation. Roosevelt's successor, Harry Truman, who as a Missouri politician had always welcomed black support as heartily as white, appointed a committee in 1946 to investigate violations of black rights. Known as the Noah's Ark commission, because it boasted pairs of businessmen, labor leaders, southerners, blacks, educators, women, Catholics, and Jews, Truman's committee urged broad federal action to end segregation.

In 1948, Truman acceded to a strong civil rights plank that liberal delegates headed by Hubert Humphrey of Minnesota had inserted in the Democratic national platform. This split the party, with many southerners defecting to a Dixiecrat faction headed by Governor Strom Thurmond of South Carolina. But, with the important support of 70 percent of the northern black vote, Truman survived for another term. Two years later he completed the desegregation of the armed forces, a policy change that acquired heightened visibility as the Korean War began. These gains were scratches on the social order, but the trend line was clear, as was the growing importance of blacks in the complex ethnic mosaic of Democratic politics.

In 1954, the Supreme Court responded to the rise in black influence and public awareness of racism by condemning the contradiction between segregation and citizenship. In four cases known collectively as *Brown* v. *Board of Education*, Chief Justice Earl Warren insisted that "the doctrine of 'separate but equal' has no place" in the nation's public schools. By confronting white supremacy so forthrightly, the verdict intensified southern resistance to civil rights progress. *Brown* was widely celebrated in liberal circles and was a cause for rejoicing among African

Americans. Racial attitudes in the white South were far too durable, however, to be softened by a mere Supreme Court decision.

But if *Brown* did not bring immediate change to the South, it did provide a new and clear yardstick of color-blind justice against which Americans could test their commitment to the ideal of equal opportunity. It also conferred an aura of legitimacy on black activists, who prepared still bolder assaults on segregation. And it demonstrated, beyond doubt, that segregation was now a national matter, no longer one that could be swept behind the convenient cover of southern culture and tradition.

Beginning in December 1955, a boycott by African Americans of segregated public buses in Montgomery, Alabama, drew support from northern white liberal papers, philanthropists, and activists, as well as predominantly black groups such as the NAACP. The triumph of the boycott late in 1956, aided mightily by a Supreme Court ruling that voided a city ordinance segregating buses, initiated a new phase in the assault on Jim Crow. It demonstrated that blacks—without political power and in the face of terrifying threats—could successfully challenge racism even in a city proud to be called the cradle of the Confederacy. The boycott also catapulted to national fame a young black minister, Martin Luther King, Jr., whose pilgrimage of nonviolence attracted a growing caravan of civil rights forces seeking inspiration and direction.

The nation watched what happened in Montgomery with growing interest. In Washington, this new attention helped a coalition of liberal, labor, religious, and minority groups to secure from Congress the first civil rights act since Reconstruction. Signed by a mildly supportive President Eisenhower in September 1957, the act created an independent federal commission to monitor civil rights violations and authorized the Justice Department to guard black voting rights through litigation against discriminatory registrars. Southern senators had used their full bag of tricks to trim away or water down the most telling provisions of the bill, but their liberal opponents saw this not as the end, but only the beginning of the struggle for meaningful civil rights legislation. Congress had joined the Supreme Court in making civil rights a national issue. Jim Crow was under attack now on several fronts.

When in 1957 Arkansas governor Orval Faubus deployed the National Guard to prevent the integration of Central High School in Little Rock, he forced the hand of President Eisenhower. Eisenhower had never been an enthusiast for federal involvement in civil rights matters. As chief of staff of the Army, he initially opposed the integration of the armed forces, and as president he had come to rue the *Brown* decision and had given little impetus to the Civil Rights Act of 1957. Some have suggested that his indifference to civil rights encouraged southern politicians to proclaim "massive resistance" to school desegregation and led, in September 1957, to mob violence against the nine black teenagers who sought to attend Central High School. But, whatever his views on the substance of civil rights policies, Eisenhower knew his duty when it came to enforcing the law. And when the situation escalated, he dispatched the 101st Airborne Division to protect the Little Rock Nine. Now the president, too, had joined the fray.

When the four North Carolina A&T students began their sit-in at Woolworth's, it was in a South that had come under intensifying scrutiny. Their efforts posed a challenge to policies and practices that had become increasingly indefensible to much of the nation. A new mood was blooming in America, a mood that combined a fear of advancing Soviet technology, rising concern over hard-core poverty, and a restless idealism that would burgeon as the Baby Boom generation came of age. No group felt these currents more keenly than young blacks in the South. Raised on the promise of *Brown* and the Montgomery campaign, they awaited only a spark to set them against the barricades of segregation, as they heralded their country's reawakening reform spirit.

THE CANDIDATE TAKES A STAND

The racial ferment rising in the South could not escape the attention of the candidates for president in 1960, both of whom probed it for advantage. John F. Kennedy in particular raised the hopes of African Americans with calls to a "New Frontier" of reform and the hint of stronger executive leadership—at least stronger than Eisenhower had offered—on civil rights. But simultaneously winning the support of black citizens and winning the election was no simple matter for a midcentury Democrat. The white South was still a core element of the Democrats' political coalition, and any appearance that Kennedy was a civil rights radical would quickly threaten his support in the southern states whose votes he needed.

In the early primaries, Kennedy's chief rival was Hubert Humphrey, a person of sterling liberal credentials whose dramatic speech for civil rights at the 1948 Democratic convention had dazzled the audience and split the party. Kennedy knew he had to challenge Humphrey's presumption that he was the "real" liberal candidate in the race, and he understood that civil rights would be the litmus test.

But Kennedy's own credentials—as a liberal and as a reliable advocate for civil rights—were suspect. So he used the campaign as an opportunity to reposition himself, making overtures to black leaders when opportunities arose and stating his views with more clarity and conviction than he had in the past. After defeating Humphrey in West Virginia and Wisconsin, Kennedy sought to pick up the civil rights torch of the fallen champion, echoing his former rival's pledge never to sacrifice civil rights for the sake of political expediency. "If anyone expects the Democratic administration to betray [the civil rights] cause," he told a black interviewer, "they can look elsewhere for a party."[1]

On the sensitive subject of the sit-ins, which were occurring even as candidates canvassed delegate support, Kennedy found another opportunity to distinguish himself from the caution of Eisenhower and other Washington leaders. Kennedy praised the sit-ins as a signal that the American spirit was "coming alive again." He added, "It is in the American tradition to stand up for one's rights—even if the new way is to sit down."[2]

At the Democratic convention in July, Kennedy employed a dual strategy. On the one hand he emphasized his northern liberal ties. He spoke forcefully of the need for vigorous action in Washington to advance the stalled liberal agenda and he supported a party platform that called for wide-ranging civil rights reforms to be implemented by "strong, active, persuasive, and inventive" presidential leadership. This helped him win the support of the party's base in the cities of the North and East, and it yielded nearly unanimous support among black delegates.

At the same time, Kennedy sought to mend his southern fences by selecting as his running mate his chief convention rival, Senate Majority Leader Lyndon Johnson. This stunned and angered some among the liberals, union leaders, and especially blacks who supported him, even as they reluctantly recognized that hard political calculations that inspired Kennedy's choice. Those with an especially sharp eye also took comfort in the understanding that the Texas senator was a very different person from the caricature that dominated his national image and that he was eager to transcend his conservative regional base. Few people in American politics had more sensitive political antennae than Lyndon Johnson, and he, too, had detected the growing force of the civil rights movement. To blacks who were critical of his nomination, Johnson offered the steady assurance that a Democratic administration would "do more in the field of civil rights than has been accomplished in the last century."[3]

The greatest civil rights test of the campaign came on October 19 when Martin Luther King, Jr., was arrested at a demonstration in Atlanta and sentenced to four months of hard labor on a convenient but gossamer legal technicality related to an earlier probation for a minor traffic violation. King's wife, Coretta, feared that he might never emerge from the rural prison where he was being held incommunicado. Nixon considered expressing sympathy for King's plight but decided that silence was the more prudent political course in his efforts to pry southern white support from his Democratic opponent.

Kennedy, too, carefully considered his options.[4] Harris Wofford, an idealistic civil rights aide who had studied Gandhian nonviolence in India, suggested that the candidate contact King's wife as a gesture of his concern. No one was sure of the political repercussions, but at the urging of Kennedy's brother-in-law Sargent Shriver, who had overall responsibility for the campaign's Civil Rights Section, Kennedy called Coretta King on October 26 to assure her of his support.

At the same time, Robert Kennedy was consulting Georgia governor Ernest Vandiver. Vandiver, a Kennedy supporter, suggested that a call to the judge who sentenced King might help get the sentence reduced. Robert Kennedy made the call to Judge Oscar Mitchell. This was no small pressure on a local judge to be called in the middle of a close presidential campaign by the brother of one of the candidates, and Mitchell relented. The day after Robert Kennedy's call, King was released from jail.[5]

On election day, Kennedy won the smallest of pluralities over Nixon, scarcely a hundred thousand votes out of some 69 million. Among African Americans, the division was far from close; 70 percent of black ballots went for Kennedy, providing the margin of success in such key industrial states as Pennsylvania and Michigan. Even in the South, where black voter registration was still small, black support exceeded Kennedy's margin of victory in Texas and South Carolina.

African Americans were thus doubly pleased by Kennedy's triumph— as a candidate pledged to vigorous leadership to achieve racial justice and as a politician indebted to blacks for their decisive loyalty. When John Kennedy captured the presidency, therefore, many in the civil rights movement believed that they had done so as well.

THE POLITICS OF EXPECTATION

President Kennedy's inaugural address stressed foreign rather than domestic affairs, but black Americans drew hope from its central theme of defending "human rights, to which this nation has always been committed, and to which we are committed today at home and around the world." The president exhorted people everywhere to "ask what together we can do for the freedom of man." Civil rights leaders rejoiced as they prepared to ask this question with growing assertiveness and impatience in the years ahead.

The most visible immediate change on race matters in Washington was a significant new interest in the appointment of blacks to government posts. Previously blacks had been largely absent from important positions in the federal service. Of 950 attorneys in the Justice Department in 1960, only 10 were black (though every single one of the department's 56 messengers was black). The more than 3,600 Foreign Service officers included only 15 blacks, and other departments showed a similar pattern of exclusion. To address this discrimination the new president created by executive order the Committee on Equal Employment Opportunity, chaired by Vice President Johnson.

Kennedy instructed the new committee "that federal money should not be spent in any way which encourages discrimination,"[6] a sharp signal not only to government administrators but also to large corporations that depended on federal contracts. Lockheed Aircraft was among the major companies that "voluntarily" began recruiting blacks, especially in southern branches that once had hired only whites.

The president also persistently pressured department and agency heads to issue periodic progress reports on their efforts to hire and promote blacks. The NAACP's Roy Wilkins underlined the impact of these actions when he began to joke that "Kennedy was so hot on the Department heads . . . that everyone was scrambling around trying to find himself a Negro in order to keep the President off his neck."[7]

In all, Kennedy appointed some forty blacks to high federal positions. Robert Weaver, chairman of the board of the NAACP, was chosen to head the Housing and Home Finance Agency, which Kennedy hoped to upgrade to cabinet status. Frank D. Reeves was named a special assistant to the president, and the campaign veteran Louis Martin became deputy chairman of the Democratic National Committee. In September 1961 the president nominated the legendary lawyer Thurgood Marshall for a judgeship on the Second Circuit Court of Appeals in New York, the most prestigious of the eleven appellate courts then existing beneath the U.S. Supreme Court. It was Marshall who had been principal litigator for the NAACP Legal Defense Fund in many of the desegregation cases, including *Brown* v. *Board of Education.* The meaning of this appointment was not lost on southern senators on the Judiciary Committee, whose delaying tactics held up confirmation for nearly a year.

Recognizing that significant new civil rights legislation would not be easily accomplished, Kennedy adopted an administrative strategy that centered on the Justice Department, under his brother Robert. The appointment of "Bobby," as the thirty-five-year-old attorney general was called with widely varying degrees of affection, generated no small amount of controversy. Some cried "Nepotism!" which, of course, it was. Other critics noted that it was rare to have an attorney general who had never tried a case in court. But Robert Kennedy quickly turned the Justice Department into a versatile and aggressive force against racism.

The Department's Civil Rights Division had plodded along to little effect since its creation in 1957. Short on staff, underfunded, and led with little boldness, it was a pure reflection of the Eisenhower administration's distaste for compelling changes in race relations. Under Robert Kennedy the division quickly assembled a staff of able and energetic deputies, headed by a soft-spoken but brilliant Washington lawyer named Burke Marshall. Bobby encouraged his aides to move frequently from their Washington offices into the field, which could be anywhere race troubles were simmering. John Doar, first assistant to the Civil Rights Division, recalled of his chief, "He was always wanting to move, get something done, accomplish something, and when I first went up to see him—probably April 1961—he was for filing seventy-five cases by Thanksgiving."[8]

Southern resistance to school desegregation was the first major test of the Kennedy Justice Department's commitment to civil rights. In 1960 New Orleans officials had pleaded with President Eisenhower to endorse a school desegregation plan that was under attack by local extremists and state leaders. Eisenhower refused to take sides, and the Justice Department disclaimed responsibility. Mob action filled the vacuum, forcing two of the New Orleans schools to close before the desegregation plan went into effect in the fall term.

Early in 1961 the new attorney general fired off a very different message of administration intent. Robert Kennedy warned Louisiana officials, who had voted to cut off the salaries of teachers in integrated schools, that he would ask the federal court to hold them in contempt and put the state superintendent in jail. He pressed them to ensure the smooth, desegregated operation of all the affected schools. They resisted. But when Burke Marshall started court proceedings, the state yielded.[9]

Justice Department leaders tried to encourage moderation by sending their southern lieutenants to reason with community leaders in cities like Dallas, Atlanta, and Memphis. "I'd go in, my Southern accent dripping sorghum and molasses," John Seigenthaler, an aide from Tennessee, recalled. "Then Burke Marshall would explain the law to them."[10] The administration's efforts were enhanced by the president's obvious and public support. Unlike Eisenhower, Kennedy endorsed school desegregation. He praised the principals, teachers, students, and parents "on the front lines of the problem." Their adherence to the Constitution, he noted, was "contributing to the education of all Americans."[11]

But there were political boundaries that Kennedy clearly recognized and was cautious about crossing. Kennedy had promised during the campaign to submit major civil rights legislation to Congress, but on that pledge he soon began to waver. He simply could not afford to alienate southern congressmen, especially key committee chairs, whose opposition could torpedo his liberal legislative program.

The political realities were clear to anyone who could count. The Democrats had lost twenty-one seats in the House and two in the Senate in 1960, and in the best of circumstances it would be a struggle to pass any of his reform measures. Even Harris Wofford, one of the administration's leading advocates of civil rights, conceded in an early memorandum that "on most controversial social and economic issues, the Republican-conservative Southern Democratic coalition could probably muster a majority in the House, and successfully invoke a filibuster in the Senate."[12]

Wofford warned that there existed virtually no chance of passing civil rights legislation, and any attempt to do so would "endanger all the rest of the administration's program, including measures of great importance to most blacks [such as the plan to raise the minimum wage]. It would demonstrate the President's weakness at a time when he needed to build strength."[13] Kennedy agreed and reneged, at least for the short term, on his pledge to send civil rights legislation to Congress. He focused instead on other social reform measures and on administrative efforts, primarily in the Justice Department, to make some progress on civil rights.

The political juggling act became especially delicate. On the one hand, the president sought to placate African American leaders by assuring them that a strategy of "minimum legislation, maximum executive action" on civil rights offered the best hope for concrete results. But he was careful to avoid a strong reaction in Congress from the southern conservatives. He'd pledged in the campaign to end housing discrimination "with the stroke of a pen." His delay in acting on that pledge was so long, however, that an "Ink for Jack" campaign deluged the White House with bottles of ink and hundreds of pens. When, after two years, he finally issued an order on housing discrimination, it was so limited in scope that he deliberately timed its announcement for maximum obscurity.

This deference to conservative southern congressmen bordered on servility in the area of judicial appointments, several of which went to advocates of white supremacy. At the urging of James Eastland of Mississippi, chairman of the powerful Senate Judiciary Committee, for example, Kennedy nominated William Harold Cox for a judgeship on Mississippi's Fifth District Court. That Cox was a strident segregationist and this court had jurisdiction over nearly a million African Americans was a dismaying lesson to civil rights leaders on the Kennedy administration's seemingly unbounded flexibility in adjusting black interests for the sake of a broader liberal program.

"A CRISIS TO BARGAIN WITH"

In the spring of 1961 the executive director of the Congress of Racial Equality (CORE), James Farmer, outlined plans for a series of interracial "freedom rides" on public buses throughout the Deep South. The goal was to test compliance with court orders to desegregate interstate transportation terminals. But this was also an effort to force the federal government to take a firmer stand on black rights by precipitating acts of racial violence in the heartland of Jim Crow. As Farmer explained the strategy of confrontation, "We put on pressure and create a crisis [for federal leaders] and then they react."[14]

Violence was not long in coming. On May 14 in Birmingham, Alabama, a gang of thirty heavyset young men attacked the thirteen passengers—six black and seven white—with baseball bats, lead pipes, and bicycle chains. Kennedy appealed for law and order while John Seigenthaler flew to Alabama to encourage state officials to protect the riders. Hearing of the violence, more freedom riders began to gather.

This distressed Kennedy, who was immersed in diplomatic crises, including an imminent summit meeting with Premier Khrushchev of the Soviet Union, and did not want to be distracted by a campaign that seemed intent on creating a crisis. "Tell [the riders] to call it off," the president commanded his civil rights aide, Harris Wofford, who had contacts with black leaders. "Stop them!"[15] But this was one executive order that no one could implement.

Six days later in Montgomery, Alabama, Seigenthaler encountered vigilantes when he tried to escort a battered young woman from the terminal. "I'm a federal man," he explained to them, as they clubbed him to the ground.

Violence threatened again later that evening when King appeared before twelve hundred blacks at a church rally in Montgomery to show support for the freedom riders. To keep order the Justice Department improvised a force of five hundred federal officers. When a mob gathered outside the church, the federal men were able to keep the crowd from burning down the church, as some had threatened.

But the challenge of protecting the freedom riders without inciting further violence was far from solved. So the Kennedys turned to Senator Eastland of Mississippi to help keep the peace. In a private conference with Bobby Kennedy, Eastland offered to ensure the safety of the riders as they traveled through Mississippi to Jackson, in exchange for assurances that the Justice Department would not contest the jailing of freedom riders on charges of traveling "for the avowed purpose of inflaming public opinion." Though it reached no moral high ground, this deal spared the riders' lives and the president's stature en route to dealing with Nikita Khrushchev.

But for all this skirmishing, the goal of moving President Kennedy toward stronger action, especially legislation, proved more elusive to civil rights advocates. Kennedy remained dubious about anything more than emergency use of federal force to keep order in the region. As Burke Marshall explained the position of the Justice Department's Civil Rights Division: "We do not have a national police force. . . . There is no substitute under the federal system for the failure of local law enforcement responsibility. There is simply a vacuum, which can be filled only rarely, with extraordinary difficulty, at monumental expense, and in a totally unsatisfactory fashion."[16]

In September 1962, however, the administration was forced to intervene yet again in a potentially explosive situation. When a black Air Force veteran named James Meredith sought to transfer from a black college to the University of Mississippi at Oxford, he was turned down. But a federal court ordered his admission, and Meredith intended to register despite the threats on his life.

When Mississippi's governor, Ross Barnett, refused to support Meredith or the federal court, a mob of students and outside vigilantes gathered in Oxford brandishing rocks and rifles. Five hundred marshals converged on Ole Miss, as the university was known, but this only inflamed the situation, with much of the violence focusing on the marshals. Scores of people were wounded and two were killed. Sensing he had few other options, the president reluctantly ordered five thousand Army troops onto the campus to restore order. Meredith remained at the school, surrounded by a federal guard, enduring threats, ostracism, and harassment of his family. He graduated the following August

The events at Ole Miss affected Kennedy's thinking about civil rights reform, diminishing any lingering faith he might have had that moral suasion could convince the southern opponents of civil rights to stand down. And it came increasingly to seem that the political constraint of squandered southern support in Congress had to be balanced against other equally pressing needs. The confrontation in Mississippi was the turning point. In attempting to deny a lone black American an education, Ole Miss instead provided one for the president of the United States. The need for more vigorous civil rights leadership could no longer be denied.

Observing Kennedy's new awareness in the aftermath of Ole Miss, the civil rights leaders expanded the pressure on their southern oppressors and on Washington. "We've got to have a crisis to bargain with," King's aide Wyatt Walker observed.[17] King agreed that unless racial tensions reached a more visibly dangerous pitch, the president's goodwill might never translate into bold deeds. "He vacillated," King wrote of Kennedy in October 1962, "trying to sense the direction his leadership could travel while retaining and building support for his administration."[18]

To create a new civil rights crisis, deeper in impact than any of the earlier confrontations, the Southern Christian Leadership Conference (SCLC) planned a campaign against segregation in Birmingham, Alabama, site of the first mass beatings of freedom riders.

On May 2, 1963, King intensified protests against segregation in Birmingham by mobilizing teenagers and children to provoke arrests by local authorities and fill up the jails. Sheriff Bull Connor, in temper and attitude the perfect foil, countered the next day by ordering police to assault a black rally outside the Sixteenth Street Baptist Church. His forces blasted adults and children with high-pressure fire hoses, ripping their clothes and leaving them bloodied on the ground. Police officers swung nightsticks into skulls indiscriminately and loosed attack dogs on the panicked crowd.

Many Birmingham whites began to fear all-out race war as Connor's officers bore down. Businessmen watched in alarm as sales dropped in the face of boycotts and the accompanying turmoil that discouraged anyone from patronizing the downtown stores. On May 10 white merchants pledged to desegregate their stores and hire blacks within three months in exchange for an immediate end to boycotts and picketing. But the police violence continued.

The Birmingham protests set broader forces in motion, especially as the nation's news media took note. Americans who had long been complacent about mistreatment of blacks despaired at the images appearing on television. One evening the national news featured film of five Birmingham policemen pinning a black woman to the ground, with one officer's knee at her throat. A photograph carried on the front pages of newspapers around the world showed a huge, snarling police dog lunging at a black woman. The sheer violence of racism, once a "southern problem," now seeped into every American home.

In Washington, government officials were besieged with calls for action. Oregon's senator Wayne Morse grumbled that the events in Birmingham would disgrace even the Union of South Africa.[19] On May 12 President Kennedy ordered three thousand Army troops to draw near the city, and he prepared to federalize the Alabama Guard by invoking his authority to take command of state militia units in a national emergency. The pressure on Birmingham began to yield results. Local merchants removed racial designations from fountains and restrooms, desegregated their lunch counters, and hired blacks for positions once reserved for whites. The city's segregation laws were repealed, and eventually the library, city golf courses, public buildings, and finally the schools opened to both races. In the nation's most segregated city, a symbol of white resistance and Ku Klux Klan power, blacks had won a victory, in the Reverend Fred Shuttlesworth's words, for "human supremacy."[20]

The impact of the Birmingham campaign convinced John and Robert Kennedy that the growth of black activism and white support had given civil rights a new urgency, that events were moving very fast. Barely twelve hundred volunteers had made the freedom rides in 1961, but in 1963 the Birmingham campaign and the other protests it helped spark over the next seven months engaged over a hundred thousand people and led to nearly fifteen thousand arrests.[21] No one could reasonably argue any longer that these were isolated incidents.

The Kennedys now found their administration tested in two critical ways. First, could it redress the injustices so glaringly exposed by black protest? Second, could it preserve national peace amid the growing polarization over the "Negro revolution"? Was it time, in effect, for the liberal reform tradition to end its long accommodation with the nation's racist heritage?

To help shape their response to the protests, the Kennedys began to meet with some of the protesters. One session, hosted by the attorney general on May 24, 1963, was notable for the rare candor—and bitterness— with which African Americans addressed the nation's political leadership. The writer James Baldwin had convened a group of blacks "other blacks listened to" for an exchange of ideas on advancing the cause of racial equality. The gathering included the playwright Lorraine Hansberry, the entertainers Lena Horne and Harry Belafonte, the psychologist Kenneth Clark, and others from varied backgrounds but—Robert Kennedy was emphatic on this point—no conventional politicians like Roy Wilkins or even Martin Luther King. The attorney general stressed that he wanted to learn what blacks were really thinking. Still, he anticipated a congenial strategy session among fellow liberal reformers.

Instead he was scorched by anger. The meeting opened with denunciations of the administration by Jerome Smith, a young freedom rider and survivor of a mob beating. In the clearest possible terms, he told Robert Kennedy how degrading it was to have to plead for rights that were supposedly guaranteed by the Constitution, pointing out how the administration had for too long held its fire on civil rights matters. Kennedy at first tried to respond by pointing out the tactical nuances of the administration's approach. Failing to make that sale, he fell into a tense silence.

Afterward Belafonte privately thanked Robert Kennedy for the administration's efforts on behalf of black rights. Asked why he had not said this at the meeting, he explained, "They would conclude I had gone over to the other side."[22] This was deeply disheartening to the attorney general, who had thought of civil rights activists as partners.

While the activists were urging acceleration, the political profession-als were urging caution. John Kennedy was sounding out aides about the possibility of a major civil rights address, to be followed by a hard push for major legislative action. But Ted Sorensen worried that this could devastate his presidency. Lyndon Johnson thought the time not yet ripe for a legislative proposal on civil rights.[23] Luther Hodges, Kennedy's secretary of commerce and a moderate from North Carolina, told the president that many southerners already resented him for apparently encouraging blacks to break the law and that southern support for his re-election would be jeopardized if he pushed for further action on civil rights.

But one aide urged the president to move ahead, and he was the most influential one of all: Robert Kennedy. Set caution aside, the attorney general counseled his brother; the time had come to rise above politics. And so it had. "There comes a time," the president told Luther Hodges, "when a man has to take a stand and history will record that he has to meet these tough situations and ultimately make a decision."[24]

Alabama, the last holdout against desegregation of its public-funded university, once again provided the opportunity that Kennedy needed to force the issue. On June 11, 1963, two black students planned to register at the main campus in Tuscaloosa. But Alabama's governor, George Wal-lace, vowed to bar the way. Determined to make his mark in southern (and soon national) politics, Wallace stood in front of the college admis-sions office—in the schoolhouse door, as he liked to say—until federal marshals accompanying the two students ordered him to stand aside. This nationally broadcast scene, a mixture of the ludicrous and the dramatic, provided John Kennedy with the perfect moment to warn the Wallaces and Connors of the land that their day was over.

Addressing the nation on television that evening, the president called civil rights "a moral issue" that was "as old as the scriptures and . . . as clear as the American Constitution." The turmoil arising from racial dis-crimination could not be "met by repressive police action," he said, but only by the efforts of Congress, state and local governments, and private citizens to see that "all Americans are to be afforded equal rights and equal opportunities. . . . " The time was past, Kennedy said, for asking black citizens to "be content with the counsels of patience and delay," nor could they tell each other that the country had "no class or caste system, no ghettoes, no master race except with respect to Negroes." The president added that he would soon ask Congress "to make a commitment it has not fully made in this century to the proposition that race has no place in American life or law."[25]

Here was the great turning point in the history of the civil rights movement, the liberation of liberal reformers from any continuing sense of obligation to the white southerners who had for so long curtailed the agenda of their political coalition. To one historian, "It marked the beginning of what can truly be called the Second Reconstruction, a coherent effort by all three branches of the government to secure blacks their full rights."[26] It marked as well the political coming of age for African Americans, whose nonviolent but confrontational politics had pressed Kennedy to act.

The weight of crisis had at last trumped political caution. But that did not mean that the legislative challenge had diminished or the electoral fear vanished. Kennedy was moving into uncertain and risky territory, and he was anxious to maintain his bearings and protect his now increasingly vulnerable flanks. Political calculations would continue to be important navigational aids in shaping civil rights policy.

The Kennedy civil rights approach that began to unfold in June 1963 included in generous measure a concern to promote human dignity, an ability to gauge the tides of history (as well as smaller ripples in Gallup surveys), and an openness to new insight based on growing experience. Like most leaders of democracies, he concluded—too readily at times—that the path to greatness was not necessarily a straight line. But in the area of civil rights his path took him in less than three years to the center of a movement that bore simultaneously the nation's highest ideals and its deepest fears.

On June 19 Kennedy requested from the Congress a broad law to bolster voting rights, ban segregation in public facilities, authorize the attorney general to initiate suits against segregated schools, and strengthen federal authority to deny funds for programs that discriminated. Soon thereafter, the president and others in the administration made personal appeals to educators, lawyers, business executives, governors, mayors, blacks, southern whites, clergymen, labor spokesmen, Republicans, and

Democrats. They met with congressional leaders and, with the aid of the national Democratic Party, formed a citizens' lobby for the civil rights bill.

Soon it became apparent that while the southern opponents in Congress were outnumbered, they had one weapon for which there might be no effective counter: the Senate filibuster. If thirty-four senators stood united against civil rights, Kennedy's bill would never make it to the floor for debate. The filibuster had undermined civil rights in earlier congressional confrontations; it loomed large in this one. But there could be no turning back. The president had fully committed the authority of his office—and his political future—to continued civil rights progress.

THE MARCH ON WASHINGTON

As the legislative process moved into gear, civil rights advocates searched for ways to accelerate it. In July 1963 A. Philip Randolph, head of the Brotherhood of Sleeping Car Porters, a predominantly black union, announced plans for a massive rally in the nation's capital. He turned to his chief aide, Bayard Rustin, to organize the rally.[27]

Though often overlooked, Rustin was an influential participant in many of the civil rights events of the time. Tall, with flaring gray hair, high cheekbones, and thin features reflecting part-Indian ancestry, his aristocratic diction shaped by long stays in England, the fifty-one-year-old Rustin cut a profile in elegance. From an early age he mingled easily with whites as one of very few blacks growing up in West Chester, a suburb of Philadelphia.

As a young man in the 1930s, Rustin, who sang in all-white clubs with such black celebrities as Josh White and "Leadbelly," clearly saw the social divide separating the races. From 1941 Rustin's résumé approximated an outline history of the black nonviolent, direct-action movement. He shared Randolph's emphasis on economic goals that could bridge racial lines, including federal measures to end poverty, and he aided Randolph's efforts to prod organized labor into the fight against Jim Crow.

Convinced that black churches held a key to mass action, Rustin went to Montgomery in 1955 to share his experience in organizing boycotts with Martin Luther King, Jr. There Rustin, the urbane activist, intrigued King with discourses on Gandhian philosophy, which he had studied with disciples of the late Mahatma while spending a year in India. It was Rustin who later persuaded King to found a regional network of black ministers and who had principal responsibility for organizing what came to be the Southern Christian Leadership Conference. An intellectual with a talent for polemic, Rustin was also a technician of change, attentive to every organizational and logistical need.

Rustin's visibility in the civil rights movement and his deserved share in the credit for its successes were always diminished by two characteristics of his life, one political and one personal. Rustin had been a member of the Young Communist League, and he was a homosexual. For all his talents and the admiration they earned from other black leaders, the politics and morality of the time could not tolerate a visible leader who was black, formerly Red, and gay. So Bayard Rustin remained largely in the shadow of the better-known civil rights leaders, the invisible pillar of the civil rights movement.

In 1963 the cresting of a national black protest movement, filled with charismatic leaders but lacking overall direction, enabled Rustin and Randolph to reassert their influence as architects of a vast coalition for change. A protest in the nation's capital with blacks and whites demanding federal action would, they believed, give much-needed focus to the civil rights movement.

Most black leaders agreed, and they joined together with a unity of purpose that had never been more evident. Randolph, Martin Luther King of the SCLC, James Farmer of CORE, Roy Wilkins of the NAACP, John Lewis of SNCC (Student Nonviolent Coordinating Committee), Whitney Young of the Urban League, and others involved in planning the rally expressed widely divergent ideas about what its character should be. Some wanted to focus on the economic suppression of blacks. Others wanted to focus instead on segregation and its legal underpinnings.

Remarkably, a compromise was achieved. Randolph and Rustin were the first to alter their vision of the march, shifting their focus from a jobs bill to passage of civil rights legislation, and from union spokesmen to black middle-class leaders like King, Wilkins, and Farmer. In exchange, they won the support of Dr. King and, with it, the chance to mobilize massive black support for their rally.

Other civil rights leaders followed King's lead. In response to the concern expressed by some that a potential confrontation with federal authorities would provoke a disastrous backlash,[28] the site of the rally was shifted from the Capitol to the Lincoln Memorial. As religious, labor, and other groups stepped forward to help sponsor or otherwise aid the march, Randolph's antigovernment protest became transmuted, in the words of the journalist Milton Viorst, from a matter of politics into "a moral witness against evil."[29]

As word of the planned march reached the White House, President Kennedy worried that it might trigger a conservative backlash and encourage the opponents of his civil rights bill. "We want success in Congress," he told a meeting with black leaders on June 22, 1963, "not just a big show at the Capitol." Farmer and Randolph countered that the march would afford an essential, nonviolent outlet for rising anger among the black masses. King added that he had never engaged in any campaign that did not seem "ill-timed." The march was inevitable, they told the president, urging him to endorse it. He did so, while seeking to discourage them from undertaking any protest against his administration while he worked to secure passage of the civil rights bill. This informal détente echoed Kennedy's concluding words to his guests: They might disagree at times over tactics, but they should always preserve "confidence in the good faith of each other."[30]

On August 28, 1963, under a nearly cloudless sky, more than a quarter of a million people gathered near the Lincoln Memorial to rally for "jobs and freedom." Fifty thousand whites mingled in the crowd and among the prominent speakers. From every area of American life leaders came to donate their talents or simply their stature: Walter Reuther, maverick labor leader and a Kennedy ally; clergymen of every faith; film stars Sidney Poitier, Charlton Heston, and Marlon Brando; folksinger Joan Baez and gospel legend Mahalia Jackson; teachers, students, professionals. It was the largest political assembly in American history. And although many Washington residents anticipated the event with terror—according to Louis Martin the Army had prepared for the rally "as if it were

World War II"[31]—the immense crowd was nonviolent and in a largely festive mood.

The sweltering afternoon featured a profusion of speakers, each allotted fifteen minutes, though more than a few found that their accumulated wisdom could not be contained in that brief span. The dominant memory of the rally, however, was the closing address by Martin Luther King, Jr. To shouts of "Tell it, doctor!" and "Amen!" the minister put aside his text and concluded in a flourish of democratic exaltation and religious exultation:

> I have a dream that one day this nation will rise up and live out the true meaning of its creed: "We hold these truths to be self-evident, that all men are created equal." . . .
>
> And . . . when we allow freedom [to] ring, when we let it ring from every village and every hamlet, from every state and every city, we will be able to speed up that day when *all* of God's children, black men and white men, Jews and Gentiles, Protestants and Catholics, will be able to join hands and to sing in the words of the old Negro spiritual, *"Free at last! Free at last! Thank God Almighty, we are free at last!"* [32]

King's dream seemed closer still because of the march's impact on the president, who publicly lauded "the deep fervor and the quiet dignity that characterizes the thousands who have gathered in the Nation's Capital from across the country to demonstrate their faith and confidence in our democratic form of government."[33] Kennedy also invited ten of the main organizers to a reception in the White House to symbolize the bond between the movement and the White House.

But the congressional challenge remained daunting, with even liberal legislators like Senator Hubert Humphrey of Minnesota doubting that the rally had changed many votes in Congress and southerners vowing an endless filibuster against the pending civil rights bill. More ominous still in the agitated atmosphere of that summer was a surge of extremist violence. In one widely noted instance in September a bomb exploded in Birmingham's famous Sixteenth Street Baptist Church, killing four black girls as they attended Sunday school.

The president's political fears seemed to be crystallizing as well. In midfall a poll showed that four and a half million white southerners had become disaffected with Kennedy's leadership, a much larger number than he could hope to gain in new black voters in 1964.[34] "He's stirred up all the colored people to get their vote," complained a North Carolina housewife. "It's terrible; he encouraged them to break state laws."[35] The apparent beneficiary of changing attitudes in the South was Arizona senator Barry Goldwater, a likely Republican nominee in 1964. Throughout the South signs sprang up, "Kennedy for King—Goldwater for President," in a bitter play on Kennedy's support for the SCLC minister.[36]

By late fall signs of racial progress increasingly broke through the pall of violence and invective. Nearly 40 percent of all southern and border-state communities of over ten thousand people had desegregated at least some public facilities. In Congress, Kennedy's search for a reform consensus took a major step forward on October 29 when the House Judiciary Committee favorably reported by a comfortable margin a bipartisan civil rights measure. The wide-ranging bill included provisions that prohibited discrimination in public facilities or employment and strengthened guarantees of black voting rights. Some of the bill's language had been trimmed to win over moderates whose votes would be crucial for House passage; still, it remained the most sweeping civil rights measure since Reconstruction.

At his last press conference before a campaign trip to Dallas in November, Kennedy was optimistic. "However dark it looks now," he said, "I think that 'westward, look, the land is bright,'" and he added, "by next summer it may be."[37] For many Americans committed to civil rights, the New Frontier at last seemed to offer that possibility.

THE CIVIL RIGHTS ACT OF 1964

As Martin Luther King, Jr., and his family sat by their television watching President Kennedy's funeral, his six-year-old son, Marty, tried to grasp the nature of their loss. "President Kennedy was your best friend, wasn't he, Daddy?" King's wife, Coretta, agreed: "In a way, he was."[38]

Surely there could not have been much confidence that the momentum so painfully gathered for civil rights legislation would continue under Kennedy's successor. Lyndon Johnson—shrewd son of the South and longtime temporizer on civil rights legislation—had finally seemed to come around on civil rights during his time as vice president. But to America's black leaders, his motives and sincerity were suspect. Civil rights leaders had lost too many battles, been encased in too many compromises, borne too many scars from the formidable legislative skills of the former majority leader of the Senate to forget all that now and embrace him as their true ally. In 1960 Johnson was the one candidate for the Democratic nomination unacceptable to most blacks, and despite his effective work in chairing Kennedy's subcabinet committee on equal employment, skepticism remained high.

But civil rights skeptics underestimated Lyndon Johnson, a common affliction in Washington in late 1963. Few political leaders of the time were better at sizing up a situation and finding the available opportunities. Keenly aware that black protest had altered the nation's political agenda, Johnson also saw that Kennedy's presidency—and his martyrdom—had made civil rights an issue no successor could safely set aside.

But there was more than political opportunism bearing on Lyndon Johnson. Black protest had also affected him personally, forcing him to recognize that he and his fellow southerners had deluded themselves into believing that the black people around them were "happy and satisfied."[39] Such belief, after years of demonstration of its unwisdom, could not be sustained.

The presidency, with its moral authority and equal moral burden, also seemed to liberate Johnson from the easy fatalism that he could do little to change race relations. "In that house of decision," Johnson found, ". . . a man becomes his commitments."[40] And in the first, difficult days of his presidency, Lyndon Johnson's commitments made him the nation's foremost champion of civil rights reform.

On November 27, having scarcely settled into the Oval Office, the new president addressed a joint session of Congress and a grieving nation. "Let us continue," Johnson said, sounding the theme of his young administration, promising, "The ideas and the ideals which [Kennedy] so nobly represented must and will be translated into effective action."[41] The message was clear: Kennedy's legacy lived on, but now with Lyndon Johnson as its steward and shepherd.

While Kennedy was president, Johnson had shared the administration's view that the civil rights bill might have to be pared considerably as it approached its final form. In particular the provisions guaranteeing equal employment opportunity appeared headed for radical surgery in the familiar committee operations dominated by southern senators. As president, however, Johnson found a new boldness and resolved to resist any compromise that could weaken the civil rights bill. "I had seen this 'moderating' process at work for many years," Johnson later wrote in his memoirs—omitting, of course, that he had been the Senate's most unstinting moderator. "... I had seen it happen in 1960 [with passage of a weakened voting rights bill]. I did not want to see it happen again."[42]

Getting a civil rights bill untainted by compromise was Johnson's immediate goal. But lurking close behind was a desire to abolish the doubts about the sincerity of his liberalism still harbored by many on the left. "I knew," he later confided, "that if I didn't get out in front on this issue, they [northern liberals] would get me. They'd throw up my background against me, they'd use it to prove that I was incapable of bringing unity to the land I loved so much. . . . I couldn't let that happen. I had to produce a civil rights bill that was even stronger than the one they'd have gotten if Kennedy had lived." "Without this," he added in a keen analysis of the political stakes, "I'd be dead before I could even begin."[43]

Two days after he asked Congress for rapid action on civil rights, Johnson summoned Roy Wilkins for a private strategy summit. As Wilkins sat down, a very somber president brought his chair to within a few inches of his visitor's knees. Wilkins "felt those mesmerizing eyes of Texas" on him as Johnson—dominating the conversation—discussed the future of the civil rights bill. He explained that he would insist on enacting a strong bill, which would require every possible Senate vote to defeat the inevitable southern filibuster. Therefore he needed Wilkins and other civil rights leaders to lobby relentlessly for the bill. "When are you going to get down here and start civil-righting?" he demanded as he delivered a heavy dose of the "Johnson treatment."[44] The president encouraged Wilkins to tell Senate Minority Leader Everett Dirksen and the entire Republican Party that black leaders would support the presidential candidate most committed to equality and would go "with a senatorial man who does the same thing."[45] Toward the end of their talk the president leaned forward, poked his finger at the civil rights leader, and said determinedly, "I want that bill passed."[46]

Wilkins left that meeting "struck by the enormous difference between Kennedy and Johnson." Kennedy had been sound on matters of principle, Wilkins concluded, but "for all his talk about the art of the possible, he didn't really know what was possible and what wasn't in Congress." But Johnson "knew exactly what was possible," and he was going to press for the last vote to get it.[47]

Through the early months of 1964 the president took his message of no compromise on civil rights to press conferences, cabinet meetings, Congress, and other sites, no matter how unlikely, including the New York World's Fair. A difficult private talk with his former mentor and patron in the Senate, Richard Russell of Georgia, was emblematic of Johnson's directness. Russell was a Senate legend who had directed successful filibusters against many other civil rights measures. Few men in his life had commanded more of Lyndon Johnson's admiration than Dick Russell.

Johnson expressed his hope for a future in which southerners would no longer stand against the rest of the nation. Russell listened respectfully, but conceded not an inch. On civil rights Johnson promised no compromise and Russell countered with no surrender. The civil rights bill would either pass with all provisions intact, or die in yet another southern filibuster. Johnson later wrote that the situation led him to consider some sound advice by a fellow Texan: "John Nance Garner, a great legislative tactician, as well as a good poker player, once told me that there comes a time in every leader's career when he has to put in all his stack. I decided to shove in all my stack on this vital measure."[48]

Johnson then instructed the lobbyists Clarence Mitchell of the NAACP and Joseph Rauh of the liberal Americans for Democratic Action, "You tell [Senate Majority Leader] Mike Mansfield to put that bill on the floor, and tell everybody that it's going to stay there until it passes. I don't care if it stays for four, six, or eight months. You can tell Mike Mansfield, and you can tell anybody else, that the President of the United States doesn't care if that bill is there forever. We are not going to have the Senate do anything else until that bill is passed. And it is going to pass."[49]

With Johnson's feet planted firmly behind him, Mansfield put his own legislative skills to work. The first obstacle was the Senate Judiciary Committee, whose chair, Mississippi's senator James Eastland, had once pledged to "protect and maintain white supremacy throughout eternity."[50] Mansfield used a rarely invoked provision of Senate rules to bypass the committee and place the civil rights bill directly on the Senate calendar in March 1964.

The expected filibuster was not long in materializing. Senator Russell started slowly, entangling the Senate, as the historian Eric Goldman noted, "in a dizzying debate over whether a motion to debate the bill was debatable." Soon these convoluted minuets gave way to a total war of delay that spared no subject of human knowledge, or ignorance. Russell organized the southerners into three platoons of six senators each. They stayed fresh by rotating their days of responsibility for tying up the business of the Senate. On and on they talked, about the "'amalgamation and mongrelization of the races,' the source of the grits that people in Minnesota eat, the living habits of Hungarian immigrants, sometimes about the bill itself, calling it, to use the phrase of Senator Russell Long, 'a mixed breed of unconstitutionality and the NAACP.'"[51]

The House of Representatives, unburdened by filibusters, moved forward on the civil rights bill at a far more rapid clip. Southern House members sought to sink the bill under the weight of over one hundred crippling amendments, but in late January a bipartisan Judiciary Committee accepted thirty-four relatively trivial ones and sent the bill to the floor. This was a real civil rights bill, little resembling the tepid imitations of the 1950s. It strengthened voting rights, banned discrimination in public facilities and in employment, empowered the attorney general to begin suits against school segregation, and authorized the withholding of federal funds from noncomplying school districts. Southern Democrats continued to rain weakening amendments on the House floor—succeeding, however, in securing only one substantial change. But it was an amendment considered so radical as to imperil passage of the entire bill.

Howard Smith of Virginia, chair of the Rules Committee and one of the great legislative tacticians of the era, offered a "perfecting" amendment that would bar employment discrimination not just against blacks, but against women as well. Summoning the full force of Virginia gallantry, he commiserated with women, who, outnumbering men by two million, already were at a disadvantage in seeking spouses. At least, he implied, they should get jobs with equal pay. Surely, he argued, they deserved as much protection in the workplace as blacks.

On the surface this appeared to be little more than a facetious rearguard action by a doomed southern leader. There had been little public discussion of including women in the protections of the bill, but Judge Smith saw the female card as a tactic for freighting the bill with more baggage than it could bear. Corporate and labor support for civil rights, he reckoned, might evaporate quickly if the new legislation required a reorganization of the entire workforce to accomplish gender equality.

The small feminist vanguard in Congress divided over the amendment. Michigan Democrat Martha W. Griffiths observed that without the protection of this amendment the civil rights bill would leave white women "at the bottom of the list in hiring," after white men and both black men and women. She added, "It would be incredible to me that white men would be willing to place white women at such a disadvantage."

Few members felt more contorted on this amendment than Edith Green, a white congresswoman from Oregon. She had fought for years to guarantee women equal pay for equal work, but she refused to let one provision jeopardize the whole civil rights bill—though she admitted that she might now be called "an Uncle Tom, or maybe an Aunt Jane."[52] She asked her colleagues to vote against the very proposition she had so long championed. Despite her plea, enough liberal representatives—including five of six women—joined with opponents of the civil rights bill to pass the amendment, 168 to 133.

Whatever rejoicing this apparent cleverness inspired in the southern Democrats was short-lived. Including women in Title VII of the Civil Rights Act turned out not to be the poison pill that opponents had hoped. A midwestern Republican who opposed the bill thought that the wily Judge Smith had "outsmarted himself. At this point there was no way you could sink the bill."[53]

Through it all Lyndon Johnson remained in the background, but even at a distance his profile was unmistakable. When the House passed the bill on February 10, by an emphatic 290–130 vote, Clarence Mitchell and Joseph Rauh stopped to celebrate in the House corridor. It wasn't long before the pay phone rang. Lyndon Johnson was on the line with terse congratulations, followed quickly by new marching orders. "All right, you fellows," he instructed. "Get over to the Senate. Get busy. We've won in the House, but there is a big job across the way."[54]

It had come to this. Passage of the most important civil rights legislation in the nation's history now rested on the ability of the liberal forces to end debate in the Senate. An unusual lobbying strategy soon emerged from the Leadership Conference on Civil Rights, a fifteen-year-old federation of over a hundred lobbying groups. It was to rely on the churches not only to keep the moral issue in view but also to sway lawmakers in central, southwestern, and far western states where labor unions and blacks wielded little political clout.

Clergymen responded with unprecedented enthusiasm for a purely political issue. They met regularly with members of Congress and pressed community leaders to do so as well. The issue became for many a test of religious sincerity, eclipsing the routines of church life and engaging local congregations in a compelling national cause. "This was the first time," marveled James Hamilton of the National Council of Churches, "that I ever recalled seeing Catholic nuns away from the convents for more than a few days."[55]

On April 19 the church pressure increased when trios of Protestant, Catholic, and Jewish seminarians staged a prayer vigil at the Lincoln Memorial. It continued around the clock throughout the Senate debate. To many of the southerners, the opposition now seemed overwhelming. It was one thing to cope with the relentless energy of Lyndon Johnson emboldened by supportive public opinion, but quite another to confront at every turn the agents of the Almighty.

The administration directed many of its own prayers to the one man who could obtain the sixty-seven votes necessary for cloture, the only effective way to end a filibuster. That man was Everett Dirksen of Illinois, the Senate minority leader. Dirksen was a complex partisan whose theatricality, shrewdness, cynicism, and patriotism all were refracted through a powerful ego of unpredictable bent. And he had previously opposed all civil rights legislation.

But Dirksen's keen political instincts, like Johnson's, told him that black activism and social turmoil were rapidly changing the nation's politics. Johnson and his aides appealed to Dirksen's desire to be on the right side of history. They played up Dirksen's importance and never missed an opportunity to flatter his formidable ego. Senator Hubert Humphrey, floor manager for the bill, recalled, "I courted Dirksen almost as persistently as I did [my wife] Muriel."[56] Humphrey's sister later said, "Hubert performed social psychology on Everett Dirksen for six months to get that bill passed."[57]

On June 10 Humphrey's persistence paid off; Dirksen announced that he would support cloture. America was changing and growing, he declared in the Senate chamber, and "on the civil rights issue we must rise with the occasion."[58]

Several days later, with every senator present, the cloture motion passed by seventy-one to twenty-nine, four more affirmative votes than the needed two-thirds. The southerners had been vanquished and the real legislative battle was over. Three weeks later Congress easily passed the Civil Rights Act of 1964 with every major provision intact, as Lyndon Johnson had predicted—and demanded.

Though feelings remained raw on both sides in the aftermath of the long congressional struggle, it was the magisterial Richard Russell who set the tone for southern reaction to the act. In a statement carrying the finality and dignity of Robert E. Lee's call for the South to accept the verdict of history, Russell wrote to his constituents, "It is the law ... and we must abide by it." He urged Georgians "to refrain from violence in dealing with this act."[59]

Russell's statesmanlike reaction came the more easily because he understood how strong national sentiment was in favor of this legislation. Roy Wilkins recalled that Senator Russell said a bit gloomily after his legislative defeat that every time he looked up he seemed to be faced with someone from the AFL-CIO, the women's groups, fraternal or civic organizations, or a minister—the great liberal coalition that had coalesced around this crusade.[60] The message was clear: the southerners' time had passed.

By permitting a lengthy floor fight, the administration had also enabled southerners to realize that their senators had been defeated fairly.

That, Russell told Clarence Mitchell just after the deciding vote, would help make the civil rights law enforceable.[61] Russell left unspoken one final, crucial factor in the acceptance of this law—the president's decision to use the full powers of his office and the full measure of his personal skills to achieve what had become a popular measure. While Senator Dirksen rightly termed the bill "an idea whose time has come,"[62] Lyndon Johnson's masterful support had surely hastened its safe arrival.

THE MOVEMENT AND THE PARTY

Among those senators who voted against the Civil Rights Act of 1964 was Barry Goldwater. Gratitude to Johnson and distrust of Goldwater impelled virtually all black leaders to support the re-election of the president in that year's election. But the question remained: How tightly should the civil rights movement tie its wagon to the Johnson administration?

Although most leaders continued to favor a coalition with white liberals as the best hope for further change, younger activists expressed suspicion of the Johnson administration and its allies. These strains in the liberal coalition peaked during the presidential campaign when Lyndon Johnson called on black leaders to set aside all protests for the sake of his candidacy and to avoid stirring a passionate conservative backlash.

Among the established black leadership, Roy Wilkins and Whitney Young especially, the view remained strong that a coalition with white liberals was the best hope for further progress on race relations. They agreed that acceptance of a moratorium seemed the only sane political course.

Bayard Rustin agreed, and helped organize a conference of black leaders in July to arrange such a moratorium,[63] but enthusiasm for the idea varied among those present, as did faith that they could effectively direct or control the actions of African American citizens. Still, the participants did agree on a carefully worded accord calling on their members voluntarily "to observe a 'broad curtailment if not total moratorium' on all mass demonstrations until after the Nov. 3 Presidential election."[64]

SNCC's chairman, John Lewis, part of the nascent younger generation of black leaders, spurned the demand for a moratorium and indi-
cated his unwillingness to submerge the civil rights revolution beneath
Lyndon Johnson's electoral ambitions. James Farmer of CORE, feeling
pressure from his members, eventually sided with Lewis. They cautioned
that if black leaders tried to stop the protest, "The kids in the street who
were demonstrating would laugh at us."[65]

Strains among civil rights leaders worsened in 1964, and within two
years they would tear the movement apart. The central issue around
which differences had begun to develop was the value of aligning the
movement with white liberals. Had the time come, younger blacks such
as Stokely Carmichael and James Forman asked, to abandon the movement's status as an appendage to the broad liberal coalition and go it
alone? It wasn't long before that question took center stage in the national
political spotlight.

As the Democratic Party convened in Atlantic City to anoint Lyndon
Johnson its nominee, blacks from Mississippi challenged the credentials
of the state's "regular" delegation. As in the past, the state party in
Mississippi had systematically excluded blacks from voting and office
holding. Whatever racial progress might be occurring in the South was
reflected in no way in the selection of that delegation. In fact, the Mississippi Democrats' opposition to racial progress was clearly evident in
the resolve of its state convention to "oppose, condemn and deplore the
Civil Rights Act of 1964" and to "reject and oppose the platforms of both
national parties and their candidates."[66]

The challenge came from the Mississippi Freedom Party, a group
born in the "Mississippi Freedom Summer" project to organize blacks
politically. Sixty-eight Freedom Party delegates reached the August convention by bus, train, dilapidated cars, and persistent hitchhiking. They
represented a fair cross section of rural and urban blacks in Mississippi,
including some sharecroppers who had only months earlier handled a
voter registration form for the first time. The delegation also included
four white activists, among them the Reverend Edwin King, a native Mis-
sissippian who had risked his safety to help found the Freedom Party in
1963. SNCC's Bob Moses doubted whether the insurgents stood much

chance in the coming struggle over credentials. Still, the tenacity of these new politicos in planning their trip to the convention had surprised many. It raised hopes that, if they could gain the support of white liberals, greater surprises lay ahead.

The confident mood of the insurgents stemmed also from their newly stimulated belief in the promise of American life, even for Mississippi blacks. The former sharecropper Fannie Lou Hamer conveyed the enthusiasm of many fellow delegates when she explained why the Freedom Party's challenge had to succeed: "When we went to Atlantic City, we didn't go there for publicity, we went there because we believed that America was what it said it was, 'the land of the free.'" She therefore believed "with all of [her] heart" in the triumph of her delegation, "because if the Constitution of this United States means something to all of us," the convention would unseat the segregated Mississippi delegation in favor of the Freedom Party's representatives.[67]

Joseph Rauh, head of the Americans for Democratic Action (ADA) and now also representing the Freedom Party to other Democrats, publicly insisted on the ouster of Mississippi's regular Democrats. But in private he suggested the possibility of a compromise allowing both delegations to be seated. To Lyndon Johnson, whose primary goal was to avoid signs of internal dissension in his party, this seemed like a reasonable solution.

But it seemed otherwise to Governor Paul Johnson of Mississippi, who personally informed the president that neither he nor any other regular Democrats would ever share their convention seats with the Freedom Party. It was not long before other southern governors aligned with Paul Johnson. John Connally of Texas and Carl Sanders of Georgia, among the more moderate southern governors, informed the president that an effort to seat the Freedom Democrats would cause them to lead their delegations out of the convention, and that other southern delegations would follow.[68]

Recalling the Dixiecrat walkout that nearly derailed Harry Truman's re-election pursuit in 1948, the president quickly calculated the politics of the situation and decided that there was little to gain from supporting the Freedom Party's challenge. Johnson picked Senator Hubert Humphrey of

Minnesota, the long-time liberal champion, for the unwelcome task of checking the Freedom Party's challenge.

At first glance, Humphrey might have seemed an odd and reluctant choice for this assignment. But Johnson had an unerring instinct for human weakness, and he knew that Humphrey's was ambition. To ensure his cooperation, Johnson sent word that Humphrey was his leading choice for a running mate, but that his selection would depend on how well he handled the convention challenge. The senator, in some anguish, agreed to do his best.[69]

The national focus grew more intense as Fannie Lou Hamer emerged as an eloquent voice of justice in the midst of the ferocious politicking. The television networks carried her testimony before the Credentials Committee and reported it extensively in their evening news broadcasts. Hamer told of her eviction from the farm where she had worked for eighteen years as a sharecropper, just after she registered to vote. She also recounted how she was jailed for encouraging others in Mississippi to register and how state highway patrolmen ordered other black prisoners to beat her as punishment for her organizing efforts. "All of this," she said, "is on account we want to register, to become first-class citizens, and if the Freedom Democratic Party is not seated now, I question America."[70]

There followed intense negotiations and a search for compromise. Humphrey offered "honorary" delegate status and two official seats for the five dozen Freedom Democrats, but Hamer and her fellow delegates overwhelmingly rejected his proposal. Their stand extended the controversy and forced white liberals and black leaders to take sides in a battle most wished had never begun.

Lyndon Johnson felt he had no choice but to pull out all the stops in this long-distance confrontation. Behind the scenes, he used all his powers of persuasion and all the instruments of influence at his command to try to keep some peace at the convention. He hurriedly called a press conference to preempt television coverage when Freedom Party members testified before the Credentials Committee. He browbeat Governor Edmund G. Brown, Sr., of California for failing to take a tough line against signs of pro–Freedom Party sentiment in his state's delegation. A delegate from the Canal Zone received a call from the secretary of the Army, informing him that if he voted to seat the Freedom Party he would be fired from his job.[71] Rauh himself, warned by the United Auto Workers chief, Walter Reuther, that his lucrative post as UAW counsel was at risk, saw his quest turning quixotic.[72]

Eventually the Freedom Democrats rejected all attempts at compromise, refusing to accept the two seats that had been offered them. Some entered the convention hall using passes provided by sympathetic delegates from other states and occupied the seats of the Mississippi delegation they had sought to replace. They found most of those seats empty. Angry that a compromise had been offered, most of the regular delegates walked out of the convention, unable to digest even the pallid offer of two delegate seats to the insurgents. (So, too, had most of Alabama's delegates, rather than abide by the party's insistence on a loyalty pledge to the national ticket.) But delegates from Georgia, Texas, and other southern states remained to support the president for re-election, satisfied that he had done everything possible to keep Mississippi's black delegates from tainting the party of the South.

In his memoirs Lyndon Johnson recalled the convention as a place of unbroken harmony. The unpleasantness of the Freedom Party challenge vanished amid memories of cheering throngs, unanimous votes, and a strengthened candidacy.[73] Thus was Lyndon Johnson's approach to all things in 1964: to brook no disharmony from any quarter, whatever the ideological or moral cavils. In July he had driven the liberal bandwagon roughshod over Senator Russell's segregationist forces to produce a historic civil rights measure. In August, feeling a chill political wind on his right, he fed the agenda of integrationist leaders into the omnivorous maw of consensus politics.

THE CAMPAIGN OF 1964

In 1964, both major-party nominees resolutely avoided the issue of race for most of the campaign, viewing the subject as too volatile to risk inflaming national tensions or undermining their own candidacies. Yet, even unspoken, the race question hovered over the campaign, a silent specter, casting doubt on the leadership of both candidates and on the nation's commitment to an integrated society.

Goldwater had opposed the Civil Rights Act on matters of constitutional principle and states' rights, but he was no racist. He resisted both the obvious temptations and the pleadings of his campaign advisors to exploit a potential white backlash against black protests and ghetto violence. Moreover, in the wake of the racial rioting in Harlem in 1964, he proposed that, for the sake of national stability, both candidates refrain from appeals to race. Johnson publicly finessed the offer but privately accepted it, pleased that his opponent was tossing aside a lever with which he could pry away conservative Democrats.

Goldwater's candidacy was nonetheless more than the sum of his own principles. From the beginning his base of support had been top-heavy with right-wing extremists, including archsegregationists such as Wallace and Eastland. Moreover, his speeches denouncing the "soul-less" monster of expanding government were at odds with the idea of benevolent federal leadership to which black leaders were committed.

So while black leaders still whispered complaints about Johnson's inconsistencies as a reformer, they saved their public tirades for Goldwater, whose consistency they found frightening. Martin Luther King, Jr., declined to endorse Johnson directly, but had no such reluctance about criticizing Goldwater. The NAACP ended its long tradition of neutrality in presidential races and stood firmly with Lyndon Johnson in 1964. Even the Mississippi Freedom Democrats, headed by the Johnson loyalist Aaron Henry, returned to their native state to work for the president's re-election.

By mid-October, the election clearly going his way, Johnson felt emboldened to work civil rights fully into the framework of consensus politics. Brushing aside the caution of his aides, he chose to give his one major speech on the subject in the Deep South city of New Orleans. "There are men down there," Johnson told one of his cabinet secretaries. "They may not like it, but at least they would like it straight." And he gave it to them straight, calling on the people of the South to move beyond a politics infected with race to a politics that focused on a promising future where people of all races could prosper together by setting aside the ancient enmities that had held their region back for so long.

The speech was well received by the audience in New Orleans, but in November Goldwater carried Louisiana's electoral votes. He carried few others, however. The legions of citizens he believed secretly shared his conservative views—the "hidden supporters"—failed to materialize. A popular avalanche returned Johnson to the White House with a record 61 percent of the vote.

The dreaded white backlash proved more apparent than real. In the Deep South the race issue helped Goldwater capture five traditionally Democratic states—Mississippi, Alabama, Louisiana, South Carolina, and Georgia. But Johnson handily won Texas, and with overwhelming black support countering the white majorities for Goldwater, he carried Virginia, North Carolina, Tennessee, and Arkansas.[74] Outside the South, Johnson won every state except his opponent's home base of Arizona.

In their zeal to blunt Goldwater's right-wing challenge, blacks cast over 95 percent of their ballots for Lyndon Johnson. That figure held for urban and rural areas, North and South, making African Americans the staunchest Democratic supporters of any ethnic, regional, or religious group. The journalist Theodore H. White noted, "Some urban Negro precincts approached 99 percent for Johnson—which can only be interpreted as meaning that several people, by mistake, pulled the wrong handle in voting booths in several big-city ghettos." It was, in White's view, "the most nearly unanimous expression of will in any community free of political surveillance anywhere in history."[75]

Combined with Democratic gains in the House and the Senate, the election results emphatically confirmed Johnson's liberal course, including his push for civil rights. They encouraged the president to hasten preparations for bolder reform measures.

BLOODY SUNDAY

Though the election of 1964 returned to office a champion of black rights, the vote totals were glaring evidence of the work that remained undone. Only two million of the South's five million voting-age blacks were registered in 1964. In Louisiana the proportion dropped to 31.8 percent, in Alabama to 19.4 percent, and in Mississippi to 6.4 percent.

The numbers formed a persuasive argument for black leaders: the judicial approach to enforcement of voting rights was too slow and ineffective, and the government would have to make good its guarantees in some new, more powerful way. The ability to vote was still a distant dream to too many black Americans

Privately Lyndon Johnson acknowledged a need to strengthen voting rights legislation, but he planned to defer such proposals for a year or more, to give the South time to digest the Civil Rights Act of 1964.[76] His patience would not prevail, however, as black protests against the last legal pillar of Jim Crow once again forced the federal government to take sides—and to take action.

The catalyst for the new campaign was the failure of existing voting rights laws to deter the familiar legal and extralegal harassment of blacks. Enforcement of these laws relied on judicial remedies that could not keep pace with state and local violations. Those who wanted to prevent blacks from voting always seemed one legal step ahead of those who sought the opposite.

The campaign for voting rights centered on Selma, Alabama, a city in which blacks made up a majority of the twenty-nine-thousand inhabitants but only 3 percent of the voting rolls. As in Birmingham, there was a white sheriff who seemed to have been ordered up from the redneck division of central casting. Jim Clark and his posse of deputies had kept black dissidents at bay with beatings and arrests when they sought to register. But on January 18, 1965, Martin Luther King, Jr., arrived to draw wider attention to the struggle in Selma and the unfinished agenda of civil rights. At a church rally, King looked past Selma to a national audience, exhorting blacks to fill the jails and arouse the federal government to assure the ballot.[77]

Before King entered Selma, Lyndon Johnson had expected the civil rights issue to lie discreetly fallow for a year while he cultivated bills for Medicare and aid to education. But as police violence against Selma's blacks worsened and public outrage grew, the president instructed Nicholas Katzenbach, who had replaced Robert Kennedy as attorney general, to accelerate his work on a voting rights bill.

On Friday, March 5, 1965, days after the murder of a twenty-six-year-old black marcher near Selma, King spent over an hour conferring with

Lyndon Johnson at the White House and received assurances that such a bill would soon be introduced in Congress. Moreover, it would bear the support of Senate Minority Leader Dirksen, all but guaranteeing an early end to a southern filibuster. It remained for civil rights leaders to solidify popular opinion in favor of rapid federal action on the voting rights issue. For this King planned a fifty-four-mile march from Selma to Montgomery to petition Governor Wallace of Alabama for protection of black registrants.

Six hundred blacks gathered outside Brown Chapel African Methodist Episcopal Church on Sunday morning, March 7, 1965, to begin the trek to Alabama's capital. State troopers' cars with Confederate insignia lined the sides of Highway 80, and troopers wearing gas masks beneath their blue helmets stood with billy clubs ready as the blacks moved in steady cadence across the Edmund Pettus Bridge. Within a minute of ordering the marchers to disperse, the troopers rushed forward in a flying wedge, clubbing blacks and firing canisters of tear gas while Sheriff Clark's mounted police charged with a rebel yell, swinging bullwhips and rubber tubing wrapped in barbed wire. That night the ABC network interrupted its feature film, *Judgment at Nuremberg*, on the Nazi war crimes trials, in order to broadcast footage of the assaults.

The march was disrupted, but its broader purpose had been served. Astonishment and anger rolled across the country and into the halls of Congress. Republican senator Jacob Javits of New York appraised law enforcement in Selma as an "exercise in terror," a fair summation of the fifty congressional speeches denouncing the city within two days of the assaults. Legislators were swept forward by a deluge of telegrams and letters, many from people normally conservative, even apolitical. William Proxmire of Wisconsin read to his Senate colleagues a plea from the publisher of the *Chippewa Herald Telegram* to send federal marshals to stop "this bloody disregard of Americans' constitutional rights." "Please understand," the publisher stated, "we and the many citizens who have contacted us, are generally not advocates of this type of intervention, but we see no other recourse."[78]

Lyndon Johnson was among the outraged, and a week after Bloody Sunday he entered the House of Representatives to make his case for a powerful new voting rights law before a joint session of Congress and a watching nation. Johnson began slowly, amid a hush so complete that even the clicks of photographers' cameras sounded clearly in the chamber. He became more animated as he warned the legislators and the public: If America defeated every enemy, doubled its wealth, conquered the stars, and yet failed to resolve this issue, "then we will have failed as a people and as a nation." Selma, he continued at a quickened pace, marked a turning point in American history equal to Lexington and Concord, equal to Appomattox. What happened there was "part of a far larger movement . . . the effort of American Negroes to secure for themselves the full blessings of American life." Then, thumbs raised, fists clenched, radiating determination, Johnson lifted consensus politics to its full moral height: "Their cause must be our cause too. Because it is not just Negroes, but really it is all of us, who must overcome the crippling legacy of bigotry and injustice. And," he concluded with a pledge that brought tears to Martin Luther King, Jr., "we shall overcome."[79]

THE VOTING RIGHTS BILL

On March 21 the protesters safely completed a four-day march from Selma to Montgomery under a federal shield that included marshals, Alabama Guard units federalized by executive order, and helicopters monitoring local residents. Their goal had been accomplished; now attention shifted to the voting rights bill beginning its own, torturous march past the gauntlet of southern legislators. The measure the administration sent to Congress on March 19 authorized the attorney general to send federal examiners to supersede local registrars and regulations wherever discrimination occurred. A provision to trigger federal intervention included counties where fewer than half the adults had voted in the 1964 presidential election and where literacy tests or similar restrictions were then in force. The bill, in short, radically streamlined the Justice Department's efforts in disenfranchisement cases by providing an alternative to the cumbersome machinery of the courts.

Johnson lined up a powerful bipartisan convoy for the bill in the Senate, partly by directing his attorney general to work closely with the Republican minority leader, Everett Dirksen, in drafting the legislation.

Selma had blown up a gust of public support for voting rights and sixty-six senators cosponsored the bill, just one vote shy of the two-thirds needed to end the expected southern filibuster. When Mississippi's James Eastland sought to bury the bill in the Judiciary Committee that he chaired, the majority once again maneuvered around him and brought the bill quickly to the floor.

The only remaining obstacle was the last-ditch filibuster led by the southerners. But the filibuster had failed a year earlier on the Civil Rights Bill, and it would fail here as well. The bill carried too much momentum, a crucial quality that, as Johnson once observed, was "not a mysterious mistress" but "a controllable fact of political life."[80]

On May 21 the cloture vote came, with Everett Dirksen ornately expressing "regrets" that he had to cut off the voices of his distinguished colleagues, "but with some measure of assurance that in the long veil of history, over the transient concerns of this fleeting day, they will find [him] not too far wrong."[81] He then brought strong Republican support behind the motion, and the Senate ended the filibuster by a vote of seventy to thirty. Roy Wilkins, by now a connoisseur of filibusters, found this one "lame" from the first. "In a way," he wrote, "I think the cloture vote saved face for the Southerners. That year they had neither their old energy nor the sympathy of the country behind them."[82]

Opponents of the bill seemed to weather their isolation better in the House of Representatives, where the Virginia Democrat Howard Smith kept the measure imprisoned in his Rules Committee for five weeks. Once remanded to custody of the full House, the bill came under fire for its method of classifying counties as guilty of disenfranchisement. A much weaker Republican substitute was offered and threatened to siphon off needed GOP support. The House debated at some length before rejecting the substitute in favor of the administration proposal.

On August 3, 1965, the House of Representatives passed the voting rights bill 328–74, better than a four-to-one margin. On the following day the Senate followed suit with nearly equal decisiveness, 79–18. For the signing ceremonies on August 6 the president invited the major civil rights leaders and two less heralded pioneers of the movement: Rosa Parks, whose quiet pride had sparked the Montgomery bus boycott in 1955, and Vivian Malone, who had enrolled at the University of Alabama in 1963 after federal marshals escorted her past Governor George Wallace.

The signing ceremony took place in the President's Room, where, on August 6, 1861, Lincoln had signed a law freeing slaves impressed into the Confederate army. "Today," Johnson said of the new, peacetime measure, "is a triumph for freedom as huge as any victory that has ever been won on any battlefield."[83]

Few doubted that the Voting Rights Act would change race relations in the South more radically than at any other time since Reconstruction. Yet despite its far-reaching implications, the legislation enjoyed broader, more sustained public support than any previous civil rights measure. Less than four months elapsed between its formal introduction in Congress and its final passage, barely half the time needed to deliberate over the civil rights bill a year earlier. Unlike many controversial bills that were whittled down in conference, this measure emerged more clearly and strongly worded than in its original draft. And both the House and the Senate gave the bill a mandate that approached unanimity outside the South and included several southern legislators casting their first vote ever for a civil rights bill. Never before had the civil rights movement exercised so commanding or prestigious a position in national politics.

As in the passage of the Civil Rights Act of 1964, legal change found its catalyst in social disorder. The historian David Garrow has argued persuasively that at Selma, Martin Luther King refined to new sophistication the tactic of precipitating racist violence in order to win media coverage and, in turn, public support that could translate into legislation. The spasm of one-sided violence at Selma helped solidify a strong, more quickly formed consensus for civil rights action than had occurred in 1963, when violence in Birmingham involved black rioters as well as rampaging white police.[84] The nation had also traveled far in those two years, becoming more sensitive to the indignities as well as the dangers blacks endured in seeking their rights.

King and his allies in protest also operated in a political climate that continued to breed an astonishing variety of reform programs. Far from standing as an isolated landmark of progressive legislation, the Voting Rights Act joined an extraordinary parade of reform bills entering the law books during this first session of the Eighty-ninth Congress.

The voting rights campaign marked, in short, the convergence of two political forces at their zenith: the black campaign for equality and the movement for liberal reform. The struggle to assure blacks the ballot coincided with the liberal call for expanded federal action to protect the rights of all citizens. At the same time the emphatic rise of the Voting Rights Bill to the top of the liberal agenda attested to the impact of non-violent direct action in dramatizing racism to the nation. Die-hard racists remained to cry "Never!" and "Segregation forever!" even after Selma. But under the insistent prodding of black demonstrators and liberal leaders, most Americans resolved that in the matter of legalized discrimination, it was indeed past time to overcome.

THE RIGHTS REVOLUTIONS

"Since I engaged in the investigation of the rights of the slave," wrote the nineteenth-century abolitionist Angelina Grimké, "I have necessarily been led to a better understanding of my own."[85] Indeed, she declared, reforms naturally "blend with each other, like the colors of the rain bow."[86] Grimké's discovery that the struggle for justice is indivisible would find repeated confirmation in the 1960s, when the example of black protest and federal measures to broaden opportunity encouraged women, Hispanics, American Indians, and other groups to assert their identity, denounce discrimination, and organize for equal rights.

Betty Friedan became the symbol of a resurgent women's rights movement with the publication in 1963 of her book *The Feminine Mystique*, which likened the sterile suburban setting of middle-class women to a "comfortable concentration camp" that confined them to the home, devalued their intellect, and eroded their aspirations and self-respect. The following year two white female activists in SNCC, Casey Hayden and Mary King, deplored the stereotypes that left women second-class citizens in the movement for racial justice. "The assumption of male superiority," they wrote, was "as widespread and deep rooted and every much as crippling to the woman as the assumptions of white supremacy are to the Negro."[87] In 1966 Friedan cofounded the National Organization for

Women (NOW), modeled on the NAACP, which demanded "full participation in the mainstream of American society now."[88]

While feminists assailed federal institutions for lagging enforcement of equal rights, they also drew energy and respectability from liberal initiatives in the government. At the urging of Esther Peterson, a trade unionist and assistant secretary of labor, President Kennedy named Eleanor Roosevelt in December 1961 to chair the nonpartisan Commission on the Status of Women. Responding to pressure from the commission, women's groups, and several unions, Congress passed an Equal Pay Act in June 1963, barring the common practice of paying women less for the same work as men. The commission's report, *American Women,* that October urged changes in state laws that excluded women from jury duty, from owning a business, or from control over their earnings, and recommended paid maternity leaves, child care centers, and equal access to education. To continue the commission's work, Kennedy created a Citizen's Advisory Council and an Interdepartmental Committee on the Status of Women.

"I believe woman's place is not only in the home," Lyndon Johnson said in 1961, "but in the House, and in the Senate and at the conference table."[89] As president, Johnson outdid Kennedy in his support for women's rights by increasing appointments of women in government and by supporting federal promotion of birth control, a commitment that, as late as 1959, Eisenhower had "emphatically" termed "not a proper political" activity.[90] While Johnson favored family planning as a way to reduce poverty rather than as a feminist cause,[91] his initiatives, according to the historian Susan Hartmann, "placed the imprimatur of the federal government on birth control and helped to legitimize reproductive rights as an issue for the burgeoning feminist movement."[92]

The climate of reform that permeated national politics in the 1960s inspired a range of minorities to stake bolder claims to their rights, pursuing what a student manifesto, the Port Huron Statement, in 1962 exalted as "participatory democracy." Hispanics, having organized for John Kennedy in 1960 and received posts in his administration, began to embrace activists like César Chávez, whose leadership of migrant workers in strikes, marches, and boycotts of grape and lettuce growers emulated the nonviolent campaigns of Martin Luther King, Jr. Mario Savio, a philosophy major fresh from the Mississippi Freedom Summer in 1964, helped galvanize student protests against the repression of political activity at Berkeley, saying, "The same rights are at stake in both places—the right to participate as citizens in a democratic society."[93] By decade's end gays and lesbians were emerging from quiescence to insist on "basic rights and equality as citizens, . . . the right as human beings to achieve our full potential and dignity, and the right as citizens to make our maximum contribution to the society in which we live."[94]

Indians, the most desperate minority, with an unemployment rate ten times the national average, the worst poverty and housing, the least access to education, and soaring rates of alcoholism and suicide, experienced the most dramatic shift in public policy and a quickening militancy across tribal lines. The Kennedy administration effectively abolished the Eisenhower administration's "termination" policy, which had withdrawn legal recognition from tribes in a disastrous bid to spur assimilation. Later, the War on Poverty created a special Indian "desk" in the Office of Economic Opportunity and provided Indians with new housing, food assistance, health counseling, rural electrification, and jobs.[95] As Native Americans increasingly staged confrontational rallies and practiced civil disobedience, Congress enacted a civil rights law in 1968 that bolstered constitutional guarantees for Indians on reservations while at the same time increasing tribal autonomy.

The pluralist creed that underlay liberal support for opportunity across all demographic boundaries found its clearest expression in an immigration reform law in 1965 that abolished quotas favoring light-skinned western Europeans over southern and eastern Europeans while nearly barring Africans and Asians. Emanuel Celler, a Jewish congressman from New York City who had denounced the national origins quotas in his maiden speech to the House forty years earlier, led the coalition for reform, while segregationists like James O. Eastland of Mississippi, chairman of the Senate Judiciary Committee, strongly opposed.[96] Karen Narasaki, who later headed the Asian American Justice Center, marveled that the bill sailed to passage despite modest public concern over aspiring immigrants. "It was really a group of political elites" who asked, "Are we going to be true to what we say our values are?"[97]

These egalitarian upheavals continued to reverberate in succeeding decades. The Civil Rights Act of 1964 knocked out the legal underpinnings of racial apartheid and eventually of sexual discrimination. Enforcement varied in intensity from one presidential administration to the next, but most of the time the federal government closely monitored state and local governments, universities, and corporations to curb racial discrimination and sexual inequities. Racial minorities and women often sought enforcement of their newly expanded rights in the federal courts. No other form of litigation expanded so rapidly. In 1960, 200 civil rights lawsuits were filed in the federal courts. By 1980 the number exceeded 25,000. By 2000 there were 40,908 such suits.[98]

The Voting Rights Act had a similarly dramatic effect on the number of registered African American voters. Before the end of the decade, black voter registration had doubled in the South. This contributed to a similar increase in the number of elected African American officeholders, especially in the South. Barely one hundred elected officials in the United States in 1965 were African American. A quarter-century later there were more than seventy-two hundred, of whom more than half were in the South.[99]

White politicians quickly came to grips with the surge of new black voters in their constituencies. Race-baiting largely disappeared as a political tactic. Strom Thurmond, who as governor of South Carolina had led the southern contingent out of the 1948 Democratic convention and then ran for president as a racist Dixiecrat candidate, later was elected to the Senate, switched parties, and fought against the civil rights legislation of the 1960s. But when it passed over his objections, he began to pay close attention to the needs of his black constituents. He was the first member of the South Carolina congressional delegation to hire a black staff member.[100]

Then there was George Wallace. Wallace was the brightest flame of the Old South in the 1960s, calling for "segregation now, segregation tomorrow, segregation forever" in his inaugural address in Alabama in 1963, "standing in the schoolhouse door" in a theatrical attempt to prevent the integration of the state's university in 1963, running for president in 1968 with thinly veiled appeals to racism. Within a decade, however, Wallace, too, worked hard to put his racist past behind him. He apologized to black leaders for his earlier segregationist views, and in his final term as governor, in the 1980s, he appointed a record number of African Americans to state government positions.

Andrew Young, an aide to Martin Luther King and then a beneficiary of the civil rights laws of the 1960s when he was elected to Congress from Georgia and then as mayor of Atlanta, captured the real impact of these laws when he said, "It used to be Southern politics was just 'nigger' politics—a question of which candidate could 'outnigger' the other. Then you registered 10% to 15% in the community, and folks would start saying 'Nigra.' Later you got 35% to 40% registered, and it was amazing how quick they learned how to say 'Nee-grow.' And now that we've got 50%, 60%, 70% of the black votes registered in the South, everybody's proud to be associated with their black brothers and sisters."[101]

Racial discrimination was the primary target of the federal civil rights policies of the 1960s. Those who proposed those policies and those who supported them rarely mentioned elimination of sexual discrimination as a significant goal. The inclusion of language banning sexual discrimination in the Civil Rights Act of 1964 was an accident of politics, not a product of heavy lobbying by women's groups or anyone else. Opponents of the Civil Rights Act of 1964 sought to undermine political support for it by including prohibitions on sexual as well as racial discrimination. The political tactic failed, but it resulted in a sweeping change in American social and economic life.

Women quickly found in Title VII of the Civil Rights Act an invaluable weapon in their efforts to be treated equitably in corporate, educational, and other settings. Some took their complaints about sexual discrimination to the Equal Employment Opportunity Commission created by that act. Others went to court. Soon the rulings began to flow: Women must get the same Social Security benefits as men; ATT, at the time the country's largest private employer, was required to pay millions in compensation to female employees who had been forced into job categories regarded as appropriate for women only and denied entry into job categories limited to men; Morgan Stanley, Wal-Mart, and many other large corporations faced lawsuits from female employees who believed they had been subject to discrimination, that their Title VII rights had been violated.

In other ways, too, the women's movement, still crystallizing in the 1960s, gained momentum during the 1970s with the repeal of abortion laws and the proliferation of women's health clinics, rape crisis centers, feminist publications, and day care centers. Women also won new guarantees from lawmakers in Washington, D.C. In 1972 Congress adopted an Equal Rights Amendment, though it narrowly failed over the next decade to win ratification by three-fourths of the states. Also in 1972 Title IX of the Education Amendments broadened the Civil Rights Act of 1964 to outlaw sexual bias in federally assisted educational programs. Strict enforcement of Title IX transformed higher education by speeding the admission of women to colleges and graduate programs while requiring schools to fund sports teams for women.

For all the gains by women and minorities, their rights revolutions secured no final victories. Bigotry and discrimination, boasting histories as long as the human race, have persisted despite mass movements, literate pleadings, and the discrediting of stereotypes. Yet in the few decades that followed the 1960s more lasting progress was achieved in America in eliminating the effects of racial and sexual bias than in any other similar period or place.

Much contributed to this transformation: first and foremost the remarkable courage of men and women whose protests forced an indifferent public to confront entrenched inequalities. But in giving tangible and lasting expression to the national revolution in attitudes, nothing mattered more than public policy, more than the law. The civil rights laws of the 1960s, slow in coming, long in gestation, created real rights and genuine procedures for protecting and enforcing those rights. And when they did, walls tumbled and glass ceilings cracked.

CHAPTER 5

TO PROTECT
THE PLANET

The trees and hills around Clear Lake were magisterial when Gaylord Nelson was growing up there. The waters of northern Wisconsin, he later remembered, were "deep and pure," the wildlife "mysterious and plentiful."[1]

The timber in that part of the country—200 billion board feet of white pine—was one of the greatest concentrations of wealth in the world.

But then came mechanization and the rapacious demands of growing economies at home and abroad—the twentieth century driving hell-bent through the natural resources of America. "We wiped it out in an eyewink of history and left behind fifty years of heartbreak and economic ruin," Nelson wrote. "Forest fires raged through the slash left behind by the loggers. Crystal clear trout streams silted in. Hundreds of thousands of acres of land became tax delinquent and local units of government faced economic chaos."[2]

The promise of progress, so powerful an attraction to Americans in the early years of the twentieth century, had revealed its dark side. The rapid expansion of industry in the middle decades of the century produced what the economist John Kenneth Galbraith called an affluent society. But to millions of Americans like Gaylord Nelson, forced to confront the by-products of that expansion, it often seemed an effluent society. Assaults on natural habitats and human health accumulated and festered in a public climate that exalted free enterprise and resisted government regimentation. As Americans increasingly demanded clean air, pure water, and scenic vistas as entitlements no less basic than consumer goods, an environmental movement was born.

Like the conservationists who flourished during the early twentieth century, postwar activists demanded that the government regulate economic activity to safeguard national resources. But municipal and state officials alone could not meet the challenge, because pollution, threats to endangered species, and blights on the landscape freely trespassed local and state boundaries. So environmentalists, as they came to be called, looked to Washington for help in restoring the air, water, and land. And there they found an emerging liberal reform movement eager to take up their cause by expanding federal authority in the public interest.

THE WASTE MAKERS

"Obsolescence Can Spell Progress," a federation of business leaders boasted of the frenzy in postwar America to acquire bigger, better, and above all, newer consumer goods. Brooks Stevens, a leading industrial designer, called "planned obsolescence" the key to prosperity: "We make good products, we induce people to buy them, and then next year we deliberately introduce something that will make those products old fashioned, out of date, obsolete." A marketing magazine, *Retailing Daily*, exhorted merchants and advertisers to ask what together they could do for "obsolescence as our contribution to a healthy, growing society."[3]

In an economy powered by the lure of new appliances and the obsolescence of last year's models, waste became the unspoken twin of abundance. The annual toll of discards was steep: 80 million tons of paper products, 100 million tires, 60 billion cans, 30 billion bottles, and millions of cars and major appliances; the total solid waste produced in 1969 alone exceeded 4 billion tons.[4] The standard repository for disposing of all this refuse was the landfill. But that innocuous name could not disguise the harsh reality: These were open pits crawling with rats and vermin, whose stench offended for miles and which often burst into flames and methane explosions.[5]

Almost everywhere, pollution clouded the postwar economic miracle. Affluence rested on expanding manufactures, accelerated use of fuel, thousands of new petrochemicals in industry and agriculture, burgeoning home and automobile ownership, and the bulldozing of forests for suburban housing and malls. All of these depleted resources, generated toxic wastes, and displaced pristine ecosystems. The testing of nuclear weapons, some over American soil, compounded these hazards by releasing carcinogenic radiation into the food chain that was deposited in human organs and bones.

World War II set in motion the advances in technology and the expansion of manufacturing, agriculture, mining, and logging that made possible the long postwar boom, but it also posed severe environmental strains. Pressed to supply vast quantities of arms, transport vehicles, and housing for more than 10 million soldiers, businesses increased the extraction of iron, aluminum, coal, uranium, oil, and timber.[6] After the war, the imperative to avoid lapsing back into depression led government and business leaders to favor continued high levels of production and new markets for cars, airplanes, and rockets, fuels, fertilizers, pesticides, synthetic fabrics, plastics, and nuclear energy.[7]

The Cold War reinforced these developments by expanding the markets for military production and by providing a national security rationale for federal policies to keep industrial production high.[8] Yet the resulting strain on resources also produced early flickers of concern at the highest levels of government about the need to temper economic growth with an ethic of environmental responsibility.

In 1952 a commission named by President Harry Truman and chaired by the head of CBS, William S. Paley, issued a five-volume report on "materials policy" that affirmed "the principle of Growth"[9] but warned of shortages of raw materials because of inefficient production and "Gargantuan—and so far, insatiable" demand.[10] The report, entitled *Resources for Freedom,* observed that although this grim prospect "would never have occurred" to the business titans who brought this nation to "greatness" at the turn of the century, "the United States must now give new and deep consideration to . . . the contents of the earth and its physical environment."[11]

While *Resources for Freedom* focused on issues of national security, it declared pollution the foul evidence of America's wasteful economy. Factories emitted more sulfur as pollution than they used in products, discarded more than a third of the average tree, and wasted enough natural gas annually to supply 11 million homes.[12] The report also criticized a cycle of wasteful production and consumption, keyed to obsolescence and status-driven excess, as in the marketing of large cars, adorned with useless chromium frills, that burned heavily leaded high-octane gasoline.[13]

Conservationists endorsed the commission report and played on its mixture of patriotic and environmental values in asking Americans to recognize limits on resources, recycle raw materials, and curb pollution. The economist Joseph Fisher, president of Resources for the Future, called the "availability of a wide variety of resource materials essential to our defense and security."[14] Fairfield Osborn, the author of *Our Plundered Planet* (1948), claimed that conservation would keep "American life what it is."[15] But the commission's warnings attracted little attention from the "'Iron Triangle' of congressional leaders, government agencies, and local development interests" that extolled unfettered production and consumption to sustain the postwar boom.[16]

In November 1952 Dwight D. Eisenhower pushed environmental concerns further to the political margins by winning the presidency on a platform that called for "restoration of the traditional Republican lands policy" of minimal federal intrusion.[17] Once in office Eisenhower removed posts in environmental agencies from the Civil Service, dismissed conservationists appointed by his Democratic predecessors, and replaced them with party loyalists who eased curbs on resource use in game preserves and wilderness lands. The president underlined his priority on development by opening all national wildlife refuges to gas and oil leasing. The Federal Power Act, amended in 1921 to bar federal licensing of waterpower projects in national parks or monuments, became a dead letter.[18] Even the Soil Conservation Service in the Department of Agriculture shifted focus from preserving the soil to enhancing productivity by developing farms and related water resources.[19]

Conservationists were few, isolated, and weak when, in December 1953, Secretary of the Interior Douglas McKay (recalled in Eisenhower's memoirs as a loyal aide "under criticism from political extremists in the West")[20] approved plans for a dam at Echo Park in the upper Colorado

River basin. The federal government had built hundreds of dams since the 1930s, and the Bureau of Reclamation aggressively lauded such projects for taming nature, building civilization, and bestowing hydroelectric power on grateful residents. But Echo Park was no ordinary site, and McKay's routine gesture at once shook conservationists—and many Americans who had not thought much about nature—from quiescence to anger.

Among the features of Echo Park was a 320-square-mile site called Dinosaur Monument. The prehistoric remains had led President Woodrow Wilson to designate the area a national monument in 1915. But later another unique feature of the park, a deep, narrow gorge, drew hydraulic engineers who proposed to build a dam that would provide hydroelectric power but deluge some sixteen hundred fossils.[21]

The plan to submerge Echo Park in the name of progress further galled conservationists because a surrounding expanse of brilliantly colored canyons, which Franklin Roosevelt had added to the park in 1938, sheltered such endangered birds as the peregrine falcon and the national symbol, the bald eagle. Anthropologist Loren Eisley wrote of the targeted land, "Once in a lifetime, if one is lucky, one so merges with sunlight and air and running water that whole eons, the eons that mountains and deserts know, might pass in a single afternoon without discomfort."[22]

Coordinating the campaign to save Echo Park, David Brower of the Sierra Club tirelessly courted the national media, presaging a key tool of conservationists for reshaping federal policy. Articles on the distinctive features of the park appeared in popular magazines such as *Life*, *Newsweek*, and the *Saturday Evening Post*, as well as in conservation publications.[23] The publicity overwhelmed the normally irresistible Bureau of Reclamation. During House debates, letters flooded congressional offices—Speaker Sam Rayburn said congressmen had received more mail on Echo Park than on any other subject[24]—and opposed the dam by eighty to one. By April 1956, when the bill at last threaded past Congress, it contained a pledge that "no dam or reservoir . . . shall be within any Park or Monument."[25]

Even Sierra Club members understood that their rescue of a single park had few legislative echoes, failing even to slow the ravages to adjoining lands. Yet this, too, energized conservationists by exposing the vulnerability of all federal land in the absence of laws to limit development. Conservationist groups and local residents increasingly coalesced to halt federal projects that, as Samuel P. Hays writes, ignored dangers "to the aesthetic and recreational use of free-flowing streams, to agricultural production, farmsteads, villages, and cemeteries that reservoirs would inundate, and to aquatic life that would be markedly altered."[26] Their insistence that economic growth not displace all other measures of the public good drew growing political support, especially among Democrats seeking new causes and constituencies in an age of mass prosperity.

"THE PROBLEM OF SOCIAL BALANCE"

President Eisenhower's hostility to federal environmental regulations handed Democrats a fertile issue as they looked to regain the White House and strengthen their hold on Congress. The party's liberal wing eagerly accepted it as a way to castigate the Republicans and redefine their identity. Liberalism had thrived in the economic crisis of the 1930s; the challenge to liberals now was to thrive in an age of growing abundance. Environmental concerns would become a potent response to that challenge. Threats to the air, water, and land were clear evidence, they argued, that government vigilance was vital to the public interest. And because pollution observed no state boundaries, the federal government would have to take the lead in crafting environmental protections.

Two Harvard professors active in the Democratic Party during the 1950s promoted conservation as part of a reform program to recharge the stalled liberal engine. Arthur M. Schlesinger, Jr., and John Kenneth Galbraith were among the founders in 1947 of Americans for Democratic Action, a liberal anticommunist pillar of the Democratic Party. Both men wrote speeches for Adlai Stevenson's presidential campaigns in 1952 and 1956, serving as an intellectual brain trust to reach an expanding educated middle class. But as Stevenson, the urbane, eloquent hope of reform Democrats, had twice failed to restore Roosevelt's majority coalition, Schlesinger and Galbraith prodded liberals to move beyond their familiar New Deal moorings.

Schlesinger, a Pulitzer Prize–winning historian at age thirty and the son of a famous scholar who charted cycles of reform and reaction in American history, wrote, voted, and spoke liberal. Schlesinger's *The Age of Jackson* in 1945 and *The Age of Roosevelt,* the three-volume paean to the New Deal published during the 1950s, both related stages in continuing American epic of democratic struggle against forces of wealth and privilege.

The battle lines for liberals might have changed since the Depression, but as Schlesinger wrote in a landmark essay, "The Future of Liberalism," in May 1956, the liberal mission remained to extend rights and opportunities while keeping in view the common good: "Instead of the quantitative liberalism of the 1930s, rightly dedicated to the struggle to secure the economic basis of life, we need now a 'qualitative liberalism' dedicated to bettering the quality of people's lives and opportunities." Schlesinger found both the physical and social environment of Americans urgently in need of reform:

> Our gross national product rises; our shops overflow with gadgets and gimmicks; consumer goods of ever-increasing ingenuity and luxuriance pour out of our ears. But our schools become more crowded and dilapidated, our teachers more weary and underpaid, our playgrounds more crowded, our cities dirtier, our roads more teeming and filthy, our national parks more unkempt, our law enforcement more overworked and inadequate.[27]

Galbraith, an economist who had helped curb inflation as President Roosevelt's deputy director of the Office of Price Administration during World War II, wrote during the 1950s of a contradiction between the overflow of consumer goods and the neglect of public services. Government, he urged, must redress "the problem of social balance." Galbraith's best-selling 1958 book, *The Affluent Society,* tapped anxieties that the postwar consumer's utopia might be a fool's paradise:

> The family which takes its mauve and cerise, air-conditioned, power-steered and power-braked automobile out for a tour passes through cities that are badly paved, made hideous by litter, blighted buildings, billboards, and posts for wires that should long since have been put under-

ground. They pass on into a countryside that has been rendered largely invisible by commercial [billboards]. . . . They picnic on exquisitely packaged food from a portable ice-box by a polluted stream and go on to spend the night at a park which is a menace to public health and morals. Just before dozing off on an air mattress, beneath a nylon tent, amid the stench of decaying refuse, they may reflect vaguely on the curious unevenness of their blessings. Is this, indeed, the American genius?[28]

While the resurgence of interest in conservation tapped misgivings about heedless growth, it paradoxically benefited from the rise in material comforts and ambitions that this growth had made possible. Popular expectations of a better life fed a rising interest in enjoying unspoiled natural vistas. Just as crowded urbanites at the turn of the twentieth century had yearned for a renewed connection with nature, midcentury suburbanites sought relief from rows of interchangeable ranch houses. As disposable income and vacation time increased, interstate highways proliferated, and Americans purchased more and bigger cars, millions flocked to nature trails, camping grounds, parks, and wilderness sites that gave tangible meaning to the value of conserving nature.

Prosperity also sustained an advanced scientific infrastructure able to detect and publicize environmental dangers hidden from the senses. Studies of radioactive fallout filtered from professional journals into popular magazines and newspapers, discrediting assurances by the Atomic Energy Commission that nuclear tests over Utah and Nevada during the 1950s posed no hazard. *Consumer Reports* warned in March 1959 that strontium-90 emitted by nuclear explosions placed children at risk: "The fact is that fresh clean milk, which looks and tastes just as it always did, nevertheless contains . . . an unseen contaminant, a toxic substance known to accumulate in human bone."[29] In September a two-part article on "Fallout: The Silent Killer" in the conservative *Saturday Evening Post* stated that radioactivity would "extort a heavy cost in disease, deformity and early death for many yet unborn."[30]

The environmental costs of modern industrial society were most apparent to Americans living in cities, the prime repositories of waste from factories. Cancer, widely linked with chemicals in the air, was twice as common in the cities as in rural areas.[31] Older industrial cities like New

York released tons of gray smog: particles of ash, soot, and sulfur from the combustion of oil or coal. Residents of sprawling metropolises like Los Angeles, whose 2.3 million cars in 1954 formed the greatest concentration of motor vehicles in the world, inhaled brown smog, caused mainly by exhaust fumes (Angelenos consumed 4.8 million gallons of gasoline a day).[32] Irritating to eyes and respiratory membranes, both kinds of smog could turn lethal whenever layers of warm air trapped the particle-laden air below for days at a time.

A day of trapped fumes in Los Angeles in 1943 known as "Black Monday" foreshadowed the postwar alarm over air pollution, and five years later a fog bearing "the smell of poison," as a resident described it, enveloped the tiny steel town of Donora, in the Monongahela Valley thirty miles southeast of Pittsburgh, causing five thousand cases of illness and twenty deaths during a six-day siege. The fumes emanated from Donora's steel plants, zinc smelter, slag processors, sulfuric acid plant, and wire and rod mills: in short, its whole industrial base.[33] Lesser plagues in succeeding years routinely punished Los Angeles and other cities and towns across the country.

Water quality suffered, too, as rivers, lakes, and reservoirs absorbed a noxious postwar brew of urban sewage, bleaches, detergents, petrochemical and metallurgical wastes, dyes, and radioactive compounds, and such land runoffs as pesticides, fertilizers, and chemicals used on highways to give traction in bad weather.[34] Detergent with phosphates, first marketed in 1948, got clothes "cleaner than clean," as the TV and magazine ads boasted, but resurfaced as foam in household tap water or as suds in distant lakes and sea shores.[35] Every region had its distinctive horror: the massive Arthur Kill "blob" of untreated sewage off Staten Island, New York, the loss of aquatic life in Lake Erie, the health bans on swimming in Boston Harbor and Santa Monica Bay, and other repositories of industrial and human waste.[36]

Even rural, sparsely settled states felt the effects of industrial and urban pollution. In 1957 the incidence of infectious hepatitis soared in eastern Nebraska wherever towns obtained drinking water from the Missouri River. State authorities, aware that waterborne agents could transmit the disease, suspected sewage from upstream communities. In Utah officials believed upstream polluters responsible for outbreaks of polio.[37]

Compounding the stress of modern life was noise pollution stemming from advances in technology that Americans had hailed for bringing comfort and convenience. Engine-driven lawnmowers, car horns blaring in snarled traffic, airports proliferating in number, size, and flight paths all assaulted people's psyches as well as their eardrums. So did the shift during the 1950s from propeller to jet engine planes that speeded air travel but repeatedly disrupted the lives of residents below.

No surprise, then, that cities, the hubs of industry and of auto and air traffic, anchored an environmental rebellion against untrammeled development. Urban residents formed the majority of members in environmental organizations[38] and they enlisted city councils, mayors, physicians, and citizen armies in campaigns to limit pollution and to insist on protection of natural spaces. Less predictably, suburban refugees from city life, though presumably sheltered from the ills afflicting their urban cousins, became equally staunch environmental advocates.

The postwar exodus to leafy streets and ranch homes had promised release from the madding city crowds and factories. Instead, the advancing technology of homebuilding that enabled the overnight appearance of inexpensive suburban developments carried a devil's bargain in blighted landscapes. Before World War II, builders had avoided wetlands and slopes, but with the wartime advent of powerful bulldozers and mass production techniques, builders could erect hundreds of thousands of homes on wetlands, hillsides, and floodplains.[39]

The new bulldozers prepared tracts for construction by flattening all vegetation, leveling rises, and filling or channeling streams and creeks. The historian Adam Rome writes of the mounting toll: "Every year, a territory roughly the size of Rhode Island was bulldozed for urban development. Forests, marshes, creeks, hills, cornfields, and orchards all were destroyed in order to create subdivisions."[40]

While suburban critics of environmental blight were predominantly liberal, their complaints resonated across the political spectrum. A leading opponent of ravaging commercialism was William H. Whyte, Jr., the assistant managing editor of *Fortune* magazine, devoted to free enterprise and powerful entrepreneurs. No friend of grand reform schemes, Whyte had hedged even his best-selling critique of corporate mores, *The Organization Man* (1956), by insisting, "This book is not a plea for non-conformity."[41] But

Whyte could not abide the erosion of nature that shadowed the postwar boom. Pained at seeing his childhood home in the Brandywine Valley of Pennsylvania overrun during the 1950s by monotonous cinderblock houses and fast-food stops, he wrote an elegy for pastoral America in *Life* magazine that conveyed the anxieties of a generation:

> Take a last look. Some summer's morning drive past the golf club on the edge of town, turn off onto a back road and go for a short trip through the open countryside. Look well at the meadows, the wooded draws, the stands of pine, the creeks and streams, and fix them in your memory. If the American standard of living goes up another notch, this is about the last chance you will have.[42]

By the late 1950s the contradictions between mounting environmental hazards and bland denials by industry and the Eisenhower White House sparked challenges by physicians, scientists, and public health officials. Dr. Robert A. Kehoe, director of the Department of Preventive Medicine at the University of Cincinnati, told a conference on "Man Versus Environment" in May 1958, "Reckless man can turn loose and build up physical forces which may destroy himself and his kind." Kehoe expressed cautious optimism that man would yet expend his "ingenuity" in "learning more of his own vulnerability and in developing the means for self-protection."[43]

Even within the Eisenhower administration, public health officials sounded a discordant counterpoint to the president's assurances. Health, Education, and Welfare secretary Arthur Flemming sponsored the first National Conference on Air Pollution in 1958 and endorsed federal regulatory powers.[44] Two years later the president's deputy surgeon general, John D. Porterfield, surveyed the nation's economic miracle with a jaundiced eye. Speaking at the annual meeting of the Air Pollution Control Association in Cincinnati, Ohio, Porterfield cautioned, "Our dazzling technological progress since World War II has yielded a random harvest of mixed blessings, and a bumper crop of new health challenges.[45] His words coincided with a report by the surgeon general that "400–500 totally new chemicals are put into use each year. . . . It is not being over dramatic to suggest that threats from our environment, actual and potential ... under certain circumstances could affect large segments of our population and conceivably threaten the very existence of our Nation."[46]

The election year 1960 witnessed an outpouring of books, articles, and speeches on the national purpose that further publicized environmental problems. Most critics did not look at these problems in isolation, but linked them with challenges of race, poverty, urban decay, limited medical care, and overburdened schools as signs of drift in public policy. "The most important continuing issue of American policy and politics over the next decade," the New York Times reported in March 1960, "will be the issue of public spending—what share of America's total resources should be devoted to public as distinct from private purposes." Echoing Schlesinger and Galbraith, the Times deplored social ills that belied claims of mass prosperity: "Education is underfinanced. Streams are polluted. There remains a shortage of hospital beds. Slums proliferate, and there is a gap in middle-income housing. We could use more and better parks, streets, detention facilities, water supply. The very quality of American life is suffering from these lacks—much more than from any lack of purely private goods and services."[47]

In a Life magazine anthology on "national purpose," Adlai Stevenson, now an elder statesman among liberal Democrats, declared, "The contrast between private opulence and public squalor on most of our panorama is now too obvious to be denied."[48]

While Schlesinger and Galbraith expressly linked environmental protection with liberal values, Vance Packard's popular exposé of planned obsolescence and pollution, The Waste Makers (1960), advocated government vigilance as a matter of nonpartisan common sense. "A person can't go down to the store and order a new park," he wrote. Americans had to stop "the growing sleaziness, dirtiness, and chaos of the nation's great exploding metropolitan areas" and face "the now poorly met challenges of reversing the shrinkage of forest lands, of conservation of the shrinking arable land, and combating the spread of pollution in both air and water.... The central challenge seems to be this: Americans must learn to live with their abundance without being ... damned fools about it."[49]

In 1960 a majority of congressmen voted, many for the first time, against being damned fools about pollution. The Democratic-controlled Senate had passed a $100 million clean water subsidy program in September 1959 over Republican opposition. House Democrats waited five more months, the better to embarrass the administration as elections approached, then enacted an amended form of the bill despite Republican warnings of "a new spending spree."[50] Eisenhower vetoed the bill, explaining, "Water pollution is a uniquely local blight,"[51] but his stand for fiscal prudence and states' rights and responsibilities seemed out of step with growing public concerns—and growing expectations of support and leadership from Washington.

Conservation surfaced only sporadically during the presidential campaign, as Republican vice president Richard Nixon and Democratic senator John Kennedy preferred to vie for credibility as Cold War leaders and as managers of a vast economy that had slowed since 1958. Intent on defending Eisenhower's eight-year record and by extension his own, Nixon ignored environmental hazards and emphasized the continued health and dynamism of the country. But Kennedy declared, "I am not part of an administration which vetoed a bill to clean our rivers from pollution."[52] In August he distilled the emerging environmental ethos in an article for *Life* magazine that warned, "Prosperity is not enough," and cited "polluted air and water, and littered parks and countrysides" among portents of a malaise that vigorous national leadership alone could overcome.[53]

FACING THE "QUIET CRISIS"

It took John Kennedy only a month in the White House to jettison his predecessor's aloof assurance that environmental problems were manageable local issues. On February 23, 1961, the president sent Congress a Special Message on Natural Resources that urged tighter curbs on industry, mining, and ranching in wilderness areas[54] and signaled a new alignment between the White House and majorities in both houses of Congress that favored tougher environmental laws.

Sensitive to the needs of urban voters and assured by his economic team that federal spending would stimulate growth, Kennedy signed with "great pleasure"[55] in July 1961 a Federal Water Pollution Act. Similar to the bill Eisenhower had vetoed, it established federal responsibility for curbing water pollution by offering a $100 million program of grants and loans to build local treatment plants. Extending this principle, Kennedy also endorsed a Clean Air Bill to subsidize construction of municipal sewage plants and to permit HEW to mediate, make recommendations, and, if necessary, sue on behalf of a state or municipality against polluters in another state.

Kennedy may have contributed most to the nascent environmental movement by appointing Stewart L. Udall as secretary of the interior.[56] The scion of a prominent Arizona family, Udall had spent two years as a Mormon missionary before serving as an Air Force gunner during World War II. On returning from the Pacific theater, he became an attorney, served three terms in the House of Representatives, and gained notice as a member of the conservation bloc in the Committee on Interior and Insular Affairs. Politics rather than ecology moved Kennedy to name Udall to a post associated with policy regarding western lands: Udall had prodded Arizona's delegates onto Kennedy's bandwagon at the 1960 Democratic convention. But on joining the cabinet, Udall became a highly visible spokesperson for a new environmental ethic and a relentless leader of an environmental wakening within the government.

Udall drafted Kennedy's conservation bills and touted them as central to the new liberalism that looked to improve the quality of life for all Americans. Udall's book *The Quiet Crisis* (1963), inspired by Galbraith's *The Affluent Society*, lamented "the disorder of our postwar priorities . . . in a land of vanishing beauty, of increasing ugliness, of shrinking open space, and of an overall environment that is diminished daily by pollution and noise and blight."[57]

Udall vowed that the Department of the Interior would shed its western preoccupation with water sites, wilderness areas, and dams and assert a "national image and a national role" that would encompass all aspects of environmental protection. Symbolizing the Interior Department's embrace of the East, President Kennedy signed a bill on August 7, 1961, creating Cape Cod National Park, which he called "a matter of great interest to me," and was the first time the park system had extended to the seashore.[58] In May 1962 the president further stoked environmental awareness by welcoming the chairmen of key committees in Congress, many governors, and conservation leaders to a White House Conference on Conservation. Most delegates publicly concurred that the nation's air and water quality were deteriorating and affirmed the urgency of federal aid and expertise.

Despite Kennedy's new directions, environmental concerns still paled in the public imagination beside questions of foreign affairs, race relations, and the economy. Conservation, espoused by small organizations of limited means, nestled near the bottom of the administration's reform agenda, and only a shock to public opinion was likely to shift its priorities. This finally came in the form of a literary event that reverberated throughout the decade: the publication of Rachel Carson's *Silent Spring* in 1962. Charting the perils of chemical pesticides and the perverse values that encouraged their use, the book awakened Americans to ravages seen and unseen, and stirred President Kennedy and his successors to give voice to the "quiet crisis."

The woman whose prose helped crystallize an environmental movement was born in 1907, at the height of President Theodore Roosevelt's conservation crusade. Young Rachel shared with her parents and younger sister a few cows, horses, and chickens on some sixty-five rural acres in the lower Allegheny Valley of western Pennsylvania. "I was rather a solitary child and spent a great deal of time in woods and beside streams, learning the birds and the insects and flowers," Carson recalled.[59]

Carson trained as a marine biologist, but her credentials proved of little value in the Depression, when private industry and academe reserved scarce jobs for male breadwinners. In 1935 she subsisted as an editor and writer in the U.S. Bureau of Fisheries and Wildlife, scripting "Seven Minute Fish Tales" for a radio show, "Romance Under the Waters." The success of her second book, *The Sea Around Us* (1951), which spent a record eighty-six weeks on the best-seller list, freed her at last to leave government and write full-time. Building a summer cottage in Maine, Carson began to research chemical toxins after the state of Massachusetts sprayed DDT from planes over Duxbury in 1957 and poisoned the bird sanctuary of a friend, Olga Owens Huckins, who described the "agonizing deaths" of several of her birds.[60]

Carson's empathy for victims of environmental recklessness fused with personal urgency as she wrote *Silent Spring* while stricken with breast cancer, to which chemical and radioactive wastes may have contributed. A radical mastectomy in 1960 failed to bring remission. Carson's ordeal reverberated through her portrait of suffering nature. "The chemical war is never won," she wrote, "and all life is caught in its violent crossfire."[61]

Serialized in the *New Yorker* in June 1962 and honored as a Book-of-the-Month Club selection, *Silent Spring* chilled more than a million and a half readers by exposing the hidden toll of DDT as it seeped from the soil and underground streams into the food chain. Such chemicals, Carson warned, "have the power to kill every insect, the 'good' and the 'bad,' to still the song of birds and the leaping of fish in the streams, to coat the leaves with a deadly film, and to linger on in soil—all this though the intended target may be only a few weeds or insects."[62]

Among the sympathetic readers of *Silent Spring* was President Kennedy. In the spring of 1962, even before the book's formal publication, the president authorized his science advisor, Jerome Wiesner, to investigate the effects of DDT. In August Kennedy fielded a reporter's question about possible "long-range side effects" of DDT, saying, "particularly, of course, since Miss Carson's book," the Public Health Service was "examining the matter."[63] The following May a special panel of the president's Science Advisory Committee endorsed Carson's view that the burden of proof properly lay with chemical companies to show that pesticides were safe.

Carson's admirers, including Supreme Court Justice William O. Douglas, Democratic senator Ernest Gruening of Alaska, and children's author E. B. White, hailed her as a latter-day Harriet Beecher Stowe, whose novel *Uncle Tom's Cabin* over a century earlier had sold three hundred thousand copies and inflamed readers against slavery with scenes of mothers torn from their children or fleeing across frozen rivers with babes in their arms. After Carson testified for forty minutes in June 1962 before a jammed Senate hearing room, Gruening predicted that just as Stowe had speeded emancipation, Carson, too, would change history as a prophet of environmental reform. [64]

A further, unspoken connection between Stowe and Carson is that both writers popularized causes others had pioneered. Abolitionists had braved northern as well as southern mobs since the 1830s, while postwar environmentalists had wandered for years in the desert of public indifference. In 1945 the nature writer Edwin Way Teale prophesied, "A spray as indiscriminate as DDT can upset the economy of nature as much as a revolution upsets social economy."[65] But Teale's warning was muffled by celebrations of record harvests and fears of a peacetime recession. By contrast the publication of *Silent Spring* coincided with national confidence in continued prosperity, rising concern with social ills, and openness to increased federal protection of the environment.

Yet timing alone cannot explain the unique impact of Carson's work. In April 1962, a book by Murray Bookchin, *Our Synthetic Environment*, anticipated by six months Carson's portrait of a planet at risk from pollution and warned that the nonselective spraying of fields and forests risked "an ecological 'boomerang.'"[66] "We are now learning," Bookchin wrote, "that the more man works against nature, the more deeply entangled he becomes in the very forces he seeks to master."[67] *Our Synthetic Environment* won plaudits from scientists for pioneering ideas of "social ecology" and bore the imprint of a distinguished publisher, Alfred A. Knopf, yet it sold poorly and soon vanished from stores. Bookchin, a former Young Communist turned libertarian socialist, blamed a corporate conspiracy, but a more immediate handicap was his eclipse by Carson's lyrical prose and her dramatic focus on pesticides that left robins convulsing in agony and slowly poisoned the water, soil, and air.

Unlike Bookchin, whose green values had emerged from a Red background, Carson's mainstream liberal ties made it harder to paint her as a communist, socialist, or other subversive. Carson had supported Kennedy for president in 1960 and, at the urging of Agnes Meyer, who owned the liberal *Washington Post*, served on the Natural Resources Committee of the Democratic Advisory Council and helped draft recommendations for a Bureau of Environmental Health within the U.S. Public Health Service. Four months later she attended the sole meeting of the Women's Committee for New Frontiers at Kennedy's home in Georgetown.[68] Illness limited Carson's involvement in the campaign, but her standing among liberal Democrats and women's groups assured vital support when chemical firms, farm organizations, and the U.S. Department of Agriculture attacked her politics, her credentials, and her state of mind.

In tones that recalled the Red Scare of the fifties, an attorney for the Velsicol Chemical Company of Chicago warned Carson's publisher, Houghton Mifflin, that "sinister influences" behind *Silent Spring* were scheming "to reduce the use of agricultural chemicals in this country and the countries of western Europe, so that our supply of food will be reduced to east-curtain parity."[69] Industry trade groups, pesticide companies, and nutritionists and entomologists, whose research was largely funded by industry, assailed Carson personally and professionally. The National Agricultural Chemicals Association, fearing that *Silent Spring* would hurt sales of pesticides, alarm the public, and prompt demands for federal regulation, alone spent $250,000 to portray Carson as an ignorant, hysterical woman.[70] Carson felt the strain but her controlled, modest demeanor belied charges of female hysteria, and the corporate fusillades seemed merely to confirm the seriousness of her warnings.

Like other successful reformers throughout American history, Carson tapped widely felt grievances in ways that appealed to common sense rather than complicated doctrine. Ordinary citizens may not have suspected the hazards posed by DDT, but they had suffered worsening air and water pollution and heard about radioactive fallout in mother's milk. *Silent Spring* expressed their fears and made plain the connections between industry, technology, and government that had endangered their families and communities.

The touchstones of American tradition—religion, patriotism, and democracy—suffused the pages of *Silent Spring* and blunted charges that the author was a dangerous radical. Carson alluded to the Bible as comfortably as she did public health reports.[71] She enlisted support from the Founding Fathers, explaining, "If the Bill of Rights contains no guarantee that a citizen shall be secure against lethal poisons distributed either by private individuals or by public officials, it is surely only because our forefathers, despite their considerable wisdom and foresight, could conceive of no such problem." And she sounded the tocsin of embattled democracy against the "little tranquilizing pills of half truth" proffered by special interests, asserting the people's right to be heard and, even more basic, to know.[72]

Those who actually read *Silent Spring* (many vehement critics admitted they had not[73]) knew that Carson's prescriptions aligned squarely with mainstream values. She did not oppose capitalism or the profit motive, nor did she demand a ban on pesticides, a fact that might have surprised some supporters. She called rather for researching biological alternatives to pesticides and for tempering their use with an informed recognition of man's dependence on nature.

While her proposals were tempered, Carson sounded a dominant chord in social criticism of the early sixties: uncompromising urgency. During the previous decade such authors as William H. Whyte, Jr., John Kenneth Galbraith, and Vance Packard had won readers and respectability by expressing wistful or ironic disapproval of growing conformity, status anxieties, policy drift, and other shortcomings of the affluent society. But the most potent critics in the turbulent 1960s aimed to shock and outrage Americans into acting against poverty (Harrington's *The Other America*, 1962), racism (Baldwin's *The Fire Next Time*, 1963), prejudice toward women (Friedan's *The Feminine Mystique*, 1963), and violations of consumer rights (Ralph Nader's *Unsafe at Any Speed*, 1966). Carson posed the ultimate stakes: planetary survival. America's "nonselective" chemical poisons "should not be called 'insecticides,' she wrote, "but 'biocides.'"[74]

Silent Spring did more than energize the environmental movement; it fostered new ways of thinking among conservationists themselves. The early movement had divided, often bitterly, between proponents of efficient resource use and preservationists like John Muir who revered nature as a higher good and a balm for the soul. These tensions between conservationists continued into the postwar era, but *Silent Spring* transcended them by showing that respect for nature had a practical value greater than any economic interest.

The conditions for a new perspective on the environment had been in place for years: worsening air and water pollution, nuclear fallout, chemical wastes, additives, and pesticides, fumes from congested auto traffic, and destruction of habitats through population growth. Scattered communities had addressed one or another problem as it became critical, and at times a flagrant offense like the plan to flood Dinosaur Monument could arouse national fervor around a single issue. It remained for Rachel Carson to dramatize in a systematic way that industry and technology had attained unprecedented destructive force. Poetry and science, passion and politics fused in *Silent Spring* to imbue the vision of John Muir with a tough-minded aura suited to the mind-set of 1960s liberals.

BATTLE OF THE WILDERNESS

Books alone could not stave off the environmental afflictions of the time. That was a role for government. And in the 1960s governments at all levels began to heed the calls for environmental protection. Lyndon Johnson, who often invoked Rachel Carson's warnings about imperiled nature, built ambitiously on Kennedy's conservation policies. As with issues of race, poverty, education, and health care, Johnson sought to expand federal responsibility for planning, funding, and enforcing environmental standards. In just over five years he secured from Congress over three hundred laws to protect nature[75] and restore "the total relation between man and the world around him."[76]

Johnson's attachment to the land was rooted in his youth on a ranch in central Texas and reinforced by his rise in politics during the 1930s as an administrator of New Deal conservation projects. Over the next two decades Johnson muted his environmental impulses as a matter of political survival. In 1948 he told the Senate's twenty-year-old principal page, Bobby Baker, that he simply could not defy the oilmen who "hold the whip hand" in Texas. "I got elected by just eighty-seven votes and I ran against a caveman. . . . [T]he New Deal spirit's gone from Texas and I'm limited in what I can do."[77] But just as Johnson sloughed off segregationist pressures and showed unsuspected fervor for black rights on becoming president, so, too, he seized the bully pulpit in the White House to proclaim the rights of nature against the ravages of heedless growth.

Stewart Udall, who had fused liberal and environmentalist convictions as Kennedy's secretary of the interior, remained in Johnson's cabinet to draft legislation and press new ideas on the President. Udall recalled that he "played the comparison" with Johnson's idol, Franklin Roosevelt, "by . . . talking about [how] this is the third wave of the conservation movement" in the tradition of Teddy Roosevelt and FDR.[78]

Perhaps, Udall hoped, the third, Johnsonian wave would change the way Americans looked at the land, from seeing only a source of profit "and therefore let her rip" to "evolving new attitudes" about the effects of mining and other economic activity "on streams, on the air." [79] As Udall summed up the new breed of conservationists in government, "We were sort of the defense attorney for the environment." [80]

Wilderness protection, a goal that echoed from the Progressive era and the New Deal, found expression in two laws that Congress passed in September 1964. The Land and Water Conservation Act created a fund to speed federal and state purchases of choice sites for new parks before private realtors carved them into suburban lots. A complementary statute, the Wilderness Act, set strict rules for preserving "primitive" federal lands. Both laws reflected the liberal ideal of federal action to improve the quality of life, and Johnson emphatically pressed them on the Congress.

In 1956, with the outcry over proposals to flood Echo Park still a potent memory, Senator Hubert Humphrey and Republican representative John Saylor of Pennsylvania introduced a bill to tighten standards for federal administration of wilderness lands. Although the bill succumbed to western resistance to "locking up" the land (a mining spokesmen said, "Certainly the Soviet Union, the enemy of the free world, would be delighted with the passage of such legislation" [81]), Congress formed a commission to "inventory and evaluate the outdoor recreation resources and opportunities . . . required by present and future generations." To chair the fifteen-member body, President Eisenhower named Laurance Rockefeller, head of the Rockefeller Brothers Fund and a longtime benefactor of conservation groups.

Since the nation's founding, the federal government had commissioned surveys of natural resources to hasten their exploitation by private interests. During the postwar era federal surveys continued to guide public policy, but increasingly they gave bipartisan sanction to protecting areas of natural beauty as a scarce resource. The Rockefeller Commission, exemplifying this shift in purpose, achieved what conservation groups had only dreamed of doing: It placed the cause of wilderness protection at the center of public policy concerns. The commission issued twenty-seven specialized reports over three years and submitted a conservation plan to

President Kennedy on January 31, 1962, that recommended creation of a wilderness system. In the tradition of mainstream conservation popularized by Theodore Roosevelt, the report claimed both an environmental and an economic mandate: "Outdoor recreation is a major land use involving a quarter of a billion acres of public land and perhaps as much private land.... It is a $20 billion-a-year industry with an annual government investment of an additional $1 billion."[82]

Ninety percent of the American people, the report observed, participated in outdoor recreation, posing intolerable strains on Yosemite and Yellowstone national parks as well as weekend facilities near large centers of population. The commission predicted a tripling of demand by the year 2000. Unless the federal government quickly coordinated federal, state, local, and private efforts, "important segments of our parks, forests and waters are in danger of being smothered by the using public."[83]

As an instrument of federal action, the commission endorsed the creation of a fund to acquire "the land and water areas best suited to outdoor recreation" before they were soon lost to "urban growth, commercial development, [and] highway construction."[84] The House Committee on Interior and Insular Affairs favorably reported the bill, citing "the support of virtually all conservationist groups and 46 state governors"[85] for replenishing the nation's vanishing refuges from the madding press of modern life.

The compromises that underlay passage of the Land and Water Conservation Fund Act advanced Udall's goal to give the cause of conservation a national rather than a western image and outlook. A Senate amendment "stipulated that at least 85 percent of the lands acquired" with federal funds "for additions to the National Forest System would be in the eastern part of the United States." A second amendment restored sectional harmony by permitting use of federal funds to develop recreational facilities on existing federal lands, most of them in the West.[86]

The Rockefeller Commission report also endorsed the idea of a Wilderness System that Humphrey and others had proposed in 1956 and that President Kennedy had revived early in his presidency.[87] Drafted by Howard Zahniser of the Wilderness Society, the bill drew a line in the forest "to assure that an increasing population, accompanied by expanding settlement and growing mechanization, does not occupy and modify all" lands, leaving none "designated for preservation and protection in their natural condition. . . ." With poetic language rare in the annals of Congress, Zahniser defined wilderness as "an area where the earth and its community of life are untrammeled by man, where man himself is a visitor who does not remain," "an area of undeveloped Federal land retaining its primeval character . . . with the imprint of man's work substantially unnoticeable," and "outstanding opportunities for solitude." The national interest required Congress "to secure for the American people of present and future generations the benefits of an enduring resource of wilderness."[88]

The Wilderness Bill won praise from conservationists, organized labor, the General Federation of Women's Clubs,[89] and large majorities in both houses of Congress eager to aid tourism and aware that 50 million Americans in 1964 were self-described wildlife watchers.[90] But the prospect of federal curbs on economic activity unleashed objections by lumber, livestock, mining, and oil and gas companies, the Chamber of Commerce, and the National Association of Manufacturers.[91]

Opponents found a champion in Representative Wayne Aspinall of Colorado, chairman of the Committee for Interior and Insular Affairs and unofficial leader of the western bloc of congressmen. Aspinall bristled at federal restrictions on local industry. Believing that Colorado and other western states must expand their economies or perish, he sized up wilderness areas as "mausoleum-like museums in which people can go to see resources that cannot be utilized."[92]

But other westerners were beginning to see a new light on conservation matters. Clinton P. Anderson of New Mexico, the new chair of the Senate Interior Committee, introduced a Wilderness Bill at the urging of conservation groups and Secretary of the Interior Udall. Anderson had earlier kept a safe distance from preservationist causes, but now, while claiming the revised Wilderness Bill would respect western economic concerns, he added, "The public has grown sufficiently alert to the need for preservation of primitive areas."[93]

Another western liberal who risked his political future to back the Wilderness Bill was Frank Church of Idaho. Church's journey was more perilous than Anderson's because, having entered the Senate only in 1957, he lacked the stature to mollify voters in a state dependent on mining, logging, and irrigation. Yet Church accepted the floor leadership of the bill that Anderson pressed on him despite fearing that that he had "thrown a shovel of dirt on his political grave every time he spoke for the bill."[94]

Though it took several years to lay the foundation of political support, the Wilderness Bill sailed through Congress in 1964 by votes of 73–12 in the Senate and 371–1 in the House. It set aside four areas totaling nine million acres in a Wilderness System and allocated 50 million more acres for review for possible inclusion over the next decade. Designated lands were to be "safeguarded permanently, subject to existing rights, against cutting of timber, livestock grazing, construction of buildings and permanent roads and mining."[95]

Some scholars have portrayed the Wilderness Act as a triumph of tourist-related enterprises over manufacturing, logging, and other interests. Influential conservationists since the Progressive era had, after all, promoted economic growth through rational management of resources, and in the postwar years outdoor recreation had become a $20 billion a year business. Yet on closer inspection, the particulars of the Wilderness Bill more nearly reflected the discomfort of liberals with enshrining growth as an absolute good than a desire to spur industry or sustain long-term profits.

Far from serving the tourist industry, the bill forbade construction of hotels, lodges, sports fields, bathhouses, permanent roads, golf courses, tennis courts, ski runs, beach houses, docks, and similar facilities. The only recreation permitted in the Wilderness System entailed minimal equipment and material comforts, such as hiking, camping, picnicking, and hunting and fishing where allowed by state law.

The bill's draconian rules for tourists suggest that its passage hinged less on advocacy by rising economic interests than on a consensus across geographical and party lines that an affluent society could afford concessions to scenic beauty. "Only a small portion of the nation's total land (at best, about 60 million acres of the 2.3 billion acres in the continental United States and Alaska), would be eligible for inclusion," defenders of the bill emphasized.[96] The nation could safely exclude millions of acres from development because vast reserves remained for miners, manufacturers, farmers, and ranchers to add to America's matchless productivity.[97]

Wilderness preservation launched President Johnson's larger program to safeguard natural beauty through federal action. On February 8, 1965, Johnson sent a special message to Congress calling for "a new conservation" to ensure that "our planning, our programs, our building, and our growth" bore "a conscious and active concern for the values of beauty." Among his proposals were measures for highway beautification, clean air and water legislation, and, to educate the public and government officials, a White House Conference on Natural Beauty in May 1965.[98]

Johnson's cause was very much a family affair. The president's wife, Lady Bird, advocated "beautification" within the administration and in speeches that reflected a love of the land rooted in childhood memories. "When I was a little girl," she recalled, "I grew up listening to the wind in the pine trees of the east Texas woods" and drawing comfort from the still mysteries of Caddo Lake.[99]

Promoting beauty was a role expected of First Ladies. Jacqueline Kennedy's elegance and patronage of the arts had set a daunting standard, and Lady Bird forged her own niche by linking beauty with America's scenic heritage and becoming the nation's best-known conservationist. Lady Bird's signature campaign, "highway beautification," evolved through years of travel between Texas and Washington as the wife of an up-and-coming politician. The postwar spread of roadside billboards obscured natural vistas and impelled her, as First Lady, to call for federal limits on such intrusive advertising. "Great roads not only get you from 'here' to 'there,'" she explained in a speech to the American Roadbuilders Association, "they afford a revelation of America's great beauty along the way."

To mobilize liberals in the Congress, Lady Bird coaxed Walter Reuther of the United Auto Workers to enlist organized labor and civil rights groups to push for highway beauty. She also made her presence felt in the White House; after winning election in November 1964, Johnson called Secretary of Commerce Luther Hodges to alert him: "Lady Bird wants to know what you are going to do about all those junkyards along the highways."[100]

The president broke with the Outdoor Advertising Council in backing a bill that required junkyards to be cleaned up or screened, regulated billboards along interstate highways, and denied federal funds to states that failed to comply.[101] Despite conservative sniping at "Lady Bird's bill," Congress passed the Highway Beautification Act by large majorities in both houses in October 1965.

A hallmark of postwar liberalism was to treat diverse social problems as interlocking, and Lady Bird absorbed this ethic in seeking to renew nature in the urban slums. After conferring with Laurance Rockefeller, whom the president had named to chair a Natural Beauty Conference in 1965, she wrote in her diary, "[It was] like picking up a tangled skein of wool—all the threads are interwoven—recreation and pollution and mental health, and the crime rate, and rapid transit, and highway beautification, and the war on poverty, and parks—national, state, and local."[102]

The spread of ghetto slums mocked Lady Bird's vision of a healthful and scenic Washington, D.C., and provoked her to launch campaigns like Project Pride in which dropouts and high-school students led residents in catching rats, removing debris, garbage, and abandoned cars, creating "play space" in housing projects, cutting nature trails in parks, and planting flowers. While cynics scoffed at such modest remedies to the ghetto's ills, Walter Washington, an African American cosponsor of a school area cleanup that brought three hundred thousand dollars in donations for a new recreation center, thought Lady Bird had done better than her critics knew, applying federal, philanthropic, and community efforts on a growing scale.[103]

Lady Bird's attention to the urban east mirrored a central postwar trend in conservation. During the 1960s, the Geological Survey, the Soil Conservation Service, and the Fish and Wildlife Service, all federal bureaus that had long cared about wildlands and rural areas, emphasized the risks of unchecked suburban growth.[104] Secretary Udall, whose Interior Department had long treated conservation as a fiefdom of the rural West, described the changing stakes in an industrialized society that generated ever deadlier poisons: "We were just increasingly driven [to see] that the big battle . . . was in and on the edge of the urban areas and that if we pretended by saving a few national parks or saving some wilderness, that we were saving the environment of this country, that we were kidding ourselves."[105]

THE CAMPAIGN FOR CLEAN AIR AND WATER

The First Lady's defense of nature resonated with the women who formed the vanguard of a nascent environmental movement. They lived mainly in the suburbs, reflecting their awareness that suburbia, in the words of historian Adam Rome, was "the most rapidly changing environment in the nation."[106] Women saw threats to their suburban environments as challenges to their role as domestic guardians.[107]

Traditional images of women as defenders of hearth and home helped female activists in cities and suburbs win respect as protectors of the land, water, and air. In 1964 a young housewife in New York City named Hazel Henderson, an English expatriate, recruited over twenty thousand members for her group, Citizens for Clean Air, by handing out leaflets to mothers in Central Park while strolling her infant daughter. Deflecting questions of ideology with disarming modesty, Henderson, like many female reformers in the early 1960s, portrayed her efforts simply as motherhood in action.[108]

Liberals increasingly sought to give local environmental campaigns national direction, funding, and when needed, enforcement. Their efforts to secure federal regulation of air and water quality coalesced around Edmund Muskie. The lanky Maine senator left his brand even on the master of legislative prodding, Lyndon Johnson, who remarked on signing an air quality bill, "Senator Muskie has been shoving me as no other person has, all these years, to do something in the pollution field."[109]

The lives of many icons of conservation, from John Muir to Rachel Carson, were linked by an early transforming experience of pure lakes, pristine mountains, and majestic forests. Edmund Muskie was an exception. Though he grew up in a thinly populated state known for its forests, lakes, and streams, his keenest memory was of "public concern and indignation" over the ruin by the timber industry of "our river," the Androscoggin. That river, he wrote, "begins its run to the ocean in the high, clear mountain streams in the northwestern corner of Maine" but ends by "picking up pulp and paper wastes in Berlin, New Hampshire, Rumford and Livermore Falls-Jay, Maine."[110]

Inspired by Franklin Roosevelt's ventures in conservation and economic reform, Muskie made environmental protection central to his political ascent in Republican Maine. His zeal drew support in a state that depended on clean water and air for its tourist industry and where an "Action Club" had formed in 1941 near the capital, Augusta, to combat pollution from paper mills. As governor during the mid-1950s, Muskie became known for his success in cleaning up Maine's streams. As a junior senator on the Public Works Committee, he deferred to Robert Kerr of Oklahoma, the chairman whose indirection on water pollution bills at times seemed reminiscent of Maine's crabs. But after Kerr died on New Year's Day, 1963, Muskie came fully into his own as the Senate's "Mr. Clean."[111]

On January 31, 1963, Muskie introduced a bill drafted by aides for the U.S. Conference of Mayors and HEW that aimed to prevent, not merely treat, pollution from industrial wastes and municipal sewage.[112] If a state failed to set satisfactory standards for all interstate waterways, HEW would. Muskie's bill passed the Senate in October by sixty-nine to eleven, gaining a solid majority of Republicans as well as Democrats. But lobbies for industry defanged the bill in the House, and the Rules Committee stalled for more than a year and then denied a rule, killing the bill before it could reach the House floor.[113]

In January 1965 Muskie's Subcommittee on Water and Air Pollution resumed its Sisyphean task of rolling the Water Quality bill back up Capitol Hill. Delegates from environmental groups, the League of Women Voters, and the National Council of Mayors came to the Senate hearings to endorse the Maine senator's reforms and call for still tougher standards.[114] In February, the president hurried after liberals in the Congress by declaring water pollution control central to his agenda. "Every major river is now polluted," Johnson said in urging passage of Muskie's national remedy.

In April the Senate voted 68–8 for Muskie's Water Quality Bill, but a phalanx of commercial interests and states' rights conservatives again waylaid the bill in the House. Because the 1964 elections had given the

House a more liberal cast, businessmen did not object outright to legal standards for water quality but argued that "'primary responsibility' for pollution control" belonged with the states and that tax revenues should lessen "the financial burden placed on industry of solving the pollution problem."[115] A spokesman for chemical firms urged flexible standards for water quality keyed to location, population, and concentration of industry rather than a uniform federal code.[116]

In April 1965 the House passed a shell of the Senate bill that would let HEW "recommend" but not set water standards. Protocol and expediency now pointed to a House-Senate conference to ready the bill for a final vote. But Muskie viewed the House bill as a betrayal, and he refused for several weeks even to request a conference rather than sacrifice the principle of federal enforcement.[117] Liberals, so often unnerved and outbluffed by delaying tactics, this time camped uneasily at the brink beside the stubborn six-foot, four-inch figure of Edmund Sixtus Muskie.

With the two versions deadlocked, the Water Quality Bill languished in a House-Senate conference for nearly four months. Muskie's ally in the House, John Blatnik, recalled that it took a presidential "nudge in the ribs . . . about as hard as you'd get from a hockey player" to prompt House and Senate leaders to resume their talks.[118] But in September 1965 Muskie salvaged a compromise that made the federal government a regulator of last resort. The final bill offered states an initial opportunity to set standards for interstate waterways, but if a state failed to act or to win federal approval of its guidelines by mid-1967, HEW could step in.[119]

On signing the act, which heralded a "national policy for the prevention, control and abatement of water pollution," President Johnson lamented that the "clean and sweet and pure" Potomac River of George Washington's day had become clogged with "decaying sewage and rotten algae." Promising to "reopen the Potomac for swimming by 1975," he added, in a Johnsonian flourish of faith and will, "water pollution is doomed in this century."[120]

Liberals in the 1960s inclined to attack social problems along a broad front, and Johnson's unconditional war on water pollution fit the mold. The Water Quality Act was one of three major laws (and a dozen lesser ones) passed in 1965 to assure a growing population and economy an adequate supply of clean water.[121] In November 1966, as the costs of local antipollution efforts spiraled, Congress provided nearly $4 billion over five years to subsidize compliance and offered financial incentives for states to set purity standards on intrastate waters.[122]

Curbs on water pollution coincided with the passage of laws to reverse the poisoning of the air. Liberals again led in pressing national remedies and drew support from moderates in both major parties, spurred by recognition of a health emergency. Once again, Kennedy established the principle of federal assistance in controlling pollution, and Johnson augmented it with a far-reaching legislative program.

Kennedy's early hopes for a clean air act faded before a two-year campaign of resistance by states' rights advocates, industries vulnerable to regulation, and budget-conscious conservatives. But just as Congress would pass civil rights laws in the wake of racial violence, an environmental disaster broke the logjam in Capitol Hill. Arthur Flemming, who had served in Eisenhower's cabinet, was presiding in December 1962 at a National Conference on Air Pollution in Washington, D.C., when word came that a wave of smog in London had killed over one hundred people. Flemming admonished the horrified participants, "Those who put selfish economic interests ahead of the health of our nation" must yield to the necessity of federal air quality standards. The American Medical Association wired agreement that the federal government must limit air pollution "in the manner of the successfully implemented Water Pollution Act."[123]

Until the London tragedy Kennedy had wavered over whether to press for federal enforcement powers in drafting a Clean Air Bill or to settle for granting subsidies to local communities. But the assistant secretary of HEW, Wilbur J. Cohen, secured Kennedy's support for a bold approach by appealing to his identity as a liberal reformer. According to James L. Sundquist, Cohen argued that the president "could not well stand to the right of Republican Flemming and the American Medical Association."[124]

A year after the smog wave in London, Lyndon Johnson signed the Clean Air Act, which allotted $95 million for study and cleanup efforts at the local, state, and federal level, and enlarged federal involvement, though not authority, in combating air pollution. The act set emissions standards for stationary sources such as power plants and steel mills but omitted deadlines for compliance and ignored the main source of pollutants, motor vehicles. It further directed HEW to identify harmful pollutant levels but relied on states to regulate these toxins, coaxing them with federal grants that paid two-thirds of the costs of starting up air pollution programs.[125]

Studies of pollution by Congress, executive agencies, and private organizations generated their own momentum for further and tougher legislation.[126] Recurring bouts of choking pollution and urban alerts against stepping outdoors on "bad" air days underlined the urgency. On the Thanksgiving holiday in 1966, a four-day wave of pollution killed over 150 New Yorkers. A report to Mayor John Lindsay credited the prevailing wind with having "spared the City an unspeakable tragedy." Had New York experienced the stagnant smog common to Los Angeles, "everyone in this city would long since have perished from the poisons in the air."[127]

On January 30, 1967, Johnson sent a special message to Congress, "Protecting Our National Heritage," that called for a strong Air Quality Bill to tighten regulations on all toxins, streamline enforcement, and increase funding of pollution programs. The next day, Muskie introduced the administration's bill in the Senate. The Department of Health, Education, and Welfare further stoked public fears by releasing on March 22, 1967, a report on "Air Quality Criteria for Sulphur Oxides," the first in a series of studies on all major air pollutants. Prepared under provisions of the Clean Air Act of 1963, the report found all major U.S. cities exposed to hazardous levels of sulphur dioxide, a by-product of burning coal or fuel oil.

In the absence of a mass environmental movement, liberals still lacked the strength to authorize the federal government to set advance limits on specific pollutants. Senator Joseph S. Clark from Pennsylvania called the power to formulate "mandatory federal emission standards" to control industrial pollution "the guts of the bill," and he implored his colleagues not to "water down" this provision.[128] But even Muskie's own Senate Public Works Committee yielded to concerted resistance by business groups and struck the offending clause in reporting the bill on July 15. Three days later the Senate passed the bill by an 88–0 vote, and on November 2 the House concurred by 362–0.

Belying conservative fears of a federal juggernaut rolling over hallowed local jurisdictions, the Air Quality Act, like earlier air pollution measures, invigorated local rule in concert with national aims. The immediate tangible impact of these laws came from the funding of state and municipal pollution programs. Congress had begun such subsidies in 1955 (a token $186,000) and cautiously raised them in 1959 ($4.4 million). Federal contributions soared, however, to $107 million by 1969. The stepped-up infusions of funds encouraged financially strained communities to invest in pollution control. As recently as 1961 only 17 states had agencies dealing with air pollution, but by 1967 more than 150 separate authorities were operating, including 34 state agencies."[129]

Johnson declared on signing the Air Quality Act that Americans must do still more to keep their air from becoming a hellish miasma. Referring to the 130 million tons of poison Americans released into the air each year, Johnson read a "weather report" to Congress. "'Dirty water and black snow pour from the dismal air to . . . the putrid slush that waits for them below,'" he intoned. "Now that is not a description of Boston, Chicago, New York, or even Washington, D.C. It is from Dante's 'Inferno.' . . . But doesn't it sound familiar?"[130]

THE ENVIRONMENTAL REVOLUTION WITHIN GOVERNMENT

In prying open a floodgate of environmental laws, Lyndon Johnson benefited from the reapportionment of electoral districts that belatedly recognized the metropolitan surge in population. According to environmental historian Richard N.L. Andrews, "Rural representatives typically viewed pro-environment legislation either as a costly new tax burden to serve other constituencies (as with urban sewers, for instance), or as an imposition of urban recreational or aesthetic preferences" over the economic interests of farmers, loggers, miners, and ranchers.

The most consistent support in the House of Representatives for environmental laws came from cities and suburbs: "The Boston-Washington corridor alone produced one-third of such votes, and the rest came predominantly from urban areas throughout the country." The environmental concerns of metropolitan centers cut across regions, parties, and ideologies, "although a higher proportion of Democratic than Republican and of 'liberal' than 'conservative' representatives favored pro-environmentalist positions."[131]

Some historians have attributed the laws regulating pollution to the very industries affected by regulation. It is true that, as in the Progressive era, corporations did not align uniformly against federal controls. Thomas J. Watson, Jr., of IBM wrote to Johnson of his dismay, during frequent air travel, on finding whole cities enveloped by contaminated air, and he urged federal action.[132] Other executives simply preferred uniform and moderate federal standards to the haphazard and potentially punitive edicts of fifty state legislatures and countless municipalities.[133] By endorsing bills after discreetly diluting them, industrialists hoped to prevent states and cities from emulating or exceeding the stringent curbs enacted by California, Pennsylvania, New York City, Los Angeles, and other vanguards of reform.[134]

The limited corporate enthusiasm for federal regulation was evident in the frequent attempts to discredit environmental spokesmen and their concerns. The frenzied reaction by chemical companies to Rachel Carson's warnings about pesticides set the mold for coal, oil, and other producers, who seemed, at times, to view knowledge as the deadliest pollutant.[135]

Lyndon Johnson, having served oil interests as a congressman, understood that corporations were the main impediments to environmental reform. As president he courted them and often deferred to their power in Congress, but he also prodded and even shamed them into accepting meaningful regulations. In preparing a speech at the signing ceremony for the Water Quality Act in 1965, Johnson told an aide, "Find out which industries are the guiltiest. I want the stockholders to know what their companies are doing to our environment." The staffer obtained from HEW "a list of the most noxious materials being poured into our water and of the industries that were responsible," and Johnson recited it to stir the public against corporate greed and misconduct.[136]

In contrast to corporate efforts to weaken environmental laws, venerable conservation groups like the Sierra Club and the Wilderness Society eagerly backed Johnson's reforms. These organizations burgeoned during the 1960s, and it is tempting to see in their revival the key to passage of so many landmark laws. Yet this conclusion, though intuitively attractive, exaggerates their impact. Just as the Poor People's March on Washington in 1968 followed rather than launched the War on Poverty, conservationists rose on a tide of Great Society legislation.

Until late in the decade, environmental issues other than nuclear fallout and the spraying of DDT failed to register in Gallup or Harris polls among the most pressing public concerns. Not until 1970 did the inaugural Earth Day rallies crystallize a sustained mass movement for the environment. By contrast, conservationist groups during Johnson's presidency remained low on members and funds. The most prestigious organizations counted far fewer members and resources than the NAACP, and— without thousands of protesters to amplify their campaigns with marches, boycotts, and civil disobedience—far less clout on Capitol Hill.[137]

The evidence instead suggests that Congress outpaced public demands for federal protection of the environment throughout the 1960s and, in concert with the Kennedy and Johnson administrations, helped educate the public and generate a mass movement. They acted on signs of looming ecological catastrophe, reinforced by reports originating on Capitol Hill or in the White House that augured lethal pollution, shortages of clean water, and assaults on nature by economic development.

The role of the federal government in documenting and dramatizing the threats to nature was essential to marshaling support for the Great Society's environmental reforms. When Edmund Muskie pressed for curbs on water pollution, he cited studies that his own Senate subcommittee had commissioned. Calculations of how reductions in pollution could maximize recycling of scarce water supplies did not readily lend themselves to popular understanding, let alone fervor. But to a critical mass of federal lawmakers, these problems were real, urgent, and susceptible to government intervention. This included an expanded federal presence in the economy and in state and local affairs, a goal that liberals championed as desirable and that others in Congress increasingly viewed as inevitable.

The wave of Great Society reforms did more than validate the goals of conservation groups; it helped redirect their efforts along lines urged by Rachel Carson and other critics of industrial and technological excess.

Goals long central to conservationists, such as respect for nature and intelligent use of limited resources, still garnered support from liberals. Yet complementing and to some degree superseding these aims, reformers now spoke of saving human beings by limiting chemical pollution, radiation, destruction of natural habitat, and other pathologies of modernization.

The shift toward a conservation movement that protected people as well as flora and fauna came more easily because liberals in the 1960s seldom distinguished sharply between natural and social landscapes. They believed the quality of American life depended on both natural and man-made environments that shaped each other. When Walter Reuther, head of a presidential task force on urban problems, proposed a Model Cities program in 1966,[138] he invoked Franklin Roosevelt's vision of saving the Tennessee River Valley from flooding and ruin. Just as the Tennessee Valley Authority had become "a worldwide symbol to combat erosion of the land," Reuther wrote to Johnson, a new presidential agency might "stop erosion of life in urban centers among the lower and middle income population."[139] Senator J. William Fulbright similarly urged passage of the bill "to arrest the human and environmental decay that blights the cities of America."[140]

Traditional conservation groups adapted, sometimes painfully, to the environmental agenda forged by government and favored by an emerging grass-roots constituency. In 1969 a poll by the National Wildlife Federation revealed that Americans were most interested in environmental issues related to air and water pollution and pesticides, least in open spaces and wildlife. "Today, concern over such amenities seems to some almost frivolous," a Sierra Club member wrote, "since we realize, as only a decade ago we did not, that there are more desperate threats and problems."

In October 1965 Johnson summed up the stakes on signing the Clean Air Act Amendments and a Solid Waste Disposal Act. "Since the beginning of the industrial revolution," he admonished, Americans had been "systematically polluting" the environment. "We have now reached the point where our factories and our automobiles, our furnaces and our municipal dumps are spewing more than 150 million tons of pollutants annually into the air that we breathe—almost one-half million tons a day. . . ." But the hour of reckoning was at hand, and with it a summons to change:

> When future historians write of this era, I believe they will note that ours was the generation that finally faced up to the accumulated problems of our American life. . . . Rachel Carson once wrote: "In biological history, no organism has survived long if its environment became in some way unfit for it. But no organism before man has deliberately polluted its own environment." . . . [T]his morning I join you in saying that together we intend to rewrite that chapter of history.[141]

Liberals in the 1960s powered this transformation of Americans' mind-set about their physical environment. If it was a revolution—and many on both sides concluded that it was—it was a revolution from the top down, with the strongest charge of reform energy coming from the highest levels of government.

THE GREENING OF AMERICAN POLITICS

Richard Nixon, who had been a Republican scourge of liberals for more than twenty years, won the presidency in 1968 with pledges to reduce federal spending, bureaucracy, and regulation. But on New Year's Day 1970, not quite a year in office, Nixon signed a bill that liberals and conservationists alike would have called utopian just a few years earlier. The National Environmental Policy Act made protection of nature a national responsibility and required the federal government to weigh the potential impact on nature before authorizing or funding any project. Three weeks later, in words that might have graced a Sierra Club publication, the president called the great question of the 1970s whether "we surrender to our surroundings" or "make our peace with nature" with "reparations for the damage we have done to our air, to our land and to our water."[142]

In asserting the rights of nature and the role of federal enforcement, Nixon looked to make his peace with the shifting political environment. As late as 1965, only 17 percent of Americans had named pollution as one of the three major governmental problems; by 1970, that figure had more than tripled, to 53 percent.[143] In a Gallup Poll months after Nixon's inauguration, Americans ranked environmental protection as their third-most-important concern after the war in Vietnam and jobs.[144] White House aides privately forecast that Edmund Muskie, the Senate's icon of conservation, would be the Democratic presidential nominee in 1972.

The rising public support for conservation was evident in the rapid birthrate of dozens of activist groups, such as the Environmental Defense Fund, the Natural Resources Defense Council, and Friends of the Earth, and in the growth of the older environmental organizations. By 1970 the Audubon Society had doubled in membership since 1962 (41,000 to 81,500), Wilderness Society membership had doubled since 1964 (27,000 to 54,000), and National Wildlife Federation membership had doubled since 1966 (271,900 to 540,000). Between 1959 and 1970, membership in the Sierra Club more than quintupled (20,000 to 113,000).[145]

These organizations also strengthened their presence on Capitol Hill, where they had long seemed an endangered species. As procedural changes opened congressional hearings to the public during the 1960s, delegates from conservation groups attended almost every stage of deliberations on key bills. The National Wildlife Federation, which pioneered in pressing environmental laws, featured subcommittee proceedings in its publication, *Conservation Report.*[146]

The tactics of conservationists became more confrontational as elements of the counterculture and the New Left looked for dramatic ways to expose the ills of industrial society. Adam Rome recounts that hippies in New York City "sprayed black mist and passed out blackened flowers at a 'soot-in' in front of the Consolidated Edison building." Hippies in Eugene, Oregon, formed Cyclists Revolting Against Pollution (CRAP) "to show people there are ways to move other than foul automobiles spewing death."[147]

Love of the land and radical politics converged in spring 1969 at People's Park, a vacant lot at the edge of the University of California, Berkeley, campus that students and residents began clearing and planting. Their common inspiration was to foster harmony with nature. But university officials called in National Guardsmen to clear the park of "trespassers" who were hoeing, planting, harvesting, building, conversing, and sleeping on university property. In May a guardsman shot and killed a youth who refused to leave the lot, an act that incensed local residents and bonded the environmental movement in memory of its first martyr.[148]

As America's anticommunist consensus unraveled, many young people emerging from the shadow of nuclear war, conditioned by duck-and-cover drills and warnings of radioactive air and milk, circulated survival readers, held survival marches, and attended courses in survival studies.[149] U.S. military strategy in Vietnam further galvanized environmental protests by relying on chemical defoliation to deprive guerrillas of shelter, a policy some American scientists called "ecocide."[150]

On the farcical fringe of the counterculture, the Yippies staged a "Festival of Life" in August 1968 to coincide with the Democratic "Convention of Death" in Chicago. The beat poet Allen Ginsberg touted the event as a way to protest the threats of "violence, overpopulation, pollution, [and] ecological destruction," Yippie leaders Abbie Hoffman and Jerry Rubin spoke about starting ecology schools, and an eighteen-point manifesto that the Yippies distributed in Chicago demanded an end to the war and the elimination of pollution.[151]

Despite these radical tendencies, the backlash that undercut so many liberal causes during the late 1960s and early 1970s scarcely slowed the Green Revolution. Surely class and race factored in this rare immunity. The predominance of middle-class whites in environmental campaigns, including many suburban home owners and housewives, made the movement appear less threatening. Unlike protests against discrimination and poverty, which had stirred group tensions, the fate of the Earth widely seemed a cause in which all Americans had a direct and urgent stake.

A quickening succession of natural disasters during the late 1960s kept the urgency of federal reform prominently in view. In 1969 alone, thermal pollution from nuclear power plants killed fish in both eastern and western rivers; DDT imperiled the national symbol, the bald eagle; the Cuyahoga River running through Cleveland burst into flames lasting three days from the dumping of industrial wastes; and a 3.5 million gallon spill from an offshore oil rig rose from the sea floor to cover the distinctive Santa Barbara coastline, "a narrow plain hugging the shore, merging into rolling hills and rising to a mountain backdrop."[152] Amid the outpouring of outrage, Park Service director George Hartzog mused, "Ecology has finally achieved currency."[153]

Even without such headline-making shocks, Americans could see, feel, and smell the toxins and clutter enveloping them. In 1969 factories discharged 165 million tons of solid waste and 172 million tons of smoke and fumes. Consumers meanwhile junked 7 million cars, 100 million tires, 20 million tons of paper, 28 billion bottles, and 48 billion cans.[154]

Mainstream publications responded with forecasts of ecological catastrophe, culminating in 1970 with front-page articles and cover stories in *Life*, *Look*, the *New York Times*, the *Washington Post*, *Time* ("Fighting to Save the Earth"), and *Newsweek* ("The Ravaged Environment").[155] *Time* reported, "The Apollo 10 astronauts could see Los Angeles as a cancerous smudge from 25,000 miles in outer space. Airline pilots say that whisky-brown miasmas, visible from 70 miles, shroud almost every U.S. city, including remote towns like Missoula in Montana's 'big sky' country."[156] *Life* warned that within a decade city residents would face a choice: wear gas masks or die from smog.[157]

Amid the surging alarm over abuses to nature, Senator Henry "Scoop" Jackson of Washington proposed in May 1969 to form a presidential council that would coordinate more than eighty executive agencies and departments with responsibility for the environment. To Jackson's surprise, his modest reorganization measure hurtled through both houses of the Congress and evolved into a far-reaching policy statement as Democrats and many Republicans scrambled to occupy the green high ground of environmental virtue. The boldest amendment required federal agencies to circulate publicly a "detailed statement" of the probable environmental impact of any project before the new president's council could approve it.

The lone serious clash over Jackson's bill, renamed the National Environmental Policy Act, came unexpectedly between Jackson and his presumed ally Edmund Muskie. Territoriality, not ideology, divided these potential contenders for the Democratic presidential nomination. A bill to hold companies liable for oil spills, which Muskie had earlier sponsored, contained a provision for a five-person executive council on the environment that Jackson's plan threatened to supersede. Muskie's aide Leon G. Billings recalled, "Scoop wanted a piece of the action" and Muskie was "not too happy about Jackson cutting into his issue."[158] But the two reformers settled for joint custody of the environmental banner, agreeing that Jackson's bill would authorize its council to coordinate policy making while Muskie's bill would give its own council enforcement powers.

The National Environmental Policy Act was passed overwhelmingly in late December 1969 and Nixon signed it on New Year's Day. Cynics looked for him to subvert the law with weak appointments to the Council on Environmental Quality, but his leading nominee included the administration's top conservationist, Undersecretary of the Interior Russell Train. A graduate of Harvard Law School and a Republican in the mold of Theodore Roosevelt, Train founded the African Wildlife Federation in the 1950s and later headed the Conservation Foundation. Train had alerted Nixon soon after his election that the environment had become a critical issue in American politics because the stakes were "no longer simply the protection of wildlife and forests" but "our standard of living, the health and quality of the life of our people."[159] Unable to ignore the Green Revolution, Nixon looked to wrest it from his Democratic critics, and one from Rumford, Maine, in particular.

"Nixon always had Muskie on his mind," Train recalled,[160] and this tended to amplify the momentum of environmental campaigns. "In the past," Muskie wryly observed of his sudden vogue, "we had to fight against all kinds of political pressure, public apathy and ignorance. Now the wind is blowing at our back."[161]

EARTH DAY AND AFTER

The lines between establishment politicians and eco-radicals further blurred in the preparations for "Earth Day" on April 22, 1970. The idea for a nationwide spectacle to focus attention on the environment was the joint project of two very different people. One was a twenty-five-year-old veteran of New Left causes named Denis Hayes. In his first year at Harvard's John F. Kennedy School of Government in 1969, Hayes was looking to do a required class project in practical politics when he read a column by Senator Gaylord Nelson about organizing campus forums on the environment.

The political insider Nelson, Earth Day's other godfather, was a generation older than Hayes but shared the younger man's resolve to rescue the environment. In 1958 he became only the second Democrat of the century to be elected governor of Wisconsin. In 1961 he created a program to acquire one million acres of Wisconsin parkland, wetlands, and other open space, funded by a penny-a-pack tax on cigarettes. Elected in 1962 to the U.S. Senate with President Kennedy's support, Nelson helped expand consumer protection, especially involving prescription medicines, and sponsored laws to preserve the twenty-one-hundred-mile Appalachian Trail corridor and to create a national hiking trails system.[162]

Nelson was frustrated, though, on finding the environment "simply a non-issue in the politics of the country." In the first stage of an idea that germinated over seven years, he turned to President Kennedy to join him on a national conservation tour "to put the environment into the political 'limelight' once and for all." Nelson discussed his proposal with Attorney General Robert Kennedy, who, Nelson recalled, "liked the idea." So did the president, who began a five-day, eleven-state conservation tour with Nelson in September 1963. But while the senator was heartened by the popular response, he found that entrenched political interests paid no attention. In 1969 he was on a conservation speaking tour out West when he thought of the campus teach-ins on Vietnam that had originated in his home state of Wisconsin. Nelson, one of three senators to vote against funding the war in 1965 and a sympathetic observer of the antiwar movement, recalled, "Suddenly, the idea occurred to me—why not organize a huge grassroots protest over what was happening to our environment?"[163]

In September 1969 Nelson announced that in spring 1970 there would be a nationwide demonstration on behalf of the environment. The response overwhelmed his Senate staff. John Gardner, the former secretary of HEW under President Johnson and founder of the public interest group Common Cause, provided temporary space for a Washington, D.C., headquarters. Nelson staffed the office with college students and reserved fifteen minutes to chat with a young volunteer, Denis Hayes, who wanted to organize the event at Harvard.

Nelson's courtesy meeting with Hayes stretched to two hours as the two found in each other a perfect political complement. Nelson had served in state government or in Congress since 1948 while Hayes had spent much of his young life protesting government policies. But Nelson believed that in Hayes he had found his Earth Day coordinator.

The Earth Day rallies drew twenty million Americans and marked the formal birth of a movement long gathering force. The turnout astonished even Gaylord Nelson, who mused afterward that no one person could claim chief credit for the scope and passion of the day. "We had neither the time nor resources to organize 20 million demonstrators and the thousands of schools and local communities that participated," Nelson said in affirming the power of grassroots democracy. "That was the remarkable thing about Earth Day. It organized itself."[164]

Earth Day defied political categories, shifting in character with each rally and speaker. Edmund Muskie, addressing a crowd in front of the Lincoln Memorial, linked Earth Day to a gamut of reform causes. Speaking in the language of the Great Society, refitted to an era of despair over the U.S. presence in Southeast Asia, Muskie declared: "Those who believe that we are talking about the Grand Canyon and the Catskills, but not Harlem and Watts, are wrong. And those who believe that we must do something about the SST and the automobile, but not ABMs and the Vietnam War, are [also] wrong."[165]

In some venues there were acts of "eco-theater," as simple as wearing flowers or as melodramatic as donning gas masks. Students at the University of Minnesota lowered a car engine into a coffin in a mock funeral service, a New Jersey housewife draped red banners with black skulls and crossbones on dredging equipment near blackened beaches, and Yippies at Indiana University plugged municipal sewage pipes with concrete.[166] In San Francisco, Adam Rome recounts, "'environmental vigilantes' poured oil into the reflecting pool at the headquarters of Standard Oil of California," and "in New York, marchers held up dead fish to dramatize the pollution of the Hudson River."[167]

Earth Day was above all educational. Teach-ins at fifteen hundred colleges and ten thousand grade schools and high schools provided formal outlets for raising awareness. Parks, streets, and corporate and government office buildings also drew people to hear talks and manifestos, dialogue and demands.

Given the range of speeches and activities, did Earth Day mark a triumph of liberal reform, radical rebellion, nonpartisan reflection, or some new vision? One could find clear continuities with the liberal hour of the 1960s in the way organizers encouraged nonviolent mass action to dramatize social ills and reshape laws, institutions, and behavior in the public interest. Yet the elastic character of Earth Day finessed the tensions inherent in so many different constituencies, ideologies, and agendas. Underlining the interdependence between man and nature and the need for private, local, and national action, Earth Day drew support across the political spectrum and among those who viewed environmental issues as personal rather than legal or political.

The environmental fervor of the early 1970s brought federal regulation to a pinnacle. In July 1970 President Nixon created the Environmental Protection Agency (EPA) to enforce the National Environmental Policy Act and related laws. A versatile watchdog, it set air and water quality standards, negotiated with and often sued polluters, and spent billions to clean up radioactive and other wastes.

EPA flourished in the salutary political climate to become the largest federal regulatory agency in history. Within a decade it had thirteen thousand workers, a budget of $5.6 billion, and authority to allot another $1.6 billion in cleanup funds.[168] Under its first director, William Ruckelshaus, whose battles against polluters as an Indiana prosecutor had taught him the need for federal enforcement, EPA referred over 150 industrial pollution cases to the Justice Department for prosecution in its first year alone. This aggressive and adversarial approach to environmental safety had no parallel in other industrial democracies or in American history.[169]

Congress joined the administration's initiatives during the early 1970s by enacting a dozen statutes against pollution that entrusted the EPA to set tough national standards for air and water quality, safeguarded habitats of endangered species, authorized a "Superfund" to clean up abandoned nuclear reactors and strip mines, and subsidized state and local efforts to implement (or in states such as California, to exceed) federal standards.[170]

Congress also gave private citizens greater access to administrative procedures and the courts, in effect encouraging activists to hold government at all levels, including EPA, to environmental rigor.[171] The new laws enabled litigants to block vast federal projects simply by citing evidence of adverse environmental consequences. In 1970 federal judges halted work on the multibillion-dollar, eight-hundred-mile-long Alaska Pipeline pending further consideration of the harm from possible oil spills. In 1977 litigants shut down construction of the nearly completed $116 million Tellico Dam on the Little Tennessee River for two years, citing the discovery by a zoology professor snorkeling in the river that the dam would imperil a four-inch-long fish called the snail darter.[172]

The snail darter succumbed on September 10, 1979, to a special exemption of the dam from environmental scrutiny, as congressmen voted for pork over fish. Yet the tenacity of the snail darter's resistance spoke to a revolution in public policy and attitudes that ceded nature a prominent place in discussions of the national interest. Americans who had entered the sixties in the shadow of a nuclear winter had emerged by decade's end intent on averting the chill of a silent spring.

CHAPTER 6

THE HOUR OF
MAXIMUM DANGER

O n October 19, 1960, CBS news anchor Howard K. Smith inaugurated the first televised presidential debate by declaring that Senator Kennedy and Vice President Nixon, by previous agreement, would restrict their comments to "internal, or domestic, issues." Prior agreement notwithstanding, Senator Kennedy dismissed the compartmentalization in his opening remarks:

> In the election of 1860, Abraham Lincoln said the question was whether this nation could exist half-slave or half-free. In the election of 1960, and with the world around us, the question is whether the world will exist half-slave or half-free.... We discuss tonight domestic issues, but I would not want ... any implication to be given that this does not involve directly our struggle with Mr. Khrushchev for survival.... The kind of country we have here, the kind of society we have, the kind of strength we build in the United States will be the defense of freedom....
>
> I want people in Latin America and Africa and Asia to start to look to America; to see how we're doing things; to wonder what the president of the United States is doing; and not to look at Khrushchev, or look at the Chinese Communists. That is the obligation upon our generation.... Can freedom be maintained under the most severe attack it has ever known?[1]

In projecting domestic issues onto a global stage, Kennedy underscored the central role that containing communist influence had come to play in postwar liberalism. But this was no mere partisan tactic. It reflected, rather, sweeping changes in world affairs to which the United States responded, at first uncertainly, then behind an emphatic bipartisan consensus for American leadership in a world shattered by war and transformed by the emergence of Soviet power and the spread of communist ideology.

As early as World War I, liberals under President Woodrow Wilson had advocated joining a new League of Nations to deter aggression, but they could not overcome resistance by isolationists and by nationalists who, like Theodore Roosevelt, refused to let the United States be dragged into war "every time a Jugoslav wishes to slap a Czechoslav."[2] The isolationist impulse prevailed until the Japanese destruction of the U.S. Pacific Fleet at Pearl Harbor in December 1941 demolished the faith that an isolated Fortress America could find ample shelter behind two oceans. Four more years of fighting in the Atlantic, North Africa, Europe, and the Pacific further convinced Americans that the perils of a shrinking world made preserving international order an inescapable national obligation.

The growing orbit of liberal internationalists included a late-blooming champion in Arthur H. Vandenberg of Michigan, the ranking Republican on the Senate Foreign Relations Committee. Vandenberg had long embodied dogged midwestern isolationism, having opposed both the draft and Lend-Lease to England, a measure that he ascribed to Roosevelt's having forced the Senate "into a goose step" worthy of a "totalitarian" regime.[3] But standing in London in 1944 while German robot bombs descended, Vandenberg asked a friend, "How can there be immunity or isolation when man can devise weapons like that?"

Early in 1945 Vandenberg rose in the Senate to declare his conversion to the principle of continuing American leadership in a new United Nations peacekeeping body. Though insisting as ever on national strength, he doubted "that any nation hereafter can immunize itself by its own exclusive action.... I want maximum American cooperation.... I want a new dignity and a new authority for international law. I think American self-interest requires it."[4]

American leaders further concluded that postwar harmony required a new emphasis on free trade across national borders. They recalled the forbidding U.S. tariffs of the interwar years that had discouraged foreign exports, aggravated a worldwide depression, and given rise to extreme German and Japanese nationalism. Principles of free trade also gratified American industrialists who sought overseas markets for their soaring production. The American economy, Truman said in 1947, could prosper only with the "early restoration of an international order in which private trade can flourish."[5]

With the surrender of Germany and Japan in 1945, the United States stood, in Winston Churchill's phrase, "at the summit of the world." In 1945 it produced nearly half the world's goods, held most of its investment capital, and counted vast reserves of oil. The U.S. Navy ruled the seas, U.S. air power dominated the skies, and only America possessed the most terrifying weapon ever produced, the atomic bomb. Yet at the moment of triumph for Americans and their British and Russian allies, the expanding dimensions of a new struggle were casting a lengthening shadow over their joint celebrations.

The common crusade against Hitler had deferred but never dispelled conflicts between the Soviet Union and the Anglo-American powers. Although Lend-Lease aid began pouring into Russia and although American public opinion converted Stalin overnight from a Red despot to a patriotic scourge of the Nazis, the Grand Alliance oozed mistrust that poisoned relations once Germany and Japan could no longer threaten either country. Even as the victors came together to shape a common destiny, their visions of a postwar order remained worlds apart. Diplomatic conferences deadlocked over Eastern Europe, where Soviet armies trumped American demands for free elections. In Germany, zones of occupation hardened into rival capitalist and communist states. Atomic power incited an escalating arms race. And the new international economy, which the United States spurred by forming an International Monetary Fund, a World Bank, and the Marshall Plan to aid Western Europe, was criticized by the Soviets as a plot to penetrate and exploit less-industrialized societies.

For Stalin as for the Russian people, the world wars taught no grand principles of international law and collective security. The lessons they drew were more earthbound and immediate: Germany must be suppressed and a ring of docile Eastern European neighbors secured as a buffer against any new invasion from the West. In contrast to the "one world" vision Americans had embraced, Stalin wanted his own world insulated against enemies and friends alike. "The war is not as in the past," he told a visiting delegation of Yugoslavian communists in April 1945; "whoever occupies a territory also imposes on it his own social system. Everyone imposes his own system as far as his army can reach. It cannot be otherwise."[6]

The American vision of free-flowing ideas and goods further repelled the Kremlin. While U.S. officials envisioned mutual benefit from such exchanges, Soviet leaders saw only a nightmare of Western economic domination, corruption of Russian values, and a weakening of communist control. In this, Stalin typified the founding generation of Bolsheviks, who looked on the West with grudging respect but unreserved antipathy. On the eve of his ruthless drive for industrialization in 1929, he told his inner circle, "We are fifty or a hundred years behind the advanced countries. We must make good this distance in ten years. Either we do it or they crush us."[7] By 1945 Stalin was already musing on the next phase of struggle. According to Soviet foreign minister Vyacheslav Molotov, "Stalin looked at it this way. World War I has wrested one country from capitalist slavery [by sparking the Russian Revolution]; World War II has created a socialist system [with the Soviet occupation of Eastern Europe]; and the third will finish off imperialism forever."[8]

In early 1946 U.S. leaders, still floundering between conciliation and conflict with Russia, sought help in decrypting the Kremlin's intentions from a hitherto obscure Foreign Service officer in Moscow, George F. Kennan. Tall, balding, intense, with blue eyes that could rivet observers or drift into a distant gaze, the forty-one-year-old Kennan sent an eight-thousand-word cable that rooted Soviet expansionism in age-old czarist imperialism and a "neurotic view of world affairs" stemming from a history of invasions, now burnished by Marxist rhetoric about "antagonistic 'capitalistic encirclement.'" As the United States was the foremost capitalist state, the Kremlin was "committed fanatically to the belief that . . . our society [must] be disrupted, our traditional way of life be destroyed, the international authority of our state be broken, if Soviet power is to be secure."⁹

In July 1947 Kennan published in the eminent journal *Foreign Affairs* a call for "the adroit and vigilant application of counter-force at a series of constantly shifting geographical and political points" wherever the Kremlin showed signs "of encroaching upon the interests of a peaceful and stable world." In advocating "containment" of Russian expansionist tendencies, Kennan introduced to public discourse a term that officials of both major parties would invoke for more than four decades as the guiding principle of American foreign policy.

It fell by chance to a liberal Democrat and heir to the New Deal coalition, Harry Truman, to lay the foundations of containment policy. Between 1946 and 1949 Truman's administration secured through diplomatic pressure the withdrawal of Soviet troops from northern Iran, provided $350 million to help Greece crush a communist insurrection and to spur the Turks to rebuff Soviet territorial claims, launched a $13 billion program of economic aid to revitalize European capitalism, conducted an eleven-month airlift to break a Soviet blockade of West Berlin, and formed the North Atlantic Treaty Organization to shore up Western Europe's defenses against a possible Soviet thrust. In 1950 American intervention to repel an invasion of South Korea by communist troops from the North, later augmented by several hundred thousand "volunteers" from Communist China, signaled an extension of containment beyond Europe and the Near East, as well as a growing reliance on military measures against communist encroachments.

While the Truman administration's strategy of containment fit a broad national consensus, its advocacy of greater military spending revealed how liberal politics could influence foreign policy, a pattern that would surge again under Presidents Kennedy and Johnson. At first glance the dramatic increase of national defense spending from $13.7 billion in fiscal 1950 to $23.6 billion in fiscal 1951 was a plain enough reaction to war in Korea. But the policy of massive permanent spending on arms took shape before the North Korean invasion and pertained as much to liberal economic theories about managed growth as to fears about Soviet military intentions.

In April 1950 Paul Nitze, an aide to President Truman's National Security Council, drafted a policy paper known as NSC-68 that justified a "massive" military buildup by citing not only Russia's growing might but also the capacity of the United States government to increase spending without incurring inflation or permanent deficits. "One of the most significant lessons of our World War II experience," the report argued, "was that the American economy, when it operates at a level approaching full efficiency, can provide enormous resources for purposes other than civilian consumption while simultaneously providing a higher standard of living."[10]

The rationale for stepped-up spending as a healthy stimulus to growth came not from the Pentagon, then wedded to orthodox ideas about the need for balanced budgets, but from liberal, "Keynesian" economists such as Leon Keyserling, soon to become head of the president's Council of Economic Advisors. Keyserling persuaded Truman that by injecting more money into the economy and embracing short-term deficits, the government could increase the gross national product by $50 billion in five years to $300 billion. "Keyserling and I discussed these matters frequently," Nitze recalled; "though he wanted to spend the money on other programs, he was convinced that the country could afford $40 billion for defense if necessary."[11]

Keyserling's tutorials in growth economics were an intoxicating lesson to the national security advisors to Truman—and later to Kennedy and Johnson. They suggested that the government could increase military spending indefinitely without severe public sacrifice, industrial shortages, or inflation. This would relieve the need for hard choices about which weapons to build, which countries and regions held greatest strategic import, and which U.S. military commitments were vital. If federal spending under the guidance of liberal economists could assure rapid increases in production of both military and consumer goods, then the United States could afford to project decisive power wherever communists threatened. During the 1960s the resurgence of this philosophy resulted in a rapid buildup of nuclear and conventional forces and an escalating commitment in Vietnam that would test the liberal faith in America's elastic resources and resolve.

1960: THE COLD WAR CAMPAIGN

John F. Kennedy had always been more interested in foreign affairs than domestic. An aide recalled, "He used to say that a domestic failure could hurt the country, but a failure in foreign affairs could kill it."[12] Kennedy's sensibility was shaped in no small part by fears of rising communist power and global upheaval that pervaded American politics during his bid for the presidency. The nation was officially at peace in 1960, but much of the world, loosed from prewar colonial anchors and caught up in a new superpower competition, was in convulsions.

"Probably not since Hitler has the average American been more concerned about the course of world affairs," Robert Spivack wrote in the *Nation* as the presidential election approached.[13] The journalist Theodore H. White found the entire Democratic National Convention in July 1960 awash in the crisis of containment: "This world of challenge and chaos and Communism, was the central theme of all oratory; and the speakers—in caucus, on TV, in convention later—seized on the theme, repeated it, hammered it, flattened it, until the entire Convention seemed a continuous drone of great worries."[14]

The sirens sounded at least as shrilly at the Republican convention in August, as Nixon accepted his party's presidential nomination with a warning that the United States could not "tolerate being pushed around by anybody, any place." Nixon's running mate, Henry Cabot Lodge, summed up the "overwhelming importance" of the presidential election "to us and to the world" as "the life and death struggle between the Communists . . . and those who insist on being free."[15]

The "drone of great worries" reverberated in the echo chamber of Khrushchev's own harsh utterances. Never had a foreign leader so brazenly injected himself into a presidential campaign as the mercurial sixty-six-year-old Soviet leader. Although Joseph Stalin had ordered millions shot or jailed and had increasingly clashed with the West, his public demeanor had been impeccable, his speeches few, dignified, and unremarkable. By contrast the stocky, bald, deep-voiced, aggressively voluble Khrushchev, chairman of the Soviet Council of Ministers and first secretary of the Communist Party, was unpredictable in his every gesture: one minute calm and jovial, the next angrily gesticulating. He presented an image that Western leaders found disconcerting and symbolic of Russia's growing dynamism and menace.[16]

Cunning and ruthless, Khrushchev was still far from being the implacable ogre of Western imagination. He denied that war between communist and capitalist states was "fatalistically inevitable," stressed instead "peaceful coexistence," and shifted resources from military to consumer growth. [17] Yet in trumpeting Soviet parity with the West in technology, military power, economic growth, and political stature, the Soviet chairman aggravated the very Cold War fears he wished to calm.

Beginning in the late 1950s Khrushchev boomed repeated threats that Soviet rockets could destroy France, England, even the United States if the "imperialists" dared aggression. The most notorious of Khrushchev's challenges to the West, "We will bury you," was much misunderstood. Coaxed by many rounds of vodka at a Polish embassy reception in Moscow in November 1956,[18] his words were an invitation to peaceful competition, not an intimation of war. Khrushchev was alluding to the march of history, which, as a good Bolshevik, he trusted would vindicate communism and leave capitalism a lifeless relic. Still, in a time of high tension between rival military alliances, his remark was often quoted—out of context—as an emblem of Soviet intentions.

"Standing up to Khrushchev" became a valued political currency during the 1960 campaign, culminating on September 19 when he arrived in the United States for an uninvited and increasingly unwelcome twenty-five-day visit. Having addressed the United Nations General Assembly, the Soviet chairman stayed to wreak havoc. After heckling British prime minister Macmillan, he expressed displeasure with the Western leanings of a Filipino delegate by removing his shoe and pounding a table. (Soviet officials at first dismissed word of this sabotage as "Western propaganda.")[19] Khrushchev assured U.N. members that his cause was peace, but as so often, he proved better at shocking his listeners than soothing them.

Khrushchev's antics conveyed added menace because Americans had only fitfully emerged from a panic beginning in October 1957, when the Russians sent the Sputnik satellite into orbit. The heft and power of this exotic entity were modest indeed, as the historians Aleksandr Fursenko and Timothy Naftali recount: "Weighing just over 184 pounds, cylindrical with splayed antennas that looked like the popular tail fins on cars of the day, Sputnik had no purpose other than to orbit and make a sound . . . a deep beep, beep, beep to radio operators in the countries that it flew over."[20] Yet this visible and audible symbol of Soviet pre-eminence in outer space shattered confidence in American technological superiority and strategic defenses. "The national ego had not been so affronted since Pearl Harbor," Ben Pearse of the *New York Times* wrote of the national trauma.[21]

Media and Main Streets across America buzzed with alarm over a Soviet threat that, said Pentagon official Paul Nitze, "may become critical in 1959 or early 1960," and Khrushchev vigorously stirred these anxieties.[22] *Time* magazine noted the Kremlin's "new offensive technique: 'missile diplomacy,'" in which "every day of every week Moscow rolls out pronouncements" of successful experiments with intercontinental ballistic missiles. In this new age of the missile, Khrushchev liked to say, Europe might become "a veritable cemetery" and the United States had become "just as vulnerable."[23]

Strategists at the RAND Corporation, an Air Force think tank in Santa Monica, did as much as popular rumors to focus the 1960 presidential campaign on questions of national survival stemming from an imminent "missile gap." Albert Wohlstetter, whose analytical clarity and reasoned tone helped make fear of vulnerability to a Russian nuclear attack intellectually respectable, wrote in *Foreign Affairs* in 1959, "The notion that a carefully planned surprise attack can be checkmated almost effortlessly, that, in short, we may resume our deep pre-Sputnik sleep, is wrong and its nearly universal acceptance is terribly dangerous. . . . [D]eterring general war in both the early and late 1960s will be hard at best."[24] Also in 1959 Bernard Brodie, the earliest pioneer in nuclear weapons theory, emphasized in his book *Strategy in the Missile Age* the shrinking limits of safety in the Cold War.

"The fact is that deterrence can fail," Brodie wrote. "The great advantage of striking first, at least under existing conditions, must be viewed as an extremely strong and persistent incentive to each side to attack the other. As long as this incentive exists, the danger of total war arising out of a crisis situation—or even from a premeditated attack by the Soviet Union—cannot be considered trivial or remote."[25]

In the presidential election year 1960, the RAND Corporation's distinctive blend of reason and terror attained still greater influence and notoriety. The catalyst was a balding, rotund mathematical physicist named Herman Kahn, who had an ear for lively phrases ("Doomsday Machine," "thinking about the unthinkable") and a bent for provocative, at times humorous references to scenarios of nuclear deterrence and destruction. In a 750-page tract, *On Thermonuclear War*,[26] Kahn portrayed nuclear war as a fact of life that Americans must prepare for, through construction of fallout shelters and periodic mass evacuations; resort to, if the Russians dared invade Western Europe; and control, by employing such "restrained" tactics as initially targeting Russian missiles rather than cities, or destroying "only" a single Russian city. Waged judiciously, Kahn suggested, a nuclear war might entail no more than a few million casualties on either side. Denounced as ghoulishly immoral (and later parodied in Stanley Kubrick's dark cinematic satire, *Dr. Strangelove*), Kahn nonetheless lectured to rows of generals, transfixed lay audiences, and became the Cold War's most widely read thinker on nuclear strategy.

Kennedy emerged during the presidential campaign as a standard bearer for the experts at RAND and for a growing core of liberal Democrats who favored hikes in defense spending as a matter of sound economics and vital strategy. The senator's literal call to arms fit the urgent mood of the electorate, though his interest in "preparedness" had been evident as early as 1940 with the publication of *Why England Slept*, a reworking of his senior thesis at Harvard on the disastrous failure to rearm against Hitler's Germany. As a member of Congress since 1947, Kennedy had consistently supported strong nuclear and conventional forces.

For all Khrushchev's boasts and RAND's laments, the so-called missile gap, like earlier cries of a "bomber gap" in the mid-1950s, was illusory. Even so, Kennedy, like the RAND experts whom he privately consulted, employed the term "missile gap" more as a shorthand reference to larger questions of military readiness than simply relative numbers of missiles. The United States, Kennedy argued, must safeguard its bombers and missiles against a Soviet attack. The country must also upgrade its conventional forces rather than rely on "massive retaliation" against Russia to deter or punish even marginal acts of communist aggression or subversion. This preference for "flexible response" endeared Kennedy to national security analysts who believed that the growing Soviet nuclear arsenal made it desirable to confine rather than brandish the "ultimate weapon."

The 1960 election affirmed the primacy of foreign affairs in national politics, but it left Kennedy struggling to ease doubts about his experience, toughness, and judgment compared with the retiring president and hero of Normandy, the seventy-year-old Dwight Eisenhower. Days before leaving office, Eisenhower cited as his proudest legacy the "firmness and readiness to take the risk [of war]" that prevented a destructive clash with the communist bloc.[27] Now Kennedy had to prove his own mettle by his readiness to "take the risk" in an age of increasingly unstable nuclear deterrence.

Nor was there a respite from the global crises that had given Kennedy's calls for national sacrifice such conviction. In January 1961 *Newsweek* expressed the national media's sympathy for the man about to inherit a world in flames:

> John Fitzgerald Kennedy will have good reason to shudder when he takes his first look at the "in" basket on the White House executive desk. . . .
> From his first day in office, he will confront an all but overpowering array of problems and dangers arising in every corner of a world in upheaval. . . .
> In each and every crisis, the world will look to the White House.[28]

ARMS AND INFLUENCE

Less than a week after Kennedy took office, Defense Secretary Robert McNamara reported that the Pentagon was unprepared either to deter a war or to fight one. Military leaders relied, he said, on "a strategy of massive nuclear retaliation as the answer to all military and political aggression, a strategy believed by few of our friends and none of our enemies and resulting in serious weaknesses in our conventional forces."[29] Only eleven combat-ready divisions existed, of which three were deployed in the United States, leaving a meager strategic reserve. Fighter-bombers lacked non-nuclear ordnance, the Army lacked ammunition to fight more than a few weeks, air transport relied on obsolescent planes that would have required nearly two months to airlift a single combat-ready infantry division to Southeast Asia.[30]

In an era when liberals shared—and amplified—the fears of vulnerability to a Soviet attack, the Pentagon, not race, poverty, or the economy, appeared the most urgent target of reform. Theodore Sorensen, a World War II pacifist and longtime activist for labor and civil rights who provided Kennedy with an early link to liberal Democrats, saw no contradiction in citing among the president's claims to greatness "the largest and swiftest [military] buildup in this country's peacetime history," providing a "versatile arsenal" that ranged, in Kennedy's words, "from the most massive deterrents to the most subtle influences."[31] Kennedy moved with equal rapidity to dampen the reliance on nuclear weapons, which he considered a deterrent of dubious value and unlimited risk.

A principal cause of Kennedy and McNamara's skepticism was SIOP-62, an operational plan for "massive retaliation" that the Joint Chiefs had completed for Eisenhower in December 1960. SIOP-62 called for incinerating the entire communist bloc with nuclear weapons if the Soviet Union crossed an unspecified threshold of misconduct. Even rumors of an impending non-nuclear Soviet action in Western Europe could trigger the pre-emptive launch of 3,423 nuclear weapons totaling 7,847 megatons (six hundred thousand times the strength of the atomic bomb that destroyed Hiroshima). Fred Kaplan, a historian of the "wizards of Armageddon" who devised nuclear strategy, wrote that the attack envisioned by SIOP-62 "would kill 285 million Russians and Chinese and severely injure 40 million more. None of these figures included the millions of casualties in Eastern Europe or the fallout victims in the free world."[32]

An aide recalled President Kennedy's shock on hearing details of the Pentagon's blueprint to target every communist-controlled city. "The plan that he inherited was, 'Mr. President, just tell us to go to nuclear war, and we'll deal with the rest.' And the plan called for devastating, indiscriminately, China, Russia, Eastern Europe—it was an orgiastic, Wagnerian plan, and he was determined, from that moment, to get the plan changed so he would have total control of it." Kennedy recoiled from his briefing by the Joint Chiefs at such "a truly monstrous event in the U.S.—let alone in world history." Afterward he said in disgust to Dean Rusk, "And we call ourselves the human race."[33]

"The Pentagon is full of papers talking about the preservation of a 'viable society' after nuclear conflict," McNamara said. "That 'viable society' phrase drives me mad. I keep trying to comb it out, but it keeps coming back."[34] At least one member of the Joint Chiefs concurred. General David Shoup of the Marines, the sole branch of the armed forces without nuclear weapons, said, "Any plan that kills millions of Chinese when it isn't even their war is not a good plan. This is not the American way."[35]

With Kennedy's encouragement, McNamara tacitly shelved SIOP-62 in favor of "flexible response," a buzzword of defense intellectuals who looked to hone proportional responses to military threats. Perhaps, Defense planners mused in strategy sessions, it would require no more than well-equipped NATO land, naval, and air forces to contain Soviet armies in Europe. Similarly the United States might counter a guerrilla war in South Vietnam by deploying a relative handful of Special Forces trained to live off the land, befriend villagers, and tutor native soldiers.

Even nuclear war might not bring the final judgment if, in accord with the tenets of flexible response, the United States initially targeted Soviet missile sites rather than cities while continuing to negotiate. But this new approach would not be cheap. Destroying enemy forces rather than population centers required much greater striking power and tended to stoke the arms race between East and West. Yet the proponents were seeking above all to control the risks of escalation rather than follow a rigid path toward unlimited nuclear war.

The enshrinement of flexible response at the Pentagon fit the vogue that was emerging in many corners of the public policy universe in the early 1960s: a belief that expertise and scientific planning could clarify and resolve any problem, domestic or foreign. Even the threat of nuclear war might be subject to precise computer simulations and mathematical modeling of military responses (Herman Kahn enthused about forty-four rungs of escalation). The *Times Literary Supplement* wrote of the reign of RAND in the Defense Department, "The military intellectuals move freely through the corridors of the Pentagon and the State Department rather as the Jesuits through the courts of Madrid and Vienna, three centuries ago."[36]

While reformers exalted the new expertise at the Pentagon, they depended still more on the new economics at the White House. Kennedy felt free to recommend far higher appropriations for conventional as well as nuclear forces because his Council of Economic Advisors assured him that increases in federal spending would act as a healthy economic stimulus. In pushing to make the armed forces "sufficient beyond doubt,"[37] therefore, Kennedy was responding as much to liberal economic wisdom as to perceptions of a threat from Moscow.

President Dwight Eisenhower's reliance on nuclear weapons rather than more costly conventional forces reflected his view of the Cold War as a marathon, not a sprint, requiring the United States to conserve its fiscal strength with "a preparedness program that will give us a respectable position without bankrupting the nation."[38] Economist James Tobin observed that Eisenhower's approach to in military spending was a doctrine "made as much in Treasury as in State."[39]

Kennedy's defense budget inverted Eisenhower's priorities. In a preinaugural task force report that revived the Keynesian tenets of the Truman years, Paul A. Samuelson wrote that "any stepping up" of federal programs "that is deemed desirable for its own sake can only help rather than hinder the health of our economy in the period immediately ahead."[40] Walter Heller, chairman of the president's Council of Economic Advisors, summed up the expansionist fiscal creed that guided Kennedy and then Johnson: "Prosperity and rapid growth ... put at [the president's] disposal, as nothing else can, the resources needed to achieve great societies at home and grand designs abroad."[41]

With Kennedy's encouragement, defense expenditures rose 10 percent in three years, from $49.6 billion in fiscal 1961 to $54.8 billion in fiscal 1964. The Department of Defense reported in 1962 that no longer would "arbitrary budget ceilings" curb arms production. Such increases were tolerable politically, it was argued, because a growing economy could absorb them. In fact, defense spending actually declined during these years as a percentage of the gross domestic product, from 9.3 percent to 8.5 percent. "The revolution at the Pentagon and the growth revolution at the White House," Robert Collins writes, "were intertwined from the beginning."[42]

THE CRISES MULTIPLY

Had fresh thinking been enough to wind down the Cold War, Kennedy appeared poised for a breakthrough. At a time when politicians routinely portrayed Soviet leaders as devils, he saw the tragic dimensions of a conflict that had trapped both sides in mutual ignorance and suspicion. In 1959, while a front-runner for the Democratic presidential nomination, he told the historian James McGregor Burns, "You have two people . . . who are both of goodwill, but neither of whom can communicate" with the other.[43] Such moderation impressed Soviet intelligence agents, who cabled Moscow expectantly from their embassy in Washington, D.C., upon Kennedy's nomination in 1960: "Considering that . . . there is a conflict of 'basic national interests' between the United States and the USSR, . . . Kennedy nevertheless grants the possibility of a mutually acceptable settlement on the basis of a joint effort to avoid nuclear war . . . rejecting as 'too fatalistic' the opinion that 'you can't trust' the Soviet Union."[44]

Yet despite his wish to find common ground with Khrushchev, Kennedy became mired in the cycle of mistrust and confrontation he had deplored. Deep-rooted tensions over Berlin; spiraling technology in nuclear weapons; competition for the allegiance of developing nations; expanding Soviet ambitions for influence beyond Eastern Europe to all points of the globe; a bid for leadership of the socialist world by the intensely anti-Western Chinese Communists; and NATO's fractious, nervous responses to U.S. initiatives all proved resistant or impervious to changes in the White House.

Two weeks to the day before Kennedy took office, Khrushchev gave a speech at Moscow's Institute for Marxist-Leninism that approvingly forecast the imminent ouster of capitalist regimes in Asia, Africa, and Latin America. The communist tide, the Soviet leader enthused, had "greatly exceeded the boldest and most optimistic predictions and expectations," so that there was "no longer any force in the world capable of barring the road to socialism." While communists must avoid nuclear holocaust, "peaceful coexistence" must nonetheless take the form of "intense economic, political and ideological struggle between the proletariat and the aggressive forces of imperialism in the world arena." This meant support "wholeheartedly and without reservation" for "wars of liberation or popular uprisings" against Western influence everywhere.[45]

Kennedy urged his aides to study Khrushchev's remarks as defining the most urgent dangers and burdens of the new administration. While Kennedy, like other liberals, believed that containing communism and extending rights and opportunities at home were inseparable goals, in practice the tensions between East and West chilled the administration's domestic reform impulses amid a preoccupation with foreign crises. On January 30, 1961, the president clarified these priorities in his first State of the Union Address, telling Congress that "in an hour of national peril" it was "by no means certain" the nation could endure. . . . Each day the crises multiply," he said. "Each day we draw nearer the hour of maximum danger, as weapons spread and hostile forces grow stronger . . . in each of the principal areas of crisis—the tide of events has been running out and time has not been our friend."[46]

The news worsened as Kennedy settled into office. On February 13 the Soviets threatened to intervene in the newly independent but faction-torn Congo. On March 9 the communist-led Pathet Lao verged on seizing all of Laos and Kennedy received plans from the Joint Chiefs for the introduction of combat troops. On March 21 the Soviet delegation at the Geneva test-ban talks demanded a veto over inspection that all but precluded nuclear disarmament. On April 12 a handsome Soviet cosmonaut, Yuri Gagarin, gained international celebrity as the first man to orbit the earth and as the symbol of Soviet superiority in rocket boosters.[47]

But the most urgent crisis was the one closest to home. In Eisenhower's last year, the CIA had initiated a plot to train and transport a force of Cuban exiles to overthrow Castro, and the plan moved steadily forward in the months following Kennedy's election. Doubts about committing a rag-tag unit, short on military experience and riven with factional strains, succumbed to CIA assurances, backed by the Joint Chiefs, that the exiles would spark a popular revolt against Castro and terminate this Soviet bridgehead in the Americas without implicating the U.S. government. After scaling down the plan from a "spectacular" operation "too much like a World War II invasion" to a "quiet" fourteen-hundred-man landing more easily disguised as a purely Cuban affair,[48] the president approved the venture. It proved, in the words of journalist Theodore Draper, "the perfect failure."[49]

Castro's vigorous leadership of his vastly superior army resulted in the death or capture of nearly the entire exile force within three days of the landing at the Bay of Pigs. The failed invasion enhanced Castro's prestige and Soviet influence in Cuba while leaving telltale American footprints that dismayed nonaligned states and fed communist propaganda mills. Kennedy suffered most with conservative politicians at home who criticized his refusal to follow through with U.S. air and naval power and, if need be, the Marines. But the president had no wish to risk a wider war to salvage a scheme so clearly exposed as unsound.

The Kennedy administration continued to fixate on Castro as a potential bridgehead for Soviet influence, an instigator of Marxist guerrillas in Latin America, and a political embarrassment. Beginning in November 1961 Bobby Kennedy oversaw secret campaigns to undermine the Cuban economy and otherwise destabilize the Castro regime. The CIA meanwhile tried repeatedly to assassinate Castro, using Mafia figures as well as Cuban dissidents; like Eisenhower before him, President Kennedy more clearly enjoyed plausible deniability in such schemes than innocence.[50]

Although covert action against Castro's Cuba continued, the failure at the Bay of Pigs deepened Kennedy's aversion to open military ventures. Only in later years would it become fashionable for scholars to bemoan the president's "machismo"[51] in foreign policy and his "conviction that great crises make great men."[52] Such judgments misread Kennedy's moderation in dangerous times by confusing his bent for activism with belligerence and by ignoring the superheated atmosphere of brinkmanship that he inherited. The narrow escape by the nation of Laos from becoming an American battleground in 1961 reveals much about Kennedy's hidden struggle to resist pressure for U.S. military intervention and to avert, in his words, "the final failure" of war with Moscow or Beijing.

The land of the Lao appeared an unlikely candidate for Armageddon.

A French colony until 1954, home to just two million people in an area twice the size of New York state, Laos was known mainly for rice, opium, and elephant, tiger, deer, and wild buffalo in the greatest natural game preserve in the world. Ravaged by seasonal monsoons "that come in torrents, coursing down the steep-sided mountains in raging floods, turning the dirt roads and trails into quagmires and washing out bridges, culverts, and fills,"[53] the country lacked modern roads, technology, and political cohesion. Kennedy's favorite iconoclast, John Kenneth Galbraith, sized up the Laotian army, which had gorged on American money and equipment, as "clearly inferior to a battalion of conscientious objectors from World War I."[54] Winthrop Brown, the U.S. ambassador to Laos, told Kennedy, "Laos was hopeless . . . a classic example of a political and economic vacuum. It had no national identity. It was just a series of lines drawn on a map."[55]

Yet in the arcane world of Cold War strategy, Laos mattered because its gentle people adjoined an American client state enveloped by revolution. "If the Communists gained possession of the Mekong valley," Arthur Schlesinger wrote of the wobbling Laotian domino, "they could materially intensify their pressure against South Vietnam. . . . If Laos was not precisely a dagger pointed at the heart of Kansas, it was very plainly a gateway to Southeast Asia." [56]

To suppress the Laotian communists, known as the Pathet Lao, by 1960 the United States had funneled into Laos $300 million in aid ($293 million for the army, a mere $7 million for technical and economic development). It was a larger per capita sum than for any other country and it nearly doubled the per capita Laotian income. The CIA meanwhile engineered the ouster of a neutralist government, only to find that the new pro-Western regime was incompetent, the army would sooner flee than fight, and the Pathet Lao were verging on a bloodless coup. The Kremlin, equally bewitched by the strategic stakes in Laos, supplied the Pathet Lao with the largest Soviet airlift operation since World War II.[57] Seeing Southeast Asia at risk, President Eisenhower hosted Kennedy at the White House on January 19, 1961, two days before leaving office, to break the grim news, "You might have to go in there and fight it out."[58]

As with the debacle in Cuba, Eisenhower's legacy hung over Kennedy's early policies toward Laos. In March 1961 he dispatched the Seventh

Fleet to the South China Sea and airlifted five hundred Marines to Thailand near the Laotian capital, Vientiane. He intended this bluff as a prelude to compromise, designed to impress on Khrushchev the urgency of an accord. But at a National Security Council meeting on April 27, the Joint Chiefs argued for an attack against the Pathet Lao with American land and naval forces. When Kennedy demurred that this might provoke the Chinese, General Lyman Lemnitzer, chairman of the Joint Chiefs, assured him, "If we are given the right to use nuclear weapons, we can guarantee victory." According to Arthur Schlesinger, this pledge jolted the gathering into silence. Then someone said, "Mr. President, perhaps you would have the General explain to us what he means by victory."[59]

Lemnitzer's advice to send U.S. troops to Laos came while the embers of Kennedy's failure at the Bay of Pigs a week earlier were still smoldering. But the risk of unchecked escalation led Kennedy to deploy instead the negotiating skills of a former ambassador to Moscow, sixty-nine-year-old Averell Harriman, to keep Laos neutral in the Cold War. By September 1961 Harriman had coaxed all factions in Laos, plus Russia and China, to approve a coalition government that welcomed the Pathet Lao while barring North Vietnamese infiltration into South Vietnam through the Laotian jungle. Another nine months of futile military maneuver passed before the exhausted Laotian leaders signed the final document in Geneva. Harriman himself called it "a good bad deal,"[60] marred by porous enforcement. But Laos emerged a more stable country, permitting a relieved Kennedy to withdraw U.S. ships and Marines from the area.

In salvaging Laos from chaos and the threat of foreign intervention, Harriman revived Kennedy's hopes of defusing through back channels the trouble spots that were snaring the superpowers in commitments fraught with "miscalculation." Yet Kennedy's prudence was bounded by the need to project firmness to Khrushchev and to the electorate. "At this point we are like the Harlem Globetrotters," National Security Advisor McGeorge Bundy wrote in the spring of 1961, "passing forward, behind, sidewise, and underneath. But nobody has made a basket yet."[61] Until this changed, the Kremlin's spires would continue to fix Kennedy's gaze.

In June 1961 a two-day summit meeting with Khrushchev appeared to offer Kennedy a chance to clarify American aims, reassure the Russians,

President John F. Kennedy meets with Premier Nikita Khrushchev of the Soviet Union at the U.S. embassy residence, Vienna, June 3, 1961.
Courtesy John F. Kennedy Presidential Library and Museum, Boston.

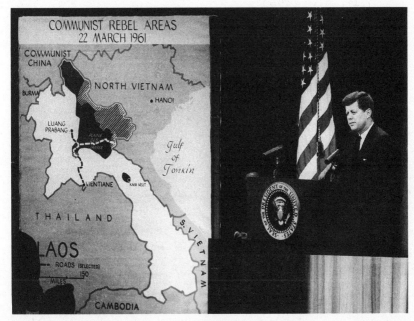

President Kennedy discussing the situation in Vietnam at his news conference on March 23, 1961. *Courtesy John F. Kennedy Presidential Library and Museum, Boston.*

President Kennedy inspects the Berlin Wall during his visit to West Berlin, June 26, 1963. *Courtesy John F. Kennedy Presidential Library and Museum, Boston.*

President Kennedy meets with leaders of the March on Washington, August 28, 1963. LEFT TO RIGHT: Secretary of Labor Willard Wirtz, Mathew Ahmann, Rev. Dr. Martin Luther King, Jr., John Lewis, Rabbi Joachim Prinz, Rev. Eugene Carson Blake, A. Philip Randolph, President Kennedy, Vice President Lyndon Johnson, Walter Reuther, Whitney Young, Floyd McKissick. *Courtesy John F. Kennedy Presidential Library and Museum, Boston.*

Wilbur Cohen, government expert on Social Security and other welfare programs, at a forum in 1961.
Courtesy Social Security Administration History Archives.

President Johnson and Senator Richard Russell (D-Georgia) at the White House, December 17, 1963.
Courtesy Lyndon B. Johnson Library.

A poster for Republican presidential nominee Barry Goldwater in 1964.
With permission of Picture History.

President Johnson hands former president Harry Truman a pen after signing the Medicare Act at the Truman Library in Independence, Missouri, July 30, 1965. Looking on (LEFT TO RIGHT): Lady Bird Johnson, Hubert Humphrey, Bess Truman.
Courtesy Lyndon B. Johnson Library.

Senate Majority Leader Mike Mansfield (D-Montana) and Senate Minority Leader Everett Dirksen (R-Illinois), April 10, 1967. *Courtesy Lyndon B. Johnson Library.*

Members of the United States Supreme Court, photographed October 23, 1967. The justices are (BACK TO FRONT, seated): John Marshall Harlan, Hugo LaFayette Black, Earl Warren, William O. Douglas, and William J. Brennan, Jr. Standing (BACK TO FRONT): Abe Fortas, Potter Stewart, Byron R. White, and Thurgood Marshall.

With permission of Bettmann/CORBIS.

Rachel Carson, a pioneer in the environmental movement, at her microscope (date unknown).

Courtesy of Rachel Carson Papers, Beinecke Rare Book and Manuscript Library, Yale University.

Governor George Wallace blocks a door at the University of Alabama on June 11, 1963, to protest the admission of two black students, Vivian Malone and James Hood. He is confronted by Deputy U.S. Attorney General Nicholas Katzenbach. *Courtesy Library of Congress Prints and Photographs Division.*

President Johnson meeting with Martin Luther King, Jr., at the White House, on March 18, 1966. *Courtesy Lyndon B. Johnson Library.*

Betty Friedan, president of the National Organization for Women, tells reporters in the New York State Assembly lobby on April 4, 1967, of her group's determination to "put sex in section 1" of the New York State Constitution. Minutes after the picture was taken, a Capitol policeman confiscated the sign. *With permission of Picture History.*

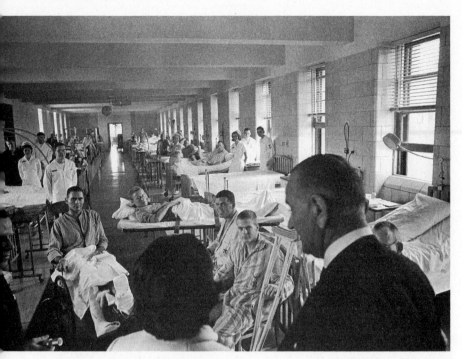

President Johnson visits injured servicemen returned from Vietnam, at Bethesda Naval Medical Center, October 21, 1965. *Courtesy Lyndon B. Johnson Library.*

Vice President Hubert Humphrey and President Johnson meet with General Creighton Abrams to discuss the situation in Vietnam, March 27, 1968. Johnson announced his decision not to seek another term four days later. *Courtesy Lyndon B. Johnson Library.*

Defense Secretary
Robert McNamara,
May 27, 1966.
*Courtesy Lyndon B.
Johnson Library.*

South Vietnamese national
police chief General Nguyen
Ngoc Loan executing a
Vietcong prisoner in the streets
of Saigon on February 1, 1968,
during the Tet Offensive. This
photograph by Associated
Press photographer Eddie
Adams was awarded the
Pulitzer Prize for spot
photography and was widely
published in the United States.
With permission of the Associated Press.

Richard M. Nixon shaking
hands with armed forces in
Vietnam, July 30, 1969.
*Courtesy Richard M. Nixon Presidential
Library and Museum.*

promote a ban on testing nuclear weapons, and lower the temperature of crisis points from Berlin to Laos. But hopes for a meeting of minds vanished in the chasm between the two governments' agendas. Aggravating the deadlock, Khrushchev's combative manner shocked Kennedy and mocked his faith that discreet, businesslike accommodation could neatly manage the volatile clash of superpowers.

Buoyed by socialist currents in many developing nations and by Soviet triumphs in missile development, space launches, and economic growth, Khrushchev saw his country—his "system"—advancing inexorably. Kennedy's recent humiliation by Castro's Cuba appeared further proof that "reactionary" capitalism was doomed. And the Soviet chairman had come to Vienna to press the point.

Conflicts over the status of Berlin dominated the waning hours of the summit and further eroded the reserves of goodwill between Kennedy and Khrushchev. To many observers Berlin symbolized the Cold War, straddling East Germany in the Soviet bloc and West Germany in the NATO alliance but lying wholly within East German territory. Crises in Soviet-American relations had repeatedly flared over West Berlin, an outpost of Western democratic capitalism in the heart of the Soviet satellite states. The provocation cut more keenly because Russians harbored traumatic memories of German invasions, as well as anxieties over West German rearmament and expressions of interest in nuclear weapons. Khrushchev called West Berlin "a bone in the throat" of the socialist world, and considered its removal a prime goal of his interactions with the West.

The immediate threat West Berlin posed to the communist bloc was economic and political rather than military. Residents enjoyed a freedom and prosperity that acted like a magnet to businessmen and professionals from East Germany (GDR), draining an already bleak economy. According to the historian Vladislav Zubok, even Khrushchev's aides joked mordantly, "Soon there will be nobody left in the GDR except for [Socialist Party boss Walter] Ulbricht and his mistress.[62]

To ensure Ulbricht's survival, in November 1958 Khrushchev demanded an end to the Western presence in Berlin. Otherwise he would sign a "peace" treaty with East Germany, ending its status as an occupied territory and, in effect, giving it control over access routes to West Berlin as a prelude to annexation. By early 1961 the unresolved tensions over Berlin made it the leading flash point of the Cold War. As Ulbricht became desperate to stem the flow of refugees, Khrushchev resolved to cajole, bluff, or threaten the new American president into concessions at Vienna.

Yet Kennedy held his ground, and the already floundering summit edged from disappointment to disaster. Khrushchev insisted that a treaty ending hostilities sixteen years after World War II was long overdue, and no power could afterward dispute East Germany's legal right to control access to West Berlin. Kennedy responded with his most forceful utterances of the summit: "We are in Berlin not because of someone's sufferance. We fought our way there . . . every President of the US since World War II has been committed by treaty and other contractual rights . . . if we were to accept the Soviet proposal US commitments would be regarded as a mere scrap of paper."[63]

Khrushchev's farewell to Kennedy included a threat of war if the United States refused to accept an "interim agreement" to end West German rule over West Berlin. Kennedy's reply was muted but resolute. "Then it would be a cold winter," he said.[64] Secretary of State Dean Rusk later reflected on "the brutality of Khrushchev's presentation,"[65] and Khrushchev himself recalled how his words on Berlin had left Kennedy "not only anxious, but deeply upset. . . . Looking at him, I couldn't help feeling a bit sorry and somewhat upset myself. . . . I would have liked very much for us to part in a different mood." But "politics," he said, "is a merciless business."[66]

"Roughest thing in my life," an exhausted Kennedy blurted to James Reston of the *New York Times* on returning to the American embassy in Vienna. In an unguarded, cathartic session with a leading member of the press, the president pondered Khrushchev's virulent behavior and his ultimatum on Berlin. "I think he thought that anyone who was so young and inexperienced as to get into that mess [at the Bay of Pigs] could be taken, and anyone who got into it, and didn't see it through, had no guts. So he just beat hell out of me. . . . I've got a terrible problem. If he thinks I'm inexperienced and have no guts, until we remove those ideas we won't get anywhere with him. So we have to act."[67]

Afraid that Khrushchev would catastrophically misread Western resolve, Kennedy warned on July 25, 1961, that Soviet action against West Berlin would mean war with the United States, asked Congress to spend billions more on defense, and announced a call-up of reservists. His speech had a tonic effect, dissuading Khrushchev from either signing a treaty with East Germany or permitting Ulbricht to move against West Berlin. But in early August, as East Germany's hemorrhaging population drain worsened, Khrushchev let Ulbricht seal the border between East and West Berlin, first with barbed wire, then a concrete wall—a wall that would soon become the pre-eminent symbol of the Cold War.

Americans were outraged. Former secretary of state Dean Acheson privately expressed dismay that the president had not ordered the wall destroyed. But although Kennedy saw the building of the wall as a brutish act (and a propaganda windfall for the West), his prime concern remained to avert a wider conflict. National Security Advisor McGeorge Bundy later acknowledged that President Kennedy's deliberately narrow reference at a press conference on August 10 to defending "West" Berlin rather than simply Berlin "may have given advance encouragement to Khrushchev" to build the wall.[68] To his friend and appointments secretary Kenneth O'Donnell, Kennedy said gently of Khrushchev, "This is his way out of his predicament. It's not a very nice solution, but a wall is a hell of a lot better than a war."[69]

A NEW DEAL FOR THE WORLD

President Kennedy began a war on poverty in developing nations some three years before President Lyndon Johnson declared unconditional war on poverty in America. Kennedy's concern sprang from fears that the difficult passage to modernity in "Third World" nations was a source of instability and discontent that communists, encouraged by the Kremlin, could exploit and possibly ride to power. The ascent of liberals in the early 1960s focused attention on these struggling nations just as reformers were stirring awareness of poverty at home and the possibilities to end it through a concerted national effort.

By 1960 some forty countries with 800 million people in Africa, Asia, and the Middle East had gained independence since World War II. Their strivings for economic growth and national strength, coupled with rising aspirations and political unrest throughout Latin America, provided a fluid arena for the United States and the Soviet Union to compete for leadership. To an emerging generation of liberals, here was an opportunity to apply the values of American reform on a world stage. "Following the war," Ambassador Chester Bowles recalled, "we were genuinely convinced that we were entering a new era, and that if we invested enough vision, energy and money, we could not only eliminate poverty and privation in the United States but ultimately extend the ideas and ideals of the American Revolution to the entire world. A permanent American Revolution, we called it; a World New Deal, a War on Want, the Century of the Common Man."[70]

What Bowles portrayed simply as a mission of American benevolence, other liberals viewed through the prism of Cold War politics and saw as a chance to prove to new nations the superiority of democratic capitalism as a path to modernity. Their ideas flourished at universities and think tanks during the late 1940s and 1950s, when the federal government and private institutions such as the Carnegie Corporation and the Ford Foundation were giving hundreds of millions of dollars for research to enhance national security. While funds went chiefly to scientists who might contribute, even indirectly, to the development of weapons systems, the government also sponsored research and projects aimed at fathoming Soviet intrigues and guiding new nations along Western lines. In 1948 the Carnegie Corporation, the CIA, and Harvard University jointly organized and funded the Russian Research Center, which sent its analyses to the federal government long before they were published. In 1952 the CIA, the Ford Foundation, and MIT cofounded the Center for International Studies, in order, as a staff member explained, "to bring to bear academic research on issues of public policy."[71]

Writing in a period of American primacy in industry, agriculture, technology, living standards, and research in natural and social science, the scholars of development expressed confidence that the United States could shape societies wisely at home and abroad. "Do we have or can we develop a knowledge of human social relations that can serve as the basis of rational, 'engineering' control?" asked the sociologist Talcott Parsons, a pioneer of modernization theory. "The evidence we have reviewed indicates that the answer is unequivocally affirmative."[72]

Economists, political scientists, historians, anthropologists, and sociologists concurred that a steep barrier separated modern Western countries from impoverished societies of Africa, Asia, Latin America, and the Middle East. These traditional states were struggling to develop productive economies, political institutions, social services, and skilled labor. The transition to a modern society entailed steep costs: It uprooted peasants seeking factory jobs in big cities, it subjected villagers to new national agencies, laws, and taxes, and it alienated intellectuals, young people, and others impatient for change. Such instability offered a window of opportunity for communists to exploit unrest. The United States could shut this window, emergent theories suggested, by hastening the birth of healthy democratic capitalist societies immune to subversion.

The flagship in this liberal scholarly armada for "nation building" was a study that glided across continents and eras called *The Stages of Economic Growth: A Non-Communist Manifesto* (1960), by W. W. Rostow. Rostow dismissed communists as "scavengers" of modernization who "know that their time to seize power in the underdeveloped areas is limited." [73] The antidote to this threat was for the United States to speed and guide the modernizing process so that nations could attain an "age of high mass consumption"[74] such as Americans enjoyed.

Rostow's exaltation of American democratic capitalism as a standard toward which other societies could aspire was characteristic of liberal thought about the developing world. As the sociologist Seymour Martin Lipset observed, new nations would do well to learn the "key values" of equality and achievement that "stem from our revolutionary origins."[75] Rostow exhorted nations in the "childhood" of modernization to learn from mature societies like the United States,[76] and invoked Louis Hartz's observation in *The Liberal Tradition in America* (1955) that America was one of a "small group of nations that were, in a sense, 'born free,'" with ideals of individual rights, democracy, and economic opportunity that favored a "natural" rise toward "modern" institutions and living standards. By emulating American values and institutions, Rostow insisted, even societies mired in poverty could attain the "preconditions" to escape their "pre-Newtonian science" and "long-run fatalism" and reach a "take-off" stage of self-sustaining economic growth.[77]

Coinciding with Kennedy's campaign calls for a vigorous American mission to the developing world, the publication of *The Stages of Economic Growth* marked Rostow as a prophet who, a reviewer for the *New York Times* wrote, had sent "a shaft of lightning through the murky mass of events which is the stuff of history." As the historian Michael Latham summed up Rostow's rebuff of Marxist rhetoric of revolution, "Liberal culture and compound interest, not class conflict, were the real engines of history,"[78] and Americans would steer aspiring nations along a safe, sound path to progress and prosperity.

The man who came to symbolize liberal faith that Americans could act as midwives in the birth of modern nations, Walt Whitman Rostow was born in Brooklyn, New York, in 1916 to an immigrant Jewish activist who had fled the czarist police. He bore his father's high aspirations for his children as the namesake of America's leading poet, just as his older brother, Eugene Debs Rostow, was named after America's leading democratic socialist. Rostow attended Yale in the 1930s as an undergraduate and a doctoral student in economics, one of a handful of Jews in an Anglo-Saxon preserve, and one who stood out even more for Marxist leanings (in sharp contrast to the fierce anticommunism he adopted during the Cold War). In World War II he volunteered for the army and helped select bombing targets in Europe for the Office of Strategic Services, a forerunner of the CIA. After the war Rostow helped develop the Marshall Plan and taught at Harvard, Oxford, Cambridge, and MIT, where his policy-driven writings and prodigious interest in world events repeatedly drew him into government service.

In 1958, while Rostow was in Washington to help write a speech for President Eisenhower on the Middle East, John Kennedy asked him to breakfast at his home in Georgetown. The senator surprised his guest by focusing the discussion on his own plans to seek the presidency, in which quest he sought Rostow's aid and support.[79] Two years later Rostow the theoretician showed an unexpected flair for marketing by contributing the main catchphrases of Kennedy's campaign, "Let's get the country moving again" and "the New Frontier." His association with the Kennedy team attested as well to the candidate's belief that developing nations were becoming central to the struggle against communism.

The Truman administration had displayed flashes of zeal to aid poor nations, though the State Department's "Point Four" program to provide Latin America with funds and technical experts paled beside the Marshall Plan's $13 billion for European recovery. Still, as the historian Melvyn Leffler has written of the Truman years, "Development itself was becoming increasingly intertwined with U.S. national security thinking."[80] In his State of the Union Address in 1948, Truman called "the most important efforts" for peace and order "those which support world economic reconstruction."[81] A year later he promised that foreign economic aid would do more for American security and at less expense than military spending. "Which is better for the country," Truman asked, "to spend twenty or thirty billion dollars [over the next four years] to keep the peace or to do as we did in 1920 [failing to aid war-ravaged nations] and then have to spend 100 billion dollars for four years to fight a war?"[82]

Eisenhower, far more than Republicans in Congress, also favored aid for global development. Yet his administration lurched between professions of sympathy for developing states and hostility toward governments that, as in Guatemala and Cuba, dared to nationalize foreign property, tolerate indigenous Communists, or accept aid from the Soviet bloc.

Kennedy made the campaign in 1960 a referendum in part on America's standing in the Third World. The nation, he suggested, faced more than a missile gap; it was losing an aid race to win hearts and minds abroad. Americans had drifted while "out of Moscow and Peiping and Czechoslovakia and Eastern Germany are hundreds of men and women, scientists, physicists, teachers, engineers, doctors, nurses . . . prepared to spend their lives abroad in the service of world communism."[83]

During a campaign stop at the University of Michigan in Ann Arbor, the candidate proposed a Peace Corps to embody America's commitment to global development. "How many of you," he asked cheering students, "are willing to spend ten years in Africa or Latin America or Asia working for the United States and working for freedom? How many of you who are going to be doctors are willing to spend your days in Ghana; technicians or engineers, how many of you are willing to work in the foreign service and spend your lives traveling around the world? On your willingness to contribute part of your life to this country will depend the answer whether we as a free country can compete."[84]

Some of Kennedy's speeches in 1960 give the impression of a man seeking votes in remote global precincts, championing a vast movement from poverty to modernity and abundance. "It is we, the American people," Kennedy exhorted, "who should be marching at the head of this world-wide revolution, counseling it, helping it come to a healthy fruition. . . . Yet we have allowed the Communists to evict us from our rightful estate."[85]

Kennedy's election marked a coming of age for liberal strategies of modernization as a key to winning the Cold War. Soon after his inauguration, Kennedy created the Agency for International Development (AID) to coordinate programs for foreign aid. The political scientist Lucian Pye, formerly a colleague of Rostow's at the Center for International Studies, became a consultant to AID and an instructor for the State Department in counterinsurgency theory, emphasizing democratic reform. Eugene Staley, an economist at the Stanford Research Institute, traveled to South Vietnam in 1961 and advised on U.S. development policy in this embattled state barely seven years old.[86] And Rostow, whose facility with ideas appealed to Kennedy ("Walt can write faster than I can read," he joked[87]), became deputy national security advisor under McGeorge Bundy and later chairman of the State Department's Policy Planning Council, a post first held by George F. Kennan.

While Rostow shared an array of high-caliber academic credentials with Bundy, a fellow Yale graduate, no one had trouble telling them apart. "In contrast to Bundy," with his reserve and acerbic wit, David Halberstam wrote, Rostow was "extremely considerate of others. . . . He seemed so ingenuously open and friendly, almost angelic. . . . The reason was simple: he was the true believer, so sure of himself, so sure of the rectitude of his ideas, that he could afford to be generous."[88] But Rostow's kind demeanor coexisted with a zeal for U.S. military intervention in Third World nations where communists threatened the government. Arthur Schlesinger referred to him as a "Chester Bowles with machine guns."[89] Later, as Lyndon Johnson's national security advisor, his die-hard support for military action in Vietnam would come to define his lasting reputation.

Rostow helped launch some of the Kennedy administration's most highly touted and best-remembered programs. The Alliance for Progress and the Peace Corps have acquired a timeless aura of idealism, sacrifice, and civic engagement, but a common historical imperative impelled their creation: the concern to revitalize American global leadership during a time of high tension with the Soviet Union and Marxist insurgencies in the Third World. Rostow's ideas about modernization as a weapon against communist agitation seemed to nestle between the soaring phrases of Kennedy's inaugural address:

> To those new States whom we welcome to the ranks of the free, we pledge our word that one form of colonial control shall not have passed away merely to be replaced by a far more iron tyranny.... To those peoples in the huts and villages of half the globe struggling to break the bonds of mass misery, we pledge our best efforts to help them help themselves.... To our sister republics south of our border, we offer a special pledge—to convert our good words into good deeds—in a new alliance for progress—to assist free men and free governments in casting off the chains of poverty. But this peaceful revolution of hope cannot become the prey of hostile powers. Let all our neighbors know that we shall join with them to oppose aggression or subversion anywhere in the Americas.[90]

As designed by Rostow, his former colleague at MIT Max Millikan, and other experts on modernization, the Alliance for Progress pledged $20 billion for Latin American development over ten years, keyed to proportional commitments by recipient governments and to reforms in land tenure and the tax structure. The plan drew on the ideas of liberal economists on two continents[91] and of such democratic leftist presidents as Rómulo Betancourt of Venezuela and Alberto Lleras Camargo of Colombia.[92] It was a visionary scheme that was a decade in the making and, as Latin Americans saw it, four centuries overdue.

"Until a hundred years ago," two students of the region wrote in 1970, "the Latin American countries were twenty poor, backward former colonies of Spain, Portugal, and France, rural-based societies that were essentially unchanged by independence."[93] But in the postwar years, the pillars of hierarchy and inertia across Latin America swayed uneasily.

Arthur Schlesinger reported on the shifting mood in 1946 for *Fortune* magazine, "The ancient oligarchies—landholders, Church, and Army—are losing their grip. There is a groundswell of inarticulate mass dissatisfaction on the part of peons, Indians, miners, plantation workers, factory hands, classes held down past all endurance and now approaching a state of revolt."[94]

Fifteen years later the spread of hope despite pervasive misery struck Schlesinger as a force for renewal that Americans could guide and redeem. "Here was a continent of 200 million souls . . . ," he wrote, "a population multiplying faster than any other in the world—where 2 per cent of the people owned 50 per cent of the wealth and 70 per cent lived in abject poverty; yet here also was a part of the west, permeated and tantalized by democratic ideals of freedom and progress."[95]

Latin economists, many trained in American graduate programs that lauded New Deal regulation of business, protection of unions, and aid to farmers, called on the United States to help fund programs for regional development.[96] During the 1950s Brazil's president Juscelino Kubitschek built on these ideas in proposing a Marshall Plan for South America. Officials in Eisenhower's State Department retorted that development must follow "free market" principles of private investment and ignored the clamor from a region they viewed as marginal. But a series of shocks in the late 1950s, stretching from Peru to Venezuela to Cuba, forced Kubitschek's "Operation Pan-America" onto the administration's political radar.

In the spring of 1958 Vice President Richard Nixon made a goodwill trip to Latin America that exposed a distinct lack of goodwill toward the United States. Students in Lima spat at Nixon, and a mob in Caracas nearly overturned his car. In January 1959 the bearded guerrilla Fidel Castro sent more tremors through the State Department when he seized Havana and sent the corrupt, American-backed dictator, Fulgencio Batista, scurrying to affluent retirement in Spain. At first hinting at accommodation with Washington, Castro veered sharply left by expropriating foreign businesses and reviling "Yankee imperialism." U.S. diplomats ridiculed him as an irrational tyrant, but Castro became an icon of social revolution among Latin Americans and a reminder of America's persistent neglect of its southern neighbors.

Eisenhower reacted to the surge in Latin American unrest and hostility by asking Congress to earmark $350 million for an Inter-American Development Bank and $500 million to fund low-cost housing, urban water-supply systems, credits to small farmers, and education.[97] In the late spring of 1960, according to Assistant Secretary of State C. Douglas Dillon, the State Department decided on an "even more radical change in U.S. policy," proposing "a $600 million fund for grants to promote social justice in Latin America." Though "far more modest in size" than Kubitschek's plan, it represented "a complete reversal of our long-standing policy of not making development grants to the countries of Latin America."[98]

Kennedy shared Eisenhower's urgency without his ambivalence about government aid for development. Surrounded by liberal economists and social theorists, he also lacked his predecessor's budgetary qualms about a southern sequel to the Marshall Plan. As a result, wrote L. Ronald Scheman, an experienced hand in inter-American relations, Kennedy's Alliance for Progress "went far beyond anything that had ever been proposed or undertaken by the United States and Latin America."[99]

In March 1961 President Kennedy heralded the Alliance to Latin American diplomats as "a vast cooperative effort, unparalleled in magnitude and nobility of purpose." By the close of the decade, he said, "The living standards of every American family will be on the rise, basic education will be available to all, hunger will be a forgotten experience, the need for massive outside help will have passed, most nations will have entered a period of self-sustaining growth, and though there will be still much to do, every American Republic will be the master of its own revolution and its own hope and progress."[100]

Kennedy's rhetoric called up a utopian future, but his gaze did not range far from the specter of Fidel Castro's Cuba. Beyond Castro's fiery exhortations to revolutionaries the world over, the very presence of his regime challenged American interests as a Soviet-supported Marxist government whose command economy, land redistribution, and seizure of foreign businesses might trigger insurrections throughout the region. The failure of the CIA-sponsored invasion at the Bay of Pigs in April 1961 added to the urgency of presenting a positive approach to development in the hemisphere.

Like many ventures in the early 1960s, the Alliance for Progress heralded great expectations but advanced with difficulty. Only seven of nineteen republics met the projected 2.5 percent annual growth for the 1960s; new schools reduced illiteracy but did not nearly end it; new health clinics improved access to medical care, but rapid population increases offset much of the benefit. Nor did Latin American elites show the requisite enthusiasm for land reform, which reached at most a million peasant families out of some 15 million, or for such New Deal landmarks as minimum-wage laws, which were often set near subsistence levels. Most discouraging, perhaps, more dictators reigned in Latin America by the end of the 1960s than when the Alliance first hailed a new era of democratization.

THE MORAL EQUIVALENT OF WAR

Obstructions in Congress that had dismayed Eisenhower intensified with Kennedy's requests for foreign aid. The resistance to increased funding for development aid found natural allies in Congress. For many members the math was troublesome: More money for foreign aid meant new taxes, but there was no offset in pork barrel spending or other domestic economic benefits.

In vain the president insisted that foreign aid for development was indispensable to national security, saying, "It is hard for any nation to focus on an external or subversive threat . . . when its energies are drained in daily combat with the forces of poverty and despair. It makes little sense for us to assail . . . the horrors of Communism, to spend $50 billion a year to prevent its military advance—and then to begrudge spending . . . less than one-tenth of that amount to help other nations . . . cure the social chaos in which Communism has always thrived."[101]

The courtly Otto Passman of Louisiana, who had gutted many an assistance bill as chairman of the House Appropriations Subcommittee on Foreign Aid, derided "the spenders, the dreamers, the internationalists"[102] who flocked to Kennedy. Under Passman's glare, Kennedy so hedged his plans for a new Agency for International Development that he said in despair to Kenny O'Donnell, "I am so busy protecting my flank from right-wing criticism that I sometimes wonder where I am getting anything done."[103]

In 1963 Kennedy gambled that a blue-ribbon presidential panel to evaluate foreign aid, stocked with Republicans and business leaders, would uphold his outreach to developing nations. It was a daring but ill-conceived stroke. In April the panel, chaired by General Lucius Clay, predictably—and publicly—chastised the administration for giving too much to too many, and recommended cutting foreign aid from a proposed $4.9 billion to $4.3 billion. The rebuke turned into a liberal rout as Congress slashed foreign aid to $3.2 billion despite Clay's efforts to temper the cuts. The president rued having called the program AID, a lightning rod for conservatives decrying giveaways. "It should have been the International Defense Fund, or something like that."[104]

Like the Alliance for Progress and the Agency for International Development, the Peace Corps was conceived as a way to counter communism by assisting developing nations. The idea of service abroad resonated with Kennedy's inaugural summons to "ask what you can do for your country" and with a national sense of urgency to reclaim the initiative in competing with the Soviet Union. Yet even in embryonic form, as a proposal voiced late in Kennedy's presidential campaign, the Peace Corps acquired an identity and an ethos unique in public service.

The paternity of the Peace Corps was complex, and not all claimants were Cold Warriors or even exclusively products of postwar culture. Individuals had summoned young people to service throughout American history. Among the oft-cited inspirations for the Peace Corps was an essay fifty years earlier by William James, "The Moral Equivalent of War," that envisioned a rite of passage for "our gilded youths" to "be drafted off, according to their choice, to get the childishness knocked out of them, and to come back into society with healthier sympathies and soberer ideas."[105] Secular and religious sponsors of overseas service proliferated in the twentieth century as though in response to James's summons. The Experiment in International Living counted among its early volunteers and organizers Kennedy's brother-in-law Sargent Shriver, who would become the founding director of the Peace Corps.

Federal forebears of the Peace Corps also thrived during the New

Deal. The Civilian Conservation Corps (CCC) organized young people in uniformed brigades to clean parks and plant trees. The National Youth Administration (NYA) set millions of students and jobless youths to build schools and hospitals, dig roads, and teach people to read and write. In January 1961 a research report on the Peace Corps proposal observed that NYA workers served when "economic conditions in some parts of the United States" during the Depression "differed little from those in underdeveloped countries today."[106]

For all the diverse ancestry of the Peace Corps, it was unmistakably a child of the Cold War that fed on alarms during the 1950s that American prestige in the developing world was ebbing. In 1952 a Democratic senator from Connecticut, Brien McMahon, called for an "army" of young Americans to go abroad as "missionaries of democracy." A fuller blueprint for overseas service came from a second-term Wisconsin congressman and longtime reformer, Henry S. Reuss, who sponsored a bill in 1960 to study the viability of a federal organization for overseas service.

Reuss had taken the road less traveled among Harvard Law School graduates in the 1930s as a municipal counsel in Milwaukee handling welfare cases, and this exposure to poverty drew him into politics as a New Deal Democrat. Like Chester Bowles and John Kenneth Galbraith, Reuss oversaw rationing of strategic materials during the war years in the Office of Price Administration until, in 1943, he had his draft exemption (as a member of OPA) revoked so he could enter the Army, serving as a major in the Seventy-fifth Infantry Division in Germany. A deputy general counsel for the Marshall Plan in Paris in 1949, Reuss renewed his interest in global relief as a congressman. On returning from a visit to Southeast Asia in 1957, he proposed a "Point Four Youth Corps" to provide technical aid and burnish America's image among nations emerging from colonial rule.

Reuss later recalled his misgivings that American aid programs in the 1950s were neglecting the mass of people they were supposed to help. "Our grandiose Eisenhower-age economic type aid projects weren't really working. For example, in Cambodia I was struck that our principal and very expensive, some $30 million aid project was something designed to curry favor with Prince Sihanouk—an enormous superhighway from

Phnom Penh."[107] But "while gratifying to the country's rulers," Reuss said, "... the superhighway's largest meaning for most Cambodian peasants lies in the use of its shoulder as a trail for their water buffalo."[108]

Heroic images of Americans living in primitive conditions to serve people in developing nations increasingly entered the popular culture. In 1958 a best-selling novel by Eugene Burdick and William Lederer, *The Ugly American*, related the exploits of a technician, Homer Atkins, who became a legend among the peasants whose lives he shared while building water pumps and digging roads. Lest readers miss the moral, Burdick and Lederer appended to their novel a plea to energize the country's foreign aid programs, calling for "a small force of well-trained, well-chosen, hard-working, and dedicated professionals. They must be willing to risk their comforts and—in some lands—their health. They must go equipped to apply a positive policy promulgated by a clear-thinking government. They must speak the language of the land of their assignment and they must be more expert in its problems than are the natives."[109] This last admonition, calling for knowledge of local cultures yet exuding confidence that superior American expertise would save these societies, fairly distilled the paradoxical liberal faith that shaped foreign policy throughout the 1960s.

In 1960 Hubert Humphrey sponsored a bill to send young volunteers to teach "basic agricultural and industrial techniques, literacy, the English language ... sanitation and health procedures in Asia, Africa, and Latin America."[110] Humphrey's presidential bid soon ebbed, but he sent his research files on an "American Peace Corps" to the man who beat him in the Wisconsin and West Virginia primaries, John Kennedy. The gesture was perfectly timed, for Kennedy was fast gaining delegates but still striving to impress the party's liberal wing and to show fresh ideas for waging the Cold War.

As happened so often in the sixties, strong leadership pushed to a boil a long-simmering idea when Kennedy's advocacy of a Peace Corps gripped the electorate and galvanized the young. "If it had been left to us," Reuss acknowledged of his and Humphrey's initiatives, "the Peace Corps idea would still be cluttering up the legislative corridors."[111]

One of Walt Rostow's first assignments from the president-elect was to team with friend and former MIT colleague Max Millikan and "[work] up a Peace Corps idea into something I could implement in the winter of '61." Kennedy named Sargent Shriver as director of the new agency.

Shriver, married to the president's sister Eunice, was known as the family idealist, committed to civil rights and aid to the poor. (Jack affectionately called him the family communist.) Shriver was also a gifted manager who had built up Joseph Kennedy, Sr.'s largest business enterprise, Merchandise Mart in Chicago. His idealism and his administrative wizardry were both in overdrive as Shriver personally conducted a whirlwind lobbying campaign for congressional approval and funds for the Peace Corps, and a twenty-six-day tour in which he persuaded Prime Minister Jawaharlal Nehru of India, Premier Kwame Nkrumah of Ghana, and leaders of six other nonaligned states to grant invitations to the first volunteers.

Shriver's lobbying was crucial to prodding Congress to approve an untested agency that Nixon had scorned during the campaign as a potential haven for draft dodgers,[112] and that Eisenhower mocked as a "juvenile experiment," asking why not send volunteers to the moon because it was underdeveloped.[113] The *Wall Street Journal* wondered at the sentiment that passed for serious policy, asking, "Who but the very young themselves can really believe that an Africa aflame with violence will have its fires quenched because some Harvard boy or Vassar girl lives in a mud hut and speaks Swahili?"[114]

Even Senator J. William Fulbright, the Democratic sponsor of a prestigious scholarly exchange program bearing his name, was cool to the prospect of an agency that might compete for talent and funds. But according to Gerard Rice, Shriver defused objections in meetings with congressmen "based on geographical region . . . rather than party affiliation" to convey that the Peace Corps was above partisan politics. In testimony before congressional committees, fiscal conservatives like Republican senator Homer Capehart from Indiana melted at Shriver's precision in accounting for jeeps (135), horses (20), outboard motors (1), and total cost ($10,712,894.58).[115]

Shriver's sheer charm, energy, and devotion to an American mission of service won over many who remained wary of the Peace Corps itself, as a member of the House Rules Committee related: "You know why I really voted for the Peace Corps? One night I was leaving at 7:30 and there was Shriver, walking up and down the halls of the House Office Building, by himself, looking into all the doors. He came in and talked to me. I still didn't like the program, but I was sold on Shriver. I voted for him."[116]

The Peace Corps was an immediate success with American youth ("the hottest topic on college campuses and among young people generally," *Life* magazine reported in March 1961). Volunteers expressed a desire to help humanity, to improve international understanding, to grow personally, and less often, to further their careers as reasons to serve two years in unfamiliar lands, forgoing amenities they had enjoyed all their lives. Beyond these specific aims, many cited a connection with President Kennedy as a spur to commitment. "Here was a man with whom I, and all young people could identify," wrote Duncan Yaggy, "a man who suddenly made being an American an exciting idea."[117]

The Corps registered equal success with host nations, which sharply stepped up their requests for volunteers. Five hundred of "Kennedy's children," as natives of the Dominican Republic called the volunteers (in Tanzania they were "*wakina* Kennedy," or "followers of Kennedy"), worked in eight developing countries in 1961, increasing to seventy-three hundred in forty-four countries two years later, and peaking at fifteen thousand in fifty-five countries in 1966. Roving ambassador Chester Bowles saw pictures of Kennedy "in remote villages of India . . . side by side with those of Gandhi and Nehru."[118]

Critics of the Peace Corps typically expressed wariness of the whole liberal enterprise in "modernizing" foreign nations. Marshall Windmiller was among the revisionist scholars who suspected that the Peace Corps was acting as a cat's paw for the United States government to open up foreign markets to American industry.[119] But as Shriver observed, the Peace Corps had no ties to big business, focused on countries so impoverished that they scarcely had enough food, and often sent volunteers to regions remote from urban markets and Western advertising.[120] A more common and reasoned criticism, as Schlesinger recorded, was "that the few thousand Peace Corpsmen were a handful of sand cast into the vast sea of underdevelopment."[121] This, of course, was true, though the volunteers had a tangible impact on the villagers and farmers they lived among, above all by spreading literacy in nations like Ethiopia, Ghana, and Nigeria that suffered from acute shortages of teachers.

One need not minimize the darker impulses of the New Frontier, evident in the zeal for covert operations and the dispatch of Special Forces into the miasma of Vietnam, to still appreciate Kennedy's gift for inspiring young Americans to exercise their best qualities "at a very special moment in history . . ." when many societies were "caught up in the adventures of asserting their independence and modernizing their old ways of life."[122] Such inspiration found daily expression in the Peace Corps, an agency rooted in the Cold War yet spared its intrigues, its dogma, and its hostilities. "Of all the agencies of the Federal Government," James Reston wrote in March 1963, "only the Peace Corps has surpassed the hopes and claims of the Kennedy administration. . . . [It] stands above the rest as something new and vigorous that has managed to avoid the pessimism of intractable problems." [123]

MISSILE CRISIS

In his Inaugural Address, President Kennedy summed up the supreme paradox of his era by observing, "Man holds in his mortal hands the power to abolish all forms of human poverty and all forms of human life."[124] The faith that energized the Alliance for Progress, the Peace Corps, Food for Peace, and other reform ventures spoke to the dreams of universal well-being that tantalized Americans in the early 1960s. An abiding fear of nuclear attack marked the grim counterpoint to this mood, which crested as Kennedy assumed office. For all the utopian strains that Kennedy channeled in his foreign policy, national survival remained his prime concern and, during the first two years of his presidency, it was far from assured.

The so-called "Thirteen Days" of the Cuban Missile Crisis in October 1962, which brought Russia and America to the edge of war, formed the critical stage of a long fever in relations between the superpowers.

For several years a cycle of fear and threat had suspended the two antagonists between war and peace by threads of uncertain resiliency. Both sides understood that this harsh limbo could not endure. In a memo to the president on August 8, 1962, called "Khrushchev at Bay," Walt Rostow forecast that with Khrushchev's ambitions stalled in Berlin, Laos, and elsewhere, he would seek a "quick success" to bolster his power in the Kremlin and raise his prestige in the international communist movement. The United States could soon face "the greatest act of risk-taking since the war."[125]

Rostow's message came several weeks after the Soviets had begun secretly to deliver more than 150 military shipments to Cuba. By late summer the island bristled with forty-two thousand Soviet troops and, among other weaponry, forty MiG-21 aircraft, batteries of surface-to-air missiles, six IL-28 bombers fitted to carry nuclear weapons, and to deter or destroy an invading force, twelve Army Luna missiles and eighty cruise missiles designed for short-range nuclear strikes. The first of several dozen surface-to-surface missiles arrived in August, capable of hitting cities as far west as Dallas, Texas. "Never before in the history of the Soviet Armed Forces and in the history of Russia had we transported so many troops to the other side of the ocean," recalled General Anatoli Gribkov, who commanded the operation. "We had to use eighty-five ships from our merchant marine, and to assemble in secrecy ships of various kinds scattered all over the seas."[126]

Several of Khrushchev's colleagues in the Politburo had opposed his Caribbean gambit as courting catastrophe. Foreign Minister Andrei Gromyko cautioned, "I must say frankly that putting our missiles in Cuba would cause a political explosion in the United States. I am absolutely certain of that."[127] Some members raised concern about nuclear war. But Khrushchev trusted that by shipping the missiles covertly, he could announce their presence as an accomplished fact that President Kennedy would have no choice but to accept.

Khrushchev trusted, too, that Kennedy was ripe for intimidation. "Nikita wouldn't have deployed missiles in Cuba unless he thought Kennedy wouldn't act," Arkady Shevchenko, a former special assistant to Gromyko, later recalled. "A few people warned him directly that the situation could lead to a blockade, and we would have no power to do anything. . . .

Nikita ignored all this—because of his opinion of Kennedy. I once heard him myself in his office saying that Kennedy was a weak man. The Cuban crisis took him completely by surprise."[128]

The Soviet leader, of course, had his own desperate reasons to place missiles in Cuba. He hoped a nuclear deterrent might protect Castro's Marxist regime in the face of covert U.S. campaigns of sabotage, assassination schemes, and amphibious exercises near Puerto Rico (to remove a mythical dictator named "Ortsac"—Castro spelled backward). He aimed, as well, to offset the lopsided American lead in nuclear weapons, which U.S. satellite photographs had exposed in September 1961 and an aide to McNamara announced in March 1962, to Khrushchev's resentment. "The Americans had surrounded our country with military bases and threatened us with nuclear weapons," he reasoned, "and now they would learn just what it feels like to have enemy missiles pointing at you."[129] Even if Khrushchev had not set out specifically to humiliate the president, still he had acted in the belief that Kennedy could be bluffed and bullied. To reverse this dangerous dynamic before it produced new gambles in Berlin and other nerve centers of the Cold War, Kennedy and his advisors perceived no alternative to firm action.

On October 16, 1962, Kennedy learned from CIA aerial photographs of the continuing deployment of nuclear missiles in Cuba, contrary to Soviet assurances and his repeated warnings. In a meeting with the ad hoc Executive Committee of the National Security Council (Ex Comm), Kennedy expressed dismay that Khrushchev had so crossed the line of acceptable conduct and risk. "But he's initiated the danger, really, hasn't he?" Kennedy remarked of this nuclear-tipped challenge just ninety miles from America's shores. "He's the one that's playing at God."[130]

The missiles posed an added challenge as the midterm elections approached. Kennedy had championed theories of flexible response and rational crisis management that looked to calibrate the use of force so precisely as to control events while curbing the risks of escalation. Yet his clouded record in foreign policy—defeat at the Bay of Pigs, concessions in Laos, acquiescence in the Berlin Wall—had troubled the public and invited charges of weakness by Republicans, conservative Democrats, and media pundits. The nuclear weapons in Cuba now posed a supreme test of the administration's strategic tenets and resolve, with Kennedy's presidency and the nation's security in the balance.

Most members of the Ex Comm, including the president and his brother Robert, inclined at first to bomb the missile sites, holding in reserve a possible follow-up invasion of Cuba. But support for an air strike faded after extended discussions notable for the president's encouragement of dissenting views. George W. Ball in particular objected to an air strike without warning as likely to kill civilians, alienate world opinion, provoke reprisals in Berlin, and risk unchecked escalation. Ball made a formidable convert in Robert Kennedy. With impassioned reference to the Japanese prime minister who had ordered the surprise attack on Pearl Harbor just over two decades earlier, he exclaimed, "My brother is not going to be the Tojo of the 1960s."[131]

At a meeting later on October 18 the president clarified the main goal: "Now, the question really is to what action we take which lessens the chances of a nuclear exchange, which obviously is the final failure—that's obvious to us—and at the same time, maintain some degree of solidarity with our allies."[132]

On Friday, October 19, Kennedy had his sole meeting during the crisis with the assembled Joint Chiefs of Staff. It was scarcely a meeting of minds. The Chiefs again pressed for a massive air strike without warning, and all except the chairman, Maxwell Taylor, favored an invasion to destroy any remaining missiles. The president instead invited them to weigh the risks. A quick strike, he conceded, would "neutralize the chance of danger to the United States of these missiles being used," but "on the other hand, we increase the chance greatly" of the Soviets' "just going in and taking Berlin by force. Which leaves me only one alternative, which is to fire nuclear weapons—which is a hell of an alternative—and begin a nuclear exchange."[133]

In contrast to his earlier deference to the military in approving the Bay of Pigs operation, Kennedy overruled their advice to bomb the missile sites and instead committed to a blockade, or "quarantine," of Cuba. Speaking to the nation on Monday evening, October 22, his demeanor grave, he said, "We will not prematurely or unnecessarily risk . . . [a] nuclear war in which even the fruits of victory would be ashes in our mouth—but neither will we shrink from that risk at any time it must be faced."[134] Nearly one in five Americans believed that World War III was imminent, according to a Gallup Poll just after the president's speech; nearly all Americans approved of Kennedy's actions.

In the tense days that followed his speech of October 22, the president pursued, in Sorensen's words, "a carefully measured combination of defense, diplomacy and dialogue."[135] Diplomacy secured Latin American and NATO support for the quarantine while on Thursday, October 25, a dramatic U.N. presentation by U.S. Ambassador Adlai Stevenson, employing photographs from CIA reconnaissance flights, dismantled Soviet denials of missile sites in Cuba. Dialogue ranged from secret correspondence with Khrushchev (twenty-two letters bearing on Cuba exchanged from October 23 through December 14) to continuing back-channel contacts between Robert Kennedy and Soviet ambassador Anatoly Dobrynin.

Defense centered on the quarantine, which President Kennedy directed with self-conscious prudence. He appealed to world opinion by exempting medical supplies, food, and oil; drew in American vessels to give Soviet ships heading toward Cuba more time to reconsider; and imposed special caution in treating foreign ships that did not clearly carry military equipment. "What would you do then," the president asked at an Ex Comm meeting on Tuesday, October 23, "if we go through all of this effort and then find out there's baby food on it?"[136]

A private letter from Khrushchev to Kennedy on Friday, October 26, hinted at a settlement based on removal of the Soviet missiles in exchange for a U.S. guarantee not to invade Cuba. But the next day a second, public letter added a demand that the United States withdraw its Jupiter missiles from Turkey. The Jupiters were obsolete (American officials jokingly wondered which way they would fire) and Kennedy had planned to remove them as provocative and without military value. Yet he did not want to antagonize the government of Turkey, a NATO member, or to appear to reward the Soviet Union for its secret nuclear deployment in Cuba.

The Ex Comm's marathon talks at the White House unfolded on Saturday afternoon in an atmosphere of growing pressure to strike at Cuba. That morning a surface-to-air (SAM) missile, fired by a local Soviet commander without approval from Moscow, had fatally downed a U-2 pilot over Cuba, Major Rudolph Anderson. Robert Kennedy later recalled the spasm of belligerence that surged through the Ex Comm: "At first, there was almost unanimous agreement that we had to attack early the next morning with bombers and fighters and destroy the SAM sites. But again the president pulled everyone back. 'It isn't the first step that concerns me,' he said, 'but both sides escalating to the fourth and fifth step—and we don't go to the sixth because there is no one around to do so. We must remind ourselves we are embarking on a very hazardous course.'"[137]

Privately he confided to his brother Bobby, "If anybody is around to write after this, they are going to understand that we made every effort to find peace and every effort to give our adversary room to move. I am not going to push the Russians an inch beyond what is necessary."[138] On Saturday evening, closeted with a small inner circle, Kennedy instructed Bobby to make a deal with Russian ambassador Dobrynin, which could include a private provision to remove the Jupiter missiles.

The attorney general welcomed Dobrynin at the Justice Department at 7:45 P.M. and conveyed the administration's proposal, embedded in warnings that time was outstripping their countries' ability to control events. If the Soviet Union halted work on the missiles and, under international control, rendered the weapons inoperable, then the United States would end the quarantine and pledge not to invade Cuba. On Sunday morning, October 28, Khrushchev broadcast his acceptance of a deal involving only a Soviet pledge to "remove weapons the United States terms offensive" (still declining to admit publicly the presence of missiles in Cuba) in return for a U.S. promise not to invade the island.

The thirteen days when, as Khrushchev wrote, "the smell of burning was in the air," had ended.

Kennedy's performance in the crisis was widely applauded. An editorial by the *New York Herald Tribune* might as easily have followed reports from Gettysburg or Appomattox: "And at the center of this great aggregation of moral and physical force was the President of the United States. This country, and free peoples everywhere, may well be grateful for the firmness and skill he has displayed in this crisis."[139] Richard Rovere declared in the *New Yorker* in November 1962 that Kennedy "has won what is perhaps the greatest personal diplomatic victory of any President in our history."[140]

The president's apparent victory still could not extinguish criticism from the Pentagon and Capitol Hill that he had been entirely too conciliatory toward Khrushchev and Castro. Military leaders fumed over the president's refusal to bomb or invade Cuba, and even the censored version of the final accord did not mollify them. Admiral George Anderson said of the news, "We have been had," and General LeMay, hoping to make the best of a bad situation, urged the president, "Why don't we go in and make a strike on Monday anyway." Kennedy politely declined the advice, and afterward remarked to Arthur Schlesinger, "The military are mad."[141]

At least the White House could count on the military to keep their mutterings about alleged presidential dereliction private. The Republican opposition, having thirsted for partisan openings throughout the crisis, did not remain so forbearing. Instead, the fading of danger appeared to dissolve any rhetorical inhibitions. George H. W. Bush, the local Republican chairman in Houston, urged Kennedy to "muster the courage" to attack Cuba. Barry Goldwater demanded that the president "do anything . . . to get rid of that cancer. If it means war, let it mean war."[142]

The president discouraged such hawkish posturing in an interview broadcast on national television on December 17, 1962. Instead of blaming the Russians, he found most troubling "that both governments were so far out of contact, really. I don't think that we expected that he [Khrushchev] would put the missiles in Cuba, because it would have seemed such an imprudent action for him to take, as it was later proved. Now, he obviously must have thought that he could do it in secret and that the United States would accept it. So that he did not judge our intentions accurately." Such "misjudgments of the intentions of others," Kennedy added, had pulled nations into war throughout the century.[143]

Khrushchev, too, felt an unaccustomed empathy with the president of the United States, as though the crucible of nuclear danger had forged a bond of unfathomable duress and responsibility. Shortly after the crisis ended, Khrushchev admitted to an American journalist, "Kennedy did just what I would have done if I had been in the White House instead of the Kremlin."[144] In his memoirs the former Soviet leader hailed Kennedy as "gifted with the ability to resolve international conflicts by negotiation, as the whole world learned during the so-called Cuban crisis. Regardless of his youth he was a real statesman."[145] As for those "clever people" who "will tell you that Kennedy was to blame for the tensions which might have resulted in war," Khrushchev said, "you have to keep in mind the era in which we live."[146]

THE TEST BAN

The peaceful settlement of the missile crisis lifted the fever that had brought the world's nuclear superpowers near the point of war. The harrowing days in October ended Khrushchev's rapture with policies based on bluff, threat, and unpredictability, and the outcome strengthened Kennedy's hand against critics who had derided "appeasement" of the Soviet Union. The gradual thaw in relations between the two countries, coupled with Kennedy's enhanced stature, brought new life to the most impassioned reform cause of his presidency: to tame the Cold War with a treaty to ban the testing of nuclear weapons.

The pursuit of a test ban revealed Cold War liberalism at the peak of political vigor. Even before his inauguration, Kennedy determined against long odds to end the Soviet and American explosions that were poisoning the atmosphere, escalating the arms race, and risking the spread of nuclear programs to other countries. This effort, which spanned most of Kennedy's thousand days in the White House, reflected the prevalent view among liberals that containment of communist power, international cooperation, and protection of vulnerable citizens were inseparable causes.

The crusade to ban nuclear tests began the night after the bombing of Hiroshima, when the thirty-one-year-old editor of *Saturday Review*, Norman Cousins, wrote an editorial called "Modern Man Is Obsolete." "Man's survival on earth is now absolutely dependent on his ability to avoid a new war," wrote Cousins, who became a clearinghouse for liberal causes centered on disarmament. Like other nuclear pacifists, he advocated a "world government" tolerant of cultural and political differences but strong enough to supersede the rivalries that inevitably led to war.

"National sovereignty is preposterous now," Cousins said in summing up the lessons of Hiroshima and Nagasaki.[147]

Opponents of nuclear tests forecast an apocalypse that could come equally from war or from poisoning of the air. Their warnings grew more urgent in the early 1950s following American and Soviet explosions of hydrogen bombs a thousand times more powerful than the ones that destroyed Hiroshima and Nagasaki. But episodes like the Bravo explosion over the Bikini atoll on February 28, 1954, which spewed radioactive ash hundreds of miles, poisoned a man on a Japanese fishing boat, and caused the Japanese government to condemn an eight-hundred-pound catch of contaminated tuna, alarmed Americans and outraged much of the world. The journalist I. F. Stone wrote, "If there is still a peace movement left in America, this must be its platform. As a first step away from mutual destruction, no more tests."[148]

The momentum of the arms race at first overwhelmed Stone's eloquent but isolated dissent. In 1955 Khrushchev proposed a ban on all nuclear explosions, but the prospects of an agreement succumbed to diplomatic tensions, objections by the U.S. Atomic Energy Commission to halting nuclear tests, doubts by U.S. scientists about the means to detect violations, and Soviet resistance to onsite inspections that could expose military weakness.

The peace movement found a clear voice during the 1956 presidential campaign when Adlai Stevenson, the liberal Democratic governor of Illinois, proposed a test ban to "reflect our determination never to plunge the world into nuclear holocaust."[149] Stevenson's gesture set loose predictable Republican charges of weakness that contributed to his lopsided defeat in the November election. Vice President Nixon called Stevenson's stand "not only naïve, but dangerous,"[150] and Eisenhower dismissed this "theatrical gesture."[151] Senator Karl Mundt observed darkly that the communist *Daily Worker* had endorsed Stevenson's proposal. Yet by making a test ban central to his candidacy, Stevenson had carried the issue through conservative resistance into the political mainstream.[152]

Worsening radioactive fallout invoked the specter of indiscriminate death and brought new life to liberal internationalism and pacifist dissent. In March 1957 the congressional Joint Committee on Atomic Energy heard public testimony by scientists detailing how strontium-90 emitted during nuclear tests "entered the atmosphere, fell to the ground, mixed with rain and snow, was ingested by cows, and entered the food cycle of humans through the milk they drank."[153] The following month Cousins visited the medical missionary Dr. Albert Schweitzer at his hospital in French Equatorial Africa and persuaded this secular saint to lend his name to the antinuclear movement.[154]

Over the next five months Cousins joined with the dean of peace activists, A. J. Muste of the War Resisters League, and diverse liberals, ministers, and scientists, to form the Committee for a Sane Nuclear Policy (SANE). Eleven thousand scientists meanwhile signed a petition in 1957 that called for immediate international agreement to halt tests of nuclear weapons. The psychoanalyst and refugee from Nazi Germany Erich Fromm explained, "The normal drive for survival" had been overwhelmed by the Cold War, and informed citizens must "try to bring the voice of sanity to the people."[155]

SANE found a champion in Hubert H. Humphrey, the Senate's leading liberal, who had long pressed with equal fervor for black rights, workers' security, aid to farmers, relief for the poor and unemployed, and universal health care. Now, as chairman of the Senate Subcommittee on Disarmament, he became a gadfly spurring Eisenhower to seek a ban on nuclear tests. This "Rembrandt with words," as Harry Truman saluted Humphrey, spoke on February 4, 1958, on the necessity of a verifiable accord on arms control, and several months later he pressed the same arguments in Moscow, engaging in an impromptu eight-and-a-half-hour dialogue with Premier Khrushchev.

By 1958 the United States had detonated 125 nuclear explosions, the Soviets 44, and the British 21. Alarm over nuclear fallout grew after the U.S. Air Force exploded a series of hydrogen bombs over Utah and Nevada. The Committee for Nuclear Information at Washington University in St. Louis underscored that nuclear testing was as much a domestic issue as a foreign policy concern by reporting the presence of a radioactive isotope, strontium-90, in baby teeth.[156] SANE advertised in the *New York Herald Tribune*, demanding, in the words of Norman Cousins, "No Contamination without Representation."

Shaken by revelations of radioactivity and pressed by world opinion, the United States, the Soviet Union, and America's junior nuclear partner, Great Britain, agreed in August 1958 to suspend further tests. When the chairman of the Atomic Energy Commission, Lewis Strauss, vehemently opposed a test ban at a meeting of advisors on disarmament, Eisenhower's secretary of state, John Foster Dulles, replied that the country must neutralize its "militaristic" image in the world. "Do we want further refinement of nuclear weapons," Dulles asked, "at the cost of the moral isolation of the United States?"[157]

For over three years the nuclear powers sustained a shaky, threat-filled moratorium while diplomats and scientists met in Geneva to seek a framework for a permanent ban. John Kennedy inherited this uncertain truce from the Eisenhower administration and created an Arms Control and Disarmament Agency to seek a permanent test ban. He remarked privately that the prospect of continued tests that poisoned the air, endangered the peace, and threatened to spread nuclear technology "haunted" him. But as East-West tensions worsened over Berlin, Khrushchev abruptly announced the resumption of nuclear testing in the atmosphere.

On September 1, 1961, the Soviet Union dropped the first of fifty hydrogen bombs in sixty days over the Siberian plains, culminating on October 30, 1961, with a record fifty-megaton blast twenty-five hundred times as powerful as the bomb dropped on Hiroshima and with ten times the power of all explosives used during World War II. Two Soviet officials reported on the bomb's transcendent physical and psychological impact: "The atmospheric disturbance generated by the explosion orbited the earth three times. The flash of light was so bright that it was visible at a distance of 1,000 kilometers, despite cloudy skies. . . . A cameraman saw 'a powerful white flash over the horizon and after a long period of time he heard a remote, indistinct and heavy blow, as if the earth has been killed!'"

"Let this device hang over the heads of the capitalists," said Khrushchev, "like a sword of Damocles."[158]

As readings of radioactivity in the atmosphere rose around the world, President Kennedy came under pressure from the military, conservatives in Congress, and the media to resume nuclear testing at once. A Gallup Poll in July 1961 favored resumption by more than a two-to-one margin.[159] Instead, Kennedy's concern over the arms race, the potential spread of nuclear technology to other countries, and increased radioactivity led him to renew his overtures to Khrushchev.

In this grim global climate, Kennedy's quest for a test ban required persistent diplomacy and nearly as vigorous courtship of Senate Republicans. It also required support from a network of liberal internationalists, nuclear pacifists, scientists, and clergy that had crystallized during the 1950s. As so often during the Kennedy presidency, the most vocal support for reform came from ordinary citizens who registered their sentiments in the street. On November 1, 1961, some ten thousand predominantly liberal and categorically indignant suburban women in Washington, D.C., and from coast to coast symbolically walked off their jobs as housewives and mothers to protest the arms race and nuclear fallout under the banner "Women Strike for Peace."

Dagmar Wilson and other leaders of Women Strike for Peace modeled their rallies on the nonviolent black demonstrations to desegregate the South that had begun a year earlier and on the campaign by "suffragettes of long ago."[160] Veterans of the peace movement, they had met in the Washington chapter of the Committee for a Sane Nuclear Policy. Yet the rank and file carried less historical and partisan baggage in their baby carriages. When a reporter asked a female marcher in Los Angeles which organization she belonged to, the woman replied with a laugh, "I don't belong to any organization. I've got a child of ten."[161]

Typical of activists in the early 1960s who balanced militancy and respectability, Women Strike for Peace carefully eyed the boundaries of acceptable protest. Unlike female abolitionists of the nineteenth century, suffragists in the Progressive era, and female pacifists during the interwar years, the leaders of Women Strike for Peace in 1961 set forth no ideology of women's rights. Wilson herself, a children's book illustrator from England, worked from home in deference to the authority on responsible motherhood, Dr. Benjamin Spock. They rejected the media's mocking parallels to an ancient Greek farce, *Lysistrata*, in which women spurned and reviled their husbands for their warlike behavior. On the contrary, they insisted, they wished only to protect their husbands, their children, and their homes.

The "female" approach of personalizing the costs of nuclear testing found an anguished ally in the White House. Jerome Wiesner, the president's science advisor, credited Women Strike for Peace and SANE with moving Kennedy more than the professional arms controllers.[162] Kennedy also kept an open channel to Cousins, whose flair for casting visionary goals in hardheaded terms made him a confidant of the president's as he navigated obstacles to a test ban treaty.

Knowing that Cousins would soon visit the Kremlin as a papal emissary to seek the release of priests interned in Eastern Europe, Kennedy told him in December 1962, "Just get across one point [to Khrushchev] . . . that there's no one in either party more anxious to get an agreement on arms control than I am."[163] The thorniest obstacle to an agreement, the president remarked of his adversary in the Kremlin, was that the same reactionary forces were buffeting Khrushchev and him to act belligerently. "[We] occupy approximately the same political positions inside our governments," Kennedy believed. "He would like to prevent a nuclear war but is under severe pressure from his hard-line crowd. . . . The hardliners in the Soviet Union and the United States feed on one another, each using the actions of the other to justify his own position."[164]

When Cousins urged the president in April 1963 to heed the people's cry to stop nuclear tests and save the earth, Kennedy replied that letters to the White House more often asked about his daughter Caroline's horse than about a treaty, and those who cared were fifteen to one against a ban."[165]

Complicating the search for consensus was the division among liberals on the merits of a test ban. While such "internationalists" as Humphrey and Stevenson backed a comprehensive treaty, Senate Democrats like Henry "Scoop" Jackson from Washington and Stuart Symington from Missouri, both stalwarts of the Armed Services Preparedness Committee, mixed support for black rights and social programs with unremitting hostility to the Soviet Union; David Riesman, a liberal critic eager to distance himself from this hawkish breed, called them "bomber liberals."[166]

Still, scattered signs pointed to growing public distaste for the hardliners' unvarying diet of anticommunist harangues. The missile crisis of October 1962 had cast doubt on the value of nuclear weapons while raising confidence in President Kennedy as a firm but temperate leader. In the spring of 1963 the nation's best-selling novel was Eugene Burdick and

Harvey Wheeler's apocalyptic *Fail-Safe*, in which the president orders a nuclear strike on New York City to avert Soviet reprisals after the accidental launch of an Air Force attack on Moscow. And as studies of radioactivity filtered from scientific journals into popular magazines, thirty-four U.S. senators introduced a Sense of the Senate Resolution on May 27 for "banning all tests that contaminate the atmosphere or the oceans."[167]

Kennedy still faced the conundrum of how to outflank the hawks in Washington and in the Kremlin. Cousins advised him to counter with "the most important speech of your Presidency ... in its breathtaking proposals for genuine peace, in its tone of friendliness for the Soviet people and its understanding of their ordeal during the last war."[168] On June 10, 1963, Kennedy did this and more in a commencement address at American University that condemned the reflexive antagonism by both sides in the Cold War and addressed the "most important topic on earth: world peace." "[W]e must reexamine our own attitude—as individuals and as a Nation—for our attitude is as essential as theirs," he said that day. "As Americans, we find communism profoundly repugnant as a negation of personal freedom and dignity. But we can still hail the Russian people for their many achievements—in science and space, in economic and industrial growth, in culture and in acts of courage."[169]

To break the "vicious and dangerous cycle in which suspicion on one side breeds suspicion on the other, and new weapons beget counterweapons," Kennedy announced an agreement to begin high-level talks in Moscow and a pledge not to resume "nuclear tests in the atmosphere so long as other states do not do so." He anticipated the stockpile of Cold War objections by conceding that no treaty could "provide absolute security against the risks of deception and evasion. But it can ... offer far more security and far fewer risks than an unabated, uncontrolled, unpredictable arms race."[170]

Kennedy's remarks at American University, though focused on Soviet-American relations, expressed the faith that national security and social justice were indivisible. Anticipating by a day the boldest speech for racial equality of any president since Lincoln, Kennedy observed "that peace and freedom walk together" and that "in too many of our cities today, the peace is not secure because freedom is incomplete." Therefore "the legislative branch at all levels" and Americans generally must "protect that freedom for all of our citizens." Envisioning freedom from war, fallout, and prejudice as intertwined, the president asked, "And is not peace, in the last analysis, basically a matter of human rights—the right to live out our lives without fear of devastation—the right to breathe air as nature provided it—the right of future generations to a healthy existence?"[171]

The domestic impact of Kennedy's overture to the Soviet Union, now widely remembered as one of the great speeches in American history, was negligible. Over the next few weeks the president received fewer than two thousand letters on his speech, compared with over fifty thousand about a freight rate bill. Kennedy told an aide, "That is why I tell people in Congress that they're crazy if they take their mail seriously."[172] Republicans in Congress fired the standard partisan salvos. Craig Hosmer, the senior Republican on the Joint Atomic Energy Committee and chairman of a House Republican Conference Committee on Nuclear Testing, called the president's speech "a soft line that can accomplish nothing." Goldwater's verdict was harsher still: "a dreadful mistake."[173]

A better reception awaited Kennedy's remarks in the Kremlin. The Soviet press published his address uncut, and the Voice of America broadcast the speech in Russian. It was "the best speech by any president since Roosevelt," Khrushchev later told Averell Harriman, the president's newly appointed emissary for test ban negotiations in Moscow.[174] Harriman, lionized by the Kennedys for having conjured a peace treaty in Laos, brought to the bargaining table toughness honed at summits with Stalin, Churchill, and other titans of diplomacy. A Soviet embassy official in Washington revealed to Arthur Schlesinger the magic of Harriman's name in the Kremlin, saying, "As soon as I heard that Harriman was going, I knew you were serious."[175]

But while Harriman conveyed the stature of a proconsul, this was the President's issue in all its minutiae. According to Richard Reeves, "Kennedy was in contact with Harriman three and four times a day. Spending hours in the cramped White House Situation Room, Kennedy personally edited the U.S. position, as if he were at the table himself."[176] When the talks deadlocked over the number of onsite inspections (Khrushchev would permit three on Soviet territory, the Americans and British would settle for eight), Kennedy, aligning with the earlier Senate resolution, secured a limited ban on tests "in the atmosphere, beyond its limits, including outer space, or under water, including territorial waters of high seas."[177] Underground tests, less dangerous to the environment and harder to detect without onsite inspections, would continue.

Remembering the failure of President Woodrow Wilson to win Senate approval of his plan for a League of Nations, Kennedy included Republican senators at the signing ceremony in Moscow on August 5, 1963.[178] Also present was U.N. Ambassador Adlai Stevenson, who had braved attacks on his patriotism and judgment in advocating a test ban during the 1950s. In Washington the president singled out Hubert Humphrey for praise, tempered by gallows humor, saying, "Hubert, this is your treaty—and it had better work."[179]

The prospect of even a limited test ban jolted the far right and others who feared Soviet cheating. The "father of the hydrogen bomb," physicist Edward Teller, testified before the Senate Foreign Relations Committee and wrote to congressmen in August 1963 that the treaty would be "a step away from safety and possibly ... toward war."[180] J. William Fulbright, chairman of the Senate Foreign Relations Committee, said to the president about Teller's effective proselytizing for deadlier weapons, "The only thing Teller had over the others is he is such an actor." Kennedy replied, "Yeah, there's no doubt that any man with complete conviction, particularly who's an expert, is bound to shake anybody who's got an open mind. That's the advantage of having a closed mind."[181]

Former military chiefs of staff Arleigh Burke, Arthur Radford, and Nathan Twining, defense contractors all, assailed the treaty for risking Soviet violations and blocking American technical advances.[182] Almost to the last, Republican Barry Goldwater tried to insert amendments to require the Soviet Union to abandon Berlin and Cuba as a precondition for Senate ratification. Among Democrats who spurned the treaty, Senator Richard Russell of Georgia held out for an absolute standard of verification, saying, "I have serious doubts that we will ever be able to persuade Russia to agree to a foolproof system of inspection."[183]

To win over doubtful senators, the president discreetly formed a bipartisan Citizens Committee for a Nuclear Test Ban Treaty, chaired by a former U.S. disarmament negotiator and U.N. delegate under Eisenhower, James J. Wadsworth, and boasting thirteen Nobel Prize winners in science, which mobilized support on Capitol Hill. Kennedy also worked to limit a different kind of nuclear fallout: the prospect that military leaders would damn the treaty in secret testimony that conservative senators could leak to the media. Kennedy asked Senator J. William Fulbright to schedule the Joint Chiefs to testify in open sessions of his Senate Foreign Relations Committee before they could meet behind closed doors in the Senate Armed Services Committee, most of whose members favored unlimited nuclear testing. Kennedy explained this precaution to Senate Majority Leader Mike Mansfield: "What they [the Joint Chiefs] will say in public would be more pro-treaty than what they will say under interrogation by [Senator Henry] Scoop Jackson with leading questions and Barry Goldwater and Strom Thurmond. . . . [Once the Chiefs are on record], they're not going to be able to leak it on us that the Chiefs have grave reservations about this treaty."[184]

The paucity of military men, active or retired, with a kind word for a test ban led Kennedy to deploy Secretary of Defense Robert McNamara and Chairman of the Joint Chiefs Maxwell Taylor as witnesses in the Senate Foreign Relations Committee. McNamara overwhelmed doubters of the nation's military readiness with numbers plucked from secret files on the U.S. nuclear arsenal: "33,000 warheads on station" and "15,000 more . . . in preparation," over 7,000 of which could strike deep inside Russia.[185]

Kennedy's hard-won victory in the battle of the generals fairly scattered all but the most unreconstructed hard liners. On August 26 former presidents Truman and Eisenhower both endorsed the limited test ban, citing the favorable testimony of the Joint Chiefs. And on September 11, the president cajoled Senate Minority Leader Everett Dirksen into backing the treaty by sending him a letter, drafted to Dirksen's written specifications, which answered objections by the military, most Republicans, and conservative Democrats.

Kennedy assured Dirksen (and in an identical letter, Majority Leader Mike Mansfield) that underground tests would move ahead "vigorously and diligently," that the United States would remain ready to resume testing in the atmosphere, and that "the treaty in no way limits the authority . . . to use nuclear weapons." The next day, the sixty-seven-year-old Dirksen rescinded his opposition to a treaty with the Russians, citing "preponderant" favorable testimony by the "most competent" scientific, military and diplomatic leaders." The shadow of Republican senator Arthur Vandenberg seemed to hover in the Senate chamber as Dirksen declared the urgency of international cooperation, saying, "I should not like to have written on my tombstone, 'He knew what happened at Hiroshima, but he did not take a first step.'"[186]

Democratic senator Jackson, after glowering skeptically at the treaty for months, also relented in response to the president's assurances. Though his shift fell short of Dirksen's in drama, it carried the weight of long expertise in military matters. Jackson remained wary of Russian gains, but he pronounced the treaty acceptable so long as the administration committed firmly to preserve the U.S. deterrent and to use the right of withdrawal to guard the nation's interest.[187]

"I don't see any political mileage in opposing the treaty," a Republican senator said in forecasting Senate ratification. A Harris Poll in September 1963 showed 81 percent of Americans favoring a test ban treaty. On September 24 the Senate approved the treaty by a nearly identical margin, 80–19; just over half the dissenters came from the South.[188]

Despite its limited scope, the treaty signaled a quickened resolve to tame the Cold War and not merely prepare for Armageddon. Sorensen tallied the change: "After 336 nuclear explosions in the atmosphere by the United States, Great Britain and the Soviet Union, after thirteen years of almost steady accumulation of radioactive poisons in the air, those three powers had formally committed themselves to no more atmospheric tests. Over a hundred other nations signed the same pledge."[189]

Scientists against the arms race took due note. Since 1945 the *Bulletin of the Atomic Scientists* had featured on its covers the hands of a doomsday clock. Upon Senate ratification of the test ban, the hands eased back from seven minutes before midnight to twelve minutes before midnight.[190]

THAW

The missile crisis and the test ban became symbols of a sea change in relations between Washington and Moscow during the last year of Kennedy's presidency. The Cold War continued, but Khrushchev joined with

Kennedy in implementing a succession of confidence-building agreements. Having stood at the brink of war, both sides resolved to hedge their rivalry in favor of predictability, accommodation of each other's vital interests, and mutual survival.

In the wake of the missile crisis, brinkmanship lost its charm for Khrushchev. On April 26, 1963, he spoke to Averell Harriman about Laos in conciliatory tones that recalled Kennedy's overtures in Vienna. According to Constantine Fursenko and Timothy Naftali, Khrushchev displayed "new priorities" of great power understanding that brooked no disruption by remote nations:

> The superpowers really had better things to worry about than tiny Laos. With a population of only two million, he told Harriman, there was "nothing really serious going on in Laos." He thought that the U.S. and the USSR should try hard to "ignore it." ... "Khrushchev impatiently exclaimed that he did not know all those silly Laotian names or the individuals to whom these names belonged," NSC staffer Michael Forrestal, who made the trip with Harriman, later reported to the White House.[191]

Even in Berlin, the potential volcano whose rumblings had recurred throughout the postwar years, things grew more quiet. In the spring of 1963 the eighty-eight-year-old West German chancellor, Konrad Adenauer, just months from retirement, secretly transmitted proposals to normalize relations. During a visit to Moscow he broached the prospect of achieving "civil peace" by freezing the status quo of two Germanys, a divided Berlin, and the postwar Polish-German border for thirty years. Khrushchev responded warmly and put the case before the Politburo that West Germany could become a closer trading partner.[192]

Much of the Cold War had centered on economic rivalry between capitalist and socialist systems, but in 1963 commerce trumped competition as Kennedy agreed to a Soviet proposal to buy 65 million bushels of American wheat. A thicket of objections blocked Kennedy's path, but as Sorensen recounts, "In time he overcame attempted Congressional restrictions, attempted longshoreman boycotts, Soviet haggling about freight rates, disagreements between Agriculture and State, disagreements between Labor and Commerce, [and] disputes over financing.... The export licenses were granted, the wheat was sold, and the President hoped that more trade in nonstrategic goods would follow."[193]

Agreements measured in symbols rather than bushels came more readily. On June 20, 1963, Soviet and American diplomats signed a memorandum of understanding to create a private teletype link between Washington and Moscow, passing through Helsinki, Stockholm, and London. This "hot line" to keep the nuclear powers talking during crises was functioning by summer's end.[194] Soviet and American delegates to the U.N. took a similar confidence-building step by voting for a United Nations resolution of October 17 banning nuclear weapons in outer space.[195]

Even where specific agreement was lacking, Kennedy looked beyond old hostilities. Speaking at the United Nations General Assembly on September 20, 1963, he proposed a joint Soviet-American expedition to the moon, observation posts to reduce the chances of surprise attack, controls on the transfer of nuclear weapons, a verifiable ban on underground testing, and freer movement of people and ideas between East and West. "But peace," the president said, "does not rest in charters and covenants alone.... [L]et us strive to build ... a desire for peace ... in the hearts and minds of all of our people."[196] Opinion polls that autumn confirmed that Americans were listening; they embraced Democrats as the "peace party," best able to keep the country out of war.[197] Conciliation toward the Kremlin, for so long a grave electoral handicap, was becoming good politics.

The verbal grappling between Soviet and American leaders over their respective readiness to use nuclear weapons never disappeared, though it shifted from public bombast toward quiet exchanges that did not derail the business of improved relations. A European political leader, struck by the emerging civility between East and West, predicted that Kennedy's stand in the missile crisis would be remembered like "the Greek stand against the Persians at Salamis in 400 B.C.—not only a great turning point in history, but the start of a true Golden Age."[198] The euphoria, so widely shared, did not long survive Kennedy's death, succumbing instead to rising casualties in Vietnam and growing divisions at home. But in the realm of domestic reform, the forecast of a golden age spoke to a coming burst of energy by intellectuals, activists, and political insiders determined to reshape American society.

This surge of reform, which spanned the last year of Kennedy's presidency and the first years of Johnson's, mirrored closely the orbit of Soviet-American relations. For much of Kennedy's time in office, foreign affairs took precedence in American politics. But as the specter of maximum danger receded for politicians and the public, the challenges of race, poverty, and economic policy came into sharper view. For a brief period in the mid-1960s, with nuclear threats subsiding and Vietnam still a manageable burden, the vision of a Great Society took root and flourished in the hollow of the Cold War.

CHAPTER 7

A TVA IN THE
MEKONG VALLEY

On November 27, 1965, as Carl Oglesby, president of Students for a Democratic Society (SDS), addressed an antiwar March on Washington, over 175,000 U.S. soldiers were in South Vietnam and U.S. Air Force pilots were running dozens of bombing sorties a day against the North. Oglesby, a lean, trimly bearded Ohio native from working-class roots, had until then comfortably affirmed the nation's Cold War verities, supporting a wife and three young children as a technical writer for a Pentagon-funded think tank. But his avid reading on the Cold War brought unsettling discoveries about CIA-sponsored coups, U.S. support for right-wing despots, and the U.S. arms buildup spanning six thousand bases overseas.

The war in Vietnam completed Oglesby's turn from mainstream reformer to indignant critic of Washington, D.C. He quit his job, joined SDS, and called on liberals at the rally to face a "crisis of conscience":[1]

The original commitment in Vietnam was made by President Truman, a mainstream liberal. It was seconded by President Eisenhower, a moderate liberal. It was intensified by the late President Kennedy, a flaming liberal. Think of the men who now engineer that war—those who study the maps, give the commands, push the buttons, and tally the dead: Bundy, McNamara, Rusk, Lodge, [Ambassador to the U.N. Arthur] Goldberg, the President himself. They are not moral monsters. They are all honorable men. They are all liberals.[2]

Oglesby urged his liberal listeners to reclaim ideals that were being subverted by the Pentagon, big business, and callous politicians. "Maybe," he suggested, "we have here two quite different liberalisms: one authentically humanist; the other not so human after all":

Not long ago I considered myself a liberal and if someone had asked me what I meant by that, I'd perhaps have quoted Thomas Jefferson or Thomas Paine, who first made plain our nation's unprovisional commitment to human rights.[3]

By contrast, Oglesby lamented, the liberals who ran the government cared only "to safeguard what they take to be American interests around the world against revolution or revolutionary change, which they always call Communism." But this was to ignore that misery and injustice fuel rebellion, whether in northern ghettos or the Mississippi Delta. "Then why can't we see that our proper human struggle is not with Communism or revolutionaries, but with the social desperation that drives good men to violence, both here and abroad?"[4]

Oglesby's warning to liberals to extricate themselves from Vietnam before it devoured their coalition foretold their ordeal over the next several years, as the widening war discredited the White House, shattered the liberal consensus, and polarized the country more than all the decade's earlier insurgencies. For two decades, liberals had championed domestic reform and unlimited military containment of communism while denying that the two agendas might be fundamentally at odds. But as Vietnam grew from a small attempt to aid a noncommunist government to the hottest theater of the Cold War, the twin pillars of liberal consensus—to "pay any price, bear any burden" for freedom both at home and abroad—buckled. Despite bluster that America could have both guns and butter, Lyndon Johnson came privately to echo Martin Luther King's lament that the Great Society had been "shot down on the battlefields of Vietnam."[5]

THE ROOTS OF CONFLICT

American intervention in Vietnam resulted from the collision between two great forces in global politics: the surge of nationalist movements against European colonial rule after World War II, and the U.S. commitment to contain communism, in the words of George F. Kennan, "at a series of constantly shifting geographical and political points." Beginning in November 1946 the Vietnamese, under the communist revolutionary Ho Chi Minh, paid for their independence with several hundred thousand lives in an eight-year war to end French control. Since first seeking vainly to enlist President Woodrow Wilson in 1919 as a champion of Vietnamese self-determination, Ho had courted American support, even beginning his nation's declaration of independence on September 2, 1945, with the words, "We hold these truths to be self-evident: that all men are created equal."[6] Yet despite professions of sympathy for colonial people, the Truman administration discreetly subsidized the French war effort in Vietnam in order to bolster a key ally against the Soviet Union.

After the triumph of communist revolutionaries in China in late 1949, the United States began openly to fund French military forces in Vietnam as part of a strategy to contain communism in Asia, a policy reinforced by the outbreak of war in Korea the following June. Ho relied on guerrilla warfare to counter French technological superiority, and he accurately foretold the course of the conflict, saying, "If ever the tiger [his army] pauses, the elephant [France] will impale him on his mighty tusks. But the tiger will not pause, and the elephant will die of exhaustion and loss of blood."[7]

By May 1954, as beleaguered French forces dug in at the remote valley fortress of Dien Bien Phu, the Eisenhower administration considered naval and air attacks to relieve the garrison. But Eisenhower found Congress reluctant and his global coalition too slender (the British had disclaimed any interest in sacrificing for a vain French colonial war while their own empire eroded). "Without allies," Eisenhower told his staff, "the leader is just an adventurer, like Genghis Khan."[8]

In his memoirs, General Matthew Ridgway, the Army chief of staff and an opponent of U.S. air strikes at Dien Bien Phu, recalled a report by a team of Army experts in 1954 that forecast disaster if the United States intervened in Vietnam. "In Korea," Ridgway wrote, "we had learned that air and naval power alone cannot win a war and that inadequate ground forces cannot win one either. . . . That error, thank God, was not repeated."[9]

The French saw no divine favor in American abandonment; shorn of air power, the elite soldiers of Dien Bien Phu succumbed to artillery bombardments from the mountains and to human-wave assaults. On May 7 the fifty-five-day resistance ended in surrender to Ho's forces, just as negotiations in Geneva to settle the war were about to open. The resulting cease-fire accords in July 1954 granted Vietnam independence and promised nationwide elections in two years. As a provisional administrative expedient, the accords partitioned Vietnam into a communist northern zone and a southern zone under Vietnamese who had served the French. The accords declared the division temporary and not to be "interpreted as constituting a political or territorial boundary." Ho had every expectation of sweeping the mandated elections, but he had not reckoned on the tenacity of U.S. hostility.

Unwilling to cede all of Indochina to the communists, the Eisenhower administration supplanted French administrators in southern Vietnam and forged a separate client state under the leadership of Ngo Dinh Diem. Robert Shaplen described Diem as "a short, broadly built man with a round face and a shock of black hair, who walked and moved jerkily, as if on strings. He always dressed in white and looked as if he were made out of ivory."[10] Though lacking the common touch, Diem had impeccable credentials for an American-backed leader. He loathed the communists, who had killed one of his brothers during the revolution, and he leaned West, having spent several years in a Catholic monastery in New Jersey before returning to Saigon in June 1954 as the prime minister of South Vietnam. But most Vietnamese, North and South, cared less about the Cold War chessboard than about unifying their land and purging foreign influence.

Diem possessed the will to power but no clear way. His fledgling nation was rich in resources but devastated by years of war; no national democratic political institutions existed after generations of French-enforced dependency; religious sects and the Binh Xuyen river pirates in Saigon fielded independent armies; Catholics made up Diem's one sure constituency but just 10 percent of the population in a largely Buddhist land; the one legendary symbol of Vietnamese nationalism, Ho Chi Minh, eclipsed Diem from his capital in Hanoi, where he ruled the more populous North.

President Eisenhower sent advisors (eight hundred by the time Kennedy came into office in January 1961) to turn Diem's nominal army into a fighting force; negotiate with, bribe, and threaten warlords and factional leaders; train civil servants; and churn out propaganda about the evils of communism and the virtues of Diem's reign. The United States also sent billions of dollars to equip the Army of the Republic of Vietnam (ARVN), as well as repair roads, railroads, and canals, pay off the national debt, supply medical facilities, and subsidize a dizzying array of imported consumer goods. A visitor wrote of the burst of affluence in Saigon, "The streets are crowded with new motor scooters and expensive automobiles; and in the upper-income residential areas new and pretentious housing is being built."[11]

Democratic senator Gale McGee of Wyoming proposed making Vietnam a "showcase" for the U.S. foreign aid program, so people from other countries could see the "wholesome effects of our efforts to help other peoples help themselves."[12] But the shopping sprees and gaudy wares in Saigon signaled reliance on American largesse rather than long-range economic development or better conditions in the villages where most Vietnamese resided. About 80 percent of American aid to South Vietnam went to the armed forces rather than to economic or technical assistance. Vietnam, Milton Taylor wrote in 1961, was the "prototype of a dependent economy, its level of national income as dependent on outside forces as was the case when the country was a French colony. . . . American aid has built a castle on sand."[13]

It did not help the U.S. effort to burnish South Vietnam's image as a showcase of democracy that Diem, descended from Mandarins at the imperial court of Hué in attitude as well as bloodlines, proved less interested in courting the masses than in cowing them. In 1955 he won 98.2 percent of the vote in a presidential election notable for police intimidation and ballot fraud; of 450,000 registered voters in Saigon, over 600,000 backed Diem.[14]

It is a measure of the alarm with which Americans surveyed the world during the early Cold War that despite Diem's manifest disabilities, his government became a rallying symbol to those who favored bold U.S. engagement in world affairs. In February 1955, over a decade before Americans first watched TV news anchors recite body counts in Vietnam, *New York Times* columnist James Reston offered "An Appraisal of the Cold War" at the University of Minnesota that dismissed a "return to the old unencumbered, unentangled days" of pre–World War II isolationism. "If anybody is looking for 'normalcy,'" he said, "let him look around the world at his leisure. This is it—what we have now. Today it is Quemoy and Matsu. Tomorrow it will be South Viet Nam. Yesterday it was Europe. Now it is Asia."[15]

Confident of U.S. support, Diem refused to allow the national elections mandated by the Geneva Accords for 1956. Instead he forcibly consolidated his rule in the South, not only smashing the rebellious Cao Dai and Hua Hao sects and the Binh Xuyen army in Saigon but also repressing the Buddhists, the peasants, the national legislature, newspaper editors, independent civil servants, and village leaders, abolishing the age-old tradition of local elections. Diem targeted for special terror the veterans of the war for independence, whom he branded communists and had tortured, jailed, and often executed by secret police and blue-shirted Republican Youth. By the late 1950s Diem had provoked a many-sided insurgency against his rule, and by extension against his American advisors in Saigon and supporters in Washington.

In December 1960 a National Liberation Front (NLF) formed to coordinate the widening rebellion to "overthrow the camouflaged colonial regime of the American imperialists and the dictatorial power of Ngo Dinh Diem."[16] Diem derisively called the rebels Viet Cong, an insulting term for Vietnamese Communists, and the U.S. government also dismissed the insurgency as masterminded by North Vietnam. Each claim had substance. Communists and noncommunists alike were rising in desperation against Diem's brutality, but Hanoi secretly advised the rebels on strategy while conducting limited efforts to supply and reinforce them. The historian William J. Duiker summed up the dual character of the uprising as "a genuine revolt based in the South" but "organized and directed from the North."[17]

The shrinking of Diem's authority and the inability of the U.S. government to restore it short of direct intervention revealed a fundamental contradiction in American policy. Fear of Vietnam's reunification under a communist hero of the war for independence had led the United States to back an isolated autocrat in the name of freedom, democracy, and nation building. Eisenhower left office in January 1961 just as this contradiction neared the breaking point. Viet Cong guerrillas dominated the countryside, and disaffected army officers stepped up their intrigues against the government. It remained for two liberal Democratic presidents to try to square the circle, to protect the shell of democracy from a communist-led revolution with widespread support.

"NO RESPECTABLE TURNING BACK"

Like Truman and Eisenhower before him, Kennedy brought to his consideration of Vietnam the core aims of containing communism in South Vietnam and containing as well the costs of U.S. commitment. He entered the White House having pledged greater vigor in handling "brushfire wars" on the periphery of the Cold War without having to resort to nuclear bluff or bombing. John Lewis Gaddis writes that budgetary constraints had "most often forced the consideration of unpalatable options" during the Cold War,[18] but Kennedy shrugged off such curbs in an age when national resources appeared ample for all tasks.

Buoyed by liberal economists who encouraged greater federal spending to stimulate growth, Kennedy rapidly built up conventional forces, including the Army "Green Berets" trained to live off the land and foil guerrilla uprisings through superior prowess and aid to indigenous peoples. Walt Rostow embodied this expansive approach to counterinsurgency in advising Kennedy in March 1961: "We must somehow bring to bear our unexploited counter-guerrilla assets on the Viet-Nam problem: armed helicopters; other Research and Development possibilities; our

Special Forces units. It is somehow wrong to be developing these capabilities but not applying them in a crucially active theater. In Knute Rockne's old phrase, we are not saving them for the Junior Prom."[19]

Kennedy still shied from sending combat units to shore up Diem's government despite persistent urging by officials in the State and Defense departments and by top military officers. The problem, in Kennedy's view, lay not with American military capabilities but with Diem's political frailty. The presence of U.S. troops simply would not make Diem an effective, popular leader, which depended on his purging corruption, implementing social reforms to aid the peasants, and motivating the ARVN, which had so far failed to defeat—or engage—much smaller enemy units.

Kennedy was not alone in preferring a negotiated solution in Vietnam. His legal counselor, Abram Chayes, the veteran diplomat Averell Harriman, and Undersecretary of State Chester Bowles all shared the president's wariness of intervention. So did John Kenneth Galbraith, now the ambassador to India, who used his back channel to Kennedy to write, "Who is the man in your administration who decides what countries are strategic? I would like to have his name and address and ask him what is so important about this real estate in the space age."[20] But the president's top civilian and military advisors argued that South Vietnam was critical to U.S. interests and that the very weakness of the Diem regime demanded an immediate military commitment to assure Saigon and to warn Hanoi, Peiping (now Beijing), and Moscow.

In October 1961 Rostow and General Maxwell D. Taylor, Kennedy's personal military advisor, toured South Vietnam. George Ball, a State Department official familiar with the French ordeal in Indochina, felt heartened by the inclusion of Taylor, a commanding presence and sound strategist, though "as I knew from experience with my French friends, there was something about Vietnam that seduced the toughest military minds into fantasy." But Ball worried that Rostow had already fallen prey to activist illusions. "A friend of mine since the Second World War," Ball recalled, "[Rostow] was an articulate amateur tactician. I thought him unduly fascinated by the then faddish theories about counter-insurgency and that intriguing new invention of the professors, 'nation building.'"[21]

Both Rostow and Taylor bore out Ball's apprehensions. They found little to praise about Diem's government but proposed sending an eight-thousand-man American "logistic task force" of engineers, medical groups, and infantry, ostensibly for flood control in the Mekong Delta but, as Taylor confided, mainly "to restore Vietnamese morale" with this "visible symbol of the seriousness of American intentions."[22] Rostow reminded Kennedy of the high stakes, predicting that the conflict in Southeast Asia "might be the last great confrontation" with communism.[23]

McNamara thought the Rostow-Taylor report did not go far enough. He doubted whether "8,000 men in a flood relief context" would suffice to "convince the other side (whether the shots are called from Moscow, Peiping, or Hanoi) that we mean business" and worried it would merely mire the United States in an "inconclusive struggle." Instead McNamara sought a "clear commitment" that risked a "prolonged" open struggle against North Vietnam and China, though he believed the United States could prevail with at most 205,000 men.[24]

Kennedy dismissed these and later recommendations for combat units as a doubtful short-term measure with lasting pitfalls. It would have been "like taking a drink," he told the historian Arthur Schlesinger. "The effect wears off, and you have to take another."[25] When Ball warned Kennedy that commitments to Vietnam might one day lead to the deployment of three hundred thousand U.S. troops, Kennedy laughed at the absurdity. "Well, George," he said, "you're supposed to be one of the smartest guys in town, but you're crazier than hell. That will never happen."[26]

While Kennedy warded off the pressures to bolster Diem's regime with a show of force, he placated the national security establishment by increasing other kinds of aid to South Vietnam. In the two years following the Rostow-Taylor mission, South Vietnam received more foreign aid than any other nation, most of it military, and the number of American advisors grew from some 1,300 to 16,700. Drawn mainly from U.S. Army Special Forces, the advisors trained ARVN soldiers, ferried them by helicopter, and often accompanied them into battle with the Viet Cong. The snares Ball had warned against were pulling the administration into a twilight stage of intervention, short of open war yet deeper than the president dared reveal.

In the ambiguity of this commitment, the Kennedy team's advocates of modernization and counterinsurgency flourished. Roger Hilsman,

Kennedy's assistant secretary of state for the Far East, exemplified the new breed of national security strategists who wielded blueprints for reform like clubs to blunt communism in the developing world. Hilsman had served in the Office of Strategic Services during World War II, studied political science at Yale, and absorbed the liberal vision of scholars like Rostow and Max Lerner that portrayed insurgency as a battle for hearts and minds as much as a military struggle. Hilsman applied this outlook in Vietnam by pressing reforms to protect villagers and raise their standard of living, in turn depriving the Viet Cong of their rural base and reducing them to "hungry, marauding bands of outlaws devoting all their energies to remaining alive."[27]

The "strategic hamlet" program, pushed by Diem with Hilsman's blessing, promised just this blend of uplift and security by relocating peasants to fortified settlements guarded by moats filled with bamboo spikes. The government would allot the residents land, fertilizer, cooking oil, and livestock, provide schools and medical clinics, and even restore village elections. As envisioned by the U.S. Agency for International Development, the U.S. Army's Military Assistance Command, and civilian advisors like political scientist Lucian Pye of MIT, such measures would turn "traditional" peasants into "modern" citizens,[28] binding the people to the national government and immunizing them against appeals by the guerrillas. It soon became apparent, however, that programs for nation building designed in Washington and at Harvard, MIT, and RAND underwent a grisly alchemy on contact with the politics and culture of Vietnam.

Diem's brother Ngo Dinh Nhu, who supervised the strategic hamlets, equated modernization and nation building with tightened police controls. When few villagers volunteered for relocation, Nhu had them uprooted from their ancestral homelands and conscripted to build fortifications, dig moats, plant spikes, and ring the settlements with barbed wire. District chiefs typically pocketed money and supplies intended to ease the villagers' migration, and settlers found that their fields and markets were impossibly distant from their new homes.

Although the strategic hamlets became symbols in Washington of imagined political progress in Vietnam, they so alienated the peasants that a Viet Cong double agent high in the government, Albert Thao, speeded their creation in order to foment rebellion. Edward Lansdale, a CIA officer who had advised a successful counterinsurgency campaign in the Philippines in the early 1950s, deplored Nhu's brutal regimentation of the populace as bad business. "I don't believe in police measures—genocide, transmigration of villages, curfews, use of force," he later told the journalist Robert Scheer. "[Y]ou don't put the people you're fighting for in a cage."[29]

Word of the disastrous impact of the strategic hamlets was slow to seep back to Washington, though it would have given clear warning that American exports to Saigon of social and political uplift did not travel well. General Paul D. Harkins, commander of the U.S. Military Assistance Advisory Group in Vietnam, suppressed pessimistic reports by his subordinates in order to stiffen the administration's resolve to persist with Diem. Army Chief of Staff General Earle Wheeler, who had earlier insisted that "the essence of the problem in Vietnam is military," not political and economic,[30] began to utter phrases from the dialect of nation building, assuring reporters that the strategic hamlets would foil an "elusive enemy" by providing "opportunities for political and economic growth." The strategic hamlets, he said, were bringing the benefits of modernity to peasants who were "beginning to appreciate more every day that they have something to fight for."[31]

Vietnamese district chiefs also plied their American supervisors with glowing claims. Hilsman cited the case of a chief in the Mekong Delta who reported all twenty-four hamlets in his region secure but admitted later that he controlled only three. *"Ah, les statistiques!"* a South Vietnamese general exclaimed to Hilsman. "Your Secretary of Defense loves statistics. We Vietnamese can give him all he wants. If you want them to go up, they will go up. If you want them to go down, they will go down."[32]

In the spring of 1963 a further indiscretion by officials in Saigon set in motion a fatal schism with their American sponsors. On May 8 Nhu's police shot to death nine Buddhists who were picketing against a ban on displaying religious flags to celebrate the 267th birthday of the Buddha. Just a week earlier Catholics had freely waved blue and white papal banners at a rally to commemorate the ordination of Diem's elder brother,

Archbishop Thuc. The killings sparked a wave of protests that culminated on June 11, when a sixty-six-year-old monk, Quang Duc, assumed a lotus position in the middle of a busy intersection in downtown Saigon and set himself on fire before shrieking crowds. Other monks followed his example. Coming barely a month after news footage of police violence against blacks in Birmingham, Alabama, the televised images of Vietnamese holy men immolating themselves shocked Americans and mocked claims that Diem, in the words of Vice President Lyndon Johnson two years earlier, was the "Winston Churchill of Southeast Asia."[33]

On August 23, 1963, Kennedy's ambassador to Saigon, the patrician Republican Henry Cabot Lodge, cabled that the administration must act boldly to remove the main impediment to victory over the communists, the regime of Ngo Dinh Diem: "We are launched on a course from which there is no respectable turning back: the overthrow of the Diem government . . . because there is no possibility . . . that the war can be won under a Diem administration, still less that Diem or any member of the family can govern the country in a way to gain the support of the people who count . . . not to mention the American people. . . . The chance of bringing off a Generals' coup depends on them to some extent; but it depends at least as much on us."[34]

The notion of defending independence and democracy in South Vietnam by toppling its president said much about the liberal paradoxes of modernization, nation building, and exporting democracy, all of which contorted to fit the priority of defeating communism. The moral and practical pitfalls of ousting Diem disconcerted Kennedy and fragmented his aides. Was it right to desert the leader who had consolidated power with American aid and had represented American interests for nine years? If Diem fell, would his successors be more competent and more responsive to the South Vietnamese people and to Washington? But as Diem continued to give Nhu free rein and as the Viet Cong gained ground, the Kennedy administration permitted Lodge to tell Vietnamese generals that Washington would not oppose a coup. On November 1 the plotters drove Diem and Nhu from the palace and had them shot the next morning. When Kennedy, too, was shot three weeks later, the U.S. government had still to determine its objectives in South Vietnam, how to attain them, and at what cost.

"STEADY ON COURSE"

Lyndon Johnson inherited chaos in South Vietnam. The strategic hamlets in late 1963 looked as though "hit by a hurricane," demolished either by the Viet Cong or by their captive residents. The government in Saigon was marginally more secure. A dozen civilian and military regimes ascended and fell between November 1963 and February 1965. None governed effectively; all relied on a demoralized army under corrupt officers "paralyzed by ineptitude" and reluctant to engage the Viet Cong.[35] In mid-1964 Hanoi added to the pressure by enlarging the jungle paths of the Ho Chi Minh Trail, which aborigines had carved through Laos and Cambodia, into a modern logistical system able to infiltrate northern combat units into the highlands of South Vietnam.

Intent on enacting programs for black rights, aid to the poor, health care, education, and economic growth, Johnson viewed foreign affairs as a vexing distraction from his Great Society. Vietnam in particular appeared a political albatross that burdened his administration with unpalatable choices. Yet Johnson shared his generation's memory of the "lessons of Munich": "that aggression unchallenged is aggression unleashed."[36] He shared, as well, the view of most Democratic and Republican leaders that communism posed an overriding threat to peace and security, whether in the heart of Europe or on the peninsula of Southeast Asia.

For a year Johnson temporized. "It's damned easy to get in a war," he remarked to McGeorge Bundy in May 1964, "but it's gonna be awfully hard to ever extricate yourself if you get in."[37] On the same day, he told his aged mentor in the Senate, Richard Russell, frail with emphysema and bronchitis but a sharp skeptic about the value of South Vietnam to U.S. security, that he could find no way to escape the cage his advisors had constructed: "I spend all my days with Rusk and McNamara and Bundy and [Averell] Harriman and [Cyrus] Vance and all those folks that are dealing with it and . . . it pretty well adds up to them now that we've got to show some power . . . that we are treaty-bound, that we are there, that this will be a domino that will kick off a whole list of others, that we've just got to prepare for the worst."[38]

Unfamiliar with the intricacies of foreign affairs, Johnson navigated the maze of Vietnamese developments by analogy with the most ominous historical episode in U.S. policy circles, the British and French appeasement of Hitler at Munich in a vain attempt to buy peace. "Everything I knew about history," he later said, "told me that if I got out of Vietnam and let Ho Chi Minh run through the streets of Saigon, then I'd be doing exactly what Chamberlain did in World War II. I'd be giving a big fat reward to aggression. . . . You see, I was as sure as any man could be that once we showed how weak we were, Moscow and Peking would move in a flash to exploit our weakness. They might move independently or they might move together. But move they would—whether through nuclear blackmail, through subversion, with regular armed forces or in some other manner. . . . And so would begin World War III."[39]

Every agency that shaped foreign policy told Johnson that withdrawing from Vietnam would gravely harm American interests. On June 9, 1964, the CIA's Board of National Estimates reported that if the dominoes of Laos and South Vietnam fell to the communists, it would be "profoundly damaging" to U.S. prestige "and would seriously debase the credibility of U.S. will and capability to contain the spread of Communism elsewhere in the area. Our enemies would be encouraged and there would be an increased tendency among other states to move toward a greater degree of accommodation with the Communists."[40]

The president also heard the unanimous warnings of military leaders that abandonment of Vietnam would be an incalculable setback in the struggle against communism. The Joint Chiefs advised Johnson on March 2, 1964, that "preventing the loss of South Vietnam" was of "overriding importance" to the United States even if nuclear weapons were needed.[41] Maxwell Taylor, whom President Kennedy had valued as his most farsighted and least bellicose commander, advised the administration to escalate in South Vietnam and propounded a theory of dominoes tumbling across three continents. "If we leave Vietnam with our tail between our legs," Taylor wrote to Rusk, "the consequences of this defeat in the rest of Asia, Africa, and Latin America would be disastrous."[42]

Even if Johnson had muzzled the hawks among his military and civilian advisors, he expected no quarter from rivals poised for signs of weakness from the White House. "The Republicans are going to make a political issue out of it, every one of them," the president said in May 1964, "even [Senate Minority Leader Everett] Dirksen." Johnson offered a still grimmer forecast of popular disapproval if he withdrew from Vietnam: "They'd impeach a President though that would run out, wouldn't they? . . . outside of [Senator Wayne] Morse, everybody I talk to says you got to go in . . . including all the Republicans."[43]

Johnson doubted that Americans cared much about South Vietnam, but he understood that retreat from communist expansion was the one mortal sin for a politician. "I don't believe the American people ever want me to run," Johnson confided to Richard Russell in June 1964. "If I lose it, I think that they'll say *I've* lost. I've pulled in. At the same time, I don't want to commit us to a war." He cited the cold wisdom of a mutual friend, A. W. Moursand, "'A fellow in Johnson City'—or Georgia or any other place—'they'll forgive you for anything except being weak.'"[44]

Recent political history sharpened Johnson's resolve to avoid the appearance of weakness, for he remembered the charges of conspiracy and appeasement that had snared more than a few Democrats following the communists' seizure of power in China in late 1949. The saying that generals always prepare to fight the last war might be extended to politicians who brace against the last political slander. Republican cries that the Democrats had "lost" China inflicted a defining trauma, littered with the careers of Foreign Service officers and the reputations of Truman, Acheson, and Marshall, whom McCarthy had virtually accused of treason.

McCarthy's ghost remained a looming presence in Johnson's deliberations on Vietnam. In February 1964 he confided to the owner of the *Miami Herald* that he was not about to "run [from Vietnam] and let the dominoes start falling over. And God Almighty, what they said about us leaving China would just be warming up, compared to what they'd say now. I see Nixon is raising hell about it today. Goldwater too."[45] In November he told Henry Cabot Lodge, his ambassador to Saigon, "I am not going to be the President who saw Southeast Asia go the way China went. . . . I don't think Congress wants us to let the Communists take over South Vietnam."[46]

Memories of the China debacle during the fifties also burdened presidential aides. Press secretary Bill Moyers recalled "a kinship, a kinetic energy between Johnson and Rusk," formerly the head of the Far East

Desk of the State Department, "on the issue of the right wing and the injury done to the body politic by that right wing attack over China and Korea."[47] McGeorge Bundy, whose brother William, a former CIA agent in West Germany, had been slandered by McCarthy as a Red agent, wrote to Johnson in 1965, "In terms of U.S. politics[,] which is better: to 'lose' now or to 'lose' after committing 100,000 men? Tentative answer: the latter."[48]

Barry Goldwater's 1964 presidential campaign added to Johnson's concern to appear firm on Vietnam. While the outspoken Republican conservative had alienated many voters with his calls to scrap Social Security and his casual references to using nuclear weapons, crowds roared their approval when he denounced liberal appeasement: "The Good Lord raised up this mighty Republic to be a home for the brave and to flourish as the land of the free . . . not to cringe before the bullying of Communism. . . . The tide has been running against freedom. Our people have followed false prophets. . . . Failures cement the wall of shame in Berlin. Failures blot the sands of shame at the Bay of Pigs. Failures mark the slow death of freedom in Laos. Failures infest the jungles of Vietnam."[49]

As Johnson looked for a way to deflect Goldwater's charges without appearing a warmonger, a naval clash in the Gulf of Tonkin off North Vietnam provided an opportunity to enlist Congress in support of his policies. Johnson had approved seven months earlier a series of covert raids by South Vietnamese gunboats on North Vietnamese radar installations while U.S. destroyers pinpointed the facilities in case the Air Force should later bomb them. During one such mission on August 2, enemy patrol boats near the coast of North Vietnam launched a torpedo at the USS *Maddox*, which escaped harm and damaged several enemy craft. Two days later sailors on the *Maddox* and a second destroyer, the *C. Turner Joy*, reported another attack by North Vietnamese ships, though they were likely reacting to radar signals and blind firing by their own crews in bad weather.

Two Air Force pilots overlooking the ships expressed doubts at intelligence debriefings about the second incident, and Johnson himself later snorted to Ball, "Hell, those dumb, stupid sailors were just shooting at flying fish." But under pressure from the Joint Chiefs urgently soliciting "evidence of second attack [to] convince the United Nations that the attack did in fact occur," one pilot changed his story. The other, Navy Commander James B. Stockdale, would not oblige. "No [enemy] boats, no boat wakes, no ricochets off boats, no boat gunfire, no torpedo wakes—nothing but black sea and American firepower," he insisted. Years later, having been shot down over North Vietnam, losing a leg in the crash, and spending the rest of the war in a Hanoi prison, Stockdale called the events of August 1964 "a tragic way to commit a nation to war."[50]

The rumored second attack provided a context—few critics then called it a pretext—for Johnson to ratchet up U.S. involvement. Hoping to avoid the woes of an earlier president, Harry Truman, whom he believed had erred by intervening in Korea without a declaration of war,[51] Johnson asked for passage of a resolution (which advisors had prudently drafted that spring) to support actions to deter aggression in Southeast Asia.

Speaking at Syracuse University on August 5, 1964, Johnson summed up the wisdom of a generation that saw itself as the front line of international order against successive threats to peace and stability: "The challenge that we face in southeast Asia today is the same challenge that we have faced with courage and that we have met with strength in Greece and Turkey, in Berlin and Korea, in Lebanon and in Cuba."[52] Johnson's words echoed his pledge earlier that year to heed the weightiest lesson of recent history, admonishing those who would abandon Vietnam that "on history's face the blotch of Munich is still visible."[53]

Only the hardiest liberals demurred. Frank Church of Idaho expressed "serious misgivings" about policies that reflected an "addiction to an ideological view of world affairs—an affliction which affects us as well as the Communists—rather than a policy based upon a detached and pragmatic view of our real national interests." Reports of North Vietnamese aggression did not ease his doubts. "Who can say," Church warned, "that these events are not the natural consequence of the hazards we have assumed by the policy we have adopted in this part of the world?"[54]

But Church made few converts in this apparent crisis. The sole holdouts in the Senate were Ernest Gruening of Alaska ("all Vietnam is not worth the life of a single American boy") and Wayne Morse of Oregon, an opponent of unchecked presidential power who had prophesied in March, "When the casualty lists of American boys in South Vietnam

increase" and the American people "start crying 'Murder,' no administration will stand."[55] But Morse, a "lean, humorless teetotaler" and "a sanc-
timonious bore . . . whose gravel voice would drone on over trivia,"[56] was
a Senate prophet with little honor and less clout. Even Church swallowed
his misgivings, and the Senate voted for the Tonkin Gulf Resolution,
88–2. The House then voted for the resolution 414–0 after just eight hours
of debate. The thunderous show of bipartisan support for Johnson neatly
deflected Goldwater's charges and effectively removed Vietnam as an
issue in the campaign.

Even now Johnson resisted a final decision for war. "I sure want more
caution on the part of these admirals and these destroyer commanders . . .
about whether they are being fired on or not," Johnson told his secretary
of defense. "A man gets enough braid on him, and he walks in a room,
and he just immediately concludes that he's being attacked." When Mc-
Namara insisted weeks after the Gulf of Tonkin incident that "there was
either an intentional attack or a substantial engagement," Johnson retorted, "Well, what is a substantial engagement? Mean that we could have
started it and they just responded?" McNamara's reply, "But they stayed
there for an hour or so," did not impress Johnson. "They would be justified in staying, though," he observed, "if we started shooting at them."[57]

On February 7, 1965, a hail of Viet Cong mortar shells struck a Special
Forces compound in Pleiku, a market town in the central highlands of
South Vietnam. The barrage killed eight Americans, wounded a hundred
others, and destroyed ten aircraft. It also overcame the vestiges of Johnson's resistance to military intervention. "Cowardice has gotten us into
more wars than response has,"[58] Johnson said in authorizing "retaliatory"
raids on North Vietnam.

Hours after the attack on Pleiku, Operation Flaming Dart sent jets
from the carrier *Ranger* to bomb a North Vietnamese army camp, the first
in a succession of strikes, officially to stop the "pattern of aggression" but
as much to stiffen the morale of the South Vietnamese government as to
punish Hanoi. Ten days later Johnson explained his tougher posture to
Senate Minority Leader Everett Dirksen, saying, "We know, from Munich on, that when you give, the dictators feed on raw meat. If they take
South Vietnam, they take Thailand, they take Indonesia, they take Burma,
they come right on back to the Philippines."[59]

On February 17, Johnson and former president Truman shared their faith in retaliation as the clearest, surest diplomacy. "I think when they go in and kill your boys," Johnson said, "you've got to hit back." Truman agreed, "You bet you have! You bust them in the nose every time you get a chance. And they understand that language better than any other kind."[60]

A hundred planes raided a North Vietnamese ammunition dump on March 2 to launch the continuous bombing of the North, Operation Rolling Thunder, which would last, with eight limited pauses, for three years. On March 8 the first two battalions of U.S. Marines, thirty-five hundred strong, landed at Danang to defend American air bases, and in April the Marines expanded their mission to "search and destroy" operations against the Viet Cong, backed by tactical air support and artillery fire. Vietnamese on both sides at once saw a decisive change in the character and scale of the war, but Johnson concealed this from Americans by telling his staff to take "all possible precautions" to "minimize any appearance of sudden changes in policy."[61]

After leaving the White House in 1969—with more than thirty-six thousand American lives lost in Vietnam and the liberal consensus in ruins—Johnson obsessively recounted his waking nightmares of being caught in a hailstorm with no place to take cover, watching the war embolden conservatives who wanted to starve his Great Society programs. Johnson's talk widely appeared self-serving and self-pitying, the more so because his self-portrait in stripes and behind bars seemed to ignore that he was the president and commander-in-chief. Still, he had moved toward war in tune with most of the nation, and—until his final year in office—in keeping with the weight of "expert" opinion.

Johnson's personal insecurities and relative inexperience in foreign affairs have led some scholars and journalists to locate the tragedy of Vietnam in an "accident of history":[62] the presidential succession on November 22, 1963. Had Kennedy lived, they believe, he would have resisted the pressures to escalate, sparing the nation a protracted, futile war and preserving the liberal coalition. Here two powerful myths converge: the degeneration of American leadership from Kennedy to Johnson and the derailment of Cold War liberalism from its true moorings. The mixed signals of Kennedy's policies permit no final verdict on whether Johnson was simply the wrong liberal at a decisive juncture, a man who, for all his legislative wizardry, lacked Kennedy's deftness and prudence in foreign affairs. Yet one is struck by Johnson's self-conscious reliance on Kennedy's "best and brightest" aides during the eighteen months when he committed the nation, by anguished stages, to an air war over North Vietnam and a ground war in the South.

It was no accident that Johnson called the first chapter on Vietnam in his memoirs "Steady on Course." In February 1964 the new president asked McGeorge Bundy, his national security advisor, whether there was anyone "that you-all ... and the President formerly consulted on these things that we're not consulting?" "Nobody," Bundy assured him.[63] A year later, having ordered the bombing of North Vietnam, Johnson told McNamara, "I would sure want to feel that every person that had an idea— that his suggestion was fully explored."[64] In June 1965, after reading a column by James Reston in the *New York Times* on the "narrowing of the basic decisions of government," Johnson asked McNamara, "Do you have any people in your outfit that ... feel that they made decisions [under Kennedy] that they're not in on now?" When McNamara said no, Johnson laughed that this was nearly true. "The only one I know that might not be is the Attorney General. And he's not my brother!"[65]

Through 1965 most Capitol Hill critics of intervention remained as bound by the imperatives of containment as the president himself. They differed mainly in doubting the feasibility of propping up the successors to Diem and in viewing the risks of an expanded war as prohibitive. But few were prepared simply to withdraw. In June 1965 the most respected dove on Capitol Hill, Senate Majority Leader Mike Mansfield, a former professor of Asian history at the University of Montana, counseled Johnson not to bomb North Vietnam but added, "You don't pull out. You try to do something to consolidate your position. ... And that may take more troops."[66]

Liberal doves alighted in the White House with Johnson's indulgence, though in token numbers and with the understanding that they would not fly to the media. The most formidable was Undersecretary of State George Ball. Ball was a former New Deal lawyer, a protégé of Adlai Stevenson's, and an experienced diplomat with NATO countries who believed that Western Europe should remain America's priority. Having failed to dissuade Kennedy from persisting in Vietnam, Ball reacted to

Johnson's drift toward war with a sixty-seven-page memo on October 5, 1964, that depicted the U.S. venture as bound for ruin. "What we might gain by establishing the steadfastness of our commitments," he wrote, "we could lose by an erosion of confidence in our judgment." Worse still, he warned, escalation in Vietnam would prove easier than disengaging. "Once on the tiger's back, we cannot be sure of picking the place to dismount."[67]

Ball's colleagues—McNamara, Bundy, Rusk, Rostow—shunned his densely argued brief as "merely an idiosyncratic diversion from the only relevant problem: how to win the war."[68] Ball tried once more during the summer of 1965 as Johnson's advisors met on whether to commit to full-scale war in Vietnam, as the Joint Chiefs were urging. In July Ball drafted a presidential memorandum, "A Compromise Solution in South Vietnam," that evoked memories of the French defeat in denying "that a white ground force of whatever size can win a guerrilla war—which is at the same time a civil war between Asians—in jungle terrain in the midst of a population that refuses cooperation to the white forces (and the South Vietnamese)." The president could still negotiate an end to U.S. involvement by acceding to a coalition government that included the Viet Cong. Otherwise, Ball predicted, a catastrophic war loomed. "Once we suffer large casualties," he wrote, "we will have started a well-nigh irreversible process. Our involvement will be so great that we cannot—without national humiliation—stop short of achieving our complete objectives. Of the two possibilities I think humiliation would be more likely than the achievement of our objectives—even after we have paid terrible costs."[69]

The memo resonated with Johnson's own deep reservations. He could not envision any policy that could bridge the discords over Vietnam rumbling just below the surface of his seemingly irresistible liberal consensus. In April 1965 he shared a sample of the voluminous, heated, and contradictory mail to the White House with an old friend, Arthur "Tex" Goldschmidt:

> Let me show you what they're saying. Atlanta, Georgia: "People are sick and tired of your lies about Vietnam. Bring these troops home." Lubbock, Texas: "We'll back down in Vietnam, as we have everywhere else under your position." ... "Your speech made me sick. Why bomb? Negotiate!"

"Your Vietnam backdown is [an] insult to U.S. men who died in the cause." . . . They're just stacked in here by the dozens.[70]

The bleak military prospects in Vietnam further dismayed the president. On June 21, barely fifteen weeks into the commitment of U.S. troops, Johnson phoned McNamara in a "depressed" mood to say that he saw no grounds for hope. The military and the State Department were "just praying" for the enemy to quit, Johnson said, "[but] I don't believe they're ever going to quit" because his administration lacked any "plan for victory—militarily or diplomatically." Yet peering into the abyss, Johnson refused to back away. "I don't think we can get out of there with our treaty like it is and with what all we've said," Johnson concluded. "I think it would just lose us face in the world. I just shudder to think what [other countries] would say."[71]

Johnson's fixation on Vietnam mirrored the position papers and memoranda of the national security establishment that aimed to preserve the credibility of U.S. global commitments. Shortly after the first U.S. Marines arrived in South Vietnam, John T. McNaughton, McNamara's assistant for international security affairs, quantified for his boss how little the South Vietnamese people mattered (10 percent) in the grand scheme of "U.S. Aims." Saving face, not freedom, must guide U.S. actions in Vietnam, according to McNaughton's ranking of war aims:

70%—To avoid a humiliating U.S. defeat (to our reputation as a guarantor [of other allies]).

20%—To keep SVN (and the adjacent) territory from Chinese hands.

10%—To permit people of SVN to enjoy a better, freer way of life.

ALSO—To emerge from crisis without unacceptable taint from methods used.

NOT—to "help a friend," although it would be hard to stay in if asked out.[72]

During a week of meetings in late July 1965 with civilian and military advisors, Johnson encouraged Ball's objections but ultimately sided with the great majority who saw no honorable alternative to expanding the war. McNamara, just back from a lightning tour of Saigon, argued that a decisive application of U.S. ground and air power could still salvage South Vietnam's deteriorating government. He dismissed Ball's claim that the war might require a quarter-million troops as "outrageous" and "dirty pool."[73] On July 28 Johnson agreed to deploy immediately forty-four more combat battalions to South Vietnam; by December the number of American troops neared two hundred thousand.

In shifting from aid to open war, Johnson promoted Lieutenant General William C. Westmoreland to commander of the U.S. Military Assistance Command (no longer a mere "Advisory Group") in South Vietnam. Not quite fifty years old, Westmoreland was a "tall, erect, handsome West Pointer with hooded eyes and a chiseled chin," decorated in World War II and in Korea, "a diligent, disciplined organization man who would obey orders."[74] His aim was to "Americanize" the war effort by deploying U.S. troops in "search and destroy" missions and by inspiring or prodding South Vietnamese leaders and soldiers to act more efficiently and energetically—in short, to act like Americans. Secretary of State Rusk summed up this approach in a directive to the U.S. embassy in Saigon to "shake" Saigon officials "by the scruff of the neck" and "somehow . . . change the pace at which these people move." "This," Rusk surmised, "can only be done with a pervasive intrusion of Americans into their affairs."[75]

Protests flared at home with the escalation in Vietnam, but Johnson at first indulged his dovish critics; his prestige as a master reformer and legislator was still soaring in 1965 and he felt able to abide this family quarrel. J. William Fulbright, the chairman of the Senate Foreign Relations Committee (whom Johnson and Truman privately dubbed "Halfbright"), was still welcome at the White House despite chafing at the expanded U.S. role in Vietnam. (Humphrey, too, expressed early doubts about the war but found the vice presidential leash much shorter; Johnson banned him from cabinet meetings for a year until, early in 1966, Humphrey declared Vietnam a crucial battleground for freedom.)

As for young demonstrators, Johnson saw them as well-meaning but ignorant of his generation's hard-earned wisdom about standing up to aggressors. "They were barely in their cradles in the dark days of World War II," he later told Doris Kearns; "they never experienced the ravages of Adolf Hitler; they were only in nursery school during the fall of

China; they were sitting in grammar school during the Korean War; they wouldn't know a Communist if they tripped over one. They simply don't understand the world the way I do."[76]

The young also did not understand Johnson's fear that ultraconservatives in Congress, the military, and the media would denounce his smallest accommodation with communists. "Here's our problem," he told his longtime confidant, attorney Abe Fortas, in May 1965. "My right wing . . . won't give me forty cents if I'm not careful."[77] In 1965 Johnson told his formidable in-house dissident, George Ball, "Don't worry about the hippies and the students and the Commies; they'll raise a lot of hell but can't do real damage. The terrible beast we have to fear is the right wing; if they ever get the idea I am selling out Vietnam, they'll do horrible things to the country, and we'll be forced to escalate the war beyond anything you've ever thought about."[78]

In the short term, Johnson's preference for appeasing the "beast" on the far right rather than Ho and the Viet Cong solidified his hold on the political center. The nation's leading pollsters revealed that public opinion rallied behind the president whenever he added more troops in South Vietnam. In August 1965 Louis Harris reported to the president an "overwhelming mandate to send as many U.S. troops there as necessary to withstand the Viet Cong attacks during Monsoon season." As for the antiwar movement, in its early stages it moved against the tide of growing support for the war. In November 1965 a Gallup Poll reported that "in sharp contrast to recent public demonstrations, survey evidence indicates that American public opinion is moving toward greater support of U.S. military action in Vietnam." In December 1965 Harris revealed Americans opposed withdrawal from Vietnam by ten to one.[79]

"SECURITY IS DEVELOPMENT"

From this early vantage point of public confidence and trust, Johnson saw the war slowly drain his reservoir of support. The nightly news reported favorable "body count" ratios of enemy dead to American dead, but this provided little illumination and less comfort about the course of the war. In the absence of front lines, grand engagements, geographical objectives, or other conventional and readily understood measures of progress, Americans looked in vain for signs that the expansion of U.S. ground forces—reaching nearly 400,000 by 1966 and peaking at more than 540,000 in 1968—was bringing tangible gains and imminent victory.

Right-wing critics then and after blamed Johnson for reining in the U.S. military for fear of provoking Russia and China, as well as provoking the media and antiwar activists. But Johnson's misgivings did not prevent him from unleashing greater American firepower than at any time since World War II. The sustained bombing campaign against North Vietnam, Operation Rolling Thunder, extending from March 1965 until November 1968, with occasional pauses, exploded roughly eight hundred tons of bombs a day for three and a half years. And, as Stanley Karnow observed, "With the exception of the nuclear weapon, nearly every piece of equipment in America's mighty arsenal was sooner or later used in Vietnam."[80]

McNamara and other strategists expected the cumulative destruction, casualties, and "pain" would compel the Viet Cong and North Vietnam to negotiate, if not surrender—an optimism that was monumentally misplaced. An independent evaluation by the Institute for Defense Analyses concluded in July 1966 that bombing North Vietnam, with its "subsistence agricultural economy," had failed to reduce "Hanoi's ability to mount and support military operations in the South at the current level. Initial plans and assessments for the Rolling Thunder program clearly tended ... to underestimate the tenacity and recuperative capabilities of the North Vietnamese," concluded the report. "This tendency, in turn, appears to reflect a general failure to appreciate the fact, well-documented in the historical and social scientific literature, that a direct, frontal attack on a society tends to strengthen the social fabric of the nation."[81]

Less than two months later McNamara reported that in view of the "thoroughly stalled" pacification program, the "apathetic" Saigon government, plagued by "corruption high and low," and ARVN "weak[ness] in dedication, direction, and discipline, [t]he prognosis is bad that the war can be brought to a satisfactory conclusion within the next two years." Yet, consistent with the administration's record of stoic persistence in Vietnam, McNamara capped his bleak remarks with a call to wade deeper: "The solution lies in girding, openly, for a longer war."[82]

By the spring of 1967 the futility of "McNamara's War" had begun to

tell on the once unflappable secretary of defense. He appeared to colleagues an emotional casualty of the bombing, which he found strategi-
cally flawed, costly in American lives and planes, and morally suspect. In
May he circulated a memorandum stating, "The picture of the world's
greatest superpower killing or seriously injuring 1,000 non-combatants a
week, while trying to pound a tiny backward nation into submission on
an issue whose merits are hotly disputed, is not a pretty one."[83]

The stated American aim to protect the South Vietnamese people
posed a further, insoluble problem for military strategists. The Viet Cong
guerrillas were drawn from these same people and enjoyed widespread
sympathy and support in battling an ineffectual regime and its foreign
backers. There simply was no way to suppress a "people's war," as Ho and
the Viet Cong called their struggle, without killing, however inadver-
tently, many innocent South Vietnamese men, women, and children. A
former Marine captain, E. J. Banks, described the vulnerability of American soldiers for whom the whole of South Vietnam was potentially hostile territory: "You never knew who was the enemy and who was the
friend. They all looked alike. They all dressed alike. They were all Vietnamese. Some of them were Vietcong. . . . It wasn't like the San Francisco
Forty-Niners on one side of the field and the Cincinnati Bengals on the
other. The enemy was all around you."[84]

Americans dismayed by the lengthening casualty lists came to refer
bitterly to "Johnson's War." The term evoked images of a swaggering,
bellicose man, indifferent to casualties on all sides, in thrall to his generals, and drunk with power, his own and the nation's. The bitterness was
understandable and the destruction undeniable, but the harsh portrait
bore little connection to the anguished occupant of the White House.
Seldom if ever in American history had a president gone to war with
greater reluctance and foreboding.

In one of history's stranger confessions, Johnson lamented to FBI Director J. Edgar Hoover the arrogance of American power, saying, "Most
people *are* anti-American because we've acted such damn fools, throwing
our weight around."[85] Nor did Johnson believe, even in the early stages
of bombing North Vietnam, that such displays would shock or awe the
enemy into submission, let alone enhance American prestige. "The more
bombs you drop, the more nations you scare, the more people you make

mad," he told his friend and mentor, Senator Richard Russell, on March 6, 1965, two days before sending the first Marines to Vietnam. When Russell commiserated, "You couldn't have inherited a worse mess," Johnson replied, "Well, if they'd say I *inherited*, I'll be lucky. But they'll all say I *created* it!"[86]

Military projections of imminent victory disgusted Johnson years before antiwar protests targeted the Pentagon. "Light at the end of the tunnel," Johnson mockingly repeated to Bill Moyers after his generals had assured him that the bombing campaign was wearing down the enemy. "Hell, we don't even have a tunnel; we don't even know where the tunnel is."[87] When the Joint Chiefs claimed on November 10, 1965, that bombing Hanoi, mining Haiphong Harbor, and blockading the whole North Vietnamese coast would spare America another protracted Asian ground war, Johnson replied with a profanity-filled tirade, as Marine Lieutenant General Charles G. Cooper recounted: "He screamed obscenities, he cursed them personally, he ridiculed them for coming to his office with their 'military advice.' . . . He then accused them of trying to pass the buck for World War III to him. It was unnerving. It was degrading. . . . He told them he was disgusted with their naïve approach toward him, that he was not going to let some military idiots talk him into World War III. It ended when he ordered them to 'get the hell out of my office!'"[88]

Physically and psychologically, the first domino to fall in the Vietnam War was Johnson himself. His press secretary, Bill Moyers, recalled that Johnson foresaw the decision to commit ground troops to Vietnam would likely mean "the end of his Presidency" and he crumpled psychologically: "It was a pronounced, prolonged depression. He would just go within himself, just disappear—morose, self-pitying, angry. . . . He was a tormented man." He often felt, Johnson told Moyers, as if he was in a Louisiana swamp "that's pulling me down."[89]

Johnson's mood brightened over a single aspect of American intervention: the effort to promote economic development, education, medical care, and democracy in Vietnam—the same bounties, in short, the Great Society was promising Americans. As President Kennedy's emissary to Southeast Asia in May 1961, Johnson had attended a U.N. meeting in Bangkok to plan regional development of the lower basin of the Mekong River. The twenty-six-hundred-mile river had alternately nourished and ravaged the land as it flowed untamed from China through Cambodia, Laos, South Vietnam, and Thailand, emptying just below Saigon into the South China Sea. Johnson, inspired by the New Deal's legacy of dams for flood control and hydroelectric power, saw the Mekong Delta as ripe for similar aid. According to the historian and presidential counselor Eric Goldman, "The Mekong project seized Lyndon Johnson's mind and emotions. Here was a chance to build something, to get Asia going the way of central Texas, to transform the law of history into the reality of bigger crops, schools, hospitals and, in the LBJ phrase, 'an extra little helping in life.'"[90]

The same restless energy to help the people of Southeast Asia marked Johnson's presidency. In March 1964 Johnson expressed to McNamara his hope that the new president of South Vietnam, Nguyen Khan, would be "socially conscious," adding, "He's getting out into the villages and talking to people and offering them something that they claim [earlier leaders] never gave them."[91] On April 7, 1965, Johnson explained the U.S. role in Vietnam in a speech at Johns Hopkins University that portrayed the fight against "aggression" as merely the first step in a billion-dollar program of American-sponsored reform:

> These countries of southeast Asia are homes for millions of impoverished people. Each day these people rise at dawn and struggle through until the night to wrestle existence from the soil. They are often wracked by disease, plagued by hunger, and death comes at the early age of 40.... The American people have helped generously in times past.... Now there must be a much more massive effort to improve the life of man in that conflict-torn corner of our world....
>
> The task is nothing less than to enrich the hopes and the existence of more than a hundred million people. And there is much to be done. The vast Mekong River can provide food and water and power on a scale to dwarf even our own TVA. The wonders of modern medicine can be spread through villages where thousands die every year from lack of care. Schools can be established to train people in the skills that are needed to manage the process of development.[92]

Johnson hoped that American plans to modernize Vietnam would prove irresistible to the masses in the South and to the government in the

North. Ho and the Viet Cong could enjoy untold prosperity if only communist forces would end their senseless fighting. But Vietnam was a land separated from the United States by ten thousand miles and a universe of values, customs, and history. Ho and his followers were intent on realizing a lifetime ambition to unify their nation and curb foreign influence. They were not likely to sacrifice their goals to let the American sway grow in the South and extend through the North. And where no common sensibility existed, trusting an adversary to act on American common sense made for reckless policy.

The dream of ending or winning the war through American aid for modernization remained, for all its elusiveness and illusions, a mainstay of U.S. policy toward Vietnam. Vice President Humphrey, an icon of postwar American liberalism, caught the spirit of the "Johnson Doctrine" for Asia in a television interview on April 19, 1966. In language echoing planks he had drafted in many a Democratic reform platform, he cited "a pledge to ourselves and to posterity to defeat aggression, to defeat social misery, to build viable, free political institutions, and to achieve peace. . . ." Humphrey said of these "great commitments," "I think there is a tremendous new opening here for realizing the dream of the Great Society in the great area of Asia, not just here at home."[93]

McNamara, too, urged U.S. aid to developing societies with a passion more likely for a liberal stump speech than for a secretary of defense known for discoursing on Mutual Assured Destruction. At a forum in Montreal in 1966, McNamara defended foreign aid to "roughly one hundred countries" of the southern hemisphere "caught up in the difficult transition from traditional to modern societies." Their economic progress, he said, was central to their nations' security and America's. "There is an irrefutable relationship between violence and economic backwardness. . . . In a modernizing society, security means development. Security is not military hardware—though it may include it. . . . Security is development, and without development there can be no security. A developing nation that does not, in fact, develop simply cannot remain secure."[94]

For all Johnson's idealism in seeking a Great Society for Vietnam, the plans to win hearts and minds by building a prosperous modern state succumbed under the rubble of villages that the U.S. military leveled in order to root out suspected Viet Cong. While each side in the war could point to enemy atrocities, the massive scale of American bombing and shelling was chiefly responsible for creating four million refugees—nearly one-quarter of the South Vietnamese population, who streamed into the cities and formed a shiftless class of slum dwellers living at the margins of subsistence.

Housed in "squalid shanties, where primitive sewers bred dysentery, malaria and other diseases," the refugees roamed the streets as "beggars and hawkers . . . whining and tugging at Americans for money," belying the Johnson administration's promises of an Asian Great Society. The journalist Stanley Karnow wrote of the "grotesque contrast" reminiscent of the French colonial era, "where limbless Vietnamese victims of the war would crawl like crabs across the handsome tile floor" of the Continental Palace Hotel in Saigon "to accost American soldiers, construction workers, journalists and visitors as they chatted and sipped their drinks under the ceiling fans."[95]

The destruction of the South Vietnamese countryside was not simply an unintended effect of indiscriminate American firepower. U.S. civilian and military strategists seeking to "pacify" the countryside purposely speeded the influx of rural refugees into the cities in order to accomplish what the strategic hamlets had failed to do: isolate the Viet Cong.[96] In 1968 the eminent journal *Foreign Affairs* published an article by the Harvard political scientist Samuel P. Huntington, a theorist of modernization and an advisor on pacification, defending the logic of killing or driving away the peasants who made up most of the population of South Vietnam.

The Viet Cong, Huntington wrote, were a "powerful force which cannot be dislodged from its constituency so long as the constituency continues to exist." If force were applied "on such a massive scale as to produce a massive migration from countryside to city," then the communist rural revolution would be "undercut by the American-sponsored urban revolution." While some might demur that turning millions of peasants into refugees was cruel, Huntington pointed to the progressive features of "forced-draft urbanization and modernization." "The urban slum, which seems so horrible to middle-class Americans," he argued, "often becomes for the poor peasant a gateway to a new and better way of life. For some poor migrants, the wartime urban boom has made possible incomes five times those which they had in the countryside."[97]

Huntington's rationale for clearing rural South Vietnam as a path to military victory through "modernization" became standard doctrine in the American "pacification" program. A civilian advisor assured Jonathan Schell that refugees had a "better standard of living than they did in their villages." The camps brought people "in closer to the urban centers, where they can have modern experiences and learn modern practices. It's a modernizing experience."[98]

American dollars did almost as much as bombs to rend Vietnamese society. According to Frances FitzGerald, "In the new economy a prostitute earned more than a GVN minister, a secretary working for USAID more than a full colonel, a taxi owner who spoke a few words of English more than a university professor. . . . The old rich of Saigon had opposed the Communists as a threat to their position in society; they found that the Americans took away that position in a much quicker and more decisive fashion—and with it, what was left of the underpinning of Vietnamese values."[99]

Why then did the United States continue to escalate in Vietnam? Year by year the futility became more apparent and the devastation to South Vietnam more appalling. The stated reasons for involvement in Vietnam seemed strained and changeable: support for our French ally; the domino theory; treaty obligations (though several administrations had freely trampled the Geneva Accords of 1954); the threat of "wars of national liberation"; the lessons of Munich; fear of Soviet aggression; fear of Chinese aggression; fear of national humiliation. Yet in speeches and in conference rooms of the Pentagon and the State Department, the administration insisted, as Johnson did early in 1966, "This nation has committed itself to help defend South Vietnam against aggression. We are determined to fulfill that commitment."[100]

The failure to realize earlier the need to contain an inconclusive war that was tearing apart American society was, in part, a matter of momentum. Each administration had built on and become prisoner to the commitments of those before it; all believed that in a bipolar world, the containment of communism must be paramount and American leadership must never betray weakness; none would risk the stigma of "losing" Vietnam and, in the case of Johnson, losing a war for the first time in American history.

The difficulty of measuring successes and setbacks in the war also inhibited clarity in gauging the costs of escalation. Pressed for "progress" (not "situation") reports, officers at every level, up to General Westmoreland, tended to undercount Viet Cong guerrillas and conclude too readily that "pacification" efforts were "winning the hearts and minds" of the Vietnamese people. American soldiers, encouraged by their superiors to record favorable "body count" ratios, often obliged by conflating civilian casualties with "enemy" dead, adhering to the widely encouraged wisdom, "If he's dead and Vietnamese, he's VC."[101]

A further impediment to sound policy was that Johnson depended on the same decision-making apparatus that had insulated earlier presidents from the flesh-and-blood costs of their policies by taking refuge in strategic abstractions, euphemisms, and metaphors. "In quiet, air-conditioned, thick-carpeted rooms," wrote a former State Department aide, James C. Thomson, Jr., "such terms as 'systematic pressure,' 'armed reconnaissance,' 'targets of opportunity,' and even 'body count' seemed to breed a sort of games-theory detachment." Thomson recalled that in 1964, "at a discussion of how heavy our bombing should be, and how extensive our strafing, an Assistant Secretary of State explained, 'It seems to me that our orchestration should be mainly violins, but with periodic touches of brass.'"[102]

The strategy of inflicting unacceptable damage on the enemy also evinced little understanding of the people Americans were fighting or those they were professing to save. U.S. officials might have found their history sobering, for the Vietnamese had waged protracted, ultimately successful struggles against larger, technologically advanced foreign armies—Chinese, French, Japanese, and French again after World War II—going back nearly two thousand years. The notion that they would desist after briefly sampling American martial valor rested on slender hopes that aligned poorly with experience. As American casualties rose, Westmoreland's assurances of "light at the end of the tunnel" acquired a surreal air among reporters and ordinary citizens who saw the war persist and the costs deepen.

"THE BEGINNING OF THE END OF THE GREAT SOCIETY"

Johnson looked back on 1965 as the year when "two great streams in our national life converged—the dream of a Great Society at home and the inescapable demands of our obligations halfway around the world."[103] He raced to satisfy these twin revolutions of rising expectations, approving a five-year National Anti-Poverty Plan even as he committed troops to South Vietnam. "In retrospect," the economist Robert Levine, who headed research and planning for the poverty program, wrote in 1970, "the fascinating thing about these [projected budgetary] figures were [sic] that we really thought they were possible." The euphoria was fleeting. In August 1965 antipoverty officials learned that the costs of the war in Vietnam would nearly preclude additional social spending.[104]

Through the end of 1966 Johnson minimized the economic impact of additional military spending and invoked the tenets of growth liberalism to justify escalating both the war in Vietnam and his wars on poverty, hunger, slums, substandard schools, scarce access to health care, and other domestic ills. In his Budget Message of January 24, 1966, he insisted that the nation could have ample guns and butter: "We are a rich nation and can afford to make progress at home while meeting obligations abroad—in fact, we can afford no other course if we are to remain strong. For this reason, I have not halted progress in the new and vital Great Society programs in order to finance the costs of our efforts in Southeast Asia."[105]

He went on, ardently affirming the prime belief of Cold War liberals that reform at home and containment of communism abroad were essential and inseparable: "We cannot fight for peace and freedom in Vietnam, while sacrificing individual dignity and opportunity at home. For it would be a hollow victory if our pursuit of world peace were carried out at the expense of domestic progress. Yet we must also recognize that a truly Great Society looks beyond its own borders. The freedom, health, and prosperity of all mankind are its proper concern."[106]

In February 1966 McNamara crunched the budgetary numbers the way his president wanted, testifying before Congress that the economy could absorb the costs of Vietnam. During the next two years, he asserted, "The defense program should not be a major factor contributing to inflationary pressures."[107] Despite McNamara's skillful marshaling of data to affirm the soundness of growth liberalism, the rising costs of social programs and the war resulted in quickening inflation and growing debt. These strains gradually dispelled the illusion of infinite plenty that had sustained the politics of affluence and contributed to the military commitment to Vietnam.

Following an era of remarkable price stability, the United States in 1966 experienced the most rapid price inflation since the Korean War, doubling from an annual rate of about 1.5 percent to more than 3 percent.[108] New and expanded entitlement programs played a part, but spending on the war had greater immediate impact. By 1970, the economic cost of Vietnam exceeded that of any other American conflict except World War II. Through fiscal 1970 the U.S. spent twice as much on Vietnam as on the Korean War, three times as much as on World War I, and more than thirty times as much as on the Civil War.[109]

In 1967 Johnson realized he could no longer mask the scope or cost of the war. In January the federal budget projected that spending on Vietnam would reach $19.4 billion in fiscal 1967 and $21.9 billion in 1968.[110] The Pentagon estimated that it would spend $72.3 billion in fiscal year 1968 for all military operations—a figure larger than for any period except the peak of World War II. Also in January, at a joint hearing of the Senate Appropriations and Armed Services committees, Robert McNamara conceded the open-ended nature of the conflict. Eschewing his customary statistical precision, he said, "I do not know of any war of any substantial size that anyone has ever been able to predict the end of it accurately, and we cannot do it here."[111]

In hearings by the Joint Economic Committee in February, Senator William Proxmire of Wisconsin scolded his fellow Democrats in the White House for grossly underestimating the costs of Vietnam. "In 1966," Proxmire said, "our Government made a serious economic policy blunder. Our fiscal policy was established . . . on the assumption that the Vietnam war would cost $10 billion . . . it is clear to me that we would have reduced spending and/or increased taxes—possibly both—if we had better and more accurate information." Gardner Ackley, chairman of the Council of Economic Advisors, explained the administration's low projections as reflecting an assumption that the war would end by June 1967.[112]

By spurring inflation, the war undermined the dollar and, in turn, the country's foreign trade balance and the international gold market. A further casualty was the faith in ever-rising abundance that had buoyed the Kennedy and Johnson presidencies. In August 1967 Johnson grudgingly requested a 10 percent tax surcharge on individual and corporate incomes, but Congress delayed for nearly a year and the budget deficit tripled while inflation soared.

Conservatives in the Congress blocked the administration's proposed tax increase, demanding that Johnson first agree to cuts in social spending as a gesture to wartime stringency. Johnson was dismayed but not surprised. "I knew the Congress as well as I know Lady Bird," he told Doris Kearns, "and I knew that the day it exploded into a major debate on the war, that day would be the beginning of the end of the Great Society."[113]

TET

Tet Nguyên Dán is the feast of the first morning, the major holiday of the Vietnamese year. It marks the beginning of spring, indeed the beginning of the new year according to the Chinese lunar calendar, and it is traditionally celebrated in Vietnam with family visits and special foods. Vietnamese who live away from their families travel home to celebrate with relatives, visit local temples, and try to put behind them the worries of the previous year.

So it was in 1968. As in previous years, both sides in the Vietnam War had called a holiday truce. Half or more of the troops from the ARVN, the regular army of South Vietnam, had left to be with their families. Most American forces were on minimal alert, looking forward to a respite from the intense fighting of the previous months.

American leaders were, as ever, upbeat in their assessments of the progress of the war. On January 31, 1968, the first day of Tet, Walt Rostow, now the president's national security advisor, was meeting with reporters from the *Washington Post*, offering them captured documents that demonstrated the progress of the war effort. President Johnson, having removed much of the language on Vietnam from his State of the Union Address on January 17, asserted: "The enemy has been defeated in battle after battle. The number of South Vietnamese living in areas under Government protection tonight has grown by more than a million since January of last year. These are all marks of progress. Yet the enemy continues to pour men and material across frontiers and into battle, despite his continuous heavy losses. He continues to hope that America's will to persevere can be broken. Well—he is wrong. America will persevere. Our patience and our perseverance will match our power. Aggression will never prevail."[114]

Westmoreland had been aware of what appeared to be a buildup of enemy strength at the end of 1967, and he had warned his superiors in Washington to be prepared for new attacks. He had been reluctant to grant the normal Tet truce in 1968. Johnson himself reflected these expectations, telling an audience in Australia that there might be some "kamikaze" attacks early in 1968.[115] But these were the normal anticipations of war and did not unduly alarm civilian and military leaders or lead them to alert the American people to unusual dangers ahead.

Americans were thus stunned to learn of the attacks that broke out all over South Vietnam on the morning of January 31, 1968. Most were assaults in heavily populated areas, including nearly all of the forty-four provincial capitals. The ancient imperial city of Hué was hit especially hard, causing heavy American casualties. Hué stayed in enemy hands for nearly a month after the initial attacks.

In Saigon, Viet Cong attacked the headquarters of the Joint General Staff, the presidential palace, and Tan San Nhut Air Base. The new American embassy was one of the first targets. Its security perimeter was quickly breached and the American military guards gunned down; fighting ensued within the embassy compound for several hours. When the first reports reached the national television networks in New York, the fate of the embassy was uncertain.

In the days that followed, the Tet offensive was repulsed by American and South Vietnamese military forces. Control of the cities, including Hué, was regained. The embassy and other targets in Saigon and its suburbs were secured. General Westmoreland, standing amid dead bodies and the detritus of the attacks on the embassy grounds, declared that the enemy assault had failed.

Indeed it had, but only in the limited, military sense.

The Tet offensive of 1968 was a shock to the American psyche, to the political process, and to Lyndon Johnson's presidency. It was the first marker in a year of unprecedented violence and turmoil that would bring a resounding end to the optimism of the 1960s and the liberal momentum in American politics. After years of upbeat pronouncements, of victory just around the corner and light at the end of the tunnel, no observer of the Tet offensive, of the apparent ease with which the Viet Cong had taken the battle to America's heart, could ever again accept predictions of success at face value.

One of the enduring images of the Tet offensive was a photograph of the murder of a Viet Cong prisoner by General Nguyen Ngoc Loan, the national commander of the South Vietnamese police. The picture showed the general casually holding a pistol to the head of a young man whose hands were tied behind his back. The thrust of the bullet had caused the prisoner's head to recoil as he expired. The photo, by Eddie Adams of the Associated Press, won a Pulitzer Prize for spot photography. It was published all over the world and quickly became a metaphor for the brutality and indifference to human rights of the ally Americans had been supporting in South Vietnam.

Backed by the Joint Chiefs, Westmoreland responded to the Tet offensive in the usual fashion, urging the president to call up 206,000 additional troops, half for immediate deployment in Vietnam and half to shore up overextended forces in other regions. The magnitude far exceeded what Johnson believed the country would tolerate, at least without giving conservatives free rein to gut his social programs. He directed his new secretary of defense, Clark Clifford (replacing the exhausted McNamara), to study the proposed troop increase.

A suave, eloquent, high-powered lawyer in his early sixties, Clifford had counseled Harry Truman and knew seemingly everyone in politics and business. But for a brief period of doubt in 1965, when he had sided with Ball against expanding the war, Clifford had consistently favored more troops and heavier bombing to vindicate America's strategy of containment and its reputation as a superpower. But on conferring with Pentagon analysts during the Tet offensive, Clifford found that acceding to Westmoreland's request would raise taxes, reduce domestic spending, further polarize the country, and still require more years of fighting. Worse still, he discovered, the generals had no clear, let alone compelling, plan for victory even with another hundred thousand troops.

On March 25 Clifford convened the "Wise Men," a group of elder statesmen in foreign policy and the armed forces spanning the Truman, Kennedy, and Johnson years. They had first met in November 1967 and endorsed the president's policy of graduated escalation, but the passage of several months had crystallized the military stalemate and a growing domestic crisis. Clifford sensed that their hard reappraisal would be just the shock treatment the president needed to curb the U.S. commitment.

After a series of diplomatic and military briefings, Dean Acheson, the secretary of state under President Truman and still a formidable presence, inaugurated the headlong retreat of the Wise Men from their earlier firm counsel. The United States, he said, could "no longer do the job we set out to" and "must begin to take steps to disengage."[116] Most of Acheson's colleagues agreed with his bleak assessment and debated mainly the dimensions and relative merits of bombing pauses, troop cutbacks, and peace talks as ways to lift the American burden in Vietnam.

Economic debacle ranked high among the Wise Men's concerns. "I now understand," Bundy told Johnson, "that the really tough problem you have is the interlock between the bad turn in the war, the critical need for a tax increase, and the crisis of public confidence at home."[117] Dean Rusk added, "If we do this [adding two hundred thousand troops] without a tax bill we are dead."[118]

Johnson did not take kindly to seeing Acheson and other living icons of America's postwar policy of global leadership renounce or reduce the commitment to Vietnam that they had long insisted on. But the president understood their concerns: The nation's resources and the electorate's patience had limits. During a recess before a lunch meeting on March 26, Rusk told Wheeler and Westmoreland, "The nation can't support a bottomless pit," which moved Johnson to offer a rambling, pained apology for denying the generals their reinforcements: "Our fiscal situation is abominable.... What will happen if we cut housing, education, poverty programs? I don't give a damn about the election.... The country's demoralized.... How can we get this job done? We need more money—in an election year; more taxes—in an election year; more troops—in an election year; and cuts in the domestic budget—in an election year. And yet I cannot tell the people what they will get in Vietnam in return for these cuts. We have no support for the war."[119]

On March 31 Johnson gave a televised speech that interwove the ideas of the Wise Men with his own concerns to heal a divided land. As gestures toward peace, he announced a bombing halt above the twentieth parallel in North Vietnam, invited talks with Hanoi, and promised to name an esteemed diplomat, Averell Harriman, as a token of good faith.

To Johnson's surprise, Hanoi welcomed his offer of talks, though as soon became evident, it regarded a conference table as one more theater of war, in accord with the ancient Vietnamese strategic perspective, "fighting and talking, talking and fighting." Nearly as many Americans would die in Vietnam between 1969 and 1973, when the last U.S. combat troops would evacuate, as during Johnson's tenure in office. Still, Johnson had taken the first clear steps to wind down a commitment that had originated more than two decades before.

The president's flurry of diplomatic initiatives and his announcement in the March 31 speech that, spurred by personal and political exhaustion and by a yearning to unify the country behind his Vietnam policy, he would not run for re-election dominated the headlines. Less heralded but resounding throughout Johnson's speech of March 31 were warnings of economic collapse, which he feared would ripple from America through every financial capital unless the Congress tightened the budgetary reins. His grim message jarred after seven years of presidential assurances that a Congress committed to tax cuts and ambitious new programs could stimulate miracles of production and provide guns and butter ample for all needs.

Johnson tacitly conceded that no longer could Keynesian magic fund social entitlements through a painless blend of tax cuts and higher federal spending. To mollify fiscal conservatives, he agreed to trim such welfare programs as Medicaid and Medicare, fixing his gaze on balanced budgets rather than growth. "The passage of a tax bill now," he said, "together with expenditure control that the Congress may desire and dictate, is absolutely necessary to protect this Nation's security, to continue our prosperity, and to meet the needs of our people." It was "unmistakably clear," Johnson said. "Our deficit just must be reduced."[120]

Johnson's urgent plea for fiscal restraint underscores how the costs of Vietnam brought a fatal reckoning to the politics of affluence. The faith in "growth liberalism" foundered on the strains of war, and its decline spurred the national security establishment to override Westmoreland's plan to raise the stakes in Vietnam yet again. "In truth," Robert Collins writes, "the decision to halt the escalation of the war was as much economic as it was political or military."[121]

The economic fallout from the war compounded a broader erosion of confidence in American power, virtue, and mission as the fighting continued without apparent progress or point. Senator J. William Fulbright, who played a leading role in educating Americans about the follies of intervention, had moved by the late 1960s from skeptically interrogating presidential aides to deploring the country's "arrogance of power": "We see the Viet Cong who cut the throats of village chiefs as savage murderers but American flyers who incinerate unseen women and children with napalm as valiant fighters for freedom; . . . we see the puritan discipline of life in Hanoi as enslavement but the chaos and corruption of life in Saigon as liberty; . . . we see China, with no troops in South Vietnam, as the real aggressor while we, with hundreds of thousands of men, are resisting foreign intervention."[122]

The larger failing of policy makers, Fulbright concluded, was to let Cold War doctrines calcify into a religious dogma that no contrary facts could shake. "Our 'faith' liberated us, like the believers of old, from the requirements of empirical thinking," he wrote. "Like medieval theologians, we had a philosophy that explained everything to us in advance, and everything that did not fit could be readily identified as a fraud or a lie or an illusion."[123]

Marine Lieutenant Philip Caputo recalled that the soldiers who fought in Vietnam had exuded this same zeal early in the war, relishing the prospect of winning glory in epic battles as they dispatched villainous communists to the cheers of grateful villagers:

For Americans who did not come of age in the early sixties, it may be hard to grasp what those years were like—the pride and overpowering self-assurance that prevailed. Most of the thirty-five hundred men in our brigade, born during or immediately after World War II, were shaped by that era, the age of Kennedy's Camelot. We went overseas full of illusions, for which the intoxicating atmosphere of those years was as much to blame as our youth.

War is always attractive to young men who know nothing about it, but we had also been seduced into uniform by Kennedy's challenge to "ask what you can do for your country" and by the missionary idealism he had awakened in us. America seemed omnipotent then: the country could still claim it had never lost a war, and we believed we were ordained to play cop to the Communists' robber and spread our own political faith around the world.

Defeat was inconceivable in an age of wondrous national achievements and lofty dreams. "So," Caputo wrote, "when we marched into the rice paddies on that damp March afternoon, we carried, along with our packs and rifles, the implicit convictions that the Viet Cong would be quickly beaten and that we were doing something altogether noble and good. We kept the packs and rifles; the convictions, we lost."[124]

CHAPTER 8

THE END OF THE LIBERAL HOUR

An appearance by an American president before the Supreme Court is a rare event, so when Richard Nixon's motorcade made its way up Capitol Hill on June 23, 1969, a large press contingent followed. As he entered the stately chamber, it seemed a triumphal return. His appointee, Warren Burger, was about to be sworn in as the nation's fifteenth chief justice, as his old political adversary, Earl Warren, was departing.

As he rose and intoned the lawyer's words, "May it please the Court..." Nixon offered a tribute to the retiring chief, saying little about the decisions of the Warren Court, focusing instead on the personal qualities of its leader. The remarks were gracious but perfunctory. "These great and simple attributes are, without question, more important than all of the controversy and the necessary debate that goes on when there is change," Nixon said of Warren. "Sixteen years have passed since the Chief Justice assumed his present position. These 16 years, without doubt, will be described by historians as years of greater change in America than any in our history."[1]

Nixon was no admirer of most of the changes wrought by the Warren Court or by the liberal majorities in Congress or his two predecessors in the White House. But now, he believed, the tide was turning. He had vanquished Hubert Humphrey, the great liberal champion, in the 1968 election, and here he was beginning to place his own stamp on the second of the nation's three great power centers. That morning at the Supreme Court was precisely the sort of symbolic occasion that Nixon treasured: the chance to demonstrate, in the gloss of formality, that the liberal hour was over. "As we consider this moment," he said, "we also think of the transition which will shortly take place. We think of what it means to America, what it means to our institutions."

Warren's departure was not the end of the Warren Court. His colleagues Black, Douglas, Brennan, White, and Marshall would remain, and much of the jurisprudence of the Warren Court would endure. But the progressive peak had passed, and new Courts would soon form, dominated by justices with different backgrounds and different goals than those of the Warren Court.

It would be a quarter-century before the Republicans captured both houses of Congress, and Nixon's own presidency would be truncated by the nation's greatest political scandal. But America was entering a new era of great partisan divide, and the policy explosion of the 1960s would not be replicated in the twentieth century.

The liberal hour was over. Its end came quickly, sharply; and it came from many directions. The perfect storm that yielded the policy explosion of 1963–66 passed as swiftly as it had formed.

CAGING THE LION

Lyndon Johnson's enormous complexity was his great charm and his great weakness. He could be generous yet vindictive, visionary yet petty, kind yet cruel. Often he could be all of these things in the same day or even the same conversation. But the very skills and traits that suited him so perfectly in the early part of his presidency served him poorly as it unraveled. Virtues became vices when Washington began to take its measure of Lyndon Johnson and when the war in Vietnam, race relations, and inflation began to spin out of his control.

Lyndon Johnson understood that he would have a real opportunity to effect policy changes and to get Congress to plow through a rich legislative agenda. But he also knew that the opportunity would pass quickly.

So he harnessed his natural impatience to the task at hand, pushing himself and those around him to act, act quickly, act now. In a speech to Congress on March 15, 1965, Johnson made no bones about his intentions. He described his early experiences teaching poor Mexican American children in Cotulla, Texas. "I never thought then, in 1928," he said, "that I would be standing here in 1965. It never even occurred to me in my fondest dreams that I might have the chance to help the sons and daughters of those students and to help people like them all over this country. But now I do have that chance—and I'll let you in on a secret—I mean to use it."[2]

The pace of activity yielded its own consequences. One, of course, was Johnson's success at producing in the Eighty-eighth and Eighty-ninth Congresses a record of legislative success rarely matched in American history. In those years following the Kennedy assassination, Johnson had his way with Congress, and nearly all of the deep liberal agenda of midcentury was enacted into public law.

But impatience bred sloppiness and contradiction. Ideas that had been barely tested and little debated were suddenly the policy of the land. Goals and visions and good intentions overwhelmed practical questions of implementation and administration. The idea of community action in the antipoverty program—that the poor would design ways to cure their poverty—had never been tested before it was implemented. Its political consequences were ill-considered, if they were considered at all. And all of the potential problems in this approach revealed themselves quickly when CAPs across the country began to bicker and founder and face the natural resistance of local political organizations and leaders.

In his rush to sell a long list of legislative goods to the American people, Lyndon Johnson overpromised. He would end poverty in his time, conquer bigotry, heal the sick, teach all the young, provide for the aged, and so on. It was an optimistic age, and disbelief was too easily suspended. As a member of the Kennedy and Johnson administrations noted, "We were all in Washington then to do social justice."[3] And there seemed to be no limit on what the government in Washington could do as long as its intentions were benign and it possessed the trust of the American people.

Lyndon Johnson rode this wave for years and never doubted his own hyperbole. When sales were good, he was the master salesman. And, as the journalist David Broder noted, Johnson would "do political business with anyone."[4] The dark side of his personality was overlooked or dismissed when his presidency was under full steam. The capacity for cruelty, the crudeness of his personal habits, the immodesty, the impatience, the burning desire to be history's darling: they were all there in those early years, but they were not the defining characteristics of this president. Nor were they yet the pathologies they would soon become.

The evolution of the Johnson presidency was under way in 1966. Johnson had made a substantial commitment to increase American forces in Vietnam in mid-1965. A year later there were 267,500 American troops there and more than a hundred were dying each week. As the opposition grew, so, too, did Johnson's defensiveness.

The legislative explosion of 1965 was followed by more modest successes in 1966. The energy had begun to seep out of the legislative process, and the agenda had thinned as well now that most of the key items had been enacted into law. In the midterm elections of that year Republicans gained forty-seven seats in the House and three in the Senate. The conservative coalition was revived by these results, and the slamming noise that Lyndon Johnson was hearing was the rapid closing of his window of opportunity on Capitol Hill.

And the booming economy of the early 1960s, the high-growth, low-inflation, low-unemployment economy that had fueled the limitless sense of possibility in those years, was also confronting the inevitabilities of the business cycle and the impacts of the combined costs of a foreign war and a Great Society. In 1964, Johnson could tell an aide, "We're the richest country in the world, the most powerful. We can do it all. . . . We can do it if we believe it."[5] Even in the White House, that kind of talk had begun to ring hollow by 1966.

When the bloom of opportunity faded and cries of opposition began to multiply, Lyndon Johnson reacted badly. David Halberstam noted:

> He was not so open, not so accessible. . . . He was, sadly, open-minded when things went well, and increasingly close-minded when things went

poorly. . . . [H]e would talk with some fatalism about the trap he had built for himself, with an almost plaintive cry for some sort of help. But these moments were rare indeed, very private, and more often than not they would soon be replaced by wild rages against any critic who might voice the most gentle doubt of the policy and the direction in which it was taking the country.

So instead of leading, he was immobilized, surrounded, seeing critics everywhere. Critics became enemies; enemies became traitors; and the press, which a year earlier had been so friendly, was now filled with enemies baying at his heels.[6]

As the president grew increasingly frustrated, his bitterness began to pervade the White House—and Washington. Kennedy aides who had stayed with him and become Johnson men—Richard Goodwin, McGeorge Bundy, even Robert McNamara—found it increasingly difficult to meet the standard of loyalty that Johnson demanded. Even Johnson's own people were often bruised and burned by the president's sour moods. By late 1966, staff departures were becoming more common, and a bunker mentality began to take hold.

Johnson could not have expected the legislative momentum of 1964 and 1965 to persist through his presidency. And even in the Ninetieth Congress, with shrunken Democratic majorities, there were high points: a major new housing act, creation of the Corporation for Public Broadcasting, a tough truth-in-lending law, some new conservation programs, appropriations increases for some Great Society programs. Congress was not the primary source of Lyndon Johnson's turning. Vietnam was. Johnson was a master of Congress, probably the greatest legislative tactician of his century. But the skills that had served him so well in dealing with members of Congress simply did not translate into foreign policy, and especially into the conduct of a war.

Johnson could understand self-interest, at least the sort of self-interest that legislators use in navigating among their own ambitions, the needs of their constituents, and the national interest. But he could not understand the self-interest of foreign leaders, especially his Vietnam adversary, Ho Chi Minh. In a telling moment, returning to the White House from Johns Hopkins University in 1965 where he had given a speech offering to help

Ho Chi Minh turn the Mekong Valley into a TVA if only Ho would be reasonable and negotiate, Johnson said to his aide Bill Moyers, "Old Ho can't turn that down, old Ho can't turn that down."

"See," said Moyers later, "if Ho Chi Minh had been [AFL-CIO leader] George Meany, Lyndon Johnson would have had a deal."[7]

This marked the boundary of Lyndon Johnson's skills. Ho Chi Minh was not George Meany, did not see the world like George Meany, would not make deals like George Meany. That made no sense to Lyndon Johnson, and it drove him mad.

Johnson's ambition to be the greatest president powered his domestic efforts where he could make reliable comparisons with his hero Franklin Roosevelt. But in managing a war, those same ambitions and comparisons drove him into blunder after blunder. The war in Vietnam was not the world war of the previous generation. Munich was the wrong analogy, Vietnam the wrong place, and simultaneously fighting a war and expanding the Great Society was the wrong strategy.

By late 1966 all of the measures of presidential success were turning south for Lyndon Johnson. His job approval ratings, which had reached as high as 80 percent and never fallen below 62 percent through 1965, had declined to 44 percent by December 1966.[8] They would never reach 50 percent again through the remainder of his presidency, save for the week in 1968 following his announcement that he would not seek re-election. Other public opinion polls showed increasing concern over the state of race relations, the war in Vietnam, and the economy. Trust in government, which had reached 76 percent in 1964, declined to 65 percent in 1966 and 61 percent in 1968.[9]

The results of the 1966 congressional elections were widely read as a repudiation by many Americans, if not of Lyndon Johnson, at least of the liberal agenda of the previous two years. Leading newspaper columnists like Walter Lippmann, James Reston, and Tom Wicker, who had cheered Lyndon Johnson in the early years of his presidency, now wrote ever-gloomier assessments of him. In spring 1966 Lippmann assessed his leadership of foreign policy as "willful, personal, arbitrary, self-opinionated."[10] A few months later, Lippmann wrote of the internal conflict that confounded Johnson's leadership: on the one hand, the "peacemaker and reformer and herald of a better world"; on the other, the "primitive frontiersman who wants to nail the coonskin to the wall, who wants to be the biggest, the best, the first, a worshipper of what William James called the bitch-goddess success."[11] If Lyndon Johnson was becoming increasingly frustrated and defensive, it was not without cause.

If Johnson had been a different person—less insecure, less driven, less omnivorous in his desires for mastery and control—the final years of his presidency might not have slipped so deeply into isolation and bitterness. The liberal hour might not have been so abruptly truncated. But if Lyndon Johnson had been that person, the legislative record of the early years would have been less rich, and the opportunities of the time less fully realized.

QUAGMIRE

When the Tet offensive occurred in January 1968, American forces had been in Vietnam for eight years. The major escalation in troop numbers that began in July 1965 was continuing. American forces in-country totaled 184,000 at the end of that year, 385,000 at the end of 1966, 485,000 at the end of 1967. They would continue to grow, to nearly 550,000 by the middle of 1969.[12]

Casualties grew apace. By the end of 1967, they numbered 19,560. In the four weeks following Tet in 1968, 1,829 more died. By the end of that year, the war's bloodiest, the total American deaths would be 36,152.[13]

The human costs were matched in scale, if not emotion, by the dollar costs. The great fiscal dividend yielded by America's growing affluence in the 1960s was being eaten away by the rapidly growing costs of the war in Vietnam—billions of dollars each month, financed primarily through supplemental appropriations.[14] And as Congress worried more and more about the costs of war, its enthusiasm for the domestic agenda diminished. "The Congress as a whole has lost interest in the Great Society and become, politically and psychologically, a 'war Congress,'" said Senator Fulbright of Arkansas in a speech at the University of Kansas in May 1967.[15]

Lyndon Johnson seemed to have persuaded himself, and he tried to persuade an increasingly skeptical country, that it could afford both the Great Society and the war in Vietnam. "The Nation has many commitments and responsibilities which make heavy demands upon our total resources," he said in his 1967 State of the Union Address. "No administration would more eagerly utilize for these programs all the resources they require than the administration that started them. So let us resolve, now, to do all that we can, with what we have—knowing that it is far, far more than we have ever done before, and far, far less than our problems will ultimately require."[16]

But the fiscal impossibility of affording both guns and butter was readily apparent by the beginning of 1968. The budget deficit for fiscal 1967 had reached $8.6 billion—more than double the deficit of the previous year—and threatened to be even larger in the year that followed. The bills were mounting, and so, too, was pressure to pay them. "The convergence of problems in early 1968 marked the end of growth liberalism's ascendancy," wrote the historian Robert M. Collins. "Johnson's guns-and-butter policy had brought the economy to the verge of financial collapse; the war in Vietnam had become a national nightmare, and the Great Society's promises had outrun its resources."[17]

After much urging by his economic advisors, Johnson had recommended in early 1967 that Congress enact a temporary 10 percent surcharge on corporate and individual income taxes—a tax increase—to help pay for the combined costs of the war and the new programs of the Great Society. Serious negotiations with Congress did not begin until late summer, and conservative opposition to the tax surcharge made this a hard sell for Lyndon Johnson, who was no longer the dominating force on Capitol Hill that he had been two years earlier. Some conservatives saw Johnson's predicament as a splendid opportunity to force a rollback in spending on the Great Society programs they disliked. And when his hard bargaining with Wilbur Mills, chairman of the tax-writing Ways and Means Committee of the House, concluded, Johnson had his tax surcharge, but he had been forced to agree to a $6 billion reduction in domestic expenditures and a cut in federal employment.

By 1968 the war was killing Americans at record rates, and it was eating into the country's financial resources at an intolerable pace. It was an ever-heavier anchor on Lyndon Johnson's job approval ratings, and it gnawed at his moods and his relations with others in Washington and the press. But it was also eroding the nation's trust in its government. Johnson's hyperbole had infected his pronouncements on the war as it had his promises about curing poverty, ending racism, fixing the cities, and educating the country's children. There emerged what the press started to call a "credibility gap."

That was a generous term. Put more plainly, the government had lied to its people. Perhaps the lies were founded in optimism more than deceit, in good intentions rather than evil, but they were lies nonetheless. And as they became apparent, Americans were no longer willing to suspend disbelief, no longer prepared to allow hope to trump experience.

The conventional measures of trust in government were in free fall. The public figure widely described as the most trusted man in America, CBS news anchor Walter Cronkite, had made an unusual but powerfully pessimistic statement about Vietnam in his broadcast on February 27, 1968: "To say that we are closer to victory today is to believe, in the face of the evidence, the optimists who have been wrong in the past. To suggest we are on the edge of defeat is to yield to unreasonable pessimism. To say that we are mired in stalemate seems the only realistic, yet unsatisfactory, conclusion."[18]

The war news continued to be bad, the predictions of success from the president and military leaders continued to be optimistic. The credibility gap widened and, as it did, the liberal surge in American public life began to recede.

UPRISING

Two boys from the neighborhood, recently returned from duty in Vietnam, were being welcomed home at a party at Clairmount Avenue and Twelfth Street in Detroit. It was July 23, 1967. Their neighbors had gathered at a "blind pig," a Detroit term for an after-hours drinking club. Blind pigs were among the few gathering places in this predominantly black neighborhood. After a while, the party grew loud and someone called the cops.

When the police arrived, they expected to find the usual few patrons and to close down the illegal club. Instead they encountered dozens of young people and arrested them all. A crowd began to gather while the police were holding their charges in the street outside, waiting for wagons to transport them to jail. Anger rose. A window was broken. The crowd grew. Soon Detroit was engulfed in one of the most destructive riots in American history. It took five days, the National Guard, and the Eighty-second Airborne Division to quell it. When the last fire had finally burned out, the toll was heavy: 43 deaths, more than 450 injuries, 7,500 arrests, and 2,000 buildings destroyed.

By 1967 the pattern had become depressingly familiar: hot summer night, minor incident in which white police officers use excessive force against black residents, angry outrage, riots follow, stores looted, fires set, neighborhoods hollowed out. The "long hot summers" of the 1960s had begun in 1964 in Harlem in New York. That riot seemed an aberration at the time. The Civil Rights Act passed Congress that year and Martin Luther King won the Nobel Peace Prize. Surely, many Americans felt, rioting in Harlem was not the true face of black expression.

But then 1965 brought a similar outbreak in Watts, a black neighborhood in Los Angeles. Dozens of lives were lost and property damage exceeded $200 million. In the years that followed, the fires of summer raged in city after city. In 1968, in the days following the assassination of King, one of the worst outbreaks occurred just a few blocks from the White House where the driving force behind the civil rights and voting rights acts was still in residence. All told, more than three hundred urban riots occurred between 1964 and 1969, resulting in more than 250 deaths and property damage in excess of a billion dollars.[19]

It seemed a cruel irony. The more the federal government did to protect the rights of African Americans, the more the ghettos burned. Journalists and sociologists searched for answers. President Johnson appointed a national commission, the Kerner Commission, to come up with an explanation. Mounting frustration in the face of rising expectations was the most common. One study found that while more than 60 percent of black citizens believed that public policy in the 1960s had contributed to black advancement, more than a third had experienced no change in their own lives. Among young people the sense that conditions had stayed the same or gotten worse was even greater.[20]

Others saw the riots as a logical outgrowth of the black power movement. For much of the decade that began with the 1955 boycott of city-owned buses in Montgomery, Alabama, the civil rights movement had enjoyed a high level of unity. Though there were ample and often angry internal debates about strategy and tactics, it had largely followed the leadership of a few groups—the NAACP, the Southern Christian Leadership Conference, and the Student Nonviolent Coordinating Committee, among others—pursuing a policy of nonviolent confrontation with the worst implementers of racial discrimination while seeking, through federal courts and the federal legislative process, to win protections of constitutional rights. With the march on Selma, Alabama, and the subsequent passage of the Voting Rights Act of 1965, that strategy seemed still to be working.

But the civil rights movement was fracturing. Some of the younger leaders scorned the strategy of nonviolence. Instead of turning the other cheek, they wanted to fight back against racism. On June 16, 1966, in Greenwood, Mississippi, a young black activist who had just been released from police custody stood before an angry crowd of supporters and said, "This is the twenty-seventh time I've been arrested, and I ain't going to jail no more! We been saying freedom for six years—and we ain't got nothin'. What we gonna' start sayin' now is 'Black Power!'"[21]

The crowd roared the phrase back, and Stokely Carmichael repeated it over and over. "Black power" caught on, though it came to mean many things. To some, black power was a call to arms. H. Rap Brown, then a twenty-three-year-old leader of SNCC, told a crowd in Cambridge, Maryland, "Don't be trying to love that honky to death. Shoot him to death. Shoot him to death, brother, because that's what he is out to do to you. Do to him like he would do to you, but do it to him first."[22] Pictures of Brown and others with automatic weapons and bandoliers of ammunition came to symbolize "black power" in the popular press.

To Eldridge Cleaver, in *Soul on Ice*, a best-selling book he wrote while in Folsom Prison, black power was an urgent retaking of the virility and freedom that had been repressed for four centuries. "Not for a single moment or for any price," he wrote, "will the black men now rising up in America settle for anything less than their full proportionate share and participation in the sovereignty of America. . . . The black man can't afford to take a chance. He can't afford to put things off."[23]

To others, like Malcolm X, who was assassinated before they became fighting words, black power was a policy of no more shuffling, of redefining African American life in indigenous terms, not the terms established by whites. If that meant black separatism, even black nationalism, he argued, so be it. "How can there ever be any white-black solidarity," he asked in his autobiography, "before there is first some black solidarity?... Black Nationalist political, economic, and social philosophies [have] the ability to instill within black men the racial dignity, the incentive, and the confidence that the black race needs today to get up off its knees, and to get on its feet, and get rid of its scars, and to take a stand for itself."[24]

To still others, black power was more practical: the need for African Americans to build their own structure of economic and political power. They were urged to start their own businesses, develop their own schools or take "local control" of the public schools in their neighborhoods, encourage black candidates for public office, and refuse to accept patronization from urban political machines.

In all of its varied meanings, the call for black power grew increasingly popular in minority neighborhoods, fueled by centuries of pent-up anger, frustration with the unmet promises of the Great Society and the civil rights movement, and the overwhelming urge to attain faster a quality of life that until very recently had not seemed possible at all.

To white advocates of civil rights and even to some black leaders of the more traditional civil rights movement, black power was a conundrum. Hadn't they done enough? Weren't the strategies of nonviolence and working within the system producing real progress? Were they now, after the ghetto eruptions, "just beginning a new ordeal," as NAACP leader Roy Wilkins suggested?[25] The answers grew increasingly uncertain and subject to debate.

Among one group, however, the response to black power and to the urban riots of the mid-1960s was very clear. Northern whites, who had been among the chief supporters of the civil rights movement and the public policies to end Jim Crow, reacted quickly and negatively. Polling in 1964 showed that 68 percent of northern whites supported President Johnson's civil rights policies. But once the riots began and the image of those became intermixed with amorphous notions of black power, northern white support quickly evaporated. By 1966 more than half of northern whites had come to believe that government was pushing too fast for integration.[26]

Serious civil rights leaders had long understood that the South was only the first battleground in the struggle for black equality. There the problem was de jure segregation in the form of Jim Crow laws that required separation of the races. Outside the South, segregation was often as severe, but the cause was different. There were no laws in Boston that required separate schools for white and black children. But, in fact, most schools in that city had student bodies that were overwhelmingly black or white—the result of neighborhood residential patterns, pupil placement policies, teacher assignment practices, and many decades of accumulated budget decisions.[27]

So long as the civil rights movement remained a southern event, northern whites could applaud its nobility. When it came to focus on their own neighborhoods, the applause quickly died and resistance rose.

After 1965 all of these developments—the emergence of newer and angrier black leaders, the growing focus on de facto segregation outside the South, the fracturing of the civil rights movement, the completion of the legislative civil rights agenda, and the growing frustration within black communities that so little seemed to have changed—had a profound effect on liberal politics. Civil rights had been the issue around which liberals could most easily coalesce. Whatever their other disagreements might be about socialism or labor unions or poverty, to be a liberal meant that one abhorred the practice of racial discrimination and thought the authority of the federal government should be employed to counteract it.

But now that authority had been exercised. The great civil rights laws had been written and passed. Southern blacks had finally been given equal rights! But the aftermath was not what most liberals imagined. There was still widespread evidence of racial discrimination across the land. Many blacks were notably cynical about these liberal efforts, and some black leaders were calling for revolution. It is no surprise that in the face of all this, civil rights was no longer the potent fuel source it had once been for liberal ideology and liberal politics.

THE GROWING FRUSTRATION in the African American community coincided with the escalation of public demonstrations against the war in Vietnam. Opposition to American wars was nothing new. But what happened in the 1960s was different. The Vietnam War was the longest American war. Opposition to it could incubate and gestate over a period of several years with effects that were not only immediate but cumulative. It was also different because it occurred in the age of television. Antiwar tactics, for the first time in the 1960s, came to focus on the creation of media spectacles.

The early expressions against the war in Vietnam grew out of traditional sources: the peace movement and some of the groups that had been pushing in the 1950s and early 1960s for control of nuclear weapons. It was easy for Washington policy-makers and journalists to dismiss these protestations as little more than "same old, same old." Weren't these peaceniks against any use of military power for any purpose?

The antiwar movement began to take a new turn, however, on March 24, 1965, when the first "teach-in" was conducted at the University of Michigan. Faculty, students, and Asian experts gathered for many hours to educate themselves about Vietnam policy and to discuss alternatives. The teach-in approach spread rapidly, and within a year such events had occurred at most of the major colleges and universities in the country.

The first significant demonstration against the war in Washington took place on April 17, 1965. It was sponsored by the Students for a Democratic Society (SDS), the organization that in 1962 had produced the Port Huron Statement. The demonstration was peaceful, almost respectful, and participation, estimated by march organizers at around twenty thousand, was noteworthy but substantially smaller than the crowds that would gather to protest the war in the years ahead.[28]

Though attracting some attention in the press, the antiwar movement remained on the fringes of public discussion until after Lyndon Johnson announced a major increase in American troop levels in Vietnam in July 1965. Antiwar activity, like the war itself, continued to escalate. As the war grew longer and hotter, it commanded the engaged attention of more and more Americans. And as victory remained elusive, frustration with the war effort spread. Increasing commitments of troops required a steady increase in the size of draft calls. More and more young men were being forced into involuntary participation in the war.

And the casualty numbers began to spiral upward: 1,863 in 1965, 6,143 in 1966, 11,153 in 1967, and 16,592 in 1968.[29]

Ironically, while much of the antiwar effort centered on college campuses, college students were protected from the draft by a policy of granting 2-S deferments to anyone enrolled in an accredited college or university. Many of those chanting "Hell no, we won't go" were in no danger of going anywhere. But position-taking on the war became inevitable among college students; it was an issue from which few found shelter.

The prominence of the antiwar movement was further accelerated by the growing sophistication of antiwar leaders in the manipulation of the mass media. The appearance of opposition to the war nearly always exceeded the breadth of opposition. Antiwar organizers could deliver tens of thousands of young people to their demonstrations. They could find young men to burn their draft cards or others to pour red liquids purporting to be blood on the records of local draft boards. None of this occurred without ample warnings to national and local news media. Protest was choreographed for its visual impact. The antiwar movement became one of the longest-running television shows of the 1960s.

Fred Halstead, a veteran of the antiwar movement, writes that "antiwar agitation and mass mobilizations spurred the radicalization of many sectors of the population ... changed the political face of the United States and ... did win over public opinion and exert enough pressure ... to bring the U.S. forces home."[30] Tom Hayden, one of the most visible activists of the decade, summarized the accomplishments of young dissidents simply: "We ended a war, toppled two presidents, and desegregated the South."[31]

But Washington policy makers were quickly inured to these demonstrations; many wrote them off as the work of radicals or crazies or even communists, and were thus immune to their effects. They went on with the war in Vietnam largely undisturbed by antiwar protests. The first antiwar demonstration in Washington occurred in the spring of 1965. The war did not end until seven years later. Adam Garfinkle, in the most extensive—and critical—study of the antiwar movement, points out that "it did not help stop the war but rather helped prolong it.... At the very time when the war's unpopularity was growing in the country at large, the image of irresponsibility and willful anti-patriotism conveyed by the antiwar movement had the general effect of muting the expression of disaffection."[32]

The antiwar movement was never a monolith. "Antiwar activists did not establish a single directing organization, coordinated leadership, or ideology," wrote the historian Charles Chatfield in another study of the antiwar movement. "They drew on varied constituencies. They offered contradictory critiques of American society and foreign policy. They argued among themselves almost as bitterly as they excoriated those they held responsible for the war."[33]

The ultimate impact of the antiwar movement on the war in Vietnam will probably never be settled. But its impact on Lyndon Johnson's presidency and on liberal politics is easier to assess. Though he unfailingly sought to dismiss his antiwar critics in his public statements, Johnson's moods and his actions were deeply affected by them. After the 1966 elections, his public appearances began to decline in number and range. More and more he sought the assurance of friendly audiences and avoided potential hostilities. He had made some of the major statements of his visions for America to university audiences in the early part of his administration; after March 1967 he made only two further appearances on college campuses.

The war and its opposition drove a sharp wedge through American liberals. Liberalism and anticommunism had been tightly welded together in the period after World War II, especially after the creation of Americans for Democratic Action as a leading liberal organization. John Kennedy's efforts to match the Soviet Union in the race to space, to force a confrontation over Soviet nuclear missiles in Cuba, to stand with Berlin in the face of Soviet saber-rattling had yielded widespread liberal applause. It was Kennedy who had taken the lead in expanding the American commitment to Vietnam in order to "deny this country to communism."[34] So it seemed only natural to Lyndon Johnson to continue that commitment and to calibrate it to the changing military situation in Southeast Asia.

But if liberals had been cheerleaders for the early phases of American engagement in Vietnam, many of them became doomsayers as the length and cost of that commitment grew. To stand by a liberal president in a cause rooted in liberal principles or to stand with the young people who opposed an expanding, deadly, costly—and unsuccessful—war? That became the liberal dilemma of the mid-1960s. "The Vietnam War was a very peculiar crisis for orthodox American liberalism," said Curtis Gans, a leader of the effort to depose Lyndon Johnson in 1968. "Their base was still liberal anticommunism, and we were fighting communism in Vietnam."[35] The war forced a deep split among American liberals just as the liberal ascendancy reached its peak.

BULLETS AND BALLOTS

Allard Lowenstein had always been a troublemaker. Not the kind who broke laws and tangled with police, but the kind who always challenged the status quo, who never accepted bad situations as permanent. Lowenstein had challenged the editor of the student paper at the University of North Carolina, headed the National Students Association in the 1950s, smuggled a critic of apartheid out of South Africa in the back of his car. But Lowenstein was no wild-eyed radical. He befriended Eleanor Roosevelt and Robert Kennedy, wrote speeches for Hubert Humphrey, and later would be elected to Congress from the Long Island district where he grew up.

"He lived on the edge of conventional liberalism," wrote his biographer, William H. Chafe, "torn between complacent New Deal–type homilies and a radical challenge to all comfortable and entrenched institutions. In effect, Lowenstein walked a line between these two options through much of his life—seeking to achieve reform from within the system, but frequently being willing to challenge established institutions and authorities as well."[36]

In 1967, Lowenstein was a man on a mission, an impossible mission in the minds of many of his friends. He wanted to challenge an incumbent president and deny Lyndon Johnson the Democratic nomination. Johnson had fallen far from his apex of support in 1965. His job approval rating had averaged 66 percent in 1965. By late 1967 it had fallen below 40 percent. A vicious satirical play about the president, *MacBird*, had opened in New York, implying that Johnson had orchestrated the assassination of President Kennedy. Most of the leading columnists found little good to say about him. And on college campuses, he had become a target of crude and cruel invective.

But the conventional wisdom still held that it was impossible to prevent an incumbent president from winning the nomination of his party. It hadn't been done at any time in the twentieth century, and even a politically wounded Lyndon Johnson was still a formidable political force.

None of that daunted Allard Lowenstein. He and Curtis Gans and a few other optimists sought to convince a limited audience of liberals that Johnson could be beaten, must be beaten. They encountered dour skepticism. Richard Goodwin, once a Johnson aide but now at the forefront of those seeking his ouster, sought in a *New Yorker* article (written under the pseudonym Bailey Laird) to convince the doubters. "The rules [of politics] are only a summary of what's happened before. The trick is in trying to see what's going to happen next." "The big prize," he argued, "is hanging right up there ready to be grabbed by the first man who fights his way to it."[37]

Lowenstein led the search for a candidate to oppose the president. One possible approach was a third party with Martin Luther King as the candidate, but King was not interested.[38] Another was to convince Robert Kennedy, by then a senator from New York, to challenge the president. But Kennedy worried that too many people would think that personal ambition had gotten the best of him and that his candidacy would split the Democratic Party.[39]

In October 1967, Lowenstein met with Eugene McCarthy, a Democratic senator from Minnesota, having heard that McCarthy might be willing to challenge Johnson. Gans had earlier met with McCarthy's daughter, Mary, at Radcliffe to try to convince her to urge her father to run. McCarthy came around, and on November 30, 1967, announced his intent to seek the Democratic nomination. "I am hopeful," he said then, "that this challenge ... may alleviate at least in some degree this sense of political helplessness and restore to many people a belief in the processes of American politics and of American government."

Although he had served in Congress for almost twenty years and was nearly chosen for the vice presidency in 1964 by Lyndon Johnson, Mc-Carthy was largely unknown outside Minnesota. He had the bearing of an intellectual, not a ward heeler. He wrote poetry and spoke in para-graphs. His sense of irony was well honed and a primary source of his humor. He often seemed diffident, and nothing about him bore the look of personal ambition. His voting record in Congress was reliably liberal and in 1964 he had written a book titled *A Liberal Answer to the Conservative Challenge*, but McCarthy had never established himself at the front rank of liberal lawmakers during the policy explosion of the mid-1960s.

McCarthy's quest quickly became a magnet for disaffected liberals and independents who could not bear the thought of another term for Lyndon Johnson. Few in the White House took the McCarthy candidacy seriously. The president never mentioned him in his speeches and did very little personal campaigning, relying on the Democratic Party organization in New Hampshire and elsewhere to manage his renomination.

But something unique was happening in New Hampshire. Young people from around the country, but from New England colleges and universities especially, were coming to the Granite State to campaign for McCarthy. Urged by Gans to "Get clean for Gene," they abandoned their beards and beads, wore skirts and suits, and went door to door urging New Hampshire citizens to use their primary votes as a statement against the war. Implicit in their pleas was the notion that a vote for Gene McCarthy was a vote against Lyndon Johnson.

McCarthy's momentum had begun to build in January as more and more young people poured into the state to work for him. He was further strengthened by the Tet offensive in Vietnam, which had begun just a few weeks before the primary and seemed to underscore all of the arguments he had been making against the war. "For the first time," said McCarthy aide Gerry Studds, "a large proportion of the country was capable of being convinced that the government had lied to them."[40]

On March 12 McCarthy won the New Hampshire primary in every way except the final vote count. Johnson received 49 percent of the Democratic votes; McCarthy 42 percent. By winning so large a percentage against an incumbent president, McCarthy persuaded Lyndon Johnson that he was in much deeper political trouble than the president had been willing to admit.

McCarthy had also established himself as a genuine candidate for the Democratic nomination, not just a protest vote or a stalking horse for Robert Kennedy or some other more "serious" candidate who might now be lured into the race. And he had made it clear, beyond all doubt, that Vietnam—not the Great Society, not civil rights, not the domestic policy accomplishments of the Eighty-ninth and Ninetieth Congresses—would be the central issue in the 1968 election.

The impact of McCarthy's candidacy began to career wildly through the political process in the weeks that followed New Hampshire. Four days later, on March 16, Robert Kennedy announced that he would join the race. On Sunday, March 31, in a stunning surprise at the end of a nationally televised speech on Vietnam, Lyndon Johnson said:

> With America's sons in the fields far away, with America's future under challenge right here at home, with our hopes and the world's hopes for peace in the balance every day, I do not believe that I should devote an hour or a day of my time to any personal partisan causes or to any duties other than the awesome duties of this office—the Presidency of your country.
>
> Accordingly, I shall not seek, and I will not accept, the nomination of my party for another term as your President.

Two days later, Eugene McCarthy received 56 percent of the vote in the Wisconsin primary. And two days after that, while McCarthy and Robert Kennedy were campaigning in Indiana, word came of the assassination of Martin Luther King in Memphis, Tennessee.

King's death occurred as he had lost much of the spotlight to more voluble black leaders. And some of his old followers had criticized him for diluting his status as a civil rights leader by entering the partisan debate as an increasingly outspoken opponent of the war in Vietnam. The movement he had helped to forge through Montgomery and Birmingham and Selma was deeply fractured in the spring of 1968. But

Martin Luther King, Jr., was still the most prominent black activist in America, and his murder made him the great martyr of the cause that had defined his life.

Violence and lawlessness broke out almost as soon as news of King's death became known. Nowhere was the angry reaction more visible than in Washington, D.C. There, in the four days it took for federal troops to quell the uprising, twelve people died, more than a thousand were injured, and over six thousand arrested. Twelve hundred buildings went up in flames, most of them stores. The symbolism was widely noted: The pain of racial torment had burned a hole in the very heart of the nation.

The death of Martin Luther King removed from the national stage the most prominent nonviolent civil rights leader, the most potent unifying symbol of the civil rights movement, and a man who had been able to work effectively with white liberal politicians in Washington. King in a Birmingham jail, King on the steps of the Lincoln Memorial, King meeting with John Kennedy and Lyndon Johnson in the White House, King at the head of the march across the Pettus Bridge in Selma: These were enduring images from the liberal hour of the mid-1960s. King's death was yet more evidence of its passing.

THE CAMPAIGN FOR THE Democratic nomination continued in earnest after King's funeral. With Johnson out of the race, Vice President Hubert Humphrey quickly entered. Now the liberal Democrats faced a Hobson's choice: Eugene McCarthy, who had dared to challenge an incumbent president when no one else would and who had inspired thousands of young people not to lose faith in the political process; Robert Kennedy, brother of a slain president and possessed of great personal magnetism; and Hubert Humphrey, liberal warhorse for more than two decades. Inevitably a contest like this tore at old bonds of friendship and political alliance. McCarthy's supporters thought Kennedy an opportunist. Kennedy's supporters attacked McCarthy's capacity to lead the country. Both groups tried to define Humphrey as a mirror image, at least on Vietnam, of Lyndon Johnson.

Humphrey, having entered late, avoided the primaries and sought to capture the delegates controlled by the political bosses. Kennedy and

McCarthy slugged it out through the remaining primaries. The last primary, in California, was on June 4, 1968, and the outcome there was critical because of the number of delegates up for grabs in the largest state. Kennedy won with 46.3 percent of the vote to 41.8 percent for McCarthy. Among Kennedy's aides, there was a sense at the victory celebration that California had propelled Kennedy to the nomination. With great enthusiasm, he ended his victory statement with a lusty "On to Chicago!"

But within seconds a young man named Sirhan Sirhan stepped toward Kennedy as he was leaving the hall and fired eight shots from a .22-caliber revolver. Three of the bullets hit Kennedy, and he died the next day.

Kennedy's assassination, so soon after that of Martin Luther King, spread a deep pall of hopelessness over many Americans. But it struck especially hard at liberals in the Democratic Party. Robert Kennedy's campaign had cast him in a new light. No longer caricatured as the ruthless younger brother of a president, he had emerged as a charismatic candidate, attracting large and boisterous crowds on the campaign trail, drawing passionate support from political insiders who had worked for John Kennedy and Lyndon Johnson, energizing the flow of disaffected Democrats back into their party. To many, his campaign had reinvigorated the sense of optimism about social justice that had been so potent in the earlier years of the decade and raised hopes for a continuation of the liberal ascendancy in national politics.

Political scientists who studied national polling data before and after Robert Kennedy's assassination believed that his chances of winning the election were substantial. "One cannot help but be impressed," notes one such study, "by the reverberations of Kennedy charisma even in the least likely quarters, such as among Southern whites or among Republicans elsewhere. . . . There is evidence of enough edge . . . to suggest that Robert Kennedy might have won election over Richard Nixon, and perhaps with even greater ease than he would have won his own party's nomination."[41] To many, Kennedy seemed the proper antidote to the corrosive effect that the war had had on liberal prospects.

But, with Kennedy gone, Humphrey was able to attract enough delegates to deny the nomination to McCarthy. McCarthy's young supporters responded angrily, as if victims of a sinister theft. They had worked hard to make popular democracy work and now Humphrey was denying them the victory they felt they deserved. And he was doing it by playing the insider's game, working hand in glove with the icons of an old politics they were hoping to demolish. It was more than most of those supporters could stomach.

When the Democrats opened their convention in Chicago on August 26, there was little prospect of a peaceful event that would reunify the party. The sides were too far apart, the anger level too elevated. McCarthy and Humphrey were both from Minnesota. They had a long relationship over many years of representing their state in Congress. But the emotions of 1968 were too strong to be set aside merely for old times' sake.

McCarthy was reluctant to concede the nomination. He was unwilling, as he said, to abandon all those people who had stood with him when there was no reason to think he had a chance. His delegates were in no compromising mood either.

But the bigger news from Chicago was happening outside the convention hall. Chicago had become a magnet for protesters of varying stripes, and they had turned out by the thousands. Each day as the Democratic delegates gathered at the International Amphitheatre, angry crowds of protesters gathered in Grant Park and in the streets of Chicago. The Chicago police gathered there as well, and violent clashes soon became the glaring image of that convention. In a memorable televised moment, Senator Abraham Ribicoff of Connecticut stood at the convention podium, glared at Richard J. Daley, the mayor of Chicago and the leader of the Illinois delegation seated right in front of him, and castigated "the Gestapo tactics in the streets of Chicago."

The convention did nominate Humphrey, but rarely in American history had a major-party candidate headed into a general election with such deep wounds.

POLITICAL GEOGRAPHY: 1968

George Corley Wallace had been a lifelong Democrat, but he was not among the Alabama delegation at the Democratic convention in 1968. Nor was he any longer a Democrat. But he was a pivotal factor in the politics of that year and that decade—and in the end of the liberal hour.

Born to a family of modest means in Clio, Alabama, Wallace became a boxer in his teens, then scratched out a law degree just as America was entering World War II. He served as an enlisted man in the Army Air Corps, flying combat missions over Japan under the command of General Curtis LeMay. After the war, he became a prosecutor, then a judge, state legislator, and governor in Alabama. But Wallace remained an obscure national figure until 1963 when his efforts to block the enrollment of two black students at the University of Alabama catapulted him into a leading symbol of the resistance to federal authority in the civil rights conflict.

In 1964 Wallace campaigned for the Democratic nomination for president. It was, of course, a hopeless quest in view of Lyndon Johnson's high public standing that year. But Wallace surprised many observers with his showing in several states outside the Deep South, winning 30 percent of the vote in Indiana, 34 percent in Wisconsin, and 45 percent in Maryland.

Four years later, Wallace mounted a different kind of campaign for president, outside the Democratic Party. He formed the American Independent Party and chose Curtis LeMay, his old general, as his running mate. Wallace intended to confront the norms of Washington politics with a campaign that touched on tender nerves in public opinion. He attacked the federal assaults on states' rights, "pointy-headed bureaucrats," white liberals, protesters, and the two major parties. "There's not a dime's worth of difference between the Democratic and Republican parties," he said often. "They're building a bridge over the Potomac," he told campaign audiences, "for all the white liberals fleeing Washington." When protesters chanted during his campaign rallies, he would say "You shout four-letter words at me, I have two for you: w-o-r-k and s-o-a-p." And he knew he could get applause whenever he said, "Any protester lies down in front of my car, that's the last car he'll ever lie down in front of."

Though the Wallace campaign did offer some positions on Social Security and health care and other issues of the day, his was a campaign of antis. He won support for the things he was against, not for the things he was for. And in his subjects and his language, he touched a significant strain of unhappiness in American politics.

Wallace won 9.4 million popular votes—13 percent of the total cast— and carried the electoral votes of five states: Alabama, Arkansas, Georgia,

Louisiana, and Mississippi. His campaign was an outlet for voters—and no small number of citizens who rarely voted—who were profoundly unhappy with the direction of their country. In the perspective of time, he appears as a transitional figure, a warning bell to politicians in both parties that politics was changing. The South had seemed ready for some time to loosen its moorings in the Democratic Party; Wallace set it fully adrift.

Wallace's candidacy also revealed changes outside the South. Among lower-income white voters all across the country, Wallace showed significant strength. His support in labor union households was three times greater than in nonunion households. He appealed most strongly to white skilled workers, a traditional Democratic constituency.[42] And that support was a powerful sign of the deep fissures that were growing in the liberal coalition that had dominated American politics since the 1930s.

The Wallace campaign was evidence less of a conservative revival than of a backlash against the liberal thrust of the previous years. Indeed, Wallace didn't call himself or think of himself as a conservative. An angry populist is closer to the mark. But a conservative revival was under way in American politics in the mid-1960s and it would later engage, and absorb, much of the constituency that George Wallace had identified and energized.

That revival took root in the Goldwater campaign of 1964. Despite his overwhelming defeat, Goldwater was a magnetic force for conservatives of many strains who had been floating unattached through the political universe. These included the anticommunist John Birch Society on the right fringe of the political spectrum, conservative college students in the Young Americans for Freedom, Republicans in the Midwest and South who were unhappy with the moderate internationalists who seemed to control their party, wealthy oil barons in the Southwest, fundamentalist Christians like those in the rapidly growing Thomas Road Baptist Church in Lynchburg, Virginia, headed by a young pastor named Jerry Falwell, the intellectual *National Review* crowd that scorned nearly all liberal policies, leaders of the country's small businesses increasingly discomfited by expanding federal regulation, and many blue collar workers who had come to feel that the leaders of their unions were taking them in the wrong direction.

Goldwater's repudiation in 1964 had led many of the leading pundits to conclude that the American people had endorsed liberalism and rejected conservatism in some kind of semipermanent judgment. Richard Rovere wrote in the *New Yorker* that the election had "finished the Goldwater school of political reaction." And James Reston of the *New York Times* concluded that Goldwater had "wrecked his party for a long time to come."[43] These seemed reasonable judgments at the time.

But the impact of the Goldwater campaign was far from fleeting. It provided a training ground for many young people who would later become candidates for office or successful political operatives. It was the stage for the political debut of Ronald Reagan, who would become one of the towering political figures of the last third of the twentieth century. It helped to tear the South away from the hold that Democrats had maintained there for a century. And, perhaps most important, Goldwater's capture of the Republican Party inspired conservatives to believe that they could compete effectively in the mainstream of American politics, that they were not doomed to inhabit its fringes.

As the liberal hour unfolded in Washington, especially in the legislative outpouring of the Eighty-ninth Congress and the increasingly liberal and activist decisions of the Warren Court, conservatives wasted no time wallowing in the darkness of 1964 and began to look to brighter days ahead. One of them was a young man named Richard Viguerie. He had been executive secretary of the Young Americans for Freedom and an active Goldwater supporter. After the election, he founded a company called American Target Advertising and became one of the nation's leaders in direct-mail fundraising. His efforts helped to fund a number of conservative candidates and political groups. Others like him became political strategists or speechwriters or organizers. By 1966 they had worked the grass roots well enough to ensure significant Republican gains in the congressional elections of that year.

There would be no Goldwater-like conservative at the top of the Republican ticket in 1968, although California governor Ronald Reagan made an eleventh-hour run for the nomination that stirred many conservative hearts at the Republican convention in Miami Beach. But the party had begun to turn. The eastern wing, the stalwarts who were internationalist in outlook and moderate on matters of social and fiscal policy, who supported civil rights initiatives, no longer dominated the party as they had in midcentury. Nelson Rockefeller of New York and George Romney of Michigan, two governors from that wing of the party, failed miserably in their efforts to win the GOP nomination that year.

The surprising nominee would be Richard Nixon—surprising because his political obituary had been written after he failed to win the presidency in 1960 and the governorship of California in 1962; surprising, too, because none of the leading pundits had predicted his success and no significant group of Republicans could really be called the Nixon constituency. Nixon was very lucky in 1968, lucky that so many of the other seekers of the nomination imploded and lucky that the events of the year made him seem like a moderate voice of reason. But Nixon left little to luck, and in the years after 1964, he logged tens of thousands of miles to Republican dinners and candidate fundraisers, doing the kind of hard political work that earns the respect of political insiders and the chits that can be cashed in at a major political convention.

Nixon was never the darling of conservatives, and though he made his initial splash in politics as a witch-hunting anticommunist, he was an internationalist in foreign policy and flexible on domestic issues. But Nixon was a sensitive political barometer. He could see how the country was changing and how the Republican Party was changing and he adapted his 1968 campaign to those new realities. The centerpiece was his "southern strategy." He chose a running mate from a border state, the barely known governor of Maryland, Spiro Agnew. He consulted closely with Strom Thurmond, the recently converted Republican senator from South Carolina, and John Tower, the Republican who had won Lyndon Johnson's Senate seat in Texas. He campaigned in the South and advertised heavily there. And he emphasized substantive themes like "law and order" that he knew would appeal to southern white voters.

Nixon understood the appeal of George Wallace, especially to that group of Americans whom Nixon would later call the "silent majority." In many ways, Nixon and Wallace were playing the same game, though Wallace was doing so in plainer language. As historian David Farber has argued, "George Wallace, in 1968, tried to mutate a racist populist politics of the Old South into a national politics of resentment. Richard Nixon, picking up on the cultural politics of Barry Goldwater and then California governor Ronald Reagan, tried to quietly unite the producing classes with the capitalist producers against the 'critical' and protesting segments of society."[44]

The politics of resentment was a potent political force in 1968, and both Wallace on the right and Nixon closer to the center sought to harness it. Between them, they captured 57 percent of the popular vote and nearly two-thirds of the electoral votes. In the South, their campaigns produced the highest voter turnout in the twentieth century.[45] They carried all the southern electoral votes, except those in Texas. And their efforts abetted the campaigns of Republican congressional candidates, adding to the long line of southern seats that had begun to swing to the Republican Party.

From the apparent ashes of 1964, a new politics was rising. In accomplishing so many of their policy goals, liberals in Washington had left their political flanks vulnerable. Goldwater in 1964 had helped to indicate those vulnerabilities; Wallace and Nixon in 1968 had exploited them. In the years that followed, the patterns established in the middle years of the 1960s would continue: conservatives ascendant, liberals on the defensive, the broad center of American politics—where elections are won and lost—leaning to the right.

In 1972, when the Democrats gathered in Miami Beach for their political convention, the changes in that party were manifest as well. The delegation from Illinois arrived at the convention as it had for years, under the sway of Richard J. Daley, mayor of Chicago, political boss of Cook County, leading grandee of the Democratic Party. But this was no longer Mayor Daley's Democratic Party, not the party of potent local leaders and union bosses and southern barons. A few of those ancients still roamed the convention hall in Miami Beach, but their days were numbered. Nothing was better evidence of that than the credentials challenge against the Daley delegation.

After the loss by Hubert Humphrey in 1968, angry Democrats resolved to fix the nominating process in the Democratic Party. Nineteen-sixty-eight had begun as a year of popular uprising for Democrats, of McCarthy and later Robert Kennedy challenging their incumbent and forcing him out of the race. But then, to their great disappointment, Hubert Humphrey won the nomination without competing in a single primary or caucus. He had gone the "boss route." To ensure that would never happen again, the Democrats formed a commission to review the party rules. Headed by Senator George McGovern of South Dakota and Representative Donald Fraser of Minnesota, the commission proposed that no more than 10 percent of a state's delegates could be named by party leaders; the remainder would have to be chosen in a process open to all those registered in the party.

But Mayor Daley went on with life as usual, as if there had been no McGovern-Fraser Commission. He handpicked the delegation from Illinois without regard to the requirement for public participation in delegate selection. His delegation was challenged when it arrived in Miami for violating the new party rules. When the party's Credentials Committee upheld the challenge, Daley and fifty-eight other Illinois delegates were sent packing. The Democratic National Convention of 1972 got under way with a collective delegation that was half men and half women, with representative proportions of ethnic minorities, with a full house of survivors of popular contests for delegate selection, but without the man who had been its highest power for a decade or more. The Democratic Party that assembled in Miami Beach in 1972 bore little resemblance to the one that had dominated American politics a decade earlier.

The changes that were overtaking the Democrats were by-products of their success in legislating a sweeping policy agenda in the 1960s. Those new policies had impacts, and one of them was to alter political perspectives. Lyndon Johnson had sagely warned that by passing the Civil Rights Act, the Democrats would lose the South. And so they did. The South did not change politically overnight, but it changed much more rapidly than informed observers expected after a century of Democratic dominance. The liberal hour was the starting point for a steep decline in the percentage of southern electoral votes won by Democratic candidates and the percentage of southern congressional seats held by Democrats. Race was not the sole factor in this change, but race remained a trenchant political issue, especially among southern whites, and it infected the politics of the South in one direction after 1964, as it had in the other for generations.

With the loss of the South, the Democratic Party not only lost its most reliable base of political strength, it also lost its ideological superego. The need to please or at least to assuage southern conservatives had long forced the liberals in the Democratic Party to trim their sails, to contain their enthusiasms. With the South growing less and less relevant to political calculations in the party, the counterweight was gone and liberals could push further and further to the left. And they did. What had been the party of the center left became for a time a party of the left.

But even on the left, things were changing rapidly in the late 1960s. In the early years of the emergence of the New Deal coalition, organized labor had been a powerful force. The leaders of the big unions were party potentates in the same way that Richard Daley, David Lawrence, Carmine DeSapio and some of the other urban political bosses were. The influence of those union leaders had a major impact on the liberal agenda of the New Deal and the decades that followed. Collective bargaining rights, a minimum wage, workplace safety, and many other liberal policies had become law. And they had altered the status of American workers. By the 1960s most unionized workers had moved into the middle class. They owned homes and cars, their children went to good schools and often to college. They had reliable jobs and pensions and health care. They paid taxes.

But much of the thrust of the liberal hour of the 1960s was to enact policies that benefited people who were not in the middle class: racial minorities, the poor, the unemployed, the sick, and the old. When the bills for those policies came due, it was the middle class that was asked to spend a larger and larger portion of its earnings to pay the costs of these new programs. The burden was growing faster on the middle class than on those at upper-income levels. Between 1953 and 1975, families with median incomes experienced a doubling of the portion of their income going to taxes. For families with incomes four times the median, the increase in the portion going to taxes was only half as large.[46]

This trend produced what the journalist David Broder called a "tax revolt," and its primary target was the Democratic Party—or what Republicans came increasingly to call the "tax and spend" Democrats. A large group of Americans, blue-collar workers who had been the beneficiaries of liberal programs of the New Deal and the Fair Deal, had undergone a significant transformation. Instead of getting benefits from the liberal programs of the 1960s, they were paying for the benefits of others—and they were not liking the change. As the political scientist Everett Carll Ladd noted in 1973, "What we now call liberalism frequently makes the old New

Deal majority contributors rather than beneficiaries. Lower-status whites more often feel threatened than encouraged by current extensions of equalitarianism. There has been a significant embourgeoisement of the working class."[47]

A major consequence of this was a tidal shift in the structure of support for the political parties. In the 1930s, and for a generation thereafter, it was a reliable rule of politics that wealth was the leading indicator of one's political preferences. This higher up the income scale, the greater the likelihood of Republican leanings. The wealthy, the business leaders, the well-educated, the professional classes all provided the core of Republican support. The lower middle class, especially those with recent immigrant connections and strong ethnic ties, the working class, and the poor provided the bulk of Democratic support.

But the 1960s turned this old rule on its head. By the end of the decade, support for Democrats was growing fastest at the upper end of the socioeconomic scale and support for Republicans was broadening in the bottom half. Among white voters, for example, 48 percent of those of high socioeconomic status had voted for Democratic congressional candidates in 1964; 57 percent of that group voted for Democrats in 1974. But among those in the lower third of the socioeconomic scale, 74 percent voted for Democratic candidates in 1964 and only 67 percent in 1974.[48]

During its midcentury ascendancy, the Democratic Party was often said to have had "more wings than a boardinghouse chicken." But a party with wings can fly. Its constituent elements may differ about some things—may, in fact, be opposites on some issues—but they agree on one very important thing: They want to win. So their differences are brokered or set aside or overlooked while they come together to win elections.

By 1968 the constituent elements of the Democratic Party looked less like wings than like factions. The difference matters. Factions are political groupings that coalesce around distinctive ideological positions or single issues. Their commitment to those original attachments is much stronger than to a party, and it is unyielding even to the compromises that might ensure a party victory. A party with wings has the capacity to attract a majority, to win elections, and to govern. But a party composed of factions only has the capacity to tear itself apart.

The Democratic Party in the late 1960s had become a party of factions. The McGovern-Fraser rules abetted this development by ensuring that sex, ethnicity, and race would be important determinants of political representation and by moving the locus of party control to a kind of popular participation that energized the party's nervous system but denied it a cerebral cortex. The bosses may never have represented the full flowering of democracy, but they could boss. And when they passed from the scene, a bossless Democratic Party teetered toward anarchy.

What was happening within the Democratic Party mirrored a trend unfolding across American politics. In ways that were not fully recognized at the time, the 1960s marked the end of an era that had endured since the founding of the Republic. The central political question of that earlier era was simply this: What is the role of government in American society?

In national politics, the question was focused somewhat more tightly: What is the role of the federal government in American society? And through that earlier era, the skirmish line was always at the boundary between the private and public sectors. What was government's jurisdiction and what was not? Conservatives—as the terms were normally defined—argued for a larger private sphere and tight limits on government encroachment. Liberals argued for "positive government," for government intervention to control the excesses of the market, to provide for those whom the market failed, to establish the rules of market competition and to referee disputes.

The New Deal and World War II yielded unprecedented expansion in the size and scope of the public sector. The Eisenhower years did little to reverse those developments. And thus it had become increasingly clear by the 1960s that the old terms of debate no longer fit the contemporary— and likely permanent—reality. Big government was here to stay. As Arthur M. Schlesinger, Jr., wrote in his review of the Kennedy administration, "The ideological debates of the past began to give way to a new agreement on the practicalities of managing a modern economy. There thus developed in the Kennedy years a national accord on economic policy—a new consensus which gave hope of harnessing government, business and labor in rational partnership for a steadily expanding American economy."[49]

The central question of national politics then became: What objectives should big government pursue? When the central question changed, the organizing dynamics of American politics were forced to change. The dynamics of politics changed faster than the rhetoric of politics. The two political parties continued to debate on the old rhetorical terms, with Democrats favoring a larger government role and Republicans arguing against it. But Americans were not fooled by this. They quickly learned that neither party was going to turn back the clock. Eisenhower didn't in the 1950s; Nixon and Ford didn't in the 1970s, and Reagan would not in the 1980s. Preferences might change, there would be recalibrations in the tilt of public policy, but the government role would not shrink in any significant way.

Recognizing that the rhetoric of the parties no longer fit the reality of politics, Americans did an apparently rational thing. They abandoned party politics in large numbers. After 1960 turnout in presidential and congressional elections began a steady decline. So, too, did citizen identification with the two major parties. The vacuum in electoral politics was quickly filled, however, by the rapid rise of organized special interest groups. It came to matter less which party controlled the large, permanent government in Washington. It came to matter more which interests would gain benefits from that government and which would not. Who would win and who would lose in the competition among interests?

This "interest-group liberalism," as the political scientist Theodore Lowi called it, assumed two things.[50] First, government would remain large and would play a major role in shaping national life. Second, the ends of government would be determined in combat among interest groups—combat that would take place in Congress, in the White House and the federal bureaucracy, in the courts, and only occasionally in elections.

Liberals in the 1960s had won the final battle in the war over government's importance in American life. Positive government was the new norm. But the major weapon in the liberal armory, the Democratic Party, was in disarray at the end of the decade and was, in any case, less and less relevant to the emergent political struggle over the kinds of policies that government would pursue.

EXCESS

The federal government took on an enormous task of social engineering in the 1960s, poking public policy into areas where it had never gone: federal aid to education, medical insurance for the elderly and indigent, a war against poverty, and so on. Had that engineering been based on tried and true notions of feasibility and limitation, it might have been more successful and less expensive. But this was also an age of experimentation. Federal initiatives often rested on foggy and incomplete ideas about human behavior and social and economic causation. Uncertainty was not much of a deterrent to decision-makers bent on changing the world.

Good intentions were often justification enough for proceeding with a program, announcing it with inflated promises of accomplishment and committing hundreds of millions of dollars to it. "It was a heady period," wrote former federal officials Marshall Kaplan and Peggy L. Cuciti, "where moral rather than strategic imperatives often governed. Policymakers and policy advocates believed that government intervention combined with money could make a difference. Faith, more often than not, substituted for the absence of predictable cause-and-effect relationships in the design and development of programs."[51]

The federal government often acted without evidence or proof because it became infected with the central and ultimately fatal germ of 1960s liberalism—that every problem has a solution and that the government in Washington is most likely to provide that solution. Once that notion inserted itself in the hearts and minds of people in power, they were immune to questioning and dissuasion. The issue for them, as for Lyndon Johnson, was not whether a programmatic solution could be found, but simply what program should be employed. And if a program did not solve the problem, then the liberal response was not to question whether the problem was solvable, but simply to try a different program.

Problems can be solved. Washington has the solution. These were the marching cadences of 1960s liberalism. We shouldn't be surprised that it came to this. Opportunity hung heavy in the air in this age of unprece-dented economic prosperity. Good intentions abounded. The confidence that derived from beating the Depression and the Axis powers propelled the nation to take on new challenges. And the maturing of the social sci-ences seemed to meet the need for ideas and directions as the social engineering unfolded.

Especially in those policy areas that involved human development, such as education, welfare, and crime, federal policies were too often rooted in assumptions that were untested, invalid, misapplied, or simply wrong. The experts, it painfully turned out, did not know as much as they professed to know. Amitai Etzioni, a prominent and chastened social sci-entist, wrote in retrospect, "Social scientists like myself have begun to reexamine our core assumption that man can be taught almost anything and quite readily. We are now confronting the uncomfortable possibility that human beings are not easily changed after all."[52]

The central idea of twentieth-century liberalism was that government could be a positive force in the lives of American citizens. Herbert Croly, a prominent Progressive, had stated the case in 1909: "The national ad-vance of the American democracy does demand an increasing amount of centralized action and responsibility."[53] But in the 1960s that basic idea inflated in liberal rhetoric into a much larger and less reliable conceit: that government action could alleviate poverty, eliminate bigotry, edu-cate all the children, cure the sick, clean the air and water, protect con-sumers, and provide a golden age for the elderly. In effect, the liberal leadership of the 1960s seemed to be saying, "Bring us your problems and we will find a way for government to solve them."

Optimism is part of the lifeblood of liberalism. When mixed with proper doses of skepticism and empiricism, optimism can be a healthy demeanor for any society. But optimism—untempered by careful analy-sis or even common sense—became the all-powerful driver of Lyndon Johnson's presidency, in domestic policy and in Vietnam. His promises overwhelmed his accomplishments, significant though some of those ac-complishments were. It devastated him when the intended beneficiaries of his policies seemed so ungrateful for his efforts. But he asked for it, by promising more than he or any government could deliver.

To many Americans, this liberal faith in the capacity of government to fix society's ills was not just a weakness, it was an arrogance. The liberals in Washington were spreading their gospel and their works with other people's money. Increasingly as the decade unfolded, it was the money of the working and middle classes.

And often they were asking the American people to suspend disbelief and abandon caution. When racial struggles turned violent in the mid-1960s, and urban riots and burning and looting replaced the earlier images of peaceful marching, many liberal leaders became apologists for what most Americans saw as criminal behavior. Pouring federal money into neighborhoods that had been destroyed by the wanton violence of their own residents made no sense to many Americans, especially those who felt it was their money that was being poured.

The years of Depression and war had seemed to teach that enough people committed to the right goals could accomplish anything. That spirit animated the Great Society and the war in Vietnam which, after all, were conducted by men who'd learned the lessons of those earlier decades. But in the 1960s they discovered that they were wrong, that no matter how lofty the goal, no matter how deep the commitment, some tasks were beyond accomplishment. Poverty, racism, ignorance, and foreign enemies would persist no matter how many programs the federal government threw at them, no matter how many bombs it dropped on their people.

Defense Secretary Robert McNamara, a man famous for his skills at sizing up and solving problems, later wrote of the lessons the 1960s taught: "We failed to recognize that in international affairs, as in other aspects of life, there may be problems for which there are no immediate solutions. For one whose life has been dedicated to the belief and practice of problem solving, this is particularly hard to admit. But at times, we may have to live with an imperfect, untidy world."[54]

When these notions of federal omnicompetence were laid bare, faith in government began to diminish and what remained was a growing fear of its omnipotence. "The stability of a democracy depends very much on the people making a careful distinction between what government can do and what it cannot do," Daniel Patrick Moynihan later wrote. "To demand what can be done is altogether in order: some may wish such things accomplished, some may not, and the majority may decide. But to seek that which cannot be provided, especially to do so with the passionate but misinformed conviction that it can be, is to create the conditions of frustration and ruin."[55]

Ronald Reagan had sought to sound the alarm about growing federal authority as Barry Goldwater's most effective advocate in 1964:

"The full power of centralized government"—this was the very thing the Founding Fathers sought to minimize. They knew that governments don't control things. A government can't control the economy without controlling people. And they know when a government sets out to do that, it must use force and coercion to achieve its purpose. They also knew, those Founding Fathers, that outside of its legitimate functions, government does nothing as well or as economically as the private sector of the economy.

But few people were listening in 1964. The liberal hour was still young. It had broad popular support. Its hard lessons had yet to be learned. Two years later, however, with no political experience, Reagan was elected governor of the nation's largest state. Republicans that year gained back most of the seats they had lost in Congress two years earlier. Public support for Lyndon Johnson began to fall.

As the bills came due for the Great Society and the war in Vietnam, the federal budget surpassed $100 billion and a tax increase was required. The real impact of Great Society spending would not be felt until the next decade, but by the end of the 1960s the liberal hour was over, done in by a combination of growing costs and growing doubts about the capacity of the federal government to fulfill its expansive promises.

Underlying the expansive promises of 1960s liberals was an inherent inconsistency. The spreading rebellions of the decade were aimed at traditional sources of authority: the corporation, the university, the military, the Catholic church, censors, and parents. The goal of most of these was to deconcentrate authority, to weaken central agents of authority and empower the people. Whether moved by the Port Huron Statement's call in 1962 for a "democracy of individual participation" where "the individual share[s] in those social decisions determining the quality and direction of his life" or by John Lennon's song "Power to the People" a decade later, the 1960s was a time when liberals craved a richer, fuller citizen role in the collective life of society.

But in Washington, the thrust of liberal politics was to concentrate authority in the federal government. Federal authority grew steadily; so, too, did the number and power of federal agencies. The latitude of state governments shrank. Corporations were subjected to thousands of new federal regulations. Local decisions about school attendance and school curricula, whether prayers could be said in public places, what could be purveyed in bookstores and movie theaters, and who could be hired by employers were increasingly subjected to federal regulation and the decisions of the Supreme Court. "Many Americans, from the self-consciously radical young people who founded the Students for a Democratic Society in the early 1960s to the proudly traditional Irish American parents in Boston who opposed busing children to end racial segregation in the schools in the late 1960s, feared the centralized, expert-oriented, and bureaucratized kind of society that America was becoming," wrote the historian David Farber.[56]

In the 1964 election, Barry Goldwater had often said, "A government big enough to give you everything you want is also big enough to take away everything you have." By the end of the decade, liberals as well as conservatives were coming to see that the federal authority that forced the end of Jim Crow segregation in the South could also be used to force white children in South Boston to get on buses to go to school in black neighborhoods or prevent devout Protestants in Arkansas or devout Jews in Brooklyn from saying prayers in their local schools. In an age where so many popular messages called for power to the people, power was coalescing in Washington. This generated a tension that liberalism and the Democratic Party ultimately could not contain.

The liberal ascendancy suffered as well from growing public awareness of and discomfort with the costs of the programs it yielded. The booming economy of the first half of the decade had contributed to a sense of relaxed economic constraints. America was a wealthy country, its president said; it could afford bold initiatives. But the costs of those bold initiatives began to accumulate. A federal deficit was becoming more common and the national debt was growing. Inflation had remained below 2 percent annually through 1965; by 1970 it was nearing 6 percent.

The conflation of all of these developments—programs failing to fully accomplish their bloated goals, concern about growing federal authority, abundant examples of administrative incompetence, and the growing costs of the war in Vietnam and the Great Society—had begun to yield a crisis of liberalism as the decade neared its end. Liberalism had come to be associated in much of the public mind not with its intentions but with its excesses and its shortfalls. Many of the goals held so high by liberals at the beginning of the decade had been accomplished. But others had not, and the costs were high. By promising much and delivering less, Johnson and the Democratic leaders of the time had contributed to a steady decline not only in political support for liberal policies but in public trust in the federal government itself. And since the success of liberal politics depended so heavily on faith in government, this last development was a sure signal that the liberal hour was nearing its end.

NIXON

By the time Richard Nixon appointed him undersecretary of Health, Education, and Welfare in 1969, John G. Veneman had built a sturdy reputation as a progressive state senator in California. Though a Republican, he had long represented a Democratic district. He was, said the president at the time of his appointment, "the California Legislature's leading authority in the areas of health care, welfare, and taxation."[57] For the next four years, Veneman and other HEW appointees from California would play leading roles in administering the social welfare programs enacted in the previous decade.

They could have been enemies of those programs; indeed there had been much in the rhetoric of the 1968 Nixon campaign to suggest that the Great Society had gone too far in extending federal authority, enlarging the role of bureaucrats, and spending taxpayers' dollars. Few would have been surprised had Nixon appointed tough fiscal conservatives to lead a counterattack.

But Nixon's real interest was foreign policy, and he was happy to leave the management of these programs to Robert Finch, an old friend who headed HEW, and to the "California mafia" that he recruited. But their views on social welfare programs bore little resemblance to Nixon's campaign rhetoric; cutting the social welfare programs they supervised was not on their agenda.

Veneman brought with him from California a man named Tom Joe who served as his special assistant. Joe was smart, a quick study, and soon came to be a major player in all determinations involving welfare programs, especially those that funded social services at the state level. Joe, in fact, had worked on those programs in California and had demonstrated remarkable ingenuity in obtaining federal funds for California programs. So successful had he been that in 1968 he had written a paper for the American Public Welfare Association titled "Finding Welfare Dollars." It was a primer for other state officials on how to milk federal appropriations for state welfare programs.

Now the country's leading genius at obtaining federal funds was sitting at the other end of the pipeline, manning the tap with no intention of slowing the flow. As the Nixon years unfolded, ever greater amounts of money moved from Washington to the state capitals funding welfare programs that many Republicans opposed. Federal grants for social services grew from $347 million in 1968 to $1.7 billion in 1972. Appointees at HEW, wrote the political scientist Martha Derthick, "took initiatives or made choices that, from the executive side of the government, laid the basis for turning social services into an uncontrolled source of fiscal relief for the states."[58]

What happened at HEW was not anomalous. Across the government, in domestic and foreign policies alike, the Nixon administration declined to truncate the momentum of the previous decade. Nixon's time out of office had given him ample opportunity to study and think about American involvement in Vietnam. He had been vice president in 1953 when Eisenhower inherited a similar war in Korea, saw its futility, and quickly ended American involvement. Nixon had no stake in the war in Vietnam and enunciated no compelling geopolitical reason for continuing it. Had he wished, he could have begun a rapid withdrawal of American forces, offering any of several justifications, even negotiating a face-saving treaty not very different from the one ultimately hammered out four years later. But he chose to continue the Kennedy-Johnson commitment in Vietnam. A draw-down of American forces began in 1969, a policy—"Vietnamization," it was called—that took more than three years to complete.

As long as the war remained Lyndon Johnson's war, Nixon had wide scope of action in ending it. But his hesitation in doing so, his very disinclination to do so, soon made it his war. His advisor Daniel Patrick Moynihan warned him in 1969, "The war in Vietnam is lost, and the sooner you get out the better we will be." But he didn't get out, and, Moynihan later noted, "it became his war. And in the end half the country seemed to think he started it."[59]

Nixon's domestic policy actions are equally difficult to explain. Few of the American voters who supported him in 1968 were fans of the Great Society or the wave of liberal programs that had had flooded through the earlier years of the decade. Among his supporters, in fact, were a number of people who were angry at the direction the country was taking, who thought that racial integration was moving too rapidly, that protesting college students were a disgrace, and that government was growing too big—and too expensive—too fast.

But just as Nixon continued the war in Vietnam and made it his own, so did he continue, and in some cases enlarge, many of the liberal domestic policies that he had seemed eager to criticize during the campaign. In no small part this resulted from Nixon's distaste for delving deeply into the details of domestic policy.

To those closest to Nixon, his lack of interest in domestic policy was legendary. "At times," wrote political scientist James Reichley, "he spoke to his staff and even to members of the press as though he regarded his domestic responsibilities as onerous burdens, as distractions from the really important work of bargaining with the Russians or holding together the Western alliance."[60]

Nixon and the senior members of his administration were reluctant to label their ideology or even to admit that they had one. They far preferred to call themselves "realists" or "pragmatists." They typically distanced themselves from the "idealists" of the previous administrations not by indicating a tectonic shift in governing ideologies, but rather by something much more limited like offering new approaches to problem solving.

Nixon seemed to believe not that the domestic programs he inherited could or should be eliminated, but that they needed to be better managed. "The idea that a team of bright, efficient administrators was coming in to clean up a mess left by woolly-headed idealists and impractical philosophers," wrote the journalist Jonathan Schell, "was reinforced by a dizzying whirl of 'reorganization,' or 'structuring,' which soon got under way in the White House. For each national problem, it seemed, the White House had an administrative answer."[61]

Nixon was happy to delegate domestic policy management to members of his White House staff. He created a Domestic Policy Council in 1970 as an analogue to the National Security Council; its primary responsibility from Nixon's perspective was to field and solve domestic problems before they got to his desk. Later he would propose a grand consolidation of domestic agencies in what came to be called his "super cabinet plan." It ultimately went aground in the storm of Watergate, but it was a unique effort to transfer domestic decision making from the line agencies to the White House staff.

This approach, focusing on the administration rather than the substance of domestic policies, permitted Nixon to appear to be the critic of his predecessors' policies at the very time he was continuing and expanding them. It was artful politics, salving the concerns of conservatives while maintaining the flow of funds to program beneficiaries. Nixon's primary assistant in domestic policy, Daniel Patrick Moynihan, noted that "Richard Nixon mostly opted for liberal policies, merely clothing them . . . in conservative rhetoric."[62]

Nixon's southern strategy in 1968 had augured an end to federal efforts to encourage racial desegregation. And there was a change in tenor and intensity in the enforcement policies of the Justice Department under Attorney General John Mitchell. But in other ways, the Nixon administration moved steadily forward in the development of new approaches to racial progress, continuing the momentum of the previous administrations. Nixon increased support for minority businesses, and in 1969 the U.S. Department of Labor announced the Philadelphia Plan, establishing quotas for hiring minority workers in federally funded construction projects.

To the surprise of many of his close associates and the consternation of many of his supporters, Nixon in the summer of 1969 proposed the most radical reform of American welfare polices since the New Deal: the Family Assistance Plan (FAP). It was an approach to welfare that even the most ardent liberals had been afraid to propose. It would replace Aid for Families with Dependent Children (AFDC), the nation's primary welfare program since the New Deal, with a new approach that some labeled a guaranteed annual income and others a negative income tax. Under the plan, a family of four would have received basic federal payments of sixteen hundred dollars a year. Even those who were working would get funding to bring their incomes up to the basic level.

Nixon liked bold strokes, and this was clearly one of those, not merely a tinkering or marginal adjustment of welfare policies. The concept of a negative income tax had long been favored by some prominent conservative economists. Milton Friedman had begun writing about it in the 1940s. The FAP seemed especially to serve the needs of the "working poor," a group close to Nixon's heart because of his own upbringing in a family that fit that categorization. And the plan seemed to promise a reduction in the size and role of the federal bureaucracy, something that Nixon always admired.

But perhaps its greatest appeal to a president with no track record of supporting such radical and expansive domestic initiatives was the sense it provided of a grand plan. In foreign policy, Nixon always seemed to be thinking in broad terms; grand designs were his policy métier. "Nixon had a sense of architecture, in both domestic and foreign policy," said Elliot Richardson, a member of his cabinet. "Some parts of the programs were more important than others, but they all belonged to the design."[63] And with FAP he had a domestic policy that fit that preference marvelously.

FAP ultimately failed, defeated by a Democratically controlled Senate, after passing the House. But it demonstrated the continuing vitality of several aspects of 1960s liberalism, even as the decade was coming to an end and the presidency had passed to Republicans.

Nixon never questioned the existence of big government or government activism to improve the quality of life for Americans. Washington bureaucrats were often the target of his rhetorical critique, and some of his darkest impulses played out in his efforts to control the bureaucrats in some of the domestic agencies (as when he ordered his aide Fred

Malek to gather the names of Jews who worked in top positions at the Labor Department). And he succeeded, largely through revenue sharing, in shifting management of some programs from Washington to the states. But the domestic policies that emerged during the Democratic administrations in the middle of the 1960s not only suffered little but, in fact, grew substantially in the Republican administrations that began at the end of that decade.

The greatest fiscal support for 1960s liberalism came not from John Kennedy and Lyndon Johnson but from Richard Nixon and Gerald Ford. The rhetorical beating that those liberal policies took from George Wallace and Nixon in 1968 was not matched by program eliminations or budget cuts once the liberals were forced from the White House. The liberals were gone, but their initiatives endured.

THE DURABLE
DECADE

I t was a rare winter storm that shut down the Austin, Texas, airport that December day in 1972. But whatever it took, the people came.

The old warhorses of the civil rights movement—Burke Marshall, Roy Wilkins, Whitney Young, Clarence Mitchell—were there. So, too, was Hubert Humphrey, the shepherd of the Civil Rights Act of 1964. The newer generation of black leaders—Julian Bond, Barbara Jordan, Henry Gonzalez—elected to public offices that people of their backgrounds had never held before; they were there. So was an even younger contingent led by Roy Innes of CORE, angry at the Nixon administration over its cutbacks in civil rights enforcement.

And then there were the lions of the law. Thurgood Marshall, whose lonely drives through the backwoods of the South had turned up black clients brave enough to challenge that region's Jim Crow laws, who had stood in triumph on the steps of the Supreme Court in May 1954 when it struck down school desegregation, then later worked inside the building as the Court's first black justice; he was there to pay homage to the man who had appointed him.

And there was Earl Warren, the legendary chief of that Court, retired now but unwilling to miss this symposium at the Lyndon Johnson Library. When the planes were grounded, he came to Austin by bus, joking that he'd come to discuss civil rights but didn't expect to be bused in order to do it.

They all came for Lyndon Johnson. But would Lyndon Johnson come? His heart had been growing steadily weaker, and he'd had a serious angina attack on December 11, the night before his planned appearance. The storm made the seventy-mile drive from the ranch even more perilous. But his political genes triumphed again, and somehow he made it.

Johnson rose cautiously to address the distinguished assembly and moved slowly toward the podium. The navy blue suit was darker than most he had worn in the White House. His face and torso were much thinner, and his hair was longer and curled over his shirt at the neck. He wore the glasses he had always hated to wear in public and his gaze struggled to form as he looked at his notes. His voice was quieter and more measured until it connected with the words, with the testimony he was to give about the continuing importance of fighting the fight for racial justice. And then the old passions stirred, singing in familiar cadences the heart songs he had sung so often, ending with the single line for which he will be most remembered.

> We know there's injustice. We know there's intolerance. We know there's discrimination and hate and suspicion. And we know there's division among us. But there is a larger truth. We have proved that great progress is possible. We know how much still remains to be done. And if our efforts continue and if our will is strong and if our hearts are right and if courage remains our constant companion, then, my fellow Americans, I am confident we shall overcome.[1]

The audience rose as one and applauded at length. And then Lyndon Johnson, politician to the end, worked the crowd. It was December 12, 1972, and this would be his last public appearance. Six weeks later, on January 22, 1973, he died at age sixty-four.

On the day he died, the U.S. Supreme Court handed down its decision in *Roe* v. *Wade*, a case that would drive new fissures through the American people for decades. On January 27, two days after General William Westmoreland laid a wreath at the grave of Lyndon Johnson, the Paris Peace

Accords were signed. Eight weeks later, the last American troops came home from Vietnam. On January 30 a Washington court convicted the burglars who broke into Democratic Party headquarters, and the country would begin its long slow slide into the sinkhole of the Watergate scandal, further undermining trust in government.

And on March 21, 1973, the Supreme Court would rule in a case involving a school district not far from the one where young Lyndon Johnson had taught in Cotulla, Texas, in 1928, that citizens had no constitutional right to an education and the fact that some school districts were poor and others rich did not discriminate against poor people.[2] The vote was five to four. All of the justices in the majority were Republican appointees.

It was, the commentators agreed, the end of an era.

THE DEPTH AND REACH of the changes wrought in the 1960s defy a neat reckoning. As the journalist Norman Cousins noted in a speech in 1968, "The trouble with trying to penetrate the vitals of the past quarter century is that 1940 was more than a hundred years ago. Into a few decades have been compressed more change, more thrust, more tossing about of men's souls and gizzards than had been spaced out over most of the human chronicle until then. The metabolism of history has gone berserk."[3]

That berserk metabolism forced Americans to take stock of themselves and their society and their government in the 1960s. Because Americans often did not like what they found, some significant sorting out was inevitable. Jim Crow, suppression of women, sexual hypocrisy, denials of democratic fairness in politics, isolation of the universities, indifference to the natural environment, disparities in the distribution of national wealth, victimization of consumers: These characteristics of the early postwar period—many of them embedded in the full course of American history—no longer seemed to fit the country that America had become by 1960. The center could hold no longer. The 1960s were bound to be a time of rapid change.

But the direction that change would take in the 1960s, the shape of it and the success of it, would be determined not by anything as abstract as the forces of history but rather by the men and women who inhabited that decade. History left them inheritances, the gathering of historical pressures created opportunities. What they did with those opportunities was up to them.

The historian Arthur Meier Schlesinger observed the importance of cycles of change that have leavened American politics since the founding of the nation. Reform energies build slowly and flower in the short spaces between periods of conservative dominance. Humans cling to sameness. What is natural is consistency, to do this year what one did last year, perhaps with incremental changes. We seem most comfortable when we develop and then persist in routines. Even when those routines are imperfect, tolerating their imperfections is often easier than trying to change them. But over time, the burdens of imperfection accumulate and fester and then become unbearable. That is the moment when reform pressures build, when the forces of the status quo can no longer defeat them, when change explodes and—as Schlesinger writes—the reformer always has "his day in court."[4] Then new norms set in and they persist until the reform cycle begins anew.

The American Revolution was such a period. The arrival of Jacksonian democracy, the Civil War, the Progressive era, the New Deal were others. But reform periods are not self-starting or self-actualizing. They don't "just happen." Trends and events may help to manufacture these moments of change, but people determine the direction of that change and play a large part in shaping its lasting impact.

Much of the history that's been written about the 1960s recognizes the vital role of personal agency, of visions and battles that shaped a decade. But too often the narratives reflexively credit for success the dissidents with the brightest plumage. They hold that a radical counterculture changed the world. Clamoring for justice, challenging the "power structure," committed to "democracy in the streets," this youthful charge against inherited evils was the decade's most powerful force. Or so the romance unfolds.

The whirligig of protest, counterculture, youthful rebellion, drugs, sex, and rock and roll may have shaped the tone and many of the images of the era. But, in the sharper focus of historical distance, it is now clear that many of the lasting effects of the 1960s had their roots in the liberal agenda and practical politics, mostly legislative policy making.

Much of this enduring change took the form of political incremental-ism. So many issues long discussed, so many social movements in long gestation, so many coalitions painstakingly constructed, so many arguments richly nurtured finally came to fruit in the great harvest of the mid-1960s. But they weren't always new or very radical. They were just ready.

And the primary midwives of these policy changes were not street demonstrators, folksingers, or the authors of the Port Huron Statement. They were journalists delving into problems like the degradation of the environment, the human costs of poverty and hunger, the dangers of consumer products. They were political organizers and the apparatchiks of the political parties whose daily work was the piece-by-piece construction of electoral majorities. And they were the elected officials and their aides who, with ingenuity and persistence, pursued their goals through the routine and often tortuous processes of politics and government.

The African American historian John Hope Franklin wrote on the death of Lyndon Johnson in 1973 that "his feverish, almost frenetic efforts to make a Great Society a reality and his constant attention to effective action in assuring freedom to the free did much to change the views of Negro Americans of what they could reasonably expect from government, in the rectification of America's racial ills. Lyndon showed what one man could do to improve conditions by using to the hilt the prestige and power of the Presidency." Franklin later said of Johnson's role in the successes of the civil rights movement, "Without the kind of leadership and context in which that leadership worked, I think almost none of these things could have been accomplished, certainly very few of them."[5]

Most of those who participated in the politics of the 1960s and have reflected upon it remember a time of passion, a time of opportunity, but especially a time of very hard work and constant struggle against powerful forces of resistance. "The achievements of the Great Society did not come easily," Joseph Califano, Lyndon Johnson's chief of staff, later said. "That kind of work in government is hard, often frustrating, sometimes exasperating. But the rewards are far greater for those in a democracy who work persistently to build and shape government to serve the people, than for those who tear it apart or lash out in despair and frustration because the task is too much for them."[6]

One of the reasons the 1960s have been made to look so radical is that cultural historians so often paint the 1950s in caricature as a time of almost sleepy self-satisfaction, of comfort, of failure to see the crises that were brewing at many of the edges of a seemingly contented society. This a mythical image, in the words of the social critic Roger Kimball, of "a sterile, soulless society, obsessed with money, stunted emotionally, negligible culturally and intellectually, brutal and hamfisted in its politics and social policy."[7]

Not so. Much of what blossomed in the 1960s was already budding in the prior decade. Only when the policy rewards were reaped in the 1960s did their significant seedtime in the 1950s come clearly into focus. The liberal hour of the 1960s was not a policy revolution so much as the conclusion of a long political struggle, some of it unfolding over decades, that relied most heavily on the practical work of determined politicians.

If the revolutionaries of the 1960s revolutionized anything it was not politics or policy, but social relationships and values. What one could read freely and see on the movie screen, what one could say in public, what one could wear, the practice of sexual relationships: These things did enjoy massive transformations in the 1960s, and the crashing sound of falling social inhibitions and prohibitions was inspired by a relentless passion for change and novelty among the generation that came of age in that decade.

To some, this was little more than the triumph of hedonism. But to others it was a long overdue rejoinder to generations of hypocrisy and intolerance. "Rather than liberating the oppressed," writes the historian Arnold Isaacs, "the peace marchers chiefly liberated themselves, from a vast array of taboos and conventions that had set boundaries for earlier generations. It was their symbols—their clothes, their shaggy hair, their dope, their music and language—that turned out to be the substance of their revolution, while their political ideas (other than on the war) proved to have been mostly fantasies, unconnected to American political realities."[8]

Legend writes large the contributions of these "revolutionaries" of the 1960s. So, too, it tends to mute the deeper and more durable changes in public policy that were the work of the very people against whom young people so often protested. Bob Dylan wrote in the protesters' anthem, "The Times They Are A-Changin'":

Come senators, congressmen
Please heed the call
Don't stand in the doorway
Don't block up the hall
For he that gets hurt
Will be he who has stalled
There's a battle outside
And it is ragin'.
It'll soon shake your windows
And rattle your walls
For the times they are a-changin'.

But the majority of those senators and congressmen were not standing in the doorway, blocking change. They were throwing open doors to cleaner air, more affordable education, better health care, higher standards of social justice, and many of the other goals of those who so lustily sang the Dylan lyrics. The times were a-changin', but more often from the inside out than the outside in.

AMERICAN LIBERALISM HAS NEVER recovered from the 1960s. As a vibrant and dominant political philosophy, it barely survived the decade in which it flourished and achieved its greatest impact. So there is much in the liberal hour that is chastening. Power invites excess, and reactions occur. A lesson is learned.

Still, the liberal hour demonstrated what democratic politics can produce when public consensus crescendos, when coherent majorities prevail, and when skilled leaders provide direction, inspiration, and relentless energy. In our own time, when so many Americans are disillusioned with our fractious, often ineffectual national politics, a glance at the 1960s reminds us of the potential of government to set lofty goals and actually build consensus to achieve them.

The sociologist Max Weber wrote, "Politics means a slow, powerful drilling through hard boards, with a mixture of passion and a sense of proportion."[9] The 1960s was a decade of heat and light, of bread and circuses. Its public spectacles—the protests, the violence, the music, the sheer sense of freedom—could be blinding and deafening. But the enduring impact of that decade was not written in shouts or songs. It was written in law and policy. More than anything else, it was the "slow, powerful drilling through hard boards" that changed the country.

The sense of proportion that had marked the liberal ascendancy of the early 1960s ultimately failed. The passion abated. But the law endures, and in it the unique and remarkable legacy of the 1960s lives on.

ACKNOWLEDGMENTS

Every page of this book bears the input of a teacher, a student, a friend, an acquaintance who shared a story or an insight about a complex decade. Each of us has a special treasure in that regard, a mentor whose experiences in the 1960s, later filtered through scholarship and teaching, never lost their hold. For Rob Weisbrot, that person was Eric F. Goldman, an aide to Lyndon Johnson and a gifted historian at Princeton University. For Cal Mackenzie, it was John C. Donovan, manpower administrator in the Kennedy and Johnson administrations and an inspiring teacher at Bowdoin College. It is a pleasure to record our intellectual debt to them and to recall warmly the pleasure of their friendship.

In our work on this book, we have been blessed with extraordinary research support. Colby students Emily Boyle and Charles Wilson served as our primary research assistants. They carried out the most taxing assignments with great intelligence, energy, care, and good humor, and were very much at the center of this joint effort. We were further aided by Melyn Heckelman, who helped to compile and verify the bibliography and notes; Tim Stenovec, present at the inception; Lokesh Todi, who aided with the research in the book's final stages; Meridith Major-Blascovich, who helped check the citations; and Randi Arsenault, who served as a thoughtful "model reader" for the manuscript.

The archivists at the Kennedy, Johnson, and Nixon libraries helped us identify and gather the collection of photographs included in this volume. We are also much indebted to the Colby Library staff. This book left many tracks in the stacks, and we could not have had better guides.

Scott Moyers, general editor of Penguin's new History of American Life series, warmly welcomed our project during the first crucial stages and enlisted the aid of Louis Menand, Harvard professor and member of the editorial board for the series. Over the next several months, Luke Menand was unfailingly generous with his time and creative suggestions in helping us shape the ideas for this book. His early guidance and his faith in the work we were about to undertake have been a lasting source of insight and encouragement.

In 2007 Laura Stickney assumed editorial responsibility for our project and proved an ideal collaborator. Laura helped measurably to refine our arguments and our prose, encouraged us throughout, and was in every way a delight to work with. In the final stages of revision our copy editor, Sean Devlin, reviewed the text with extraordinary thoroughness and an enviable gift for clarity and precision.

In all of our work, we have been supported, inspired, challenged, and comforted by our colleagues and by the administration of Colby College. We happily acknowledge the debts we have accumulated there over the past three decades. We are grateful, as well, for the direct support and encouragement we have received in our research and teaching from Julie Kidd and the Christian A. Johnson Endeavor Foundation and from William R. Goldfarb and the Goldfarb family.

Finally, we would like to express a word of personal appreciation to Ivan R. Dee; to Lucy, Rob, Daisy, Julius, and Judah Tapert; and to our family, friends, and colleagues, for their invaluable support throughout.

G. CALVIN MACKENZIE   ROBERT WEISBROT

Waterville, Maine
November 2007

NOTES

INTRODUCTION

1. Alan Brinkley, *The End of Reform: New Deal Liberalism in Recession and War* (New York: Vintage, 1996), pp. 6, 226.

CHAPTER 1. AMERICA IN THE POSTWAR YEARS

1. J. Hector St. John de Crèvecoeur, *Letters from an American Farmer and Sketches of Eighteenth Century America* (New York: Penguin Books, 1986), p. 81.
2. Alexis de Tocqueville, *Democracy in America* (Cambridge, Mass.: Sever and Francis, 1863), p. 22.
3. AT&T: Sears, Roebuck Catalog, Franklin D. Roosevelt, The New Deal, 1933 (http://home.att.net/~jrhsc/fdr.html; accessed July 5, 2007).
4. U.S. Department of Commerce, Bureau of the Census, *Statistical Abstract of the United States, 1961* (Washington, D.C.: U.S. Government Printing Office, 1961), p. 301.
5. Iwan W. Morgan, *Beyond the Liberal Consensus: A Political History of the United States Since 1965* (New York: St. Martin's, 1994), p. 4. Dollar amounts in constant 1968 dollars.
6. U.S. Department of Commerce, Bureau of the Census, *Statistical Abstract of the United States, 1961*, p. 220.
7. John Kenneth Galbraith, *The Affluent Society* (Boston, Mass.: Houghton Mifflin, 1958), p. 2.
8. *Economic Report of the President, 1971* (Washington, D.C.: U.S. Government Printing Office, 1971), p. 215.
9. Data on labor union membership are from U.S. Department of Commerce, Bureau of the Census, *Historical Statistics of the United States: Colonial Times to 1970* (Washington, D.C.: U.S. Government Printing Office, 1975), Part 1, p. 178.
10. *Economic Report of the President, 1961*, p. 192.
11. Jesse H. Ausubel and Arnulf Grübler, "Working Less And Living Longer: Long-Term Trends in Working Time and Time Budgets" (http://phe.rockefeller.edu/work_less/; accessed March 20, 2006).
12. U.S. Department of Commerce, Bureau of the Census, *Historical Statistics of the United States: Colonial Times to 1970*, Part 1, p. 132.
13. See Lloyd A. Free and Hadley Cantril, *The Political Beliefs of Americans: A Study of Public Opinion* (New Brunswick, N.J.: Rutgers University Press, 1967), pp. 11–13. The polling data reported here show substantial majorities of the American people supporting specific social-welfare programs even after the 1966 midterm elections in which Republicans made major gains in Congress.
14. Daniel Patrick Moynihan, *Maximum Feasible Misunderstanding: Community Action in the War on Poverty* (New York: Free Press, 1969), p. 23.
15. U.S. Department of Commerce, Bureau of the Census, *Historical Statistics of the United States: Colonial Times to 1970*, Part 1, p. 55.

16. United States Census Office, *Census Reports* (Washington, D.C.: U.S. Government Printing Office, 1902), Volume 2, pp. 2–3.

17. U.S. Department of Commerce, Bureau of the Census, *Historical Statistics of the United States: Colonial Times to 1970*, Part 1, p. 345.

18. AARP Web site (http://www.aarp.org/about_aarp/aarp_overview/a2003-01-13-aarphistory.html; accessed July 5, 2007).

19. Andrea Louise Campbell, *How Policies Make Citizens: Senior Political Activism and the American Welfare State* (Princeton, N.J.: Princeton University Press, 2003), p. 76.

20. U.S. Department of Commerce, Bureau of the Census, *Historical Statistics of the United States: Colonial Times to 1970*, Part 1, p. 49.

21. Ibid, p. 368.

22. U.S. Department of Commerce, Bureau of the Census, *Statistical Abstract of the United States, 1971* (Washington, D.C.: U.S. Government Printing Office, 1971), p. 122.

23. Jeane Kirkpatrick, "Representation in the American National Conventions: The Case of 1972," *British Journal of Political Science*, Volume 5, Number 3, July 1975, p. 284.

24. U.S. Department of Commerce, Bureau of the Census, *Statistical Abstract of the United States, 1971*, p. 102; U.S. Department of Commerce, Bureau of the Census, *Statistical Abstract of the United States, 1981* (Washington, D.C.: U.S. Government Printing Office, 1981), p. 134.

25. U.S. Department of Commerce, Bureau of the Census, *Statistical Abstract of the United States, 1981*, p. 132.

26. U.S. Department of Commerce, Bureau of the Census, *Historical Statistics of the United States: Colonial Times to 1970*, Part 1, p. 385.

27. U.S. Department of Commerce, Bureau of the Census, *Statistical Abstract of the United States, 1990* (Washington, D.C.: U.S. Government Printing Office, 1990), p. 161.

28. A. A. Berle, Jr., "Case for the Professor in Washington," *New York Times*, February 5, 1961, p. SM17.

29. Clark Kerr, "The Worth of Intellect," Inaugural Address as president of the University of California, September 29, 1958 (http://www.higher-ed.org/resources/inaugural_kerr.html; accessed February 27, 2006).

30. National Interstate and Defense Highways Act of 1956 (http://www.ourdocuments.gov/doc.php?flash=old&doc=88; accessed July 5, 2007).

31. U.S. Department of Commerce, Bureau of the Census, *Statistical Abstract of the United States, 1981*, p. 614.

32. See T. Stanton Dietrich, "Nature and Directions of Suburbanization in the South," *Social Forces*, Volume 39, Number 2 (December 1960), pp. 181–86; and Sylvia F. Fava, "Beyond Suburbia," *Annals of the American Academy of Political and Social Science*, Volume 422 (November 1975), pp. 10–24.

33. U.S. Department of Commerce, Bureau of the Census, "Demographic Trends in the Twentieth Century" (http://www.census.gov/prod/2002pubs/censr-4.pdf; accessed March 21, 2006), p. 33.

34. James C. Massey and Shirley Maxwell, "After the War: How the Rush to House Returning Vets Recast Suburbia," *Old House Online Journal*, April 2004 (http://www.oldhousejournal.com/magazine/2004/april/after_war.shtml; accessed February 27, 2006).

35. Dietrich, "Nature and Directions of Suburbanization in the South," p. 181.

36. Fava, "Beyond Suburbia," p. 11.

37. U.S. Department of Commerce, Bureau of the Census, *Statistical Abstract of the United States, 1981*, p. 761; U.S. Department of Commerce, Bureau of the Census, *Statistical Abstract of the United States, 1950* (Washington, D.C.: U.S. Government Printing Office, 1950), p. 739.

38. See, for example, Edward C. Banfield, "The Politics of Metropolitan Area Organization," *Midwest Journal of Political Science*, Volume 1 (May 1957); Louis Harris, *Is There a Republican Majority?* (New York: Harper and Row, 1954); and Edward Janosik, "The New Suburbia," *Current History*, Volume 31 (August 1956).

39. Frederick M. Wirt, "The Political Sociology of American Suburbia: A Reinterpretation," *Journal of Politics*, Volume 27, Number 3 (August 1965), p. 648.

40. Ibid, p. 666.

41. Charles G. Bell, "A New Suburban Politics," *Social Forces*, Volume 47, Number 3 (March 1969), p. 288.

42. Richard Lehne, "Suburban Foundations of the New Congress," *Annals of the American Academy of Political and Social Science*, Volume 422 (November 1975), p. 146.

43. Ibid, p. 151.
44. William J. Collins, "When the Tide Turned: Immigration and the Delay of the Great Black Migration," *Journal of Economic History*, Volume 57, Number 3 (September 1997), p. 608.
45. Karl E. Taeuber and Alma Taeuber, "The Negro Population in the United States," in John P. Davis, ed., *The American Negro Reference Book* (Englewood Cliffs, N.J.: Prentice-Hall, 1964), p. 110.
46. Collins, "When the Tide Turned: Immigration and the Delay of the Great Black Migration," p. 607.
47. Francis Fox Piven and Richard A. Cloward, "The Politics of the Great Society," in Sidney M. Milkis and Jerome M. Mileur, eds., *The Great Society and the High Tide of Liberalism* (Amherst, Mass.: University of Massachusetts Press, 2005), p. 256.
48. Bill Clinton, *My Life* (New York: Alfred A. Knopf, 2004), pp. 35, 55, 64.
49. Harold Mendelsohn and Irving Crespi, *Polls, Television, and the New Politics* (Scranton, Pa.: Chandler Publishing Company, 1970), p. 264. U.S. Department of Commerce, Bureau of the Census, "50th Anniversary of 'Wonderful World of Color' TV," March 11, 2004 (http://www.census.gov/Press-Release/www/releases/archives/facts_for_features/001702.html; accessed March 20, 2006).
50. Yale Roe, *The Television Dilemma* (New York: Hastings House, 1962), p. 7.
51. U.S. Department of Commerce, Bureau of the Census, *Statistical Abstract of the United States, 1971*, p. 488.
52. Matie Molinaro et al., *Letters of Marshall McLuhan* (New York: Oxford University Press, 1987), pp. 286–87.
53. Martin Luther King, Jr., "Letter from a Birmingham Jail," April 16, 1963 (http://www.sas.upenn.edu/African_Studies/Articles_Gen/Letter_Birmingham.html; accessed October 22, 2006).

CHAPTER 2. POLITICS AND THE LIBERAL ARC

1. Quoted in John F. Manley, "Wilbur D. Mills: A Study in Congressional Influence," *American Political Science Review*, Volume 63, Number 2 (June 1969), p. 448.
2. Richard Bolling, *House Out of Order* (New York: E. P. Dutton, 1964), p. 13.
3. In 1912, Maine Republicans split their votes between William Howard Taft (20.5 percent) and Theodore Roosevelt (37.4 percent). Woodrow Wilson, the Democrat, actually carried the state's electoral votes that year, even though he received only 39.4 percent of the popular vote.
4. Even in the aftermath of the 1966 midterm elections—widely interpreted at the time as a setback to the liberal programs of the Great Society—a national Gallup Poll found that 36 percent of respondents agreed that "the Federal Government is now using just about the right amount of power for meeting today's needs," while another 31 percent preferred the statement that "the Federal Government should use its powers even more vigorously to promote the well being of all segments of the people." Lloyd A. Free and Hadley Cantril, *The Political Beliefs of Americans: A Study of Public Opinion* (New Brunswick, N.J.: Rutgers University Press, 1967), p. 19.
5. Iwan W. Morgan, *Beyond the Liberal Consensus: A Political History of the United States Since 1965* (New York: St. Martin's Press, 1994), p. 1.
6. Alan Brinkley, *The End of Reform: New Deal Liberalism in Recession and War* (New York: Alfred A. Knopf, 1995), pp. 228, 234–35.
7. Godfrey Hodgson, *America in Our Time* (New York: Doubleday, 1976), p. 492.
8. H. F. Gosnell, *Machine Politics* (Chicago, Ill.: University of Chicago Press, 1968), is the classic work on the politics of the urban party machines.
9. Joseph Cooper, "Congress and Political Change: From Congressional to Presidential Preeminence: Power and Politics in Late Nineteenth-Century America and Today" in Lawrence C. Dodd and Bruce I. Oppenheimer, eds., *Congress Reconsidered* (Washington, D.C.: CQ Press, 2005), p. 377.
10. U.S. Department of Commerce, Bureau of the Census, *Historical Statistics of the United States: Colonial Times to 1970* (Washington, D.C.: U.S. Government Printing Office, 1975), Part 1, p. 178.
11. David S. Broder, *The Party's Over: The Failure of Politics in America* (New York: Harper & Row, 1971), p. 17.
12. See Nelson W. Polsby, *How Congress Evolves: Social Bases of Institutional Change* (New York:

Oxford University Press, 2004), pp. 82ff for an excellent discussion of the ways demographic and technological changes affected southern politics.

13. Quoted in Maggie Riechers, "Racism to Redemption: The Path of George Wallace" (http://www.neh.gov/news/humanities/2000-03/wallace.html; accessed September 27, 2006).

14. "County Unit System, *The New Georgia Encyclopedia* (http://www.georgiaencyclopedia.org/nge/Article.jsp?id=h-1381; accessed September 27, 2006).

15. Burns Roper, "Emerging Profiles of Television and Other Mass Media," *Public Attitudes* (New York: Television Information Office, April 5, 1967).

16. Eric R. A. N. Smith, *The Unchanging American Voter* (Berkeley, Calif.: University of California Press, 1989), p. 185.

17. Harold Mendelsohn and Irving Crespi, *Polls, Television, and the New Politics* (Scranton, Pa.: Chandler, 1970), pp. 6–7.

18. Angus Campbell et al., *The American Voter* (New York: John Wiley and Sons, 1964), p. 67.

19. Martin P. Wattenberg, *The Decline of American Political Parties, 1952–1996* (Cambridge, Mass.: Harvard University Press, 1996), p. 23.

20. U.S. Department of Commerce, Bureau of the Census, *Statistical Abstract of the United States, 1963* (Washington, D.C.: U.S. Government Printing Office, 1963), p. 523.

21. Howard Smith's life is detailed in Bruce J. Dierenfield, *Keeper of the Rules: Congressman Howard W. Smith of Virginia* (Charlottesville, Va.: University of Virginia Press, 1987).

22. Ibid, Foreword.

23. Bolling, *House Out of Order*, p. 81. Bolling excepted Sam Rayburn, the Speaker of the House, from this assessment.

24. The story is oft told, but cited here from Bolling, *House Out of Order*, pp. 85–86.

25. John D. Morris, "Congress Chiefs Forecast Gains," *New York Times*, January 4, 1959, p. 40.

26. James L. Sundquist, *Politics and Policy: The Eisenhower, Kennedy and Johnson Years* (Washington, D.C.: Brookings Institution, 1968), p. 405.

27. Bolling, *House Out of Order*, p. 56.

28. D. B. Hardeman and Donald C. Bacon, *Rayburn: A Biography* (Austin, Tex.: Texas Monthly Press, 1987), pp. 448, 451.

29. Theodore C. Sorensen, *Kennedy* (New York: Harper and Row, 1965), p. 341.

30. An insightful description of these changes in Congress is provided in Polsby, *How Congress Evolves: Social Bases of Institutional Change*.

31. See Julian E. Zelizer, *On Capitol Hill: The Struggle to Reform Congress and Its Consequences, 1948–2000* (New York: Cambridge University Press, 2004), pp. 63ff.

32. This change is documented in Gordon E. Baker, *The Reapportionment Revolution: Representation, Political Power, and the Supreme Court* (New York: Random House, 1966), pp. 92–93.

33. Richard Neustadt, "Memo on Presidential Transition," *American Prospect*, Volume 3, Number 11, September 1, 1992 (http://www.prospect.org/print/V3/11/neustadt-r.html; accessed March 21, 2007).

34. Richard Neustadt, *Presidential Power and the Modern Presidents* (New York: Free Press, 1990), p. 155.

35. James Bryce, *The American Commonwealth* (New York: Macmillan, 1989), Volume 1, p. 206.

36. George F. Hoar, *Autobiography of Seventy Years* (New York: Scribner's, 1903), Volume 2, p. 46.

37. Woodrow Wilson, *Congressional Government: A Study in American Politics* (New York: World, 1956), pp. 31, 82.

38. See Stephen Hess, *Organizing the Presidency* (Washington, D.C.: Brookings Institution Press, 3rd ed., 2002), pp. 49–64; and Emmet John Hughes, *The Ordeal of Power: A Political Memoir of the Eisenhower Years* (New York: Atheneum, 1963).

39. David McCullough, *Truman* (New York: Simon & Schuster, 1992), p. 228.

40. Doris Kearns, *Lyndon Johnson and the American Dream* (New York: Harper & Row, 1976), p. 36.

41. Sorensen, *Kennedy*, p. 345.

42. Arthur M. Schlesinger, Jr., *A Thousand Days: John F. Kennedy in the White House* (Boston: Mass.: Houghton Mifflin, 1965), p. 709.

43. Vaughn Davis Bornet, *The Presidency of Lyndon B. Johnson* (Lawrence, Kans.: University Press of Kansas, 1983), p. 130.

44. See Broder, *The Party's Over: The Failure of Politics in America*, pp. 32–33. For a description of the efforts to construct effective relations with Congress, see Lawrence F. O'Brien, *No Final Victories* (New York: Ballantine Books, 1974), pp. 106–38.

45. William Barry Furlong, "The Senate's Wizard of Ooze: Dirksen of Illinois," *Harper's*, December 1959.

46. Quoted in Edward L. Schapsmeier and Frederick H. Schapsmeier, *Dirksen of Illinois: Senatorial Statesman* (Urbana, Ill.: University of Illinois Press, 1985), p. 151.

47. Quoted by Frank H. Mackaman, Introduction to Everett McKinley Dirksen, *The Education of a Senator* (Urbana, Ill.: University of Illinois Press, 1998), p. xxx.

48. Edgar Driscoll, Jr., "Leverett Saltonstall: United States Senator," *Boston Globe*, June 18, 1970 (http://www.harvardsquarelibrary.org/unitarians/saltonstall.html; accessed September 27, 2006).

49. Personal observation by the author.

50. Quoted by Broder, *The Party's Over: The Failure of Politics in America*, p. 41.

51. Quoted in Robert A. Caro, *The Years of Lyndon Johnson: Master of the Senate* (New York: Alfred A. Knopf, 2002), pp. 737–38.

52. Ibid, p. 599.

53. Ibid, p. 1005.

54. M. Stanton Evans II, *The Liberal Establishment* (New York: Devin-Adair, 1965), pp. 56–65.

55. Ibid, p. 56.

56. See *The Handbook of Texas Online* (http://www.tsha.utexas.edu/handbook/online/articles/DD/fda94_print.html; accessed March 20, 2006).

57. Walter Heller, "Notes on Meeting With President Johnson, 7:40 pm, November 23, 1963," Heller Papers, John F. Kennedy Library. Quoted in Irving Bernstein, *Guns or Butter: The Presidency of Lyndon Johnson* (New York: Oxford University Press, 1996), p. 30.

58. James MacGregor Burns, *The Deadlock of Democracy: Four-Party Politics in America* (Upper Saddle River, N.J.: Prentice-Hall, 1963).

59. Cited in Lyn Ragsdale, *Vital Statistics on the Presidency: Washington to Clinton* (Washington, D.C.: CQ Press, 1996), p. 197.

60. Quoted in *Congressional Quarterly*, "Congress and the Nation, 1945–1964" (Washington, D.C.: 1965), p. 49.

61. Lyndon B. Johnson, "Address to a Joint Session of Congress," November 27, 1963.

62. Quotations are from transcripts of tape-recorded phone conversations. See Michael Beschloss, ed., *Taking Charge: The Johnson White House Tapes, 1963–1964* (New York: Simon & Schuster, 1997), pp. 25–48.

63. Vaughn Davis Bornet, *The Presidency of Lyndon B. Johnson* (Lawrence, Kans.: University Press of Kansas, 1983), p. 9.

64. Johnson's job approval ratings in the Gallup polls averaged over 75 percent for the first six months of 1964. See Ragsdale, *Vital Statistics on the Presidency: Washington to Clinton*, pp. 197–98.

65. Quoted in *Congressional Quarterly*, "Congress and the Nation, 1945–1964," p. 50.

66. Quoted in Rowland Evans and Robert Novak, *Lyndon B. Johnson: The Exercise of Power* (New York: New American Library, 1966), p. 490.

CHAPTER 3. THE FEDERAL COLOSSUS

1. "Shame in Georgia," *Time*, January 20, 1961. (http://www.time.com/time/archive/preview/0,10987,871979,00.html; accessed August 2, 2006).

2. Quoted in *Life*, May 23, 1960, p. 24.

3. John K. Jessup, ed., *The National Purpose: America in Crisis: An Urgent Summons* (New York: Holt, Rinehart and Winston, 1960), p. 1.

4. Richard Neustadt, "Memo on Presidential Transition," September 15, 1960 (http://www.prospect.org/print/V3/11/neustadt-r.html; accessed August 3, 2006).

5. See David Steigerwald, *The Sixties and the End of Modern America* (New York: St. Martin's Press, 1995), p. 9.

6. Irwin Unger, *The Best of Intentions: The Triumphs and Failures of the Great Society Under Kennedy, Johnson, and Nixon* (New York: Doubleday, 1996), p. 22.

7. Arthur M. Schlesinger, Jr., *A Thousand Days: John F. Kennedy in the White House* (Boston, Mass.: Houghton Mifflin, 1965), p. 14.

8. Joseph Kraft, *Profiles in Power: A Washington Insight* (New York: New American Library, 1966), p. 6.

9. Lawrence F. O'Brien, *No Final Victories: A Life in Politics from John F. Kennedy to Watergate* (New York: Ballantine Books, 1974), p. 111.
10. Data from *Economic Report of the President, 2003* (Washington, D.C.: U.S. Government Printing Office, 2003).
11. Theodore C. Sorensen, *Kennedy* (New York: Harper & Row, 1965), p. 395.
12. David P. Calleo, *The Imperious Economy* (Cambridge, Mass.: Harvard University Press, 1982), p. 12.
13. Quoted in Gerald S. and Deborah H. Strober, *Let Us Begin Anew: An Oral History of the Kennedy Presidency* (New York: HarperCollins, 1993), p. 243.
14. Edmund S. Phelps, "Economic Policy and Unemployment in the 1960s," in Eli Ginzberg and Robert M. Solow II, eds., *The Great Society: Lessons for the Future* (New York: Basic Books, 1974), p. 32.
15. Kennedy may not have actually read Harrington's book. Godfrey Hodgson suggests that his familiarity with Harrington's arguments came from reading Dwight McDonald's lengthy review of it in the *New Yorker*. See Godfrey Hodgson, *America in Our Time* (Garden City, N.Y.: Doubleday, 1976), pp. 172–73.
16. Michael Harrington, *The Other America: Poverty in the United States* (New York: Penguin Books, 1981), p. 7. The book was originally published by Macmillan in 1962.
17. Unger, *The Best of Intentions: The Triumphs and Failures of the Great Society Under Kennedy, Johnson, and Nixon*, p. 69.
18. While legislative enactment of most of the major elements in Kennedy's program had not occurred at the time of his death, his success rate in dealing with Congress, as measured by legislative support for bills he endorsed, was higher than that of most other presidents of the modern era. *Congressional Quarterly* calculates annual scores of presidential success rates, the frequency with which the Congress approves positions taken by the president. In his three years in office, Kennedy was successful 81 percent (1961), 85 percent (1962), and 87 percent (1963) percent of the time. That compares favorably with the average presidential success score in the years 1953–2000 of 67 percent.
19. Kraft, *Profiles in Power: A Washington Insight*, pp. 9, 18.
20. Jack Valenti, "Lyndon Johnson: An Awesome Engine of a Man," in Thomas W. Cowger and Sherwin J. Markman, eds., *Lyndon Johnson Remembered: An Intimate Portrait of a Presidency* (Lanham, Colo.: Rowman & Littlefield, 2003), p. 34.
21. Eric F. Goldman, *The Tragedy of Lyndon Johnson* (New York: Alfred A. Knopf, 1969), pp. 20–21.
22. William E. Leuchtenberg, "Lyndon Johnson in the Shadow of FDR," in Sidney M. Milkis and Jerome M. Mileur, eds., *The Great Society and the High Tide of Liberalism* (Amherst, Mass.: University of Massachusetts Press, 2005), p. 200.
23. Valenti, "Lyndon Johnson: An Awesome Engine of a Man," p. 34.
24. Quoted in Joseph A. Califano, Jr., *The Triumph & Tragedy of Lyndon Johnson: The White House Years* (New York: Simon & Schuster, 1991), p. 341.
25. Edward D. Berkowitz, *Mr. Social Security: The Life of Wilbur J. Cohen* (Lawrence, Kans.: University of Kansas Press, 1995), p. xi.
26. Lyndon B. Johnson, "Remarks on the Occasion of the 50th Anniversary of the Brookings Institution," September 29, 1966, *Public Papers of the President, 1966* (http://www.presidency.ucsb.edu/ws/index.php?pid=27896&st=&st1=; accessed August 4, 2006).
27. Goldman, *The Tragedy of Lyndon Johnson*, p. 9.
28. Richard N. Goodwin, *Remembering America: A Voice from the Sixties* (Boston, Mass.: Little, Brown, 1988), p. 285.
29. Daniel Patrick Moynihan, "The Professionalization of Reform," in Marvin E. Gettleman and David Mermelstein, eds., *The Great Society Reader: The Failure of American Liberalism* (New York: Random House, 1967), pp. 464–65.
30. Quoted by Lawrence Friedman, "The Social and Political Context of the War on Poverty: An Overview," in Robert Haveman, ed., *A Decade of Federal Antipoverty Programs* (New York: Academic Press, 1977), p. 51.
31. "LBJ," PBS Video for *The American Experience*, 1991.
32. Ibid.
33. Gallup Poll data reported in Lyn Ragsdale, *Vital Statistics on the Presidency* (Washington, D.C.: CQ Press, 1996), pp. 197–98.
34. Goodwin, *Remembering America: A Voice from the Sixties*, p. 272.
35. Lyndon B. Johnson, "Remarks at the University of Michigan," Ann Arbor, Michigan, May

22, 1964, *Public Papers of the President, 1964* (http://www.presidency.ucsb.edu/ws/index.php?pid=26262&st=&st1=; accessed August 4, 2006).

36. See Arthur M. Schlesinger, Jr., "The Future of Liberalism: The Challenge of Abundance," *Reporter,* May 3, 1956, p. 9.

37. "The War on Poverty: The Economic Opportunity Act of 1964," *Senate Document No. 86* (Washington, D.C., 1964).

38. See Hyman Bookbinder, "We Can No Longer Ignore Poverty in Our Midst: LBJ's Other War," in Thomas W. Cowger and Sherwin J. Markman, eds., *Lyndon Johnson Remembered: An Intimate Portrait of a Presidency* (Lanham, Colo.: Rowman & Littlefield, 2003), p. 96; and Mark I. Gelfand, "Elevating or Ignoring the Underclass" in Robert H. Bremner, Gary W. Reichard, and Richard J. Hopkins, eds., *American Choices: Social Dilemmas and Public Policy Since 1960* (Columbus, Ohio: Ohio State University Press, 1986), p. 4.

39. Lyndon Baines Johnson, *The Vantage Point: Perspectives of the Presidency, 1963–1969* (New York: Holt, Rinehart and Winston, 1971), p. 73.

40. See Gelfand, "Elevating or Ignoring the Underclass," p. 10.

41. Ibid., pp. 9–10.

42. As reported by the U.S. Food and Nutrition Service, "In 2004, a total of 38 million individuals were eligible to receive benefits. Throughout the year, 60 percent of those who were eligible participated in the program and 71 percent of the total benefits possible were distributed. Participation rates were higher than average among families with children and people in the poorest households." United States Department of Agriculture, Food and Nutrition Service, "Food Stamp Participation Rate Increases for Third Consecutive Year" (http://www.fns.usda.gov/cga/PressReleases/2006/PR-0234.htm; accessed August 4, 2006).

43. David Burner, *Making Peace with the Sixties* (Princeton, N.J.: Princeton University Press, 1996), p. 169.

44. Robert Wood, "The Great Society in 1984: Relic or Reality?" in Marshall Kaplan and Peggy L. Cuciti, eds., *The Great Society and its Legacy: Twenty Years of U.S. Social Policy* (Durham, N.C.: Duke University Press, 1986) , p. 19.

45. Johnson, *The Vantage Point: Perspectives of the Presidency, 1963–1969,* p. 327.

46. Barry Goldwater's 1964 Acceptance Speech (http://www.nationalcenter.org/Goldwater.html; accessed July 27, 2006).

47. See John Osgood Field and Ronald E. Anderson, "Ideology in the Public's Conceptualization of the 1964 Election," *Public Opinion Quarterly,* Volume 33, Number 3 (Autumn 1969), p. 380.

48. Aaron Wildavsky, *The Revolt Against the Masses* (New Brunswick, N.J.: Transaction Books, 2003), p. 250.

49. Theodore H. White, *The Making of the President 1964* (New York: Atheneum, 1969), p. 281.

50. Johnson, *The Vantage Point: Perspectives of the Presidency, 1963–1969,* pp. 104–5.

51. "The Voters Answer," *Washington Post,* November 4, 1964, p. A20.

52. Walter Lippmann, "Return to Normal Political Setup After Election Seems Unlikely," *Los Angeles Times,* November 4, 1964, p. A5.

53. "The Johnson Landslide," *New York Times,* November 4, 1964, p. 38.

54. Field and Anderson, "Ideology in the Public's Conceptualization of the 1964 Election," pp. 381–82.

55. Califano, *The Triumph & Tragedy of Lyndon Johnson: The White House Years,* p. 55.

56. Robert Mason, *Richard Nixon and the Quest for a New Majority* (Chapel Hill, N.C.: University of North Carolina Press, 2004), p. 87.

57. President Lyndon B. Johnson, "State of the Union," January 4, 1965 (http://www.presidency.ucsb.edu/ws/index.php?pid=26907; accessed July 28, 2006).

58. President Lyndon B. Johnson, "State of the Union," January 12, 1966 (http://www.presidency.ucsb.edu/ws/index.php?pid=28015; accessed July 28, 2006).

59. Gallup Poll data reported in Lyn Ragsdale, *Vital Statistics on the Presidency* (Washington, D.C.: CQ Press, 1996), p. 193.

60. Tom Wicker, "The President—What Will He Do for an Encore?" *New York Times,* August 10, 1965, p. 28.

61. President Lyndon B. Johnson, Remarks with President Truman at the Signing in Independence of the Medicare Bill, July 30, 1965 (http://www.presidency.ucsb.edu/ws/index.php?pid=27123&st=&st1=; accessed July 28, 2006).

62. *Colegrove* v. *Green,* 328 US 549 (1946).

63. Felix Frankfurter, "John Marshall," in *Government Under Law* (Cambridge, Mass.: Harvard University Press, 1956), p. 30.

64. *Colegrove v. Green*, 328 U.S. 549 (1946).

65. *Baker v. Carr*, 369 U. S. 186 (1962).

66. Lucas A. Powe, Jr., *The Warren Court and American Politics* (Cambridge, Mass.: Harvard University Press, 2000), p. 90.

67. Frank Norris, *The Octopus: A Story of California* (New York: Penguin Books, 1986), p. 51.

68. Bernard Schwartz, *Super Chief: Earl Warren and His Supreme Court—A Judicial Biography* (New York: New York University Press, 1983), p. 9.

69. Earl Warren, *The Memoirs of Earl Warren* (New York: Doubleday, 1977), pp. 30–31.

70. G. Edward White, *Earl Warren: A Public Life* (New York: Oxford University Press, 1982), p. 18.

71. Warren, *The Memoirs of Earl Warren*, p. 248.

72. John Aubrey Douglass, "Earl Warren's New Deal: Economic Transition, Postwar Planning, and Higher Education in California," *Journal of Policy History*, Volume 12, Number 2 (2000), p. 475.

73. "California Speeds Postwar Planning," *New York Times*, March 23, 1944.

74. Dwight D. Eisenhower, *The White House Years, 1953–1956: Mandate for Change* (New York: Doubleday, 1963), p. 228.

75. David Halberstam, "Earl Warren and His America," in Bernard Schwartz, ed., *The Warren Court: A Retrospective* (New York: Oxford University Press, 1996), p. 15.

76. William J. Brennan, Jr., "A Personal Remembrance," in Bernard Schwartz, ed., *The Warren Court: A Retrospective* (New York: Oxford University Press, 1996), p. 10.

77. Powe, *The Warren Court and American Politics*, p. 482.

78. Robert G. McCloskey, "Reflections on the Warren Court," *Virginia Law Review*, Volume 51, Issue 7, November 1965, p. 1231.

79. *United States v. Carolene Products Co.* 304 US 144 (1938).

80. Morton J. Horwitz, *The Warren Court and the Pursuit of Justice* (New York: Hill and Wang, 1998), pp. 77ff, provides an insightful discussion of this dilemma.

81. Everett Carll Ladd, Jr., "The Polls: The Question of Confidence," *Public Opinion Quarterly*, Volume 40, Number 4 (Winter 1976–77), p. 545.

82. Philip B. Kurland, *Politics, the Constitution and the Warren Court* (Chicago, Ill.: University of Chicago Press, 1970). p. 98.

83. Warren, *The Memoirs of Earl Warren*, p. 306.

84. In 1973, in *Miller v. California* (413 U.S. 15), the Supreme Court affirmed that the First Amendment did not protect obscene works and laid out a three-part test for determining what is obscene.

85. Robert Shogan, *A Question of Judgment: The Fortas Case and the Struggle for the Supreme Court* (New York: Bobbs-Merrill, 1972), p. 172.

86. Quoted by Sandra Day O'Connor in "Justice O'Connor Speaks on the Judiciary," *The Third Branch: Newsletter of the Federal Courts*, Volume 37, Number 8 (August 2005), p. 2.

87. Leonard W. Levy, ed., *The Supreme Court Under Earl Warren* (New York: Quadrangle Books, 1972), p. 16.

88. Mark Tushnet, ed., *The Warren Court in Historical and Political Perspective* (Charlottesville, Va.: University Press of Virginia, 1993), p. 3.

CHAPTER 4. FREE AT LAST

Although it is not directly cited here, this chapter draws significantly on Robert Weisbrot, *Freedom Bound: A History of America's Civil Rights Movement* (New York: Plume, 1991; original ed., W. W. Norton, 1990).

1. Carl M. Brauer, *John F. Kennedy and the Second Reconstruction* (New York: Columbia University Press, 1977), p. 33.

2. Ibid.

3. "LBJ 'Bares Soul' over Civil Rights," *Pittsburgh Courier*, July 23, 1960, p. 6.

4. On King's arrest and its impact on the 1960 presidential election, see Harris Wofford, *Of Kennedys and Kings: Making Sense of the Sixties* (New York: Farrar, Straus, and Giroux, 1980), pp. 11–28; Theodore H. White, *The Making of the President, 1960* (New York: Atheneum, 1961), pp. 345–52; and Richard M. Nixon, *Six Crises* (New York: Doubleday, 1962), pp. 362–63, 403.

5. Wofford, *Of Kennedys and Kings*, pp. 21–22.

6. Ibid., p. 141.

7. Brauer, *John F. Kennedy and the Second Reconstruction*, p. 84.

8. Victor S. Navasky, *Kennedy Justice* (New York: Atheneum, 1971), p. 96.

9. Wofford, *Of Kennedys and Kings*, pp. 134–35.

10. Ibid., p. 135.

11. Ibid.

12. Wofford, *Of Kennedys and Kings*, p. 136.

13. Ibid., p. 138.

14. Ibid., p. 151.

15. Ibid., pp. 152–53.

16. Ibid., p. 160.

17. David L. Lewis, *King: A Critical Biography*, 2nd ed. (Urbana: University of Illinois, 1978), p. 173.

18. Martin Luther King, Jr., *Why We Can't Wait* (New York: Mentor Books, 1964), p. 158.

19. Stephen B. Oates, *Let the Trumpet Sound: The Life of Martin Luther King, Jr.* (New York: Harper and Row, 1982), p. 235.

20. Pat Watters, *Down to Now: Reflections on the Southern Civil Rights Movement* (New York: Pantheon, 1974), p. 242.

21. According to the Southern Regional Council there were 14,733 arrests related to civil rights protests in eleven southern states between April and November 1, 1963; 10,420 of these arrests occurred between April 3 and June 24. See *New South* 18 (October–November 1963), p. 20.

22. Arthur M. Schlesinger, Jr., *A Thousand Days: John F. Kennedy in the White House* (New York: Ballantine Books, 1965), p. 963.

23. Telephone conversation between Johnson and Theodore Sorensen, June 3, 1963, Lyndon Baines Johnson Library, Pre-Presidential Files.

24. Brauer, *John F. Kennedy and the Second Reconstruction*, p. 247.

25. "Radio Television Report to the American People on Civil Rights," June 11, 1963, *Public Papers of the Presidents of the United States: John F. Kennedy, 1963* (Washington, D.C.: U.S. Government Printing Office, 1964), pp. 468–71.

26. Brauer, *John F. Kennedy and the Second Reconstruction*, pp. 259–60.

27. In the past decade, Bayard Rustin has gained fuller recognition as an architect of the civil rights movement. Among recent, widely divergent interpretations, see John D'Emilio, *Lost Prophet: The Life and Times of Bayard Rustin* (Chicago: University of Chicago Press, 2004); Daniel Levine, *Bayard Rustin and the Civil Rights Movement* (New Brunswick: Rutgers University Press, 1999); and Jervis Anderson, *Bayard Rustin: Troubles I've Seen: A Biography* (New York: HarperCollins, 1997). See also the insightful account by Milton Viorst, *Fire in the Streets: America in the 1960s* (New York: Simon & Schuster, 1979).

28. Roy Wilkins with Tom Matthews, *Standing Fast: The Autobiography of Roy Wilkins* (New York: Viking Press, 1982), pp. 291–92.

29. Milton Viorst, *Fire in the Streets*, p. 226.

30. Schlesinger, *A Thousand Days*, pp. 969–71.

31. Wilkins, *Standing Fast*, p. 292.

32. King's speech read and heard online at http://www.americanrhetoric.com/speeches/mlkihaveadream.htm.

33. "Statement by the President on the March on Washington for Jobs and Freedom," *Public Papers of the Presidents of the United States: John F. Kennedy, 1963* (Washington, D.C.: U.S. Government Printing Office, 1964), p. 645.

34. Schlesinger, *A Thousand Days*, p. 968.

35. Brauer, *John F. Kennedy and the Second Reconstruction*, p. 299.

36. Ibid., p. 297.

37. "The President's News Conference of November 14, 1963," *Public Papers of the Presidents of the United States: John F. Kennedy, 1963*, p. 849.

38. Coretta Scott King, *My Life with Martin Luther King, Jr.* (New York: Holt, Rinehart and Winston, 1969), pp. 243–45.

39. Johnson, *The Vantage Point*, p. 155.
40. Ibid., p. 157.
41. "Address Before a Joint Session of the Congress," November 27, 1963, *Public Papers of the Presidents of the United States: Lyndon B. Johnson, 1963–64*, Book I (Washington, D.C.: U.S. Government Printing Office, 1965), pp. 8–9.
42. Johnson, *The Vantage Point*, p. 157.
43. Doris Kearns, *Lyndon Johnson and the American Dream* (New York: Harper & Row, 1976), p. 191.
44. Ibid., p. 192; Wilkins, *Standing Fast*, p. 296.
45. Kearns, *Lyndon Johnson and the American Dream*, p. 192.
46. Wilkins, *Standing Fast*, p. 296.
47. Ibid.
48. Johnson, *The Vantage Point*, p. 37.
49. Wilkins, *Standing Fast*, pp. 299–300.
50. Ibid., pp. 233–34.
51. Eric F. Goldman, *The Tragedy of Lyndon Johnson* (New York: Alfred A. Knopf, 1969), p. 69.
52. *New York Times*, February 9, 1964, p. 52.
53. Charles Whalen and Barbara Whalen, *The Longest Debate: A Legislative History of the 1964 Civil Rights Act* (Cabin John, Md.: Seven Locks Press, 1985), p. 117.
54. Wilkins, *Standing Fast*, pp. 300–301.
55. Whalen and Whalen, *The Longest Debate*, p. 165.
56. Ibid., p. 201.
57. Frances Humphrey Howard, interview with the author (Mackenzie).
58. Speech by Senator Dirksen, on June 10, 1964, reprinted in *Congressional Record*, Volume 110, Part 10, 88th Cong., 2nd sess. (Washington, D.C.: U.S. Government Printing Office, 1964), p. 13319.
59. Whalen and Whalen, *The Longest Debate*, p. 205.
60. Wilkins, *Standing Fast*, pp. 302.
61. Whalen and Whalen, *The Longest Debate*, p. 205.
62. *New York Times*, May 20, 1964, p. 1.
63. August Meier and Elliott Rudwick, *CORE: A Study in the Civil Rights Movement, 1942–1968* (New York: Oxford University Press, 1973), p. 324.
64. *New York Times*, July 30, 1964, p. 1.
65. Interview with James Farmer by Paige Mulhollan, July 20, 1971, tape 2, p. 3, Lyndon Baines Johnson Presidential Library.
66. Stokely Carmichael and Charles V. Hamilton, *Black Power: The Politics of Liberation in America* (New York: Vintage Books, 1967), p. 93; Len Holt, *The Summer That Didn't End* (London: William Heinemann, 1965), p. 163.
67. Interview with Fannie Lou Hamer, November 1966, in Anne Cooke Romaine, "The Mississippi Freedom Democratic Party through August, 1964" (M.A. thesis, University of Virginia, 1969), pp. 213–14.
68. Interview with Joseph Rauh, June 1967, ibid., pp. 306–7.
69. Seth Cagin and Philip Dray, *We Are Not Afraid: The Story of Goodman, Schwerner, and Chaney and the Civil Rights Campaign for Mississippi* (New York: Macmillan, 1988), pp. 413–14.
70. Clayborne Carson, *In Struggle: SNCC and the Black Awakening of the 1960s* (Cambridge, Mass.: Harvard University Press, 1981), p. 125.
71. Interview with Joseph Rauh, June 1967, in Romaine, "The Mississippi Freedom Democratic Parts through August, 19644," pp. 336–37.
72. David J. Garrow, *Bearing the Cross: Martin Luther King, Jr., and the Southern Christian Leadership Conference* (New York: William Morrow, 1986), p. 348; Rauh discusses his convention role, in Romaine, "The Mississippi Freedom Democratic Party through 1964," pp. 301–53, and with Paige Mulhollan, August 8, 1969, pp. 12–23, Oral History, Lyndon Baines Johnson Presidential Library.
73. Johnson, *The Vantage Point*, p. 101.
74. Theodore H. White, *The Making of the President, 1964* (New York: Atheneum, 1965), pp. 400–401.
75. Ibid., p. 403.
76. Goldman, *The Tragedy of Lyndon Johnson*, p. 318.

77. Oates, *Let the Trumpet Sound*, p. 328; see also Charles Fager, *Selma 1965: The March That Changed the South* (New York: Scribner's, 1974), p. 9.
78. David J. Garrow, *Protest at Selma: Martin Luther King, Jr., and the Voting Rights Act of 1965* (New Haven, Conn.: Yale University Press, 1978), pp. 177–78.
79. "Special Message to the Congress: The American Promise," March 15, 1965, *Public Papers of the Presidents of the United States: Lyndon B. Johnson, 1965,* Book I (Washington, D.C.: U.S. Government Printing Office, 1966), pp. 281–87. Quotations are from pp. 281, 284.
80. Kearns, *Lyndon Johnson and the American Dream*, p. 226.
81. Goldman, *The Tragedy of Lyndon Johnson*, p. 328.
82. Wilkins, *Standing Fast*, p. 311.
83. "Remarks in the Capitol Rotunda at the Signing of the Voting Rights Act," August 6, 1965, *Public Papers of the Presidents of the United States: Lyndon B. Johnson, 1965,* Book II (Washington, D.C.: U.S. Government Printing Office, 1966), p. 840.
84. Garrow, *Protest at Selma*, pp. 27–28.
85. Angelina Grimké, letter to Catharine Beecher, August 2, 1837, in Kathryn Kish Sklar, *Women's Rights Emerges within the Antislavery Movement, 1830–1870: A Brief History with Documents* (Boston and New York: Bedford/St. Martin's, 2000), p. 142.
86. Sklar, *Women's Rights Emerges within the Antislavery Movement, 1830–1870,* p. 133.
87. Alexander Bloom and Wini Breines, eds., *"Takin' It to the Streets": A Sixties Reader,* 2nd ed. (New York: Oxford University, 2003), p. 39.
88. http://www.feminist.org/chronicles/early1.html.
89. Susan M. Hartmann, "Women's Issues and the Johnson Administration," in Robert A. Divine, ed., *The Johnson Years,* Volume 3: *LBJ at Home and Abroad* (Lawrence: University Press of Kansas, 1994), p. 57.
90. Ibid., p. 65.
91. Ibid., p. 67.
92. Ibid., p. 68.
93. James A. Henretta, David Brody, Lynn Dumenil, Susan Ware, *America's History,* Volume 2: *Since 1865,* 5th ed. (Boston: Bedford/St. Martin's, 2004), p. 857.
94. Franklin Kameny, "Gay Is Good" (1969), in Mark Blasius and Shane Phelan, eds., *We Are Everywhere: A Historical Sourcebook of Gay and Lesbian Politics* (New York: Routledge, 1997), p. 375.
95. Pauline Maier et al., *Inventing America: A History of the United States,* Volume 2: *From 1865* (New York: W. W. Norton, 2003), p. 962.
96. Irving Bernstein, *Guns or Butter: The Presidency of Lyndon Johnson* (New York: Oxford University Press, 1996), p. 260.
97. "Immigration Law Changed Face of Nation," National Public Radio, May 9, 2006, http://www.npr.org/templates/story/story.php?storyId=5391395, accessed September 10, 2007.
98. Data for year 2000 from the administrator of the U.S. Courts (http://www.uscourts.gov/judicialfactsfigures/Table404.pdf).
99. National Park Service (http://www.cr.nps.gov/nr/travel/civilrights/prize.htm).
100. See Earl Black and Merle Black, *The Rise of Southern Republicans* (Cambridge, Mass.: Harvard University Press, 2002), p. 115.
101. Quoted in *Time,* September 27, 1976 (http://www.time.com/time/magazine/article/0,9171,918352-2,00.html; accessed March 4, 2007).

CHAPTER 5. TO PROTECT THE PLANET

1. Gaylord Nelson and the editors of *Country Beautiful, America's Last Chance* (Waukesha, Wisc.: Country Beautiful Corporation, 1970), p. 8.
2. Ibid.
3. Vance Packard, *The Waste Makers* (New York: David McKay, 1960), p. 54.
4. John C. Whitaker, *Striking a Balance: Environment and Natural Resources Policy in the Nixon-Ford Years* (Washington, D.C.: American Enterprise Institute, 1976), p. 22.
5. Robert Gottlieb, *Forcing the Spring: The Transformation of the American Environmental Movement* (Washington, D.C.: Island Press, 1993), p. 78.
6. Richard N. L. Andrews, *Managing the Environment, Managing Ourselves: A History of American Environmental Policy* (New Haven, Conn.: Yale University Press, 1999), p. 180.

7. Ibid., p. 182.
8. Ibid.
9. The President's Materials Policy Commission, *Resources for Freedom: A Report to the President*, Volume I, *Foundations for Growth and Security* (Washington, D.C.: U.S. Government Printing Office, 1952), p. 3.
10. Ibid., p. 4.
11. Ibid., p. 1.
12. Ibid., p. 8.
13. Ibid., p. 11.
14. Gottlieb, *Forcing the Spring*, p. 309, citing Joseph L. Fisher, "Long-Range Research in Times Like These," in Resources for the Future, *Annual Report* (for the year ending September 30, 1961) (Washington, D.C.: Resources for the Future, December 1961), p. 4.
15. Peter Collier and David Horowitz, *The Rockefellers: An American Dynasty* (New York: Holt, Rinehart and Winston, 1976), p. 305.
16. Gottlieb, *Forcing the Spring*, p. 40.
17. Stephen Fox, *John Muir and His Legacy: The American Conservation Movement* (Madison, Wisc.: University of Wisconsin Press, 1981), p. 283.
18. Ibid.
19. Samuel P. Hays in collaboration with Barbara D. Hays, *Beauty, Health, and Permanence: Environmental Politics in the United States, 1955–1985* (Cambridge, Mass.: Harvard University Press, 1987), pp. 17–18.
20. Dwight D. Eisenhower, *Mandate for Change: The White House Years, 1953–1956* (Garden City, N.Y.: Doubleday, 1963), p. 550.
21. Joseph M. Petulla, *American Environmental History: The Exploitation and Conservation of Natural Resources*, 2nd ed. (Columbus, Ohio: Merrill, 1988), p. 408.
22. Loren Eisley, *The Immense Journey* (New York: Franklin Watts, 1946), p. 16.
23. Petulla, *American Environmental History*, p. 408.
24. James L. Sundquist, *Politics and Policy: The Eisenhower, Kennedy, and Johnson Years* (Washington, D.C.: Brookings Institution, 1968), p. 337.
25. Petulla, *American Environmental History*, p. 41.
26. Hays, *Beauty, Health, and Permanence*, p. 139.
27. Arthur M. Schlesinger, Jr., "The Future of Liberalism: The Challenge of Abundance," *Reporter*, May 3, 1956, p. 10.
28. John Kenneth Galbraith, *The Affluent Society* (Boston: Houghton Mifflin, 1958), 40th anniversary edition (Boston: Houghton Mifflin, 1998), pp. 186–87.
29. "The Milk All of Us Drink—and Fallout," *Consumer Reports*, Volume 24, Number 3 (March 1959), p. 103.
30. Steven M. Spencer, "Fallout: The Silent Killer," *Saturday Evening Post*, Volume 232, Number 10 (September 5, 1959), p. 86.
31. Hays, *Beauty, Health, and Permanence*, p. 25.
32. Scott Hamilton Dewey, *Don't Breathe the Air: Air Pollution and U.S. Environmental Politics, 1945–1970* (College Station, Tex.: Texas A&M University Press, 2000), pp. 58–59.
33. Gottlieb, *Forcing the Spring*, p. 76.
34. "Anti-Water Pollution Law Strengthened," *CQ Almanac*, 1965 (Washington, D.C.: Congressional Quarterly Service, 1966), p. 745; Murray Bookchin, *Our Synthetic Environment*, rev. ed. (New York: Harper & Row, 1974), pp. 83–84.
35. Gottlieb, *Forcing the Spring*, p. 78.
36. Ibid.; on the Arthur Kill blob, see Frank Graham, Jr., *Disaster by Default: Politics and Water Pollution* (New York: M. Evans & Co., 1966), pp. 90–96.
37. Murray Bookchin, *Our Synthetic Environment*, rev. ed. (New York: Harper & Row, 1974), p. 85.
38. Hays, *Beauty, Health, and Permanence*, p. 71.
39. Adam Rome, *The Bulldozer in the Countryside: Suburban Sprawl and the Rise of American Environmentalism* (Cambridge: Cambridge University Press, 2001), pp. 3, 121.
40. Ibid., p. 8.
41. William H. Whyte, Jr., *The Organization Man* (New York: Simon & Schuster, 1956), p. 10.
42. William H. Whyte, Jr., "A Plan to Save Vanishing U.S. Countryside," *Life* 47 (August 17, 1959), p. 88.
43. Lewis Herber [a pseudonym of Murray Bookchin], *Our Synthetic Environment* (New York: Alfred A. Knopf, 1962), p. 253, Appendix B, "Excerpt from Public Health in an Industrial

Society," by Robert A. Kehoe, *Proceedings of the Conference on "Man Versus Environment," May 5–6, 1958,* published with support by the U.S. Public Health Service, Department of Health, Education, and Welfare.

44. Sundquist, *Politics and Policy,* p. 332.
45. Herber [Bookchin], *Our Synthetic Environment,* p. 247, Appendix A, John D. Porterfield, "Changing Concepts of Illness—An Excerpt From 'The Healthy Environment,'" presented at the Fifty-third Annual Meeting of the Air Pollution Control Association, Cincinnati, Ohio, May 24, 1960.
46. United States Congress, House Committee on Appropriations, *Report on Environmental Health Problems,* Hearings before the Subcommittee of the Committee on Appropriations, House of Representatives, 86th Congress, 2nd Session (Washington, D.C.: U.S. Government Printing Office, 1960), pp. 6, 9.
47. Edwin L. Dale, Jr., "Big Debate: Public Vs. Private Spending; Critics Charge Government Policies Allot Too Much of Our Resources to Private Sector," *New York Times,* March 13, 1960, p. E5.
48. Adlai Stevenson, "Extend Our Vision . . . to all Mankind," in John K. Jessup et al., *The National Purpose: America in Crisis: An Urgent Summons* (New York: Holt, Rinehart and Winston, 1960), p. 27.
49. Packard, *The Waste Makers,* pp. 297, 307, 313.
50. Ibid., pp. 326–27.
51. "Veto of Bill to Amend the Federal Water Pollution Control Act," February 23, 1960, *Public Papers of the Presidents of the United States: Dwight D. Eisenhower, 1960–1961* (Washington, D.C.: U.S. Government Printing Office, 1961), p. 208.
52. Sundquist, *Politics and Policy,* p. 331.
53. John F. Kennedy, "We Must Climb to the Hilltop," *Life,* Volume 49, Number 8 (August 22, 1960), pp. 70B–77, esp. p. 75; see also Richard M. Nixon, "Our Resolve Is Running Strong," *Life,* Volume 49, Number 9 (August 29, 1960), pp. 87–94.
54. "Special Message to the Congress on Natural Resources," February 23, 1961, *Public Papers of the Presidents of the United States: John F. Kennedy, 1961* (Washington, D.C.: U.S. Government Printing Office, 1962), pp. 114–21.
55. "Remarks Upon Signing the Federal Water Pollution Control Act Amendments," July 20, 1961, *Public Papers of the Presidents of the United States: John F. Kennedy, 1961,* p. 524.
56. See Thomas G. Smith, "John Kennedy, Stewart Udall, and New Frontier Conservation," *Pacific Historical Review,* Volume 64, Number 3 (August 1995), pp. 329–62.
57. Stewart L. Udall, *The Quiet Crisis* (New York: Holt, Rinehart and Winston, 1963), p. viii.
58. "Remarks Upon Signing Bill Authorizing the Cape Cod National Seashore Park," August 7, 1961, *Public Papers of the Presidents of the United States: John F. Kennedy, 1961,* p. 552.
59. Linda Lear, ed., *Lost Woods: The Discovered Writings of Rachel Carson* (Boston: Beacon Press, 1998), p. 148.
60. Gottlieb, *Forcing the Spring,* p. 83.
61. Rachel Carson, *Silent Spring* (Boston: Houghton Mifflin, 1962), p. 8.
62. Ibid., p. 7.
63. "The President's News Conference of August 29, 1962," *Public Papers of the Presidents of the United States: John F. Kennedy, 1962* (Washington, D.C.: U.S. Government Printing Office, 1963), p. 655.
64. Linda Lear, *Rachel Carson: Witness for Nature* (New York: Henry Holt, 1997), pp. 453–54.
65. "The Talk of the Town: DDT," *New Yorker,* May 26, 1945, p. 18.
66. Bookchin, *Our Synthetic Environment,* rev. ed., p. 55.
67. Ibid., p. 53.
68. Lear, *Rachel Carson,* p. 376.
69. Ibid., p. 417.
70. Ibid., pp. 428–29.
71. Carson, *Silent Spring,* p. 86.
72. Ibid., pp. 12–13.
73. Lear, *Rachel Carson,* p. 426.
74. Carson, *Silent Spring,* pp. 7–8.
75. Martin V. Melosi, "Lyndon Johnson and Environmental Policy," in Robert A. Divine, ed., *The Johnson Years,* Volume II: *Vietnam, the Environment, and Science* (Lawrence: University of Kansas Press, 1987), p. 113.

76. "Special Message to the Congress on Conservation and Restoration of Natural Beauty," February 8, 1965, *Public Papers of the Presidents of the United States: Lyndon B. Johnson, 1965*, Book I, 1965 (Washington, D.C.: U.S. Government Printing Office, 1966), p. 156.

77. Bobby Baker, *Wheeling and Dealing: Confessions of a Capitol Hill Operator* (New York: W.W. Norton, 1978), pp. 40–41; Dallek, *Lone Star Rising*, p. 372.

78. Udall, Oral History, I, p. 19, Lyndon Baines Johnson Library.

79. Ibid., V, p. 3.

80. Ibid., V, p. 19.

81. Frank Graham, Jr., *Man's Dominion: The Story of Conservation in America* (New York: M. Evans, 1971), p. 302.

82. Outdoor Recreation Resources Review Commission, *Outdoor Recreation for America: A Report to the President and to the Congress* (Washington, D.C.: U.S. Government Printing Office, 1962).

83. "Land and Water Conservation Act Passed," *CQ Almanac, 1964* (Washington, D.C.: Congressional Quarterly Service, 1965), p. 480.

84. *CQ Almanac, 1962*, p. 463, cited in "Major Recreation Legislation of 1964," *CQ Almanac, 1964*, p. 474.

85. "Land and Water Conservation Act Passed," *CQ Almanac, 1964*, p. 480.

86. Ibid., p. 483.

87. "Special Message to the Congress on Natural Resources," February 23, 1961, *Public Papers of the Presidents of the United States*, pp. 114–21.

88. http://www.wilderness.net/index.cfm?fuse=NWPS&sec=legisact; accessed July 6, 2007. Citing Public Law 88–577, 88th Congress, S. 4, September 3, 1964, Sec. 2(C).

89. "Congress Passes Wilderness Act," *CQ Almanac, 1964*, p. 488.

90. Hays, *Beauty, Health, and Permanence*, p. 111.

91. "Congress Passes Wilderness Act," *CQ Almanac, 1964*, pp. 488–89.

92. Stephen C. Sturgeon, *The Politics of Western Water: The Congressional Career of Wayne Aspinall* (Tucson: University of Arizona Press, 2002), p. 63; Thomas G. Smith, "John Kennedy, Stewart Udall, and New Frontier Conservation," p. 341.

93. Steven C. Schulte, *Wayne Aspinall and the Shaping of the American West* (Boulder: University Press of Colorado, 2002), pp. 123–24; the quotation is on p. 124.

94. LeRoy Ashby and Rod Gramer, *Fighting the Odds: The Life of Senator Frank Church* (Pullman: Washington State University, 1994), pp. 145–53, quotation on p. 149.

95. "Congress Passes Wilderness Act," *CQ Almanac, 1964*, p. 485.

96. Ibid.

97. The belief in America's unlimited bounty was easier to sustain because politicians in the White House and on Capitol Hill routinely undercounted the costs of government beneficence. "We would authorize a national park [or] national seashore and Congress would authorize as they did with Point Reyes [near San Francisco, in September 1962], fourteen million dollars," Udall related. "Then it turned out today, eight years later, that it is going to cost over seventy-five million. . . . I think we ought to have been honest with ourselves. If we think it's important to conserve land, conserve open space, we're just going to have to pay whatever the cost is." See Udall, Oral History, V, p. 14, Lyndon Baines Johnson Library.

98. "Special Message to the Congress on Conservation and Restoration of Natural Beauty," February 8, 1965, *Public Papers of the Presidents of the United States*, pp. 155–65; the quotations are on p. 156.

99. Lewis L. Gould, "Lady Bird Johnson and Beautification," in Robert A. Divine, ed., *The Johnson Years*, Volume II, p. 151.

100. Hal K. Rothman, *The Greening of a Nation? Environmentalism in America since 1945* (New York: Harcourt, Brace, 1998), p. 97.

101. John A. Andrew III, *Lyndon Johnson and the Great Society* (Chicago: Ivan R. Dee, 1998), p. 173.

102. Ibid., p. 234.

103. Joseph Judge, "New Grandeur for Flowering Washington," *National Geographic*, Volume 131, Number 4 (April 1967), p. 520.

104. Rome, *The Bulldozer in the Countryside*, p. 217.

105. Udall, LBJ Library, OH, V, pp. 13–14.

106. Adam Rome, "'Give Earth a Chance': The Environmental Movement and the Sixties," *Journal of American History*, September 2003, p. 538.

107. Ibid., pp. 534–41.

108. Mrs. Carter F. Henderson, "What You Can Do to Combat Air Pollution," *Parents' Magazine and Better Homemaking*, Volume 41, Number 10 (October 1966), pp. 76–77, 96–98.

109. "Remarks Upon Signing the Air Quality Act of 1967," November 21, 1967, *Public Papers of the Presidents of the United States: Lyndon B. Johnson*, 1967, Book II, p. 1069.

110. On Muskie see *Current Biography, 1968*, pp. 276–78; Nelson Lichtenstein, Eleanora W. Schoenebaum, and Michael L. Levine, *Political Profiles: The Johnson Years* (New York: Facts on File, 1976), pp. 447–49; Edmund Muskie, *Journeys* (Garden City, N.Y.: Doubleday, 1972), p. 31; David Nevin, *Muskie of Maine* (New York: Random House, 1972), Chapter 5, quotations at pp. 31, 104–5; Theo Lippman, Jr., and D. C. Hansen, *Muskie* (New York: W.W. Norton, 1971), Chapter 7; Frederic N. Cleaveland and associates, *Congress and Urban Problems* (Washington, D.C.: Brookings Institution, 1969), pp. 259–60.

111. Bernstein, *Guns or Butter*, pp. 281–82.

112. "Anti-Water Pollution Law Strengthened," *CQ Almanac, 1965* (Washington, D.C.: Congressional Quarterly Service, 1966), p. 743.

113. Bernstein, *Guns or Butter*, p. 283.

114. Petulla, *American Environmental History*, p. 412.

115. "Anti-Water Pollution Law Strengthened," *CQ Almanac, 1965*, p. 747, citing William R. Adams, president of the St. Regis Paper Co. and director of the Pulp, Paper, and Paperboard Institute (U.S.A.), Inc.

116. Ibid., p. 747, citing A. J. von Frank of the Manufacturing Chemists' Association, Inc.

117. Sundquist, *Politics and Policy*, p. 364.

118. Ibid., p. 364.

119. "Anti-Water Pollution Law Strengthened," *CQ Almanac, 1965*, pp. 743, 744.

120. "Remarks at the Signing of the Water Quality Act of 1965," October 2, 1965, *Public Papers of the Presidents of the United States: Lyndon B. Johnson*, 1965, Book II (Washington, D.C.: U.S. Government Printing Office, 1966), p. 1035.

121. "Water Resources Planning Act Passed by Congress," *CQ Almanac, 1965*, p. 759.

122. "Water Pollution Control Funds Expanded," *CQ Almanac, 1966* (Washington, D.C.: Congressional Quarterly Service, 1967), p. 632, on the Clean Water Restoration Act, passed on October 17, 1966, and signed into law on November 3.

123. Sundquist, *Politics and Policy*, p. 352.

124. Ibid., p. 352.

125. Andrews, *Managing the Environment, Managing Ourselves*, p. 208; Edmund S. Muskie, "NEPA to CERCLA: The Clean Air Act: A Commitment to Public Health," originally published in the January/February 1990 issue of *Environmental Forum*, http://www.cleanairtrust.org/nepa2cercla.html; accessed July 7, 2007.

126. Petulla, *American Environmental History*, p. 419.

127. John C. Esposito, *Vanishing Air* (New York: Grossman, 1970), p. 204. See also Scott Hamilton Dewey, *Don't Breathe the Air*, p. 133.

128. "Congress Strengthens Air Pollution Control Power," *CQ Almanac, 1967* (Washington D.C.: Congressional Quarterly Service, 1968), p. 881, citing Joseph S. Clark, May 2, 1967.

129. Ibid., p. 877; majority report by the House Interstate and Foreign Commerce Committee, p. 885.

130. "Remarks Upon Signing the Air Quality Act of 1967," November 21, 1967, *Public Papers of the Presidents of the United States*, 1967, Book II, pp. 1067–68.

131. Andrews, *Managing the Environment, Managing Ourselves*, p. 222, citing Kenneth C. Martis, *The History of Natural Resources Roll Call Voting in the United States House of Representatives*, Ph.D. diss., University of Michigan, 1976.

132. Bernstein, *Guns or Butter*, p. 294.

133. Thomas C. Mann, president of the Automobile Manufacturers Association and former undersecretary of state for economic affairs, in reply to a question by Edmund Muskie, praised the federal antipollution standards for the 1968 model year and welcomed "a series of stated goals, projecting what will be required of the industry as far ahead as 1975 or 1980," for helping the industry to focus research and development on specific problems. See "Congress Strengthens Air Pollution Control Powers," in *CQ Almanac, 1967*, p. 879, citing Thomas C. Mann to Edmund Muskie, February 20, 1967.

134. Andrews, *Managing the Environment, Managing Ourselves*, p. 209.

135. See, for example, the Senate testimony in 1965 by the nuclear geochemist Clair Patterson, assailing fraudulent inhouse studies by the Ethyl Corporation, the major producer of lead

additives in gasoline, http://www.radford.edu/~wkovarik/envhist/8sixties.html; accessed July 7, 2007.

136. Lyndon Johnson, *The Vantage Point: Perspectives of the Presidency, 1963–1969* (New York: Holt, Rinehart and Winston, 1971), pp. 337–38. The speech is quoted on p. 338.

137. Even environmental science rose on the tide of liberal reform. According to Samuel P. Hays, "As late as the 1960s environmental science was still in its infancy," but flourished quickly. "The central journal in the field of environmental pollution, *Environmental Science and Technology*, published by the American Chemical Society beginning in 1967, became by the 1990s the society's journal of largest circulation save for its lead publication, *Chemical and Engineering News*." See Samuel P. Hays, *A History of Environmental Politics since 1945* (Pittsburgh: University of Pittsburgh Press, 2000), p. 137.

138. Reuther called the program "Demonstration Cities" until Johnson ridiculed the term for implying that it would generate protests.

139. Robert Dallek, *Flawed Giant: Lyndon Johnson and His Times, 1961–1973* (New York: Oxford University Press, 1998), p. 317.

140. Bernstein, *Guns or Butter*, p. 466. Senator Gaylord Nelson, the founder of Earth Day, similarly viewed urban congestion and homelessness as environmental hazards that required federal housing for low-income families and "care to ensure that in any massive reshaping of our cities, we do not simply build in the ingredients for new slums and new human misery." See Nelson, *America's Last Chance*, p. 8.

141. "Remarks in the Hospital at the Signing of the Clean Air Act Amendments and Solid Waste Disposal Bill," October 20, 1965, *Public Papers of the Presidents of the United States, Lyndon B. Johnson, 1965*, Book II, pp. 1066–67.

142. "Annual Message to the Congress on the State of the Union," January 22, 1970, *Public Papers of the Presidents of the United States: Richard Nixon, 1970* (Washington, D.C.: U.S. Government Printing Office, 1971), p. 12.

143. G. Ray Funkhouser, "The Issues of the Sixties: An Exploratory Study in the Dynamics of Public Opinion," *Public Opinion Quarterly*, Volume 37, Number 1 (Spring 1973), p. 70.

144. Petulla, *American Environmental History*, p. 416.

145. Kirkpatrick Sale, *The Green Revolution: The American Environmental Revolution, 1962 to 1992* (New York: Hill and Wang, 1993), p. 23.

146. Hays, *Beauty, Health, and Permanence*, pp. 460–61.

147. Rome, "'Give Earth a Chance,'" p. 544.

148. Ibid.

149. Ibid., p. 542, n. 48.

150. Ibid., p. 546, citing Barry Weisberg, ed., *Ecocide in Indochina: The Ecology of War* (San Francisco: Canfield Press, 1970); John Lewallen, *Ecology of Devastation: Indochina* (New York: Penguin Books, 1971).

151. Ibid., p. 548.

152. On Santa Barbara, Malcolm F. Baldwin and James K. Page, Jr., *Law and the Environment* (New York: Walker and Company, 1970), p. 11, citing Statement by Richard Whitehead, planning director of Santa Barbara County, to Assistant Secretary of Interior Cordell Moore, February 28, 1967.

153. J. Brooks Flippen, *Nixon and the Environment* (Albuquerque, N.M.: University of New Mexico Press, 2000), p. 25.

154. "Fighting to Save the Earth from Man," *Time*, Volume 95, Number 5 (February 2, 1970), p. 59.

155. Sale, *The Green Revolution*, p. 23.

156. "Fighting to Save the Earth from Man," *Time*, p. 56.

157. Petulla, *American Environmental History*, p. 420.

158. J. Brooks Flippen, *Nixon and the Environment*, p. 47.

159. Ibid., pp. 21–22.

160. Ibid., p. 27.

161. "Fighting to Save the Earth from Man," *Time*, p. 56.

162. Remembrance of Gaylord Nelson by the Wilderness Society, at http://www.wilderness.org/AboutUs/Nelson_Bio.cfm; accessed July 7, 2007.

163. "All About Earth Day," http://earthday.wilderness.org/history/; accessed July 7, 2007.

164. Ibid.

165. Gottlieb, *Forcing the Spring*, p. 112.

166. Flippen, *Nixon and the Environment*, pp. 7–8.

167. Rome, "'Give Earth a Chance,'"p. 550, citing Philip Shabecoff, *A Fierce Green Fire: The American Environmental Movement* (New York: Island Press, 1993), pp. 111, 113.
168. Sale, *The Green Revolution*, p. 36.
169. Andrews, *Managing the Environment, Managing Ourselves*, p. 231. Also see Andrews, p. 458, n. 6.
170. Ibid., pp. 227–28.
171. Ibid., pp. 227–28, 237.
172. Rothman, *The Greening of a Nation?*, pp. 120–21, 127.

CHAPTER 6. THE HOUR OF MAXIMUM DANGER

1. Transcript of first presidential debate, September 26, 1960, http://www.debates.org/pages/trans60a.html.
2. John Gerard Ruggie, "The Past as Prologue? Interests, Identity, and American Foreign Policy," *International Security*, Volume 21, Number 4 (Spring 1997), p. 96.
3. Arthur H. Vandenberg, *The Private Papers of Senator Vandenberg*, ed. Arthur H. Vandenberg, Jr., with the collaboration of Alex Morris (Boston: Houghton Mifflin, 1952), pp. 9–11.
4. Eric F. Goldman, *The Crucial Decade—and After* (New York: Alfred A. Knopf, 1960), p. 30.
5. "Address on Foreign Economic Policy, Delivered at Baylor University," March 6, 1947, *Public Papers of the Presidents: Harry S. Truman, 1947* (Washington, D.C.: U.S. Government Printing Office, 1948), p. 171.
6. Milovan Djilas, *Conversations with Stalin*, tr. Michael B. Petrovich (New York: Harcourt, Brace & World, 1962), p. 114.
7. David Holloway, *Stalin and the Bomb: The Soviet Union and Atomic Energy, 1939–1956* (New Haven, Conn.: Yale University Press, 1994), p. 15.
8. Vyacheslav Molotov, *Molotov Remembers: Inside Kremlin Politics: Conversations with Felix Chuev*, ed. Albert Resis (Chicago: Ivan R. Dee, 1993), p. 63.
9. Kenneth M. Jensen, ed., *Origins of the Cold War: The Novikov, Kennan, and Roberts "Long Telegrams" of 1946*, rev. ed. (Washington, D.C.: United States Institute of Peace, 1993), pp. 17, 20, 28.
10. John Lewis Gaddis, *Strategies of Containment: A Critical Appraisal of American National Security Policy*, rev. and expanded ed. (Oxford: Oxford University Press, 2005), p. 91.
11. Paul Nitze, "The Development of NSC 68," *International Security*, Volume 4, Number 4 (Spring, 1980), p. 173.
12. Roger Hilsman, *To Move a Nation: The Politics of Foreign Policy in the Administration of John F. Kennedy* (Garden City, N.Y.: Doubleday, 1967), p. 53. See also Theodore C. Sorensen, *Kennedy* (New York: Harper & Row, 1965), p. 509.
13. Robert G. Spivack, "It's Up to Kennedy," *Nation*, CXCI (October 8, 1960), pp. 220–21.
14. Theodore H. White, *The Making of the President 1960* (New York: Atheneum, 1961), p. 153.
15. Robert A. Divine, *Foreign Policy and U.S. Presidential Elections, 1952–1960* (New York: New Viewpoints, 1974), pp. 228–29.
16. See, for example, Averell Harriman, "My Alarming Interview with Khrushchev," *Life*, Volume 47, Number 2 (July 13, 1959), pp. 33–36; "Peaceful Coexistence," *Time*, Volume 74, Number 2 (July 13, 1959), p. 10.
17. John Newhouse, *War and Peace in the Nuclear Age* (New York: Alfred A. Knopf, 1989), p. 125.
18. The reference to Khrushchev's inebriated state is in John Newhouse, *War and Peace in the Nuclear Age* (New York: Alfred A. Knopf, 1989), p. 125.
19. Vladislav Zubok and Constantine Pleshakov, *Inside the Kremlin's Cold War: From Stalin to Khrushchev* (Cambridge, Mass.: Harvard University Press, 1996), p. 207.
20. Aleksandr Fursenko and Timothy Naftali, *Khrushchev's Cold War: The Inside Story of an American Adversary* (New York: W. W. Norton, 2006), p. 148.
21. Ben Pearse, "Defense Chief in the Sputnik Age," *New York Times Magazine*, November 10, 1957, p. 20.
22. "The Gaither Report: Deterrence & Survival in the Nuclear Age," November 7, 1957, p. 5, online at http://www.honors.umd.edu/HONR269J/images/Etc/GaitherReport.pdf (viewed July 12, 2007).
23. "The Power for Now," *Time*, Volume 70, Number 22 (November 25, 1957), p. 27.
24. Albert Wohlstetter, "The Delicate Balance of Terror," *Foreign Affairs*, Volume 37, Number 2 (January 1959), p. 234.

25. Bernard Brodie, *Strategy in the Missile Age* (Santa Monica, Calif.: The RAND Corporation, 1960), pp. 393–94.
26. See Herman Kahn, *On Thermonuclear War* (Princeton N.J.: Princeton University Press, 1960).
27. "The President's News Conference of January 18, 1961," *Public Papers of the Presidents of the United States: Dwight D. Eisenhower, 1960–1961* (Washington, D.C.: U.S. Government Printing Office, 1961), p. 1043.
28. "Global Crises Stacked Up for Mr. Kennedy: A Special Section," *Newsweek*, Volume 57, Number 4 (January 23, 1961), p. 25.
29. Theodore C. Sorensen, *Kennedy* (New York: Harper & Row, 1965), p. 603.
30. Arthur M. Schlesinger, Jr., *A Thousand Days: John F. Kennedy in the White House* (Boston: Houghton Mifflin, 1965), p. 316.
31. Sorensen, *Kennedy*, pp. 608–9.
32. Fred Kaplan, *The Wizards of Armageddon* (New York: Simon & Schuster, 1983), p. 269.
33. Robert Dallek, *An Unfinished Life: John F. Kennedy 1917–1963* (Boston: Little, Brown, 2003), pp. 345–46.
34. Schlesinger, *A Thousand Days*, p. 315.
35. Kaplan, *The Wizards of Armageddon*, p. 270.
36. Schlesinger, *A Thousand Days*, p. 315.
37. "Inaugural Address," January 20, 1961, *Public Papers of the Presidents: John F. Kennedy, 1961* (Washington, D.C.: U.S. Government Printing Office, 1962), p. 2.
38. Robert M. Collins, "Growth Liberalism in the Sixties: Great Societies at Home and Grand Designs Abroad," in David Farber, ed., *The Sixties: From Memory to History* (Chapel Hill and London: University of North Carolina Press, 1994), p. 57.
39. James Tobin, "Defense, Dollars, and Doctrines," *Yale Review*, Volume 47, Number 3 (Spring 1958), pp. 324–25.
40. Gaddis, *Strategies of Containment*, p. 203, citing Samuelson report, "Prospects and Policies for the 1961 American Economy," January 6, 1961, Kennedy Papers, Pre-Presidential File, Box 1071, "Economy-Samuelson Report," John F. Kennedy Library.
41. Walter W. Heller, *New Dimensions of Political Economy* (Cambridge, Mass.: Harvard University Press 1966), p. 11.
42. Collins, "Growth Liberalism in the Sixties," p. 21.
43. Michael R. Beschloss, *The Crisis Years: Kennedy and Khrushchev, 1960–1963* (New York: HarperCollins, 1991), p. 20.
44. Zubok and Pleshakov, *Inside the Kremlin's Cold War*, p. 239.
45. Schlesinger, *A Thousand Days*, p. 303.
46. "Annual Message to the Congress on the State of the Union," January 30, 1961, *Public Papers of the Presidents: John F. Kennedy, 1961*, pp. 19, 22–23.
47. Sorensen, *Kennedy*, pp. 292–93.
48. Peter Wyden, *Bay of Pigs: The Untold Story* (New York: Simon & Schuster, 1979), p. 100.
49. Trumbull Higgins, *A Perfect Failure: Kennedy, Eisenhower and the CIA at the Bay of Pigs* (New York: W. W. Norton, 1987), p. 13.
50. Stephen G. Rabe, *Eisenhower and Latin America: The Foreign Policy of Anticommunism* (Chapel Hill, N.C.: University of North Carolina Press, 1988), p. 168.
51. Richard J. Walton, *Cold War and Counter-Revolution: The Foreign Policy of John F. Kennedy* (Baltimore: Penguin, 1972), p. 116.
52. Beschloss, *The Crisis Years*, p. 350.
53. Hilsman, *To Move a Nation*, pp. 95–96.
54. John Kenneth Galbraith to President Kennedy, May 10, 1961, reprinted in Galbraith, *Ambassador's Journal* (Boston: Houghton Mifflin: 1969), p. 107.
55. Winthrop G. Brown, Oral History, John F. Kennedy Library.
56. Schlesinger, *A Thousand Days*, p. 324.
57. Ibid., pp. 325, 331.
58. Michael P. Riccards, *The Presidency and the Middle Kingdom: China, the United States, and Executive Leadership* (Lanham, Md.: Lexington, 2000), p. 161.
59. Schlesinger, *A Thousand Days*, p. 338.
60. Walter Isaacson and Evan Thomas, *The Wise Men: Six Friends and the World They Made: Acheson, Bohlen, Harriman, Kennan, Lovett, McCloy* (New York: Simon & Schuster, 1986), p. 618.
61. Henry Fairlie, *The Kennedy Promise: The Politics of Expectation* (Garden City, N.Y.: Doubleday, 1973), p. 180.

62. Vladislav Zubok, "Working Paper #6: Khrushchev and the Berlin Crisis (1958–62)," Cold War International History Project (http://cwihp.si.edu), citing his interview with Khrushchev's interpreter, Oleg Troyanovsky, March 23, 1993.

63. Memorandum of Conversation, Vienna Meeting Between the President and Chairman Khrushchev, June 4, 1961, 10:15 A.M., p. 13, Box 126, President's Office Files, John F. Kennedy Library.

64. Ibid.

65. Beschloss, *The Crisis Years*, p. 224, citing author's interview with Rusk. See also Dean Rusk, as told to Richard Rusk, *As I Saw It*, ed. Daniel S. Papp (New York: W. W. Norton, 1990), p. 221.

66. Nikita S. Khrushchev, *Khrushchev Remembers: The Last Testament*, tr. and ed. Strobe Talbott (Boston: Little, Brown, 1974), p. 499.

67. David Halberstam, *The Best and the Brightest* (Greenwich, Conn.: Fawcett, 1973), pp. 96–97.

68. McGeorge Bundy, *Danger and Survival: Choices About the Bomb in the First Fifty Years* (New York: Random House, 1988), p. 368.

69. Kenneth P. O'Donnell and David F. Powers with Joe McCarthy, *"Johnny, We Hardly Knew Ye": Memories of John Fitzgerald Kennedy* (Boston: Little, Brown, 1970), p. 303.

70. Chester Bowles, *Promises to Keep: My Years in Public Life, 1941–1969* (New York: Harper & Row, 1971), pp. 1–2.

71. Michael E. Latham, *Modernization as Ideology: American Social Science and "Nation Building" in the Kennedy Era* (Chapel Hill, N.C.: University of North Carolina Press, 2000), p. 54.

72. Ibid., p. 49.

73. W. W. Rostow, "Countering Guerrilla Attack," in Franklin Mark Osanka, ed., *Modern Guerrilla Warfare: Fighting Communist Guerrilla Movements, 1941–1961* (New York: Free Press, 1962) pp. 465–66.

74. W. W. Rostow, *The Stages of Economic Growth: A Non-Communist Manifesto* (Cambridge: Cambridge University Press, 1960), p. 10.

75. Seymour Martin Lipset, *The First New Nation: The United States in Historical and Comparative Perspective* (New York: Basic Books, 1963), p. 2.

76. Latham, *Modernization as Ideology*, p. 92.

77. Rostow, *The Stages of Economic Growth*, pp. 4–6. 17.

78. Latham, *Modernization as Ideology*, p. 45.

79. Godfrey Hodgson, obituary for Walt Rostow, *The Guardian*, February 17, 2003.

80. Melvyn P. Leffler, *A Preponderance of Power: National Security, the Truman Administration, and the Cold War* (Stanford, Calif.: Stanford University Press, 1992), p. 293.

81. "Annual Message to the Congress on the State of the Union," January 7, 1948, *Public Papers of the Presidents: Harry S. Truman*, 1948 (Washington, D.C.: U.S. Government Printing Office, 1949), p. 8.

82. Gaddis, *Strategies of Containment*, p. 61.

83. Theodore C. Sorensen, *"Let the Word Go Forth": The Statements, Speeches, and Writings of John F. Kennedy, 1947–1963* (New York: Dell, 1988), p. 119.

84. Latham, *Modernization as Ideology*, p. 114.

85. John F. Kennedy, *The Strategy of Peace*, ed. Allan Nevins (New York: Harper & Brothers, 1960), p. 6.

86. Latham, *Modernization as Ideology*, pp. 7–8

87. Gaddis, *Strategies of Containment*, p. 199.

88. David Halberstam, *The Best and the Brightest* (New York: Random House, 1969), pp. 156–57.

89. Schlesinger, *A Thousand Days*, p. 422.

90. "Inaugural Address," January 20, 1961, *Public Papers of the Presidents: John F. Kennedy, 1961*, p. 1.

91. According to Arthur M. Schlesinger, Jr., "A thoughtful memorandum in March 1961 from ten leading Latin American economists had particular impact on President Kennedy's decision to launch the Alliance for Progress." See Schlesinger, "Myth and Reality," in L. Ronald Scheman, ed., *The Alliance for Progress: A Retrospective* (New York: Praeger, 1988), p. 67. See also Lincoln Gordon, "The Alliance at Birth: Hopes and Fears," in Scheman, *The Alliance for Progress*, p. 73.

92. Carlos Sanz de Santamaria, "Making the Alliance Work," in Scheman, *The Alliance for Progress*, p. 121.

93. Jerome Levinson and Juan de Onis, *The Alliance that Lost Its Way: A Critical Report on the Alliance for Progress*, a Twentieth Century Fund Study (Chicago: Quadrangle Books, 1970), p. 17.

94. Schlesinger, *A Thousand Days*, p. 172.

95. Ibid., p. 186.
96. Scheman, *The Alliance for Progress*, p. 64. See also Howard J. Wiarda, "Did the Alliance 'Lose Its Way,' or Were Its Assumptions All Wrong from the Beginning and Are Those Assumptions Still with Us?" in Scheman, *The Alliance for Progress*, pp. 95–97. Wiarda observed that even among indigenous Latin specialists, the liberal aura was pervasive because "many had attended U.S. universities, they had read Lipset and Rostow, their writings were full of citations of the newest developmentalist literature."
97. Levinson and de Onis, *The Alliance that Lost Its Way*, p. 6.
98. C. Douglas Dillon, "The Prelude," in Scheman, *The Alliance for Progress*, p. 64.
99. Scheman, *The Alliance for Progress*, p. 5.
100. "Address at a White House Reception for Members of Congress and for the Diplomatic Corps of the Latin American Republics," March 13, 1961, *Public Papers of the Presidents: John F. Kennedy, 1961*, p. 172.
101. Sorensen, *Kennedy*, p. 530.
102. Schlesinger, *A Thousand Days*, p. 595.
103. Ibid., p. 599.
104. Jim F. Heath, *Decade of Disillusionment: The Kennedy-Johnson Years* (Bloomington, Ind.: Indiana University Press, 1975), p. 148.
105. William James, "The Moral Equivalent of War," in *Memories and Studies* (New York: Longmans, Green, 1911), p. 291.
106. Ibid., pp. 7–8.
107. Henry Reuss, Oral History, p. 70, John F. Kennedy Library.
108. Henry S. Reuss, "A Point Four Youth Corps," *Commonweal*, Volume 72, Number 6 (May 6, 1960), p. 146.
109. William J. Lederer and Eugene Burdick, *The Ugly American* (New York, London: W. W. Norton, 1958), p. 284.
110. Rice, *The Bold Experiment*, pp. 10–11.
111. Henry Reuss, Oral History, p. 71, John F. Kennedy Library.
112. *New York Times*, November 7, 1960, p. 31.
113. Irving Bernstein, *Promises Kept: John F. Kennedy's New Frontier* (New York: Oxford University Press, 1991), p. 269.
114. "It's a Puzzlement," *Wall Street Journal*, March 6, 1961, p. 10, cited in Karen Schwarz, *What You Can Do for Your Country: An Oral History of the Peace Corps* (New York: William Morrow, 1991), p. 29.
115. Rice, *The Bold Experiment*, pp. 80–81, citing U.S. Senate, Committee on Foreign Relations, *Hearings on S. 2935: "Peace Corps Act Amendments*, 87th Cong., 2nd Sess., Volume 5, p. 21.
116. William F. Haddad, "Mr. Shriver and the Savage Politics of Poverty," *Harper's*, Volume 231, Number 1387 (December 1965), pp. 45, 48.
117. Rice, *The Bold Experiment*, pp. 67, 169. See also comments by Michael Tudor, a volunteer in Nigeria, 1961–63, Roger Landrum (Nigeria, 1961–63), and Michael Moore (Togo, 1962–64), in Karen Schwarz, *What You Can Do for Your Country: An Oral History of the Peace Corps*, pp. 36–38.
118. Chester Bowles, *Promises to Keep*, p. 453.
119. Marshall Windmiller, *The Peace Corps and Pax Americana* (Washington, D.C.: Public Affairs Press, 1970), pp. 1–2.
120. Rice, *The Bold Experiment*, pp. 269–70.
121. Schlesinger, *A Thousand Days*, p. 608.
122. "Special Message to the Congress on Foreign Aid," March 22, 1961, *Public Papers of the Presidents: John F. Kennedy, 1961*, p. 205.
123. James Reston, "Shriver's Peace Corps and the New Frontier," *New York Times*, March 6, 1963, p. 8.
124. "Inaugural Address," January 20, 1961, *Public Papers of the Presidents: John F. Kennedy, 1961*, p. 1.
125. W. W. Rostow, *The Diffusion of Power: An Essay in Recent History* (New York: Macmillan, 1972), pp. 252, 259.
126. James G. Blight, Bruce J. Allyn, and David A. Welch, with the assistance of David Lewis, eds., *Cuba on the Brink: Castro, the Missile Crisis, and the Soviet Collapse* (New York: Pantheon, 1993), pp. 59–60.
127. Beschloss, *The Crisis Years*, p. 387.
128. John Newhouse, *War and Peace in the Nuclear Age*, p. 170, citing conversation with Arkady Shevchenko, November 11, 1986.

129. Nikita S. Khrushchev, *Khrushchev Remembers*, ed. and trans. by Strobe Talbott (Boston: Little, Brown, 1970), p. 494.
130. Ernest R. May and Philip D. Zelikow, eds., *The Kennedy Tapes: Inside the White House During the Cuban Missile Crisis* (Cambridge, Mass.: The Belknap Press of Harvard University Press, 1997), p. 88.
131. George W. Ball, *The Past Has Another Pattern: Memoirs* (New York: W.W. Norton, 1982), p. 291.
132. May and Zelikow, *The Kennedy Tapes*, p. 145; the quotation is emended by Sheldon M. Stern, *Averting "The Final Failure": John F. Kennedy and the Secret Cuban Missile Crisis Meetings* (Stanford, Calif.: Stanford University Press, 2003), pp. 105–6.
133. Ibid., p. 176.
134. "Radio and Television Report to the American People on the Soviet Arms Buildup in Cuba," October 22, 1962, *Public Papers of the Presidents: John F. Kennedy, 1962* (Washington, D.C.: U.S. Government Printing Office, 1963), p. 807.
135. Sorensen, *Kennedy*, p. 717.
136. Robert F. Kennedy, *Thirteen Days: A Memoir of the Cuban Missile Crisis* (New York: W. W. Norton, 1969), p. 61.
137. Ibid., p. 98.
138. Ibid., p. 127.
139. "'A Contribution to Peace," *New York Herald Tribune*, October 29, 1962, p. 24.
140. Richard H. Rovere, "Letter from Washington," *New Yorker*, Volume 38, Number 39 (November 17, 1962), p. 200.
141. Arthur M. Schlesinger, Jr., *Robert Kennedy and His Times* (Boston: Houghton Mifflin, 1978), p. 524, citing author's journal, October 29, 1962. Admiral Anderson and General LeMay had earlier objected to the president's agreement at a meeting of the Joint Chiefs: see notes from transcripts of JCS meetings, October 28, 1962 [at 0900], p. 1, Dept. of Defense, Office of the Chairman of the Joint Chiefs of Staff, Office of Joint History, reprinted in U.S. State Department, *Foreign Relations of the United States, 1961–1963*, Volume 10–12, microfiche supplement, document 441.
142. Beschloss, *The Crisis Years*, p. 581.
143. "Television and Radio Interview: After Two Years—a Conversation with the President," December 17, 1962, in *Public Papers of the Presidents: John F. Kennedy, 1962*, p. 898.
144. "When One Man Sizes Up Another," *Newsweek*, Volume 60, Number 23 (December 3, 1962), p. 23.
145. Khrushchev, *Khrushchev Remembers*, p. 505.
146. Khrushchev, *Khrushchev Remembers: The Last Testament*, p. 513.
147. Milton S. Katz, *Ban the Bomb: A History of SANE, the Committee for a Sane Nuclear Policy, 1957–1985* (New York: Greenwood, 1986), pp. 1–2.
148. I. F. Stone, "The Fatal Decisions Have Already Been Made," *I.F. Stone's Weekly*, Volume 2, Number 39 (November 1, 1954), p. 1.
149. Katz, *Ban the Bomb*, p. 15.
150. Charles A. H. Thomson and Frances M. Shattuck, *The 1956 Presidential Campaign* (Ann Arbor, Mich.: Univeristy of Michigan Press, 1960), p. 236.
151. Schlesinger, *A Thousand Days*, p. 451.
152. Katz, *Ban the Bomb*, p. 16.
153. Amy Swerdlow, *Women Strike for Peace: Traditional Motherhood and Radical Politics in the 1960s* (Chicago: University of Chicago Press, 1993), p. 43.
154. Katz, *Ban the Bomb*, p. 16.
155. Ibid., p. 24.
156. Steven M. Spencer, "Fallout: The Silent Killer," *Saturday Evening Post*, Volume 232, Number 9 (August 29, 1959), p. 27.
157. "Department of State memorandum of conversation, "Meeting with Disarmament Advisors," April 28, 1958, excised copy, Dwight D. Eisenhower Library, Office of the Special Assistant for Science and Technology, box 1, Disarmament—General April 1958," reprinted as Document 4 in William Burr and Hector L. Montford, eds., "The Making of the Limited Test Ban Treaty, 1958–1963," National Security Archive, http://www.gwu.edu/~nsarchiv/NSAEBB/NSAEBB94/.
158. Viktor Adamsky and Yuri Smirnov, "Moscow's Biggest Bomb: The 50-Megaton Test of October 1961," *Cold War International History Project Bulletin* Number 4 (Fall 1994), pp. 3, 19, 20.

159. Sorensen, *Kennedy*, p. 618.
160. Swerdlow, *Women Strike for Peace*, p. 19.
161. Ibid., p. 16.
162. Andrew Hamilton, "MIT: March 4 Revisited amid Political Turmoil," *Science*, March 13, 1970, p. 1476.
163. Richard Reeves, *President Kennedy: Profile of Power* (New York: Simon & Schuster, 1993), p. 440.
164. Dallek, *An Unfinished Life*, p. 618, citing author's interview with Norman Cousins.
165. Reeves, *President Kennedy*, p. 476.
166. Todd Gitlin, *The Sixties: Years of Hope, Days of Rage* (New York: Bantam, 1989; orig. Bantam 1987), p. 92.
167. *New York Times*, May 28, 1963, p. 1.
168. Reeves, *President Kennedy*, p. 512, citing Cousins letter to JFK, April 30, 1963, Sorensen Papers, Box 36, John F. Kennedy Library. See also Glenn T. Seaborg, with the assistance of Benjamin S. Loeb, *Kennedy, Khrushchev and the Test Ban* (Berkeley, Calif: University of California Press, 1974), p. 212.
169. "Commencement Address at American University in Washington," June 10, 1963, *Public Papers of the Presidents: John F. Kennedy, 1963* (Washington, D.C.: U.S Government Printing Office, 1964), pp. 460, 461.
170. Ibid., pp. 462–64.
171. Ibid., p. 464.
172. Schlesinger, *A Thousand Days*, p. 910.
173. *CQ Almanac, 1963* (Washington, D.C.: U.S Government Printing Office, 1964), p. 250.
174. William Taubman, *Khrushchev: The Man and His Era* (New York: W. W. Norton, 2003), p. 602.
175. Schlesinger, *A Thousand Days*, p. 903.
176. Reeves, *President Kennedy*, p. 545.
177. *CQ Almanac, 1963*, p. 249. According to Fursenko and Naftali, *Khrushchev's Cold War*, p. 520, Khrushchev had decided in April 1963, as part of his rethinking of Soviet-American relations, to accept a partial ban on nuclear tests if a comprehensive ban proved unworkable.
178. Two Republicans, George D. Aiken of Vermont and Leverett Saltonstall of Massachusetts, though uncommitted on the treaty, attended the signing ceremony; Dirksen and Bourke B. Hickenlooper of Iowa declined invitations. *Congressional Quarterly Almanac*, Volume XIX, *88th Congress, 1st Session, 1963*, p. 251.
179. Mark O. Hatfield, with the Senate Historical Office, *Vice Presidents of the United States, 1789–1993* (Washington: U.S. Government Printing Office, 1997), p. 467.
180. *CQ Almanac, 1963*, p. 252.
181. Reeves, *President Kennedy*, p. 555.
182. Herbert S. Parmet, *JFK: The Presidency of John F. Kennedy* (New York: Dial, 1983), p. 315.
183. Ibid., p. 311.
184. Reeves, *President Kennedy*, p. 554.
185. "The Atomic Arsenal," *Time*, August 23, 1963, p. 11.
186. Reeves, *President Kennedy*, p. 594.
187. Seaborg, *Kennedy, Khrushchev and the Test Ban*, p. 280.
188. Dallek, *An Unfinished Life*, p. 629.
189. Sorensen, *Kennedy*, p. 740.
190. Dallek, *An Unfinished Life*, p. 630.
191. Fursenko and Naftali, *Khrushchev's Cold War*, p. 521.
192. Ibid., pp. 522–25.
193. Sorensen, *Kennedy*, pp. 742–43.
194. Seaborg, *Kennedy, Khrushchev and the Test Ban*, p. 207.
195. Sorensen, *Kennedy*, p. 743.
196. "Address Before the 18th General Assembly of the United Nations," September 20, 1963, *Public Papers of the Presidents: John F. Kennedy, 1963* (Washington, D.C.: U.S. Government Printing Office, 1964), pp. 693–698; the quotation is on p. 698.
197. Sorensen, *Kennedy*, p. 745.
198. Ibid.

CHAPTER 7. A TVA IN THE MEKONG VALLEY

1. Alexander Bloom and Wini Breines, eds., *"Takin' It to the Streets": A Sixties Reader* (New York: Oxford University Press, 1995), p. 225. Oglesby spoke on November 27, 1965, according to James Miller, *"Democracy Is in the Street": From Port Huron to the Siege of Chicago* (Cambridge, Mass.: Harvard, 1994; orig. 1987), p. 255.

2. Ibid., pp. 220–21.

3. Ibid., p. 221.

4. Ibid., pp. 221–22.

5. *New York Times*, April 2, 1967, p. 76.

6. Andrew J. Rotter, ed., *Light at the End of the Tunnel: A Vietnam War Anthology* (New York: Rowman and Littlefield, 1999), p. xvi.

7. Jean Lacouture, *Ho Chi Minh: A Political Biography* (New York: Random House, 1968), p. 171.

8. Stanley Karnow, *Vietnam: A History*, rev. ed. (New York: Penguin, 1983), pp. 213–14.

9. Matthew B. Ridgway, *Soldier: The Memoirs of Matthew B. Ridgway*, as told to Harold H. Martin (New York: Harper, 1956), p. 277.

10. Robert Shaplen, *The Lost Revolution: The U.S. in Vietnam: 1946–1966* (New York: Harper & Row, 1967), p. 104.

11. Milton C. Taylor, "South Vietnam: Lavish Aid, Limited Progress," *Pacific Affairs*, Volume 34, Number 3 (Autumn 1961), p. 242.

12. George C. Herring, *America's Longest War: The United States and Vietnam, 1950–1975*, 2nd ed. (New York: Alfred A. Knopf, 1986), p. 61.

13. Taylor, "South Vietnam: Lavish Aid, Limited Progress," pp. 62–63.

14. Marilyn B. Young, *The Vietnam Wars, 1945–1990* (New York: HarperCollins, 1991), p. 53.

15. James B. Reston, *An Appraisal of the Cold War*, February 22, 1955 (Minneapolis: University of Minnesota, 1955), p. 5.

16. "Founding Program of the National Liberation Front of South Vietnam," in Marvin E. Gettleman et al., eds., *Vietnam and America: A Documented History*, rev. and enlarged 2nd ed. (New York: Grove Press, 1995), p. 189.

17. William J. Duiker, *The Communist Road to Power in Vietnam* (Boulder, Colo.: Westview, 1981), p. 198. See also Truong Nhu Tang with David Chanoff and Doan Van Toai, *A Vietcong Memoir: An Inside Account of the Vietnam War and Its Aftermath* (New York: Vintage, 1986), p. 68. Tang, an anticommunist southerner well placed in the NLF, elaborates on how "Ho was the spiritual father" of the movement against Diem and for national unification, "And yet, this struggle was also our own."

18. John Lewis Gaddis, *Strategies of Containment: A Critical Appraisal of Postwar American National Security Policy*, rev. and expanded ed. (New York: Oxford University Press, 2005), p. 259.

19. George McT. Kahin, *Intervention: How America Became Involved in Vietnam* (New York: Alfred A. Knopf, 1986), 131.

20. John Kenneth Galbraith, *Ambassador's Journal: A Personal Account of the Kennedy Years* (Boston: Houghton Mifflin, 1969), p. 311.

21. George Ball, *The Past Has Another Pattern: Memoirs* (New York: W. W. Norton, 1982), p. 365.

22. Maxwell D. Taylor, *Swords and Plowshares* (New York: W. W. Norton, 1972) p. 239; Herring, *America's Longest War*, p. 81.

23. Karnow, *Vietnam*, p. 373.

24. Robert S. McNamara to President Kennedy, November 8, 1961, in *The Pentagon Papers: The Defense Department History of United States Decision Making on Vietnam*, Senator Gravel, ed. (Boston: Beacon, 1971–72), Volume II, p. 108.

25. Arthur M. Schlesinger, Jr., *A Thousand Days: John F. Kennedy in the White House* (Boston: Houghton Mifflin, 1965), p. 547.

26. Karnow, *Vietnam*, p. 366.

27. Roger Hilsman, *To Move a Nation: The Politics of Foreign Policy in the Administration of John F. Kennedy* (Garden City, N.Y.: Doubleday, 1967), p. 432.

28. Michael E. Latham, *Modernization as Ideology: American Social Science and "Nation Building" in the Kennedy Era* (Chapel Hill, N.C.: University of North Carolina Press, 2000), p. 190.

29. Robert Scheer, "Behind the Miracle of South Vietnam," in Gettleman et al., eds., p. 153.

30. Hilsman, *To Move a Nation*, p. 432, citing a speech by Wheeler in November 1962 at Fordham University.

31. Latham, *Modernization as Ideology*, p. 190, citing Wheeler, Press Statement, February 4, 1963, Hilsman Papers, box 3, "Vietnam, 3/1-8/21/63," John F. Kennedy Library.
32. Hilsman, *To Move a Nation*, pp. 522–23.
33. Young, *The Vietnam Wars, 1945–1990*, p. 79.
34. Henry Cabot Lodge to Dean Rusk, August 29, 1963, in *The Pentagon Papers*, Volume II, p. 738.
35. Karnow, *Vietnam*, pp. 339–40.
36. "Remarks at Syracuse University on the Communist Challenge in Southeast Asia," August 5, 1964, *Public Papers of the Presidents of the Unites States: Lyndon Baines Johnson, 1963–1964*, Book II (Washington, D.C.: U.S. Government Printing Office, 1965), pp. 928, 930.
37. Conversation with McGeorge Bundy, May 27, 1964, in Michael R. Beschloss, ed., *Taking Charge: The Johnson White House Tapes, 1963–1964* (New York: Simon & Schuster, 1997), p. 372.
38. Conversation with Richard Russell, May 27, 1964, ibid., p. 364 (first quotation), p. 365 (other quotations).
39. Doris Kearns, *Lyndon Johnson and the American Dream* (New York: Harper & Row, 1976), pp. 252–53.
40. *The Pentagon Papers*, III, p. 178.
41. Joint Chiefs to Lyndon Johnson, March 2, 1964, in *Foreign Relations of the United States*, Volume I, *Vietnam 1964* (Washington, D.C.: U.S. Government Printing Office, 1992), pp. 112–18, esp. p. 115; the quoted words are on p. 118.
42. Maxwell Taylor to Dean Rusk, September 6, 1964, in *The Pentagon Papers*, Volume II, p. 336.
43. Conversation with Richard Russell, May 27, 1964, in Beschloss, *Taking Charge*, pp. 365, 369.
44. Conversation with Richard Russell, June 11, 1964, ibid., pp. 401, 402.
45. Conversation with John S. Knight, February 3, 1964, ibid., p. 213.
46. Robert Dallek, *Flawed Giant: Lyndon Johnson and His Times, 1961–1973* (New York: Oxford University Press, 1998), p. 99.
47. Ibid., p 88, citing interview with Moyers, May 14, 1997.
48. William J. Duiker, *U.S. Containment Policy and the Conflict in Indochina* (Stanford, Calif.: Stanford University Press, 1994), p. 344.
49. Eric F. Goldman, *The Tragedy of Lyndon Johnson* (New York: Alfred A. Knopf, 1969), p. 176.
50. Ibid., pp. 386, 390.
51. Beschloss, *Taking Charge*, p. 267.
52. "Remarks at Syracuse University on the Communist Challenge in Southeast Asia," August 5, 1964, *Public Papers of the Presidents of the United States*, p. 930.
53. "Remarks at Miami Beach at a Democratic Party Dinner," February 27, 1964, *Public Papers of the Presidents of the United States: Lyndon Baines Johnson, 1963–1964*, Book I (Washington, D.C.: U.S. Government Printing Office, 1965), p. 320.
54. Goldman, *The Tragedy of Lyndon Johnson*, pp. 181–82.
55. Young, *The Vietnam Wars, 1945–1990*, p. 110.
56. Karnow, *Vietnam*, p. 390. Goldman, *The Tragedy of Lyndon Johnson*, pp. 178–82, surveys the objections by Gruening, Morse, Church, and other congressmen.
57. Conversation with McNamara, September 18, 1964, in Michael R. Beschloss, ed., *Reaching for Glory: Lyndon Johnson's Secret White House Tapes, 1964–1965* (New York: Simon & Schuster, 2001), pp. 38–39.
58. "Memorandum for the Record," Washington, February 6, 1945, 7:45–9 P.M., *Foreign Relations of the United States, 1964–1968*, Volume II, Vietnam, January–June, 1965 (Washington, D.C.: U.S. Government Printing Office, 1996), p. 160.
59. Conversation with Everett Dirksen, February 17, 1965, in Beschloss, *Reaching for Glory*, pp. 181–82.
60. Conversation with Harry Truman, February 15, 1965, ibid., p. 180.
61. Karnow, *Vietnam*, p. 433.
62. See Bernard Brodie, "Accidents of History: JFK and LBJ Compared," in Jeffrey P. Kimball, *To Reason Why: The Debate About the Causes of U.S. Involvement in the Vietnam War* (Philadelphia: Temple University Press, 1990), p. 94.
63. Conversation with McGeorge Bundy, February 6, 1964, in Beschloss, *Taking Charge*, p. 227.
64. Conversation with Robert McNamara, February 26, 1965, in Beschloss, *Reaching for Glory*, p. 194.
65. Conversation with Robert McNamara, June 10, 1965, ibid., p. 350.
66. Conversation with Mike Mansfield, June 8, 1965, ibid., p. 347.
67. George Ball, *The Past Has Another Pattern: Memoirs* (New York: W. W. Norton, 1982), p. 382.

68. Ibid., p. 384.
69. George W. Ball to President Johnson, "A Compromise Solution in South Vietnam," July 1, 1965, in *The Pentagon Papers*, Volume IV, pp. 615–19; the quotations are on pp. 615–16.
70. Conversation with Arthur "Tex" Goldschmidt, April 8, 1965, in Beschloss, *Reaching for Glory*, p. 272.
71. Conversation with Robert McNamara, June 21, 1965, ibid., pp. 365, 366.
72. John T. McNaughton to Robert McNamara, March 24, 1965, first draft, "Proposed Course of Action," in *The Pentagon Papers*, Volume III, pp. 694–702; the quotation is on p. 695.
73. Transcript, Benjamin Read Oral History Interview II, March 1970, by Paige E Mulhollan, p. 6, LBJ Library. Online: http://www.lbjlib.utexas.edu/johnson/ archives.hom/oralhistory .hom/ReadB/read-b2.pdf (June 20, 2007).
74. Karnow, *Vietnam*, p. 361.
75. Ibid., p. 361.
76. Kearns, *Lyndon Johnson and the American Dream*, p. 312.
77. Conversation with Abe Fortas, May 14, 1965, in Beschloss, *Reaching for Glory*, p. 325.
78. Merle Miller, *Lyndon: An Oral Biography* (New York: G. P. Putnam's Sons, 1980), p. 488. See also Clark Clifford with Richard Holbrooke, *Counsel to the President: A Memoir* (New York: Random House, 1991), p. 417.
79. Dallek, *Flawed Giant*, p. 290.
80. Ibid., p. 452.
81. *The Pentagon Papers*, Volume IV, pp. 116, 119. According to Gaddis, *Strategies of Containment*, p. 258, intelligence forecasts that bombing North Vietnam could not curb infiltration were in fact plentiful. They included a CIA report in November 1961 and a series of war games in 1964 that confirmed the CIA's predictions. But the demand in Washington for such prescient reading did not match the supply.
82. Robert McNamara, "Actions Recommended for Vietnam," draft presidential memorandum, October 14, 1966, in *The Pentagon Papers*, pp. 350, 351, 353.
83. John McNaughton, "Future Actions in Vietnam," draft presidential memorandum, May 19, 1967, in *The Pentagon Papers*, Volume IV, p. 484.
84. Karnow, *Vietnam*, p. 481.
85. Conversation with J. Edgar Hoover, May 19, 1965, in Beschloss, *Reaching for Glory*, p. 334.
86. Conversation with Richard Russell, March 6, 1965, ibid., p. 213.
87. Dallek, *Flawed Giant*, pp. 254–5.
88. Lt. Gen. Charles G. Cooper, "The Day It Became the Longest War," *Naval Institute Proceedings*, Volume 122, Number 5 (May 1996), p. 80.
89. Dallek, *Flawed Giant*, p. 282.
90. Goldman, *The Tragedy of Lyndon Johnson*. p. 393.
91. Conversation with McNamara, March 2, 1964, in Beschloss, *Taking Charge*, p. 259.
92. "Address at Johns Hopkins University: 'Peace Without Conquest,'" April 7, 1965, *Public Papers of the Presidents of the United States: Lyndon B. Johnson: 1965*, Book I (Washington, D.C.: U.S. Government Printing Office, 1966), pp. 396–97.
93. Fulbright, *The Arrogance of Power*, p. 53.
94. Robert S. McNamara, *The Essence of Security: Reflections in Office* (New York: Harper & Row, 1968), pp. 144–45, 149.
95. Karnow, *Vietnam*, p. 454.
96. Young, *The Vietnam Wars, 1945–1990*, p. 177.
97. Samuel P. Huntington, "The Bases of Accommodation," *Foreign Affairs* 46: 4 (July 1968), pp. 642–56; quotations are on pp. 653, 650, 652, 649.
98. Jonathan Schell, *The Real War: The Classic Reporting on the Vietnam War* (New York: Pantheon Books, 1988), pp. 112, 119, 120, 188, cited in Young, *The Vietnam Wars, 1945–1990*, p. 393.
99. Frances FitzGerald, *Fire in the Lake: The Vietnamese and the Americans in Vietnam* (New York: Vintage, 1972), pp. 440–41.
100. "Annual Budget Message to the Congress, Fiscal Year 1967," January 24, 1966, *Public Papers of the Presidents: Lyndon B. Johnson, 1966*, Book I (Washington, D.C.: U.S. Government Printing Office, 1967), p. 68.
101. Philip Caputo, *A Rumor of War* (New York: Owl, 1996; originally published by Holt, Rinehart and Winston, 1977), p. 74.
102. James C. Thomson, Jr., "How Could Vietnam Happen—An Autopsy," *Atlantic Monthly*, Volume 221, Number 4 (April 1968), p. 51.

103. Lyndon Baines Johnson, *The Vantage Point: Perspectives of the Presidency, 1963–1969* (New York: Holt, Rinehart and Winston, 1971), p. 324.

104. Alice O'Connor, *Poverty Knowledge: Social Science, Social Policy, and the Poor in Twentieth-Century U.S. History* (Princeton and Oxford: Princeton University Press, 2001), p. 179.

105. "Annual Budget Message to the Congress, Fiscal Year 1967," January 24, 1966, *Public Papers of the Presidents of the United States: Lyndon B. Johnson, 1966,* p. 48.

106. Ibid, p. 68.

107. James L. Clayton, ed., *The Economic Impact of the Cold War* (New York: Harcourt, Brace & World, 1970), p. 201.

108. Ibid., p. 201.

109. Ibid., p. 179.

110. Ibid., p. 199.

111. Ibid., p. 198.

112. Ibid., p. 205.

113. Kearns, *Lyndon Johnson and the American Dream,* pp. 282–83.

114. "Annual Message to the Congress on the State of the Union," January 17, 1968, *Public Papers of the Presidents of the United States.* Lyndon B. Johnson, 1968–69, Book I (Washington, D.C.: U.S. Government Printing Office, 1970), p. 25.

115. Herbert Y. Schandler, *The Unmaking of a President: Lyndon Johnson and Vietnam* (Princeton, N.J.: Princeton University Press, 1977). p. 80.

116. Herring, *America's Longest War,* p. 206.

117. Larry Berman, *Lyndon Johnson's War: The Road to Stalemate in Vietnam* (New York: W.W. Norton, 1989), p. 193.

118. Johnson, *The Vantage Point,* p. 407.

119. Karnow, *Vietnam,* p. 576.

120. "The President's Address to the Nation Announcing Steps to Limit the War in Vietnam and Reporting His Decision Not to Seek Reelection," March 31, 1968," *Public Papers of the Presidents of the United States: Lyndon B. Johnson, 1968–69,* Book I (Washington, D.C.: U.S. Government Printing Office, 1969), esp. pp. 472, 473.

121. Robert M. Collins, "Growth Liberalism in the Sixties: Great Societies at Home and Grand Designs Abroad," in David Farber, ed., *The Sixties: From Memory to History* (Chapel Hill and London: University of North Carolina Press, 1994), p. 34.

122. Fulbright, *The Arrogance of Power,* pp. 107–8.

123. J. William Fulbright, "In Thrall to Fear," *New Yorker,* January 8, 1972, p. 43.

124. Caputo, *A Rumor of War,* p. xiv.

CHAPTER 8. THE END OF THE LIBERAL HOUR

1. Richard Nixon, "Remarks at the Swearing In of Warren E. Burger as Chief Justice of the United States," June 23, 1969 (http://www.presidency.ucsb.edu/ws/index.php?pid=2107; accessed September 20, 2007).

2. Lyndon Baines Johnson, "Special Message to Congress: The American Promise," March 15, 1965, Public Papers of the President, 1965 (http://www.presidency.ucsb.edu/ws/index .php?pid=26805&st=&sti=; accessed August 4, 1965).

3. John C. Donovan, former manpower administrator, U.S. Department of Labor, interview with the author, Brunswick, Maine, 1966.

4. David Broder, "Consensus Politics: End of an Experiment," *Atlantic Monthly,* October 1966, p. 62. Broder's article helpfully informs this discussion of Johnson's consensus politics.

5. Quoted in Richard Goodwin, *Remembering America: A Voice from the Sixties* (Boston: Little, Brown, 1988), p. 258.

6. David Halberstam, *The Best and the Brightest* (New York: Random House, 1969), p. 622–23.

7. Public Broadcasting System, *The American Experience,* Vietnam Online, Transcript of "LBJ Goes to War (1964–1965)" (http://www.pbs.org/wgbh/amex/vietnam/series/pt_03.html; accessed September 30, 2006).

8. Data are from Gallup Polls (http://www.ropercenter.uconn.edu/cgi-bin/hsrun.exe/ Roperweb/PresJob/PresJob.htx;start=HS_fullresults?pr=Johnson; accessed September 11, 2006).

9. Data are from the American National Election Study. The standard "trust in government" measure combines two responses to the question: "How much of the time do you think you can trust the government in Washington to do what is right—just about always, most of the time or only some of the time?" (http://www.umich.edu/~nes/nesguide/toptable/tab5a_1.htm; accessed September 11, 2006).

10. Walter Lippmann, "Today and Tomorrow," *New York Herald Tribune*, May 17, 1966.

11. *Newsweek*, February 27, 1967.

12. Herbert Y. Schandler, *The Unmaking of a President: Lyndon Johnson and Vietnam* (Princeton, N.J.: Princeton University Press, 1977), p. 352.

13. Data are from the National Archives (http://www.archives.gov/research/vietnam-war/casualty-statistics.html#year; accessed September 11, 2006).

14. A recent estimate is that the Vietnam War cost an average of $5.1 billon a month (in 2005 dollars) over its eight-year duration. See Phyllis Bennis and Erik Leaver, *The Iraq Quagmire: The Mounting Costs of War and the Case for Bringing Home the Troops* (Washington, D.C.: Institute of Policy Studies, 2005), p. 13.

15. J. W. Fulbright, "What Kind of Country Do You Want America to Be?" in William W. Boyer, ed., *Issues 1968* (Lawrence, Kans.: University Press of Kansas, 1968), p. 24.

16. Lyndon B. Johnson, "Annual Message to Congress on the State of the Union," January 10, 1967 (http://www.presidency.ucsb.edu/ws/index.php?pid=28338&st= &st1=; accessed September 20, 2006).

17. Robert M. Collins, "Growth Liberalism in the Sixties: Great Societies at Home and Grand Designs Abroad" in David Farber, ed., *The Sixties: From Memory to History* (Chapel Hill, N.C.: University of North Carolina Press, 1994), p. 33.

18. Walter Cronkite, *CBS Evening News*, February 27, 1968.

19. David R. Colburn and George E. Pozzetta, "Race, Ethnicity, and the Evolution of Political Legitimacy" in David Farber, ed., *The Sixties: From Memory to History* (Chapel Hill, N.C.: University of North Carolina Press, 1994), p. 137.

20. Ibid., p. 128.

21. Robert Weisbrot, *Freedom Bound: A History of America's Civil Rights Movement* (New York: Penguin, 1990), p. 199.

22. Quoted in "The Cambridge Convergence: How a Night in Maryland 30 Years Ago Changed the Nation's Course of Racial Politics" (http://www.stanford.edu/group/King/about_the_project/ccarson/articles/cambridge_convergence.htm; accessed September 20, 2006).

23. Eldridge Cleaver, *Soul on Ice* (New York: McGraw-Hill, 1968), p. 125.

24. Malcolm X, as told to Alex Haley, *The Autobiography of Malcolm X* (New York: Ballantine Books, 1965), p. 410.

25. Roy Wilkins with Tom Mathews, *Standing Fast: The Autobiography of Roy Wilkins* (New York: Viking Press, 1982), p. 313.

26. Maurice Isserman and Michael Kazin, *America Divided: The Civil War of the 1960s*, 2nd ed. (New York: Oxford University Press, 2004), p. 207.

27. J. Anthony Lukas, *Common Ground: A Turbulent Decade in the Lives of Three American Families* (New York: Random House, 1985), pp. 238ff.

28. Crowd estimates from Fred Halstead, *Out Now! A Participant's Account of the Movement in the U.S. Against the Vietnam War* (New York: Pathfinder Press, 1978), p. 40.

29. National Archives Vietnam Casualty Statistics (http://www.archives.gov/research/vietnam war/casualty-statistics.html#year; accessed July 7, 2007).

30. Halstead, *Out Now!* pp. 728–729.

31. Quoted in "An Elegy for the New Left," *Time*, August 15, 1977, p. 67.

32. Adam Garfinkle, *Telltale Hearts: The Origins and Impact of the Vietnam Antiwar Movement* (New York: St. Martin's Press, 1995), pp. 1–2.

33. Charles Chatfield, "The Antiwar Movement and America" in Charles DeBenedetti, *An American Ordeal: The Antiwar Movement of the Vietnam Era* (Syracuse, N.Y.: Syracuse University Press, 1990), p. 389.

34. President John F. Kennedy, "White House Statement Following the Return of a Special Mission to South Viet-Nam," October 2, 1963 (http://www.presidency.ucsb.edu/ws/index.php?pid=9452&st=&st1=; accessed September 20, 2006).

35. Quoted in Charles Kaiser, *1968 in America: Music, Politics, Chaos, Counterculture, and the Shaping of a Generation* (New York: Grove Press, 1988), pp. 32–33.
36. William H. Chafe, *Never Stop Running: Allard Lowenstein and the Struggle to Save American Liberalism* (New York: Basic Books, 1993), p. xvii.
37. Bailey Laird (Richard Goodwin), "A Political Fiction," *New Yorker*, September 16, 1967, pp. 42, 46.
38. Thomas Powers, *The War at Home* (New York: Grossman, 1973), p. 272.
39. Jack Newfield, *Robert F. Kennedy: A Memoir* (New York: Bantam Books, 1970), pp. 206–7.
40. Quoted in Lewis Chester, Godfrey Hodgson, and Bruce Page, *An American Melodrama: The Presidential Campaign of 1968* (New York: Viking, 1969), p. 93.
41. Philip E. Converse, Warren E. Miller, Jerrold G. Rusk, and Arthur C. Wolfe, "Continuity and Change in American Politics: Parties and Issues in the 1968 Election," *American Political Science Review*, Volume 63, Number 4 (December, 1969), pp. 1089–90.
42. Ibid., p. 1102.
43. Quoted in Rick Perlstein, *Before the Storm: Barry Goldwater and the Unmaking of the American Consensus* (New York: Hill and Wang, 2001), p. xi.
44. David Farber, "The Silent Majority," in David Farber, ed., *The Sixties: From Memory to History* (Chapel Hill, N.C.: University of North Carolina Press, 1994), p. 302.
45. Donald S. Strong, "Further Reflections on Southern Politics," *Journal of Politics*, Volume 33, Number 2 (May 1971), p. 244.
46. Advisory Commission on Intergovernmental Relations, *Significant Features of Fiscal Federalism* (Washington, D.C., 1976).
47. Everett Carll Ladd, Jr., "Liberalism Upside Down: The Inversion of the New Deal Order," *Political Science Quarterly*, Volume 91, Number 4 (Winter 1976–1977), p. 597.
48. Ibid., p. 581.
49. Quoted in Theodore J. Lowi, *The End of Liberalism* (New York: W. W. Norton, 1969), p. 78.
50. Theodore Lowi, "The Public Philosophy: Interest-Group Liberalism," *American Political Science Review*, Volume 61, Number 1 (March 1967), pp. 5–24.
51. Marshall Kaplan and Peggy L. Cuciti, eds., *The Great Society And Its Legacy: Twenty Years of U.S. Social Policy* (Durham, N.C.: Duke University Press, 1986), p. 217.
52. Amitai Etzioni, "Human Beings Are Not Very Easy to Change After All," *Saturday Review*, June 3, 1972, p. 45.
53. Herbert Croly, *The Promise of American Life* (Indianapolis, Ind.: Bobbs-Merrill, 1965), p. 274. Originally published in 1909.
54. Robert S. McNamara, *In Retrospect: The Tragedy and Lessons of Vietnam* (New York: Random House, 1995), p. 323.
55. Daniel P. Moynihan, *Coping: Essays on the Practice of Government* (New York: Random House, 1973), pp. 255–56.
56. Farber, ed., *The Sixties: From Memory to History*, p. 3.
57. Richard Nixon, "Statement Announcing the Nomination of John G. Veneman as Under Secretary of Health, Education, and Welfare," February 7, 1969 (http://www.presidency.ucsb.edu/ws/print.php?pid=2241; accessed October 10, 2006).
58. Martha Derthick, *Uncontrollable Spending for Social Services Grants* (Washington, D.C.: Brookings Institution, 1975), p. 108.
59. Moynihan speaking in "Nixon," PBS Video for *The American Experience*.
60. James Reichley, *Conservatives in an Age of Change: The Nixon and Ford Administrations* (Washington, D.C.: Brookings Institution, 1981), p. 130.
61. Jonathan Schell, *The Time of Illusion* (New York: Alfred A. Knopf, 1976), p. 28.
62. Moynihan, *Coping*, p. 23.
63. Quoted in Reichley, *Conservatives in an Age of Change*, p. 130.

CONCLUSION: THE DURABLE DECADE

1. Quoted in Merle Miller, *Lyndon: An Oral Biography* (New York: G. P. Putnam's Sons, 1980), p. 562.
2. *San Antonio Independent School District v. Rodriguez*, 411 U.S. 1 (1973).

3. Norman Cousins, "The Age of Acceleration," in William W. Boyer, ed., *Issues 1968* (Lawrence, Kans.: University Press of Kansas, 1968), p. 3.

4. Arthur Meier Schlesinger, *The American as Reformer* (Cambridge, Mass.: Harvard University Press, 1950), p. 96.

5. John Hope Franklin statement in Barbara C. Jordan and Elspeth D. Rostow, eds., *The Great Society: A Twenty Year Critique* (Austin, Tex.: Lyndon Baines Johnson Library, 1986), p. 141.

6. Joseph Califano statement, ibid., p. 130.

7. Roger Kimball, *The Long March: How the Cultural Revolution of the 1960s Changed America* (San Francisco: Encounter Books, 2000), p. 27.

8. Arnold R. Isaacs, *The War, Its Ghosts, and Its Legacy* (Baltimore, Md.: Johns Hopkins University Press, 1997), p. 57.

9. Max Weber, "Politics as a Vocation," in *The Vocation Lectures*, trans. Rodney Livingstone (Indianapolis, Ind.: Hackett Publishing, 2004), p. 93.